Twenty-First Century Theologies of Religions

Currents of Encounter

STUDIES ON THE CONTACT BETWEEN CHRISTIANITY AND OTHER
RELIGIONS, BELIEFS, AND CULTURES

VOLUME 54

The titles published in this series are listed at *brill.com/coe*

Twenty-First Century Theologies of Religions

Retrospection and Future Prospects

Edited by

Elizabeth J. Harris
Paul Hedges
Shanthikumar Hettiarachchi

Editorial Assistant

Juhi Ahuja

BRILL

RODOPI

LEIDEN | BOSTON

Cover illustration: The painting on the front cover is entitled 'Pluralism' and is by the artist and priest Sonya Wratten. It is intended to represent the dynamic meeting and encounter that pluralism implies. It was presented by the artist to the Rev Dr Alan Race at the 'Thirty Years of the Theology of Religions Typology: Retrospection and Future Prospects' Conference, Winchester, UK, September 2013.

Library of Congress Cataloging-in-Publication Data

Names: Harris, Elizabeth J. (Elizabeth June), 1950- editor.
Title: Twenty-first century theologies of religions : retrospection and
    future prospects / edited by Elizabeth J. Harris, Paul Hedges, Shanthikumar Hettiarachchi.
Description: Leiden ; Boston : Brill-Rodopi, 2016. | Series: Currents of
    encounter, ISSN 0923-6201 ; VOLUME 54 | Includes index.
Identifiers: LCCN 2016030028 | ISBN 9789004322462 (pbk. : alk. paper)
Subjects: LCSH: Christianity and other religions.
Classification: LCC BR127 .T89 2016 | DDC 261.2--dc23
LC record available at https://lccn.loc.gov/2016030028

Want or need Open Access? Brill Open offers you the choice to make your research freely accessible online in exchange for a publication charge. Review your various options on brill.com/brill-open.

Typeface for the Latin, Greek, and Cyrillic scripts: "Brill". See and download: brill.com/brill-typeface.

ISSN 0923-6201
ISBN 978-90-04-32246-2 (paperback)
ISBN 978-90-04-32407-7 (e-book)

Printed by Printforce, the Netherlands

This volume is dedicated in deep appreciation to, and in honour of, Alan Race for his seminal contribution to the theology of religions and the development of Christian engagement with our sisters and brothers in other religious traditions. We salute his pioneering work as colleagues and co-pilgrims.

∴

Contents

Foreword

Leonard Swidler

Three Paths–Whither?

With this volume we are celebrating the thirtieth anniversary of a new articulation of the religious understanding of the ultimate meaning of life as coined by Alan Race: *Exclusivism, Inclusivism, Pluralism*. This tablature has been both insightful and 'inciteful,' as can be seen by its almost universal reference among theologians. Many simply accept it as obvious, now that it has been stated; some emphasize its perspicacity by denouncing it, and still others by presenting it as "variations on a theme," such as "Inclusivist Pluralism" or "Pluralist Inclusivism." Doubtless Alan has created theological categories that every serious contemporary religious thinker has had to wrestle with for the past three decades, and doubtless will have to for still more decades to come positively, negatively, or variationally.

Simply put, the exclusivist position claims that its institution (or religious tradition) alone contains the means of 'salvation.' This was expressed as early as the third century by the Christian bishop Cyprian of Carthage with the words: *Salus extra ecclesiam non est*, "Salvation outside the church does not exist," and was repeated regularly over the centuries, in various forms, right into the present for conservative Protestants, and into the middle of the twentieth century for conservative Catholics.

Even just a half-dozen years ago, I had a white Protestant undergraduate student at Temple University (despite its name, a state university) who, somewhat embarrassedly stated in class that sadly his non-Protestant classmates (and presumably me as well!) were all going to go to hell upon their demise unless they converted to his evangelical brand of Protestantism. I have also met Muslims with a similar exclusivist position. Then there is the odd kind of exclusivist atheist who claims that s/he *knows* that at death we all just "evaporate."

The inclusivist position is considerably more nuanced, admitting that, yes, there are religions/ideologies which contain *some* of the means of salvation, but my religion includes *all* of those means. In a Catholic primary school in the 1930s, I was taught by "Sister Mary Holy Card" and "Monsignor O'Hooligan" that there were three kinds of Baptism: 1. Baptism of Water, 2. Baptism of Blood, and 3. Baptism of Desire.

1. *Baptism of Water* was the standard one which made you a Catholic.
2. *Baptism of Blood* was the one of persons who were martyred for committing themselves to Christ, even though they had not yet been baptized–like the catechumens, who in the early Christian centuries had to go through a long instruction period before being baptized.
3. *Baptism of Desire* was of persons who through no fault of their own did not learn that Jesus was the Savior of Humankind, but if they had, and lived properly according to their consciences, they would have *desired* to be baptized–and hence, were reckoned by God to have done so virtually.

An ironic twist on that Catholic inclusivist teaching occurred in the late 1940s when I was an undergraduate at St. Norbert's College in DePere, Wisconsin. Jesuit Father Leonard (I am embarrassed by this eponymous connection) Feeney had gained a certain minor fame as a poet and was the Catholic chaplain at Harvard University. He rejected the inclusivist position I had learned in Catholic primary schools and publicly proclaimed a rigid exclusivist position based on the above-mentioned doctrine *extra ecclesiam nulla salus* (outside the Church no salvation)–as noted, first articulated by third century St. Cyprian (also the name given to me as a Norbertine novice–is there a message in these two coincidences?). Cardinal Cushing of Boston, whose favorite nephew by marriage was a non-Catholic, could not stomach the idea that he would be destined for hell, and after vainly trying to quiet down Father Feeney, petitioned the Holy Office in Rome to render a decision on the matter. Cardinal Marchetti-Selvaggiani of the Holy Office wrote back in 1949, and told Feeney to desist such teaching; he refused, and on February 13, 1953, he—in strange irony—was excommunicated from the Catholic Church for continuing to claim that outside it no one could be saved! Shortly before his death (1978) he was reconciled to the Catholic Church.

The question continued to be raised within Catholicism, as for example in the form of the Holy Office's silencing of another American Jesuit, John Courtney Murray, in 1954. However, this silencing was for the opposite reason of that of Feeney. Murray had been writing in favor of religious freedom (in the face of Popes Gregory XVI and Pius IX condemnations of the same as "madness" [*deliramentum*] in 1832 and 1864 respectively), and was forbidden to publish on the subject by Cardinal Ottaviani of the Holy Office. He was later vindicated by being invited by Pope John XXIII to Vatican Council II in 1963 to write the counciliar *Declaration on Religious Freedom* which definitively declared *freedom of religion as part of the essence of Catholic Christianity*. This Declaration, signed by almost all the Catholic bishops of the world, including the Bishop of Rome, the Pope, clearly diametrically contradicted what had all the appearances of an "Infallible Dogma" previously declared by two successive popes, but no overt notice was taken of the contradiction.

The position of the Catholic Church as articulated in Vatican Council II (1962–1965), then, definitively rejected the exclusivist position, though a number of hyper-conservative members, even in high places, continue to do their best to hold onto and even reinstate it; but it is a past paradigm that is dying with them. At the same time, the exclusivist position is definitely alive and well with conservative Protestants and Muslims, of which there are a great number in the world. However, as a historian, I am convinced that world trajectory is also pulling that position into near-total oblivion, though it will doubtless go more slowly than many would wish. Further, although Vatican II Catholicism formally adopted inclusivism, again, in my opinion, the trajectory of history clearly is ineluctably directed toward pluralism.

The pluralist position is that certain basic questions naturally occur to humans, like: Does life have meaning, and if so, what is it? How should we live so as to realize that meaning? Where did we, and everything else, come from? What happens after we die?....? These are what I call "limit questions," that is, questions that virtually "ask themselves," but by their nature we finite ("limited") humans cannot answer, and which we cannot avoid trying to answer. The answers we come up with produce what we in the West call "religions." However, because the climatic, physical, cultural, etc. A conditions differ across the globe, we thus have different ways of articulating the answers, that is, different religions. For example, did the fact that Judaism, Christianity, and Islam all were formed in a desert like climate have any influence on those three articulations of the "explanation of the ultimate meaning of life, and how to live accordingly" (my succinct definition of religion)? Well, ask yourself, for instance: Had these three religions been developed by Eskimos instead of semi-desert people, would "hell" be a place of extreme heat?

Some long-term attempts to answer these basic human limit questions eventually made sense to a significant number of people over a long period of time, and thereby produced the so-called World Religions, e.g., Judaism, Hinduism, Buddhism, Confucianism, Christianity, Islam, etc. Pluralists judge, after serious study/experience of at least a number of these World Religions, that they all provide valid/helpful "Ways" of living, leading persons to relatively happy, non-violent lives. Simply by observation they seem to be more or less equally effective in leading humans to "salvation," and hence provide plural paths to the ultimate human goal of "happiness" (what authentic human happiness is, of course, is the subject of serious–ongoing, in fact, endless–dialogue.

'Salvation' comes from the Latin root *salus*, meaning 'health,' whence the English cognates 'salutary,' 'salubrious,' 'salute.' The parallel Germanic rooted

English term comes from *Heil*, meaning precisely 'health,' 'healthy,' 'hale,' 'whole'—further behind it is the Greek *holos*, meaning 'whole.' This is where our English word 'holy' derives from; hence, to be 'holy' means to be 'healthy,' 'whole,' not being engaged in externals, like fasting, going to church/mosque/temple, wearing costumes, beards, or formally proclaiming certain doctrines.

I am inclined to agree with Kenneth Rose (2013) when he claims that the future is already decided, as the title of his new book reflects: *Pluralism: The Future of Religion*. Rose argues persuasively, philosophically and historically, that of the tripartite division that Alan Race devised thirty years ago, exclusivism is already—except for now numerically expanding but intellectually ineffectual fundamentalist groups—*passé*, and inclusivism is experiencing increasing intellectual abandonment. He, however, makes no prediction when the inevitable embrace of pluralism will come to bodies like the Catholic Church–but come it will.

Let me close my reflections here with a slightly ironic note. In the Christian world, except for conservative Protestants, almost no serious Christian theologian or thinker focuses on 'salvation,' as in 'going to heaven or hell' when we die. Luther's overwhelming question of 'Justification' which played a significant role in launching what we call the Protestant Reformation, is a question today only of some slight historical interest, but no more a 'live' question. Rather, Alan's tripartite division is about which institution holds the exclusive or inclusive or parallel possession of the means of 'salvation,' means leading its adherents to an authentic, 'happy' human life now, *before* the grave (for all religions claim that whatever lies beyond the grave is determined by how we live this side of the grave). All need to heed Paul's admonition, "*Now* is the time of salvation!"

Bibliography

Rose, Kenneth (2013). *Pluralism: The Future of Religion*. New York: Continuum International Publishing.

List of Contributors

Graham Adams
Tutor in World Christianity (including Mission Studies) and World Faith Traditions, Northern College, Luther King House, Manchester, UK.

Tony Bayfield
Rabbi and Professor of Jewish Theology and Thought, Leo Baeck College, London and President, Movement for Reform Judaism, UK.

Abraham Veléz de Cea
Professor, Department of Philosophy and Religion, Eastern Kentucky University, USA.

Gavin D'Costa
Professor of Catholic Theology, Department of Religion and Theology, University of Bristol, UK.

Reuven Firestone
Regenstein Professor in Medieval Judaism and Islam, Hebrew Union College-Jewish Institute of Religion, California, USA.

Ray Gaston
Tutor in Interfaith Engagement, Queen's Foundation for Ecumenical Theological Education, Birmingham, and a Team Vicar, Parish of Central Wolverhampton, UK.

Elizabeth J. Harris
Associate Professor in Religious Studies, Liverpool Hope University, UK.

Paul Hedges
Associate Professor in Interreligious Studies, Studies in Inter-Religious Relations in Plural Societies Programme, S. Rajaratnam School of International Studies, Nanyang Technological University, Singapore.

Shanthikumar Hettiarachchi
Director, In Reach Consult (IC), Political Columnist on South Asia, and Visiting Lecturer, Universities of Colombo and Kelaniya, Sri Lanka.

Haifaa Jawad
Senior Lecturer in Islamic and Middle Eastern Studies, and Director of Centre for Islamic and Middle Eastern Studies, Department of Theology and Religion, University of Birmingham, UK.

Kristin Beise Kiblinger
Professor of Religious Studies, and Director of the International and Global Studies Program, Winthrop University, South Carolina, USA.

Paul F. Knitter
Emeritus Paul Tillich Professor of Theology, World Religions, and Culture, Union Theological Seminary, New York, USA.

Oddbjørn Leirvik
Professor of Interreligious Studies, Faculty of Theology, University of Oslo, Norway.

Marianne Moyaert
Professor of Comparative Theology and Hermeneutics of Interreligious Dialogue, Faculty of Theology, VU University, Amsterdam, Netherlands, and Guest Lecturer in Jewish-Christian Relations and Post-Holocaust Theology, Faculty of Theology and Religious Studies, Catholic University of (KU) Leuven, Belgium.

Mark Owen
Director, Centre of Religions, Reconciliation and Peace, University of Winchester, UK.

Alan Race
Rector of St Margaret's Church, Lee, South London, UK.

Sigrid Rettenbacher
Director, Centre for Students of Theology, Theological Faculty, University of Salzburg, Supervisor of the diocesan education of students of theology in the Archdiocese of Salzburg, Vice Chairwoman of the Salzburger Hochschul-wochen, and Project Coordinator of the Salzburger Religionstriennale, Department of Systematic Theology, University of Salzburg, Austria.

Perry Schmidt-Leukel
Professor of Religious Studies and Intercultural Theology, and a Principal Investigator in the Cluster of Excellence 'Religion and Politics', University of Muenster, Germany.

Leonard Swidler
Professor of Catholic Thought and Interreligious Dialogue, Temple University, Philadelphia, Pennsylvania, USA.

Philip Whitehead
PhD Candidate and Teaching Affiliate, Department of Theology and Religious Studies, University of Nottingham, UK.

Janet P. Williams
Dean of West of England Ministry Training Course, Ripon College, Cuddesdon, UK.

Ulrich Winkler
Professor of Systematic Theology, Initiator and Co-Director of the Centre for the Study of Intercultural Theology and the Study of Religions, Director of the Postdoctoral Studies "Spiritual Theology in Interreligious Process and Encounter", University of Salzburg, and Vice President of the European Society for Intercultural Theology and Interreligious Studies (ESITIS), Austria.

Introduction: Theologies of Religions in the Twenty-First Century

Elizabeth J. Harris, Paul Hedges and Shanthikumar Hettiarachchi

The question of the theology of religions has become a key part of discussions over the last thirty or so years. We should note that this is a discussion that began in, and is still dominated by, the Christian tradition. As such, the fact that this text reflects this is seen as more a survey of the situation than a normative situation we would wish to perpetuate. Indeed, as discussed below, we have attempted to widen the debate into the context of, and in relation to, other religions. From a fringe interest it has become something that has to be addressed. We should note that we speak very much from a Western (European-North American) context here. The relation of Christianity to the religious Other has been of central concern in other parts of the world for far longer, but for better or worse the Western context still has a certain global hegemony despite the shift in demographics to the Global South. Christian systematic theology now seems incomplete without a discussion on both the religious Other and the changing demographics of Christianity and what this means. Introductions to Christianity or theology will address religious Others as an area of concern, while ecclesial communities have committees and forums to address and engage the religious Other. Over that time a central focus of those discussions has been the typology of exclusivisms-inclusivisms-pluralisms[1] (often now with particularities added as a fourth paradigm), which was first introduced by Alan Race in his classic 1983 book *Christians and Religious Pluralism: Patterns in the Christian Theology of Religions*. It was, indeed, the thirtieth anniversary of that book which saw two initiatives come together which led to the current volume. On one side, Elizabeth Harris and Shanthikumar Hettiarachchi were putting together an edited book. On the other, Paul Hedges, with Alan Race, was planning a conference with a follow up publication. Inevitably, the two ventures started to call on the same people and the organisers of each (and the contributors) soon saw the merits of combining forces to produce the current volume. However, the result is far from a simple paean to the typology or a festschrift to Alan Race, although we offer this volume in honour of his landmark contribution. Rather, it marks the deep and growing conversation around the

---

1 Although initially used in the singular, Race later suggested using the plural to indicate that each paradigm does not indicate simply one standpoint, but rather includes a range of views. This usage first appeared and was explained in Hedges and Race (2008).

theology of religions that continues beyond the thirtieth anniversary of that work.

It would be useful if we say something to contextualise and provide a background for these debates. First, Alan's typology (his "patterns") of the 1983 volume has become the standard marker for debates and classifications. In brief we can describe these patterns as follows.

> *Exclusivisms*: only my religion is true; all other religions are false and lead people astray. God or a transcendent reality has ordained one path to lead people to Him (Her/It) and failure to follow this means you are not included in the chosen or elect.
> *Inclusivisms*: while my religion is the most true, God or a transcendent reality is known to all humanity and so other religions are ways leading towards the truth found in my tradition. True followers of other religions will come to the truth in my religion eventually.
> *Pluralisms*: I simply do not know if there is only one true religion or many true religions. Followers of other religions have a depth of prayer life, insight into truth, spiritual aspirations, and ethical ideals which at least equal my own. If God is as loving and big as I believe Her/Him to be, or if liberation is intended for all, I cannot limit truth to just the path I know.

However, since then various people have suggested that these paradigms can be understood in different ways. Some argue that these three options are the range of all religiously possible options. They are, therefore, logical markers of the debate. Such a position is most associated with Perry Schmidt-Leukel (2005).[2] Others suggest that the terms are more descriptive and heuristic and represent a range of standpoints which are not always clearly distinct, and that, at the borders, each merges into the next. In these terms, it is possible to add on further categories, like particularities. Such a position has been argued by, for instance, Hedges (2008, 2010) and Paul Knitter (2002). Still others have suggested various other permutations of the typology or alternative typologies (see Hedges 2008). The typology has also been the subject of often bitter dispute, with some suggesting it is fundamentally flawed or biased, although some telling rebukes of these criticisms have been made (see Hedges 2008, Schmidt-Leukel 2005). Perhaps, most significant amongst these critics are advocates of comparative theology who suggest that engaging other religions using the tools of comparative theology bypasses the typology and its

---

2   It should be noted that Schmidt-Leukel would add that another logical possibility would be that no religion is true, but he suggests this is not a religious option in the way the others are.

judgments altogether (see Fredericks 1999: 8). However, it has been convincingly argued that to engage in the act of comparative theology requires an initial
prejudgement of the type implied by the typology (see Hedges 2010: 53–4, Kiblinger 2010, Schmidt-Leukel 2009: 90–104). This merely scratches the surface
of the debates, many of which are engaged more fully, and often in new ways,
within the following chapters.

The theology of religions, moreover, is not simply limited to a discussion
around the typology and its paradigms and so the chapters herein also extend
the discussion further, by examining, for instance, the insights of comparative
theology or what multiple religious belongings or identities may contribute.
The volume also explores traditions beyond Christianity, partly by looking at
their responses to the Christian discussion but also thereby asking what the
character of a 'theology of religions' developed within these traditions would
be (or even if such a concept or venture makes sense within their terms). Of
course, some people from other traditions have employed the typology to refer
to their own tradition. Rita Gross for instance identifies as a Buddhist pluralist
while Mohammad Hassan Khalil has used the terms in his discussion of Muslim views of salvation (Khalil 2012: 7–24).[3] The chapters offered here just touch
a potentially much larger debate which has not always been as much discussed
as it might have been. All of these debates show that discussions within the
theology of religions are alive and well as we head into the twenty-first century.
Arguably, they are becoming more relevant than they have ever been before.
Indeed, in an increasingly globalised world it is clear that what have been, as
we mentioned above, rather marginal discussions in the Western theological
sphere have not just become ones which cannot be ignored there, but also
have great resonances elsewhere. Indeed, the wider global discussion and the
resources it holds for Christian theological thinking have not yet been fully
explored. Certainly this volume holds voices from beyond the Western world,
but as with many other areas there is still far more to be explored here. While
the text focuses upon the Christian discussion, voices from other religious traditions are raised or foregrounded in various chapters.

We turn now to look at the individual chapters and the structure of
this book. The book is divided into four parts. The first looks at disputes and
contentions around the typology itself in terms of how it is understood and
employed. The second looks at the pluralist position within the typology—it
should be stressed that this is not because the pluralist position is privileged

---

3 This is discussed in the present volume by Jawad who notes that Khalil extends Race's typology by adding a universalist category, which is part of the wider extension and general usage
   within the paradigms (see, e.g., Hedges 2010: 22).

in the volume but because it simply reflects the papers offered and received. The third looks at disputes relating to the theology of religions but which go beyond the traditional discussions of the typology and its paradigms. The final part explores reactions from various non-Christian religions towards the Christian theology of religions. The whole is introduced by a Foreword by Leonard Swidler and concludes with an Afterword by Race on the essays included in the volume. Swidler's Foreword, which argues strongly for a pluralist hegemony, represents his own personal reflection on Race's typology and views, and is not included as the views of the editors nor as setting the scene for the text. Race, meanwhile, also offers his own personal reflection on the chapters and views on where the debate stands. Within each part the chapters are arranged alphabetically and so there is no explicit order and readers should feel free to dip in and read in whichever order they wish.

In the first part "Disputing and Using the Typology" we begin with a chapter by Graham Adams which uses his reflections on Jesus as the 'Shaken One', inspired by Shanks' work, to look at how the positions within the typology may themselves be 'shaken' and to question the construction of the typology. The next chapter by Abraham Veléz de Cea uses ideas he had previously developed for a Buddhist typology, or theology of religions, to examine Christianity and suggests that we need a further category between pluralisms and inclusivisms. The third chapter sees Ray Gaston looking at how the typology can be constructively used in theological education using his own experience in training ministers, which suggests that it is not simply an abstract academic construct but something with practical usefulness in allowing Christians to reflect upon their own views and those of the tradition they represent. Elizabeth Harris then develops a spatial analysis of the typology showing how different theological positions across the paradigms map onto actual practices in terms of how space in lived reality is negotiated. Following this, Paul Hedges offers a different vision for the typology conceived in terms of tendencies and degrees of openness, suggesting that some perspectives on the typology are more fruitful in terms of employing it for practical applications. Finally in this part, Philip Whitehead uses Paul's epistles to revaluate Christian approaches to religious Others and suggests a reading of those texts that calls into question whether the typology can fully reflect what he takes to be a Christian attitude. As such, these chapters include voices that both affirm and critique the typology, while suggesting ways it can be rethought and employed.

The second part, "Pluralist Voices and Contestations," looks at various debates in and around the pluralist paradigm. It begins with Tony Bayfield examining the problems of religious absolutism leading to tensions and aggression, suggesting, therefore, that we need a pluralist approach for harmonious co-existence in the world. Gavin D'Costa then argues a very different position, that the pluralist position should be seen as post-Christian rather than a stance within the Christian theology of religions, arguing that it necessitates abandoning the primary essence of that tradition. In the next contribution, Paul Knitter explores how pluralism has developed within primarily the Christian tradition, arguing that it has faced adversity but remains central to Christian thought today. The final chapter in this part, by Perry Schmidt-Leukel, looks at manifestations of, and resources for, pluralism within non-Christian religious traditions, surveying Judaism, Islam, Hinduism, and Buddhism. This part, therefore, offers both support for, and critiques, an understanding of pluralisms as Christian theological positions, as well as looking at how the pluralist paradigm operates outside of the Christian tradition.

The third part is "Beyond the Typology: New Debates, New Vistas," which looks at a range of areas which have largely grown up subsequent to the typology's introduction in 1983, showing something of the range and expanse of the theology of religions debate today. It begins with Shanthikumar Hettiarachchi looking at the effects of imperialism and colonialism on perceptions of the religious Other and taking a post-colonial approach to the deconstruction of these narratives and approaches. Next, Kristin Beise Kiblinger uses John Caputo's philosophical theology to argue for what she terms a 'weak' theology of religions that takes a post-modern indeterminacy as its starting point and so avoids what can be seen as the clear-cut positions of the traditional typological paradigms. Oddbjørn Leirvik then discusses how an ethical interreligious approach to Islam that emphasises relationality offers an alternative and useful perspective. In the following chapter, Marianne Moyaert takes a different approach, analysing the category 'religion' itself and showing how Western thought has used a Christian model to define the religious Other. She sees the theology of religions as traditionally trapped within a hegemonic and textual paradigm that needs to take material religion more seriously. Sigrid Rettenbacher also employs a postcolonial perspective, but this time to analyse a German Roman Catholic attitude to the theology of religions, showing that it has failed to fully respect religious Others in their own right. Janet Williams, meanwhile, looks at dual religious belonging and uses a personal reflection on her own use of the Chalcedonian adverbs as a model for a Christian approach to such border crossing. Finally in this part, Ulrich Winkler raises the issue of comparative theology as an alternative to the theology of religions, but shows that the two should not stand in opposition but may usefully complement each other. This part takes a diverse set of approaches, although quite a number emphasize the post-colonial context and critique of religion and theology. The contributors address the typology critically or affirmatively, showing how such debates may relate to this issue but also go beyond it.

The final part is entitled "Some Responses to the Christian Theology of Religions" and begins with Reuven Firestone giving a Jewish response. He shows both how the Jewish tradition has envisaged its own attitude to religious Others, but also how it has responded to Christian attitudes towards 'Judaism' noting that these are often entwined, and usefully noting that one reason some Jews today engage in dialogue with Christians is "so they won't kill us" [anymore]. Haifaa Jawad in her Islamic response notes that Islam has never developed a theology of religions in the way that Christianity has but looks at traditional Islamic resources, especially from the Qur'an, for approaching the religious Other and making sense of diversity. She especially looks at the variety of contemporary Muslim responses to this issue. Finally, Mark Owen offers a Buddhist response, noting that the terms 'Buddhist' and 'Christian' are far from simple and mean many different things. He suggests that, while Buddhism may be sympathetic to a theology of religions as envisaged from within Christianity, it would also be critical of the way that it shapes the debate. He brings in his own work in peace-building to ask whether the theological specificities of much discussion on the typology are really helpful to fostering and maintaining positive on-the-ground relations. This part shows some of the issues and problems that have arisen in the way Christians have engaged religious Others, and also that the theology of religions shapes the debates in ways that may not be helpful or familiar to those of other traditions. It also looks at ways in which the religious Other can respond and has reacted to Christianity, and suggests resources for dialogue and engagement.

The editors hope that this volume will provide an important critical account of the current state of play across the broad theology of religions debate, mainly within the Christian tradition, at the beginning of the twenty-first century, including many new perspectives and approaches. Of course, it cannot survey the entire field and the editors recognise that some significant areas and important voices are not included, but of course no single volume could contain everything without making it prohibitively large. We nevertheless hope that this volume will become an important resource for students and scholars of the theology of religions that provides both a suitable retrospective over the last thirty or so years and a pointer to future research and developments that may appear as we move towards the middle of the twenty-first century.

Bibliography

Fredericks, James. (1999). *Faith Among Faiths: Christian Theology and Non-Christian Religions*. New York, NY: Paulist Press.

Hedges, Paul. (2008). "A Reflection on Typologies: Negotiating a Fast Moving Debate." In: Paul Hedges and Alan Race (eds.). *Christian Approaches to Other Faiths*. SCM Core Text Series. London: SCM Press. Pp. 17–33.

———. (2010). *Controversies in Interreligious Dialogue and the Theology of Religions*. London: SCM Press.

Hedges, Paul, and Alan Race (eds). (2008). *Christian Approaches to Other Faiths*. SCM Core Text Series. London: SCM Press.

Khalil, Mohammad Hassan. (2012). *Islam and the Fate of Others: The Salvation Question*. Oxford: Oxford University Press.

Kiblinger, Kirsten Bleise. (2010). "Relating Theology of Religions and Comparative Theology." In: Francis X. Clooney (ed.). *The New Comparative Theology: Voices from the Next Generation*. London and New York, NY: T & T Clark. Pp. 21–42.

Knitter, Paul F. (2002). *Introducing Theologies of Religions*. Maryknoll, NY: Orbis.

Race, Alan. (1983). *Christian and Religious Pluralism: Patterns in the Christian Theology of Religions*. London: SCM Press.

Schmidt-Leukel, Perry. (2005). "Exclusivism, Inclusivism, Pluralism: The Tripolar Typology—Clarified and Reaffirmed." In: Paul F. Knitter (ed.). *The Myth of Religious Superiority: A Multifaith Exploration*. Maryknoll, NY: Orbis. Pp. 13–27.

———. (2009). *Transformation by Integration: How Inter-Faith Encounter Changes Christianity*. London: SCM Press.

PART 1

Disputing and Using the Typology

∵

CHAPTER 1

Shaking the Typology: Being Honest and Hospitable

Graham Adams

Introduction

How should we assess the truth and salvific efficacy of religious traditions? Christian theologies of religions respond to this question on the basis of varied presuppositions. The task of a typology of those theologies is obviously to categorise the range of responses. I contend that Race's typology implicitly assumes one presupposition to be the dominant basis for these responses: namely, that Christian assessment of the religions focuses on whether a particular tradition constitutes, defines, or represents what is universally true and saving. In other words, the challenge of the *scandal of particularity* is presumed to be uppermost. As a consequence of this, whilst Race personally encourages pluralistic theologies,[1] the typology implicitly requires pluralists to redefine the territory and thus work harder for Christian legitimacy. By contrast, building on the theological concerns of Andrew Shanks, I propose that the truth and effectiveness of religious traditions depends on the interaction between *three scandals*—those of particularity, plurality, and universality. The interaction of these necessarily 'shakes' us out of various 'dishonesties', by virtue of self-critical and hospitable impulses which are intrinsic to Christian faith and which arguably foster dialogical and pluralistic theologies.

Affirming Three Implicit Goals

I begin by affirming three implicit goals of the typology. Firstly, it rightly helps to remind us, even if this may be self-evident, that Christian self-understanding is integral to our assessment of other religious traditions. That is, one cannot separate our view of others from our location in the particularity, and otherness, of Christian identity. Secondly, related to that, the typology reminds us that Christian self-understanding is pluriform, and the recognition of this broad church of Christian identity impresses on us the need, wherever we locate ourselves, to attend to the otherness *within* our tradition. But thirdly, the typology can be interpreted as having an agenda, quite legitimately, which

---

1 I prefer *pluralistic theologies* to *pluralism* as the latter suggests a somewhat singular agenda and some of its manifestations are often less pluralistic than intended, whereas the notion of 'pluralistic theologies' is inherently more plural and open-ended.

is to nudge people in the direction of pluralistic theologies. This is illustrated by the fact that, as Strange acknowledges (2011: 95–6), the term 'exclusivism' is often associated with "sensationalist terms (intolerant, arrogant, 'fundamentalist')," whereas 'pluralist' appears "more benign, enlightened, tolerant."[2] However, I assert that the typology's pluralistic aspirations are impeded by certain presuppositions. I appreciate that Race's typology is logically comprehensive (Yong 2008: 66), but because it does not address the interdependence of the three scandals in its understanding of what constitutes true and saving religion, it paradoxically requires pluralistic theologies to work harder for their legitimacy, and it is increasingly clear that several theologies do not neatly fit the types. Its presuppositions should therefore be 'shaken.'

Being Shaken in Pursuit of Honesty

The following is a summary of the particular concerns of Andrew Shanks, which shape and underpin my argument. Shanks explains that his understanding of 'shakenness,' or being shaken, is rooted in the notion of the "solidarity of the shaken," coined by the philosopher and activist Jan Patočka in what was Czechoslovakia under Soviet rule (Shanks 2000: 5).[3] We all live within certain, culturally-conditioned presuppositions and prejudices; but various traumatic experiences can shake us out of such half-truths and open us up towards transcendence, or to a moral authority greater than that which is contained by any cultural or ideological mind-set or practice (Shanks 2000: 5–6).[4] Of course, not everyone will refer to this shaking power in theological or theistic terms, but for Shanks these moments of trauma and shakenness are very much part of the story and revelatory power of God (Shanks 2000: 15). For shakenness, like revelation, is about "the shaking away of that which conceals" (Shanks 2000: 36).

However, shakenness is not as such the end in itself; rather, "[w]hat 'shakes' the 'shaken'... is the sheer imperative of Honesty" (Shanks 2007: 27). Shanks

---

2 Previously Strange accepted 'exclusivism' (2008: 36–7), but as with his later comments, I am simply highlighting the inevitability of value judgments and preferences in the typology's terminology.

3 He cites Jan Patočka, *Heretical Essays on the Philosophy of History*, the final chapter of which is translated into English as "Wars of the Twentieth Century and the Twentieth Century as War" (1976–77).

4 He cites Jan Patočka, "What Charter 77 Is. and What It Is Not," in H. Gordon Skilling (1981) *Charter 77 and Human Rights in Czechoslovakia*, Winchester, MA: Allen and Unwin, p. 219.

capitalises "Honesty" to denote its radicality: for true Honesty, or "truth-as-Honesty," is more than simply being frank (saying what you mean) or sincere (meaning what you say); it is about being truly open to what *others* have to say (Shanks 2005: 2), hence his later term, "truth-as-openness" (Shanks 2014: 3). Such Honesty, "a quality of sheer conversational *receptivity*" (Shanks 2014: 3), contrasts with "truth-as-correctness," which is manifest in much church theology. The latter is more about impatiently closing down the conversation, claiming that particular knowledge is enough; whereas truth-as-Honesty or truth-as-openness consists in being ever further shaken out of each impatient "correctness."[5]

Truth-as-Honesty, then, is inherently hospitable; for it is not about making others sufficiently at home simply so we may subject them to what *we* have to say, but consists of being truly open to what *they* have to say, on their terms. For example, we witness Jesus' commendation of Mary's hospitality, as she demonstrates openness to receive from the Other (in this case, Jesus), whilst Martha's hospitality is more defined, to distraction, by what she strives to give (Luke 10:38–42). Or, in situations where Jesus models the hospitality, rather than receives it, we see him share table fellowship with those widely regarded as having nothing godly to give (Mark 2:13–17), or make himself open and vulnerable to the initiative and desires of cultural Others, such as a centurion (Matthew 8:5–13) and a Syro-Phoenician woman (Mark 7:24–30).

We must ask, though, whether this notion of being shaken in pursuit of ever greater Honesty is an invasive virus re-wiring the internal circuitry of Christian faith. For Shanks, in fact, it illuminates something which is *intrinsic* to the Gospel, and it is a mark of truly Christian community. Much as I began to illustrate from Jesus' ministry, Shanks too argues that this reality goes to the heart of the Gospel; that Jesus is not a community-builder in the sense of creating a bounded-set, but the profoundest of anti-sectarians (Shanks 2001: 21). His Beatitudes can in fact be understood as the blessing of shaken people; those who have been shaken out of life-as-taken-for-granted and opened up to alternative horizons, both painful and hopeful (Shanks 2000: 16–17). (I develop this by suggesting Jesus is 'the Shaken One,' not only initiating others' shakenness, but

---

5 Arguably this distinction is akin to that of Wilfred Cantwell Smith (1979: 122–5, 140–1): 'belief' being truth-as-correctness and 'Faith' truth-as-Honesty. In fact, Shanks argues (2014: 38–9) that faith must not be confused with metaphysical truth-as-correctness, but often is. Rather, as that which "saves," it should be understood as what responds to the "imperatives of perfect truth-as-openness," so saves us from "the condition of being inwardly closed-down... [i]t is just a being opened-up; an infusion of agape, expressed as trust in God, into the soul. And, really, nothing more!"

receiving the truth, experience and trauma of a whole range of others [Adams 2010]. This is discussed further below.) More systematically, in *Faith in Honesty* Shanks argues that the sensibilities effected by the shaking God can be understood in Trinitarian terms (Shanks 2005), and that, since truth-as-openness "is the defining essence of the truly sacred," Christian theology's proper calling is thus "the systematic consideration of strategies for the promotion of truth-as-openness, recognised as God's will revealed in Christ" (Shanks 2014: 66–7).

Intuitively does it not ring true that the Gospel of reconciliation is *fundamentally* shaking us out of culturally-conditioned half-truths and forming us in community, not by virtue of human prejudices, but in solidarity with others beyond the limits of our own bounded correctness? In terms of the relationship between Christian faith/theology and Honesty, Shanks explains:

> The best theology of all is that which most explicitly seeks to serve the universal *solidarity of the shaken*, as such. An alliance, that is to say, embracing all comers. The solidarity of those shaken—out of complacency, out of inertia, out of dumb despair—into a serious pursuit of true Honesty;
>
> SHANKS 2007: 18

and this thus requires the development of:

> a grand narrative whose central theme would be the historic emergence of the possibility of the solidarity of the shaken—a church which would explicitly identify its vocation as a kenotic contribution to that larger ideal.
>
> SHANKS 2005: 104

Not unlike how the Global Ethic is said to transcend its own roots in the Christian tradition (Race 2001: 124), so, too, for Shanks, Christian faith is fundamentally about a distinctive—namely, kenotic—contribution to a larger ideal, the pursuit of Honesty. That is to say, as I shall elaborate below, Christian particularity contributes to the Universal but only in and through relationships with other, plural, particularities.

Shaking Dishonesties: Turning to the Typology

In short, the implication of Shanks's insights for the typology is that each 'type' will tend to manifest only partial shakenness. Exclusivists may be shaken by other Christians who impress on them the question of the breadth of God's grace (at least to embrace a wider range of Christians), or may be shaken by the Christ-like ethic to show love to those who do not share one's theological commitments; and inclusivists may be shaken further by the conviction that dialogue with those of other traditions may illuminate hidden depths in the Gospel; but the presumption is nevertheless in both cases a solidarity of shaken Christians, for neither type is truly open to receiving the *otherness* of what the Other has to say (Shanks 2000: 43). Meanwhile, pluralists, by virtue of their own desire for pluralistic correctness and the innocence untainted by perspectives they too find disagreeable, may simply be a solidarity of shaken liberals, though inclusive of liberal Hindus, Muslims, Buddhists alongside liberal Christians. For example, Shanks is critical of Hick's form of pluralism on the grounds that the otherness of the Other is not truly heard; that is, there is something of an impatience to incorporate the traditions in an Esperanto-style religious/language framework (Shanks 2000: 44–7). This 'superficial' rather than 'deep' pluralism (Griffin 2005: 5, 29), and its concomitant solidarity of shaken liberals—with their own 'confessional' and 'exclusivist' commitments, as Moyaert incisively judges them (Moyaert 2011: 86–120; also see D' Costa 2000: 30)—is very much about pluralists' desire for innocence, free from the intolerant absolutism of exclusivists, and as such, so-called pluralism is limited by its own "truth-as-correctness." By contrast, Shanks insists that Christian identity demands more of us: to be open to solidarity with all-comers, including those very different from us; all who are being shaken out of cultural and ideological half-truths. The problem, though, is that, like any tradition, we tend towards dishonesty, since Honesty as such is so demanding. (Note, the openness required by Honesty and effected through shakenness is not easy at all; it is not a lazy or sentimental openness, or indifference, but the most demanding anti-sectarianism.) Our tendency is rather to build barriers around ourselves, even as new encounters with the Other invite us to be shaken.

In particular, we resist the shaking power of revelation in three ways (Shanks 2005: 11):[6] the first, which Shanks calls "dishonesty-as-disowning," is that tendency to disown or evade responsibility for our chequered past; that desire to sanitise our story, so we may boast about our innocence and neglect other voices which witness to messier truths; or that individualism which tries to remain free from a tradition's "burdensome... corporate history." The second, which Shanks calls "dishonesty-as-banality," is that "low-key unreflectiveness;" that satisfaction with merely belonging; that "herd mentality" which moulds our indifference to the reality and truth of other herds. The third dishonesty

---

6 My summary places them in a different order from that of Shanks.

is that which comes from "manipulation," the seductive agenda or threats of a gang or powers-that-be, feeding us the inhospitable lies which impede our capacity to be open and receptive to the truth, gifts and pain of others.

What, then, of the signs of these dishonesties in the typology, and how might they be shaken, so its own goal of encouraging pluralistic theologies may be more achievable?

The Scandal of Particularity: God's Mission and Our Non-Innocence

The first issue is the most difficult to outline briefly, but it is concerned specifically with the particular criteria Christians use for assessing the truth and power of religious traditions. In three respects, however, I appreciate the typology's approach. Firstly, it rightly refers to explicitly Christian criteria, since it is addressing the diversity of viewpoints within the Christian tradition. As Cobb argues, this is the appropriate thing to do: to assess other traditions using the norms intrinsic to whom we are, while humbly expecting others to assess our tradition according to their norms (Cobb 1999: 79, 127, 137). For there is no neutral or objective standpoint from which to assess religion; we are instead committed to our particular subjectivity. Secondly, the typology wisely refers, if only in part, to a range of Christian criteria, particularly in the context of pluralism (Cobb 1999: 31–3, 132–3). Thirdly, it is good that Race considers the gulf between, on the one hand, our criteria, ideals and judgments, and, on the other, the actuality of our religious practice (Race 1983: 12ff.), because Christian faith demands not only awareness that we fall short of our own ideals but due confession, especially if we are measuring others by those ideals.

Nevertheless, regarding its implicit assessment criteria, the typology manifests a degree of "dishonesty-as-disowning." For how *should* Christians judge what constitutes true and saving religion? Through its discussion of exclusivism and then inclusivism, the typology colludes with the dominant impression that the Christian tradition has a core or default lens through which to assess the truth and efficacy of religious traditions. This lens, which by implication constitutes the Christian tradition's 'correct' assessment criterion, consists fundamentally of God's self-revelation in Christ (or the Christ-Event) and the saving faith of individuals in that revelation. This is deemed to be the primary answer to the question of the 'scandal of particularity', that is, how the particular event relates to God's universal will. In other words, the impression is that religious traditions must be judged by their capacity to enable people (essentially individuals) to affirm the truth and saving power of God in Christ. Pluralism, however, challenges the presumption that God's self-revelation in Christ is definitive of all true religion, allowing instead for God to self-reveal in many traditions, so a range of commitments can be salvific. It therefore dissents from the default criterion and must work harder for its legitimacy. While it apparently still accepts that the scandal of particularity is the focus for assessing true religion, it alters the terms of the Christian response.

There are, I argue, three signs of "dishonesty-as-disowning" here. First, by implicitly accepting the centrality of one criterion, the typology makes a particular choice, and disowns more expansive possibilities. It is a choice which Milbank would criticise for its fetishizing of the role of Christ in Christian faith, since Milbank reminds us that Christian faith is also a social project (1990: 179). Christian visions of social relationships can therefore legitimately be criteria for assessing true religion. I propose, though, that a more comprehensive biblical measure of true and saving religion is the question of whether the *Missio Dei* is being fulfilled (Bosch 1991).[7] I define the *Missio Dei* simply as the pursuit of God's purposes or goals for creation—God's kingdom realised on earth— which God is acting to fulfil and in which God invites us to participate. (Incidentally, the revelatory invitation *shakes* us and our ongoing shakenness is demonstrated through our participation.) True and saving religion thus consists of our participation in the fulfilment of God's purposes for creation— a particular Way with a scandalously universal vision for all things: God's kingdom. The narrower focus on whether an individual affirms God's self-revelation in Christ may well disregard, or 'disown,' this deeper and broader Christian concern. Of course, the notion of the *Missio Dei* begs Christian questions about the nature of the God concerned—essentially whether or not we must affirm that it is the triune God whose incarnation in Christ is definitive for our participation—so Christological answers to the scandal of particularity are not displaced by embracing this more comprehensive criterion. Nevertheless, the recovery of this expansive vision requires Christians to respond to its multi-faceted nature, as I explore further below, so it is understandable that Christians should respond diversely.

While Race discusses the *Missio Dei* (2001: 8–10), this does not clearly impact on the typology as such; whereas I propose that it should determine the first of three questions which a Christian theologies of religions typology ought to ask: "To what extent do the religious traditions fulfil the *Missio Dei*?" Answers to this question would necessarily attend to a whole range of biblical issues, from the coming to transformative faith "in Christ," to the practices of mercy, hospitality, and 'true fasting,' or worship, as embodied in the pursuit of social

---

7   On the comprehensiveness of mission within the biblical witness, see also: Wright (2006), Bauckham (2003).

justice, and even the very renewal of creation. Of course, even if they advocate and practise in many of these areas, as many indeed do very substantially, non-theistic traditions may struggle with the criterion of 'the mission *of God*;' but, rather than imagining a 'universal theology of religions,' I seek to legitimise intrinsically Christian assessment criteria which are nevertheless expansive, while inviting others to assess Christian faith with their criteria. In fact, were I to strive for criteria which were purportedly 'common' among more religions, it would be understandable were I suspected of not taking difference seriously enough. Furthermore, I will go on to explain that this criterion itself invites others to assess Christian fulfilment of it, and my second criterion more explicitly is concerned with hospitality to others' norms; so even as they are rooted in Christian faith, the intent of these criteria is to reflect the truth-as-openness of such faith. I recognise that Race coins his own term, "transcendent vision and human transformation" (Race 2001: 3), which alludes to the transforming effects of religious traditions, but it is not the typology's criterion for assessment, certainly not one which springs specifically from the Christian tradition as such, but is rather his encapsulation of what is universal to the religious traditions. In this respect, it is a significant contribution to the claims of religious pluralism, but it does not speak to the question of the typology's criteria or act as an alternative to either God's self-revelation in Christ or the fulfilment of the *Missio Dei*.

Secondly, a consequence of the typology's implicit acceptance of a dominant assessment criterion is that pluralism must work harder for legitimacy in Christian terms. For pluralism must innately challenge the very definitiveness of the Christological norm. By contrast, were the typology to begin with the more multi-faceted question of *Missio Dei* fulfilment, it would underscore the plural nature of the Christian criterion in itself, since the *Missio Dei*—as embodied in Christ—consists in multiple transformations of human, social and cosmic realities. This shift, from Christ in himself to the mission to which Christ contributes, would also affirm the authenticity of many of the concerns frequently stressed by pluralists, such as well-being and eco-justice.[8]

Thirdly, and most clearly indicative of "dishonesty-as-disowning," the acceptance of God's self-revelation in Christ as the dominant assessment criterion is an attempt to disown Christianity's lack of innocence. For our acceptance of God's self-revelation in Christ as the default criterion is arguably an assertion of our innocence by association with the Christ-Event, God in Christ being understood as wholly free from sin. Making the acceptance of this unique event

---

8   See, for instance, Suchocki on 'well-being' (2003: 79–80); or Knitter on 'eco-human suffering' (1995).

the primary measure of religious activity allows us to hold at bay the issue of Christian obstruction of the *Missio Dei*. For the history of Christian faith is, in fact, irrefutably riddled with our failures to fulfil the *Missio Dei*, if not our subversion of it—from anti-Semitism, Crusades, Inquisitions, to slavery, imperial violence, racism, sexism, and ecological damage—and by deprioritising such concerns, we allow ourselves to enjoy an innocence which non-Christians are denied, by virtue of their rejection of our core assessment criterion.[9] Far from such self-criticism being the eccentric obsession of over-sensitive pluralists, the confrontation with our messy history ought to be understood as intrinsic to who we are, by virtue of the grace upon which we purport to depend. For grace is not a license for bad behaviour, or the means by which we may excuse our shortcomings while judging others, but the foundation of our self-reflexivity and activism as we aspire to participate more fully in the *Missio Dei*.

In other words, to ask of religious traditions whether they contribute to the *Missio Dei* is also to ask Christians whether we contribute to it, and is to incorporate due confession into our assessment of all religion. This can even be rooted in the Christ-Event itself; for Jesus the Shaken One not only shakes others but is shaken by others, so does not profess to have innocently and perfectly fulfilled the *Missio Dei*. This non-innocence is manifest in three respects: firstly, as a human being, embedded in social relationships and systems (Adams 2010: 11), conditioned by culture and limited by geography, Jesus displayed his "shadow side" through dualistic, sometimes violent, imagery (Pattison 1995: 56–7) and showed that he himself had lessons to learn about his vocation (e.g. Mark 7:24–30, as discussed too by Hedges (2010: 233–7) where he argues that Jesus' hospitality had to incorporate his being opened up by the Other). Secondly, being embedded in social relationships, his stories and actions inevitably had unforeseen consequences, some of which were negative (Adams 2010: 135, 146): for example, what of the feelings of those who missed out on being healed? Thirdly, of course, we cannot easily speak of a singular Jesus; for he formed a diverse community which continually re-forms him in plural ways, as illustrated for example by the typology's different types. Christology is thus a social practice, not only fracturing the wholeness of Christ but actually reflecting his fractured wholeness. Such is the Shaken One, initiating our shakenness but constantly receiving others' initiatives; so the fulfilment of the *Missio Dei* remains fragmentary and incomplete. Even as the Christian's model for the fulfilment of God's purposes, Jesus points us towards it, defining

---

9   Cobb, amongst others, identifies the sins of Christian history and the need for repentance and continual self-criticism (1987: 91).

the trajectory, but is not the figure of "superman" christologies who leaves us nothing to do (Wink 2002: 32).

In summary, I suggest that by naming and owning more directly and honestly the multiple criteria intrinsic to the fulfilment of the *Missio Dei*, criteria by which the Christian scriptures foster assessment of true and saving religion, the typology could resist Christian innocence—that is, it could help us to remain profoundly self-critical—and affirm that our very particularity consists of a real plurality of goals to be fulfilled.

The Scandal of Plurality: Engaging Hospitably with Others

The first dishonesty comprises the typology's presumption that Christians answer the question of the 'scandal of particularity' by focusing on the definitiveness of God in Christ. The second dishonesty consists in the typology's presumption that this 'scandal,' concerning the relationship between particularity and universality, is in itself the only question when measuring religions. Is a given religion the exhaustive, constitutive, or definitive embodiment of what is universal, or merely one representative of the universal among others? This focus is a form of "dishonesty-as-banality," in the specific sense that it betrays a low-key unreflectiveness vis-à-vis the intrinsic relations *between* particularities. For this (modernist) concern with the scandal of particularity obscures the interrelationships among religious traditions, including shared histories, syncretism and symbiosis regarding key symbols or stories (see, e.g., Hedges 2010: 237–42). Furthermore, the real possibility is overlooked that a tradition may be *only truly itself*—true to its particular embodiment of the universal—when it is deeply self-critical and hospitable towards others (Shanks 2014; Newlands and Smith 2010; Yong 2008).[10] The point is that (religious) reality is not simply about the relationship between particularity and universality, but demands proper appreciation of and engagement with what I maintain is the *scandal* of genuine *plurality* too.

Race's discussion of "the Jewish-Christian filter" illustrates a difficulty here (2001: 43–64). On the one hand, he is right that, whenever Christians have effectively treated the transition from Judaism to Christian faith as a transferable model to underpin any supersessionist or fulfilment theology, they have profoundly abused their indebtedness to Judaism. On the other hand, his

---

10   Concerning the intrinsic hospitableness of Christian faith, see also: the self-critical "Christocentric catholicity" of John B. Cobb Jr. (1987); Kosuke Koyama (1999: 64–8) on 'neighborology;' and Suchocki (2003: 109–21) on 'friendship.'

conclusion, that we should consequently emphasise the separateness of the two religions, risks wrenching us from our constant indebtedness to Judaism. To over-emphasise the separation of the two traditions is not only to overlook the wider reality of religious traditions' interdependence, and, more narrowly in the Judaeo-Christian context, the fact that Jesus essentially binds the traditions. Such an over-emphasis may also cause us to pay insufficient attention to a vision in the Jewish worldview of how the particular Way is meant to be a Blessing not only for those affiliated to it but for the whole world. Judaism is, after all, a self-critical Way, repeatedly reminding itself to be mindful of insider complacency and sensitive to the presence, truth and trauma of the alien or stranger. It is arguably integral to faith in YHWH that although the particular community is chosen, it is called to bear the cost of witnessing to the universal scope of YHWH's blessing, which does not require outsiders to become insiders, but inspires all to live in light of God's trans-tribal purposes. Such a focus on the blessing of the Way necessitates a readiness to be hospitable, which is both to give of one's particular tradition and to create space where other particularities may give of themselves too.[11]

Certainly, we see such Jewish engagement with the Other embodied in the ministry of Jesus—an engagement with those of other particularities, such as Samaritans, Syro-Phoenicians, and centurions, as a mark of the prophetic particularity's vocational trajectory towards the universal. The Other's faith in transformative possibilities is both received as such and affirmed as a means of revealing to insiders the truly expansive scope of God's hospitable purposes. This further resonates with Hedges's identification of hospitality to the Religious Other as a significant dimension of the Biblical tradition (2010:138–40, 231–7) and Shanks's (2015) emphasis on the Gospel's intrinsic 'xenophilia': love-for-strangeness.

Incidentally, it is because this kind of hospitality entails receiving the gifts of others on their own terms, that pluralists are mistaken if they presume the *equality* of religious traditions. For equality would necessitate a common, neutral numeracy, a way of measuring the wide range of traditions' norms which could be agreed amongst all; whereas the hospitality of truth-as-Honesty demands that we are open to receiving the truths, gifts and norms of traditions which are each the best according to their own measurements, rather than

---

11   This may idealise somewhat the Jewish pattern of engagement with the Other: for example, Reuven Firestone (2016: 239–42) emphasises Judaism's particularism. Cobb, too, warns that it is not for Christians to judge on the respective weight of Judaism's particularist and universalist impulses (Cobb 1987: 93). Nevertheless, because Christian engagement with Judaism is linked with our engagement with Jesus, we may be disposed to receive this hospitable pattern gratefully.

comparable ways of achieving similar ends. For instance, there are transformations which Buddhist paths can achieve far more fruitfully than Christians,
others better achieved by Muslims than Hindus, and so on. Even where they
all encourage similar practices, as in the good of hospitality, the value of such
an ethic within the pattern of each tradition cannot be equated by a measure
common to all. The presumption of equality is more a mark of our impatience
than a sign of truth-as-Honesty.

Within the typology currently, the focus on the scandal of particularity requires no assessment to be made of a tradition's disposition towards or interrelatedness with other particularities. This silence vis-à-vis a tradition's potential
engagement with the Other is surely problematic, especially as the *Missio Dei*
includes the demand for hospitality-or xenophilia (See also Moyaert 2011: 175).
For instance, Christian exclusivism (even if it ethically affirms hospitableness)
need only say that others probably have nothing salvific to contribute; inclusivism simply affirms that which confirms Christian truth; and even pluralism,
if it simply presumes the legitimacy of others, can thus be indifferent to what
others actually have to say. Also, the acceptance of the dominance of the scandal of particularity—without due regard for a tradition's engagement with the
'scandal of plurality'—further defines pluralistic theology as deviant. Whereas,
if Christian faith involves true hospitality (truth-as-Honesty), genuine openness to receive the truth of others is innately legitimate.

So, I propose a second question, one which reflects the scandal of plurality, that is, the Christian belief that true and saving religion consists in constructive, hospitable relationships with the plurality of traditions, including
a readiness to hear humbly the critiques of us by others' norms. There will
be a diversity of Christian responses to this question's legitimacy—concerned
not least with whether or not Jesus epitomises such hospitality—and a range
of interpretations of the hospitableness of other traditions, thus further prob-
lematizing the typology.

The Scandal of Universality: Transforming Systems of Exclusion

I hope it is becoming evident that, even though this reappraisal of the typology
primarily involves my questioning the way Christology is allowed to define, if
not monopolise, the terrain, my proposals are nevertheless shaped by christological praxis: namely, so far, Jesus' particular contribution to the *Missio Dei* and
his hospitable engagement with people of other particularities. The vision of
Jesus as the Shaken One, running through this, is thus more "christomorphic",
or Christ-shaped (Hodgson 1994: 243). In respect of the third dishonesty, this is

particularly clear. It concerns the *scandal of universality*, by which I mean the presumption of a more universal reality, beyond the particularities of religious traditions, on the basis of *common humanity* (Min 2004: 66–82)[12]—and that this universality affirms human interrelatedness with the whole of creation. This *political* conception, transcending religious differences, is discernible in christological praxis but arguably the typology presumes its absence. How is this so?

Signifying "dishonesty-as-manipulation", the typology colludes with a predominant manipulation of Jesus as *either* the ultimate barrier *or* ultimate bridge to pluralism.[13] Namely, in 'constitutive' christologies, which maintain his ontological uniqueness, he inevitably excludes some people's faith, and in 'representative' (or 'expressive') christologies, in which he represents or expresses what God more generally is doing, he potentially embraces all faith. I appreciate Race's discussion of the factors affecting and distorting our understandings of Jesus (2001: 65–84), but essentially he retains the choice between these two christological options (Race 2001: 75–6). This contrast appears logical, except that it does not engage honestly enough with the politics of these theological judgments. For Jesus cannot be reduced to one who either excludes or includes. His ministry excluded certain attitudes and habits while transforming religio-political systems of exclusion and oppression, as I shall argue further. In fact, in his very humanity, shaped by and shaping others, or *shaken* by and *shaking* others, he 'constitutes' the scandal of universality—the presumption that our common humanity demands to be realised. For this Jew, steeped in Mosaic, jubilee and prophetic traditions, offers us hope of a deeply anti-sectarian solidarity of the shaken, a community where insiders and outsiders, oppressors and oppressed, are honestly opened up to each other's truth and trauma, and recreated in each other.

Let me be clear what is generated by the typology's collusion with the polarised christological options. It forces us to choose a Jesus who either, in constitutive christologies, massages our moral assurance that relativism must be held at bay, or, in representative christologies, confirms our moral catholicity which transcends humankind's little but dangerous empires. Each manifests the sectarianism of truth-as-correctness, with its related desire for innocence. The constitutive approaches manifest in exclusivist and inclusivist solidarities-of-the-like-minded, and the representative approaches manifest in pluralist solidarities-of-the-like-minded. By contrast, Jesus of the Gospels does not fit.

---

12   For Min, this is about the philosophical, historical and strategic coherence of our *solidarity* on the basis of shared human nature.

13   Mona Siddiqui also questions this polarity between Jesus as a bridge and a gulf (2005: 130).

Specifically, the exclusive and oppressive debt and purity codes, embodied by the Temple, were targets of his transformative ministry.[14] Thus, as signs of his shaking mission, he practised subversive hospitality for tax collectors and sinners, commended women and made children definitive. He sought the uprooting of 'the mountain,' that is, the Temple (Mark 11:23), and affirmed mercy not sacrifice. He sat 'opposite,' in judgment of, the Temple treasury (Mark 12:41), and ultimately overturned tables of religio-economic exclusion, reclaiming the Temple's purpose as "a house... for all the nations" (Mark 11:17), which triggered his arrest. This confrontation with the Temple also provoked the Roman Empire, because of the conspiracy between the temple-state's aristocracy and imperial authorities. So he died a death designed by the Empire to impress on any dissidents its violent capacity to silence critical honesty. Yet even this authority—resting on imperial theology—would be shaken: for God raised Christ in defiance of such violence, giving the lie to the Empire's manipulative claim on people's mortality, announcing instead that no such imperial power is the last word. Neither the religio-political correctness of the Temple nor of the Empire could contain or suppress the sheer Honesty of Jesus the Shaken One. As such, he continues to shake us out of our dishonest versions of him and his relationships with others.

Steeped, then, in self-critical and ever-renewing streams of prophetic, emancipatory Judaism, Jesus engages with religious tradition and the imperial context. Both those fields are theological and political, and in both respects, Jesus shakes any sectarian 'correctness' and reorients people towards scandalous universality: the presumption of solidarity on the basis of our common humanity. This defies the manipulation of him as either a barrier or a bridge to pluralism, and impresses on us the theo-political question, relevant to all theologies of religions: 'To what extent are religious traditions themselves transforming systems of religio-political exclusion and oppression?'[15] This question, for Christians, is defined by christological/christomorphic praxis, but signifies the commitment of such praxis to the scandal of universality. This has problematic consequences for the traditional division between constitutive and representative christologies, but is a universal concern which, together with

---

14   Regarding the following articulation of Jesus' political and anti-imperial ministry, see Ched Myers (1988), and Richard A. Horsley's edited collection (2008).

15   The point is that socio-political systems have a 'theology' or religious character which justifies their preservation, and which needs exposing and transforming: see, eg, Miguez, Rieger and Sung (2009).

the two previous questions, ought to shape Christian assessment of the truth and salvific efficacy of religious traditions.

Conclusion: The Shaking Questions

I have been arguing that the dominant typology rests on the centrality of a certain presupposition, namely that true and saving religion is best assessed by its response to the 'scandal of particularity,' and that the default Christian response is focused on God's self-revelation in Christ. Pluralists must therefore work harder to achieve Christian legitimacy, and the wide range of Christian theologies of religions must try to fit categories which rest on the centrality of this presupposition.

I propose instead that true and saving religion, if understood in more comprehensively Christian terms, may be better assessed by the interaction between three 'scandalous' concerns. The first *is* focused on the particular goals of the religion, but for Christians, rather than understanding these simply in terms of faith in God's self-revelation in Christ, they may comprise the fulfilment of God's purposes for creation (the *Missio Dei*). The second is a focus on the interrelatedness amongst the plural particularities, that is, the xenophile hospitality one shows to the others, including those whom it criticises most. The third consists of the transformation of systems of religio-political exclusion, affecting those beyond the particular tradition, and effecting solidarity on the basis of our common humanity within creation.

In essence, a Christian typology of the theology of religions must ask Christians (whether exclusivist, inclusivist, pluralist or however one may self-identify) to consider: firstly, to what extent do you believe other religious traditions contribute to the *Missio Dei*? In the second place, to what extent do you believe other religious traditions relate constructively—'hospitably'—with people of the other religious traditions? And thirdly, to what extent do you believe other religious traditions transform systems of religious and political exclusion and oppression?

Of course, these questions would be answered diversely by Christians, not least as they draw our attention to the subtleties within as well as between other traditions: for a given tradition may be judged more positively in the light of one 'scandal' than another, and in relation to each scandal, a tradition's internal diversity should be recognised (for example, Hindu traditions are not all equally inclined to transform systems of exclusion). The reactions would thus be complex. While certain exclusivists, inclusivists, and pluralists may remain identifiable, the varied and overlapping responses to the three scandals should expose the fact that Christian theology of religions, and thus Christian identity, is founded on a wide range of presuppositions—and divergent views of Jesus Christ, who continues to be shaken.

Moreover, the questions implicitly urge Christians to reflect on Christian achievements and failures in each respect. After all, these concerns are shaped by the definitive commitment that the Gospel shakes us out of dishonesties of disowning, banality and manipulation, towards ever greater truth-as-Honesty: so if we presume to assess others, we must assess ourselves at least as honestly. Consequently, as corollaries of the three questions above, I propose that a typology of Christian theologies of religions ought also to engage Christians in considering: firstly, in what ways do we contribute to the *Missio Dei*, and fail to do so? Secondly, what of our hospitable engagement with those of other traditions, including those we judge most harshly? And thirdly, what of our commitment and action to transform systems of religio-political exclusion and oppression, on the basis of our common humanity within creation?

Both triadic sets of questions are extremely demanding, not only for those whom Christians presume to assess, but for Christians themselves, as they invite us to recognise our own degrees of shakenness and realise the capacity for solidarity with others which shakenness fosters in us. As such, even as they remain rooted in Christian tradition, especially christological/christomorphic praxis, these questions encourage us to do theology dialogically. For, with regards to the Christian tradition, they challenge us to reflect: firstly, are we being shaken out of any pretensions to be innocent, reminded of our harmfully partial versions of the Gospel, and opened up to participation in God's comprehensively creation-renewing mission? Secondly, are we being shaken out of our inhospitable fears, and urged to realise we are only fully ourselves when in constructive relationships with those painfully different from us? And thirdly, are we being shaken out of our collusion with systems of exclusion and oppression, collusion forged by our political manipulation, but which can be overcome, and opened up to God whose love for humanity within creation is scandalously universal? To be Honest, such are my hopes.

Bibliography

Adams, Graham. (2010). *Christ and the Other: In Dialogue with Hick and Newbigin*. Farnham: Ashgate.

Bauckham, Richard. (2003). *Bible and Mission: Christian Witness in a Postmodern World*. Milton Keynes: Paternoster Press.

Bosch, David. (1991). *Transforming Mission: Paradigm Shifts in Theology of Mission.* Maryknoll, NY: Orbis.

Cobb, John B Jr.. (1987). "Toward a Christocentric Catholic Theology." In: Leonard Swidler (ed.). *Toward a Universal Theology of Religion.* Maryknoll, NY: Orbis Books. Pp. 86–100.

———. (1999). *Transforming Christianity and the World: A Way Beyond Absolutism and Relativism.* Maryknoll, NY: Orbis Books.

D'Costa, Gavin. (2000). *The Meeting of Religions and the Trinity.* Edinburgh: T&T Clark.

Firestone, Reuven. (2016). "Christian Theology of Religions: A Jewish Response." In: Elizabeth Harris, Paul Hedges, and Shanthikumar Hettiarachchi (eds.). *Twenty-First Century Theologies of Religions: Retrospection and New Frontiers.* Leiden: E. J. Brill. Pp. 239–42

Griffin, David Ray. (2005). "Religious Pluralism: Generic, Identist, and Deep." In: David Ray Griffin (ed.). *Deep Religious Pluralism.* Louisville, KY: Westminster John Knox Press. Pp. 3–38.

Hedges, Paul. (2010). *Controversies in Interreligious Dialogue and the Theology of Religions.* London: SCM.

Hodgson, Peter C. (1994). *Winds of the Spirit: A Constructive Christian Theology.* London: SCM.

Horsley, Richard A. (ed.). (2008). *In the Shadow of Empire: Reclaiming the Bible as a History of Faithful Resistance.* Louisville, KY: Westminster John Knox Press.

Knitter, Paul. (1995). *One Earth, Many Religions: Multifaith Dialogue and Global Responsibility.* Maryknoll, NY: Orbis Books.

Koyama, Kosuke. (1999). *Water Buffalo Theology.* Rev. ed. Maryknoll, NY: Orbis Books.

Miguez, Nestor, Rieger, Joerg, and Sung, Jung Mo. (2009). *Beyond the Spirit of Empire: Theology and Politics in a New Key* London: SCM.

Milbank, John. (1990). "The End of Dialogue." In: Gavin D'Costa (ed.). *Christian Uniqueness Reconsidered: The Myth of a Pluralistic Theology of Religions.* Maryknoll, NY: Orbis. Pp. 174–90.

Min, Anselm Kyongsuk. (2004). *The Solidarity of Others in a Divided World: A Postmodern Theology After Postmodernism.* London and New York, NY: T&T Clark International.

Moyaert, Marianne. (2011). *Fragile Identities: Towards a Theology of Interreligious Hospitality.* Amsterdam and New York, NY: Rodopi.

Myers, Ched. (1988). *Binding the Strong Man: A Political Reading of Mark's Story of Jesus.* Maryknoll, NY: Orbis Books.

Newlands, George and Allen Smith. (2010). *Hospitable God: The Transformative Dream.* Farnham: Ashgate.

Pattison, Stephen. (1995). "The Shadow Side of Jesus." *Studies in Christian Ethics* 8.2: 54–67.

Race, Alan. (1983). *Christians and Religious Pluralism: Patterns in the Christian Theology of Religions*. London: SCM.

———. (2001). *Interfaith Encounter: The Twin Tracks of Theology and Dialogue*. London: SCM.

Shanks, Andrew. (2000). *God and Modernity: A New and Better Way to do Theology*. London: Routledge.

———. (2001). *What is Truth? Towards a Theological Poetics*. London and New York, NY: Routledge.

———. (2005). *Faith in Honesty: The Essential Nature of Theology*. Aldershot: Ashgate.

———. (2007). *The Other Calling: Theology, Intellectual Vocation and Truth*. Oxford: Blackwell.

———. (2014). *A Neo-Hegelian Theology: The God of Greatest Hospitality*. Farnham: Ashgate.

Sharks, Andrew (2015). Hegel versus 'Inter-Faith Dialogue': A General Theory of True Xenophilia New York: Cambridge University Press.

Siddiqui, Mona. (2005). "Jesus in Popular Muslim Thought." In: Gregory A. Barker (ed.). *Jesus in the World's Faiths: Leading Thinkers from Five Religions Reflect on His Meaning*. Maryknoll, NY: Orbis. Pp. 125–31.

Smith, Wilfred Cantwell. (1979). *Faith ad Belief*. Princeton, NJ: Princeton University Press.

Strange, Daniel. (2008). "Exclusivisms: 'Indeed Their Rock is Not like Our Rock'." In: Paul Hedges and Alan Race (eds.). *Christian Approaches to Other Faiths*. London: SCM. Pp. 36–62.

Strange, Daniel. (2011). "Perilous Exchange, Precious Good News: A 'Subversive Fulfilment' Interpretation of Other Religions." In: Gavin D'Costa, Paul F. Knitter, and Daniel Strange. *Only One Way? Three Christian Responses on the Uniqueness of Christ in a Religiously Plural World*. London: SCM. Pp. 91–136.

Suchocki, Marjorie Hewitt. (2003). *Divinity and Diversity: A Christian Affirmation of Religious Pluralism*. Nashville, TN: Abingdon Press.

Wink, Walter. (1992). *Engaging the Powers: Discernment and Resistance in a World of Domination*. Minneapolis, MN: Fortress Press.

Wink, Walter. (2002). *The Human Being: Jesus and the Enigma of the Son of the Man*. Minneapolis, MN: Fortress Press.

Wright, Christopher J.H. (2006). *The Mission of God: Unlocking the Bible's Grand Narrative*. Nottingham: Inter-Varsity Press.

Comparative Theology of Religions and the Typology Exclusivisms-Inclusivisms-Pluralisms

Abraham Veléz de Cea

Introduction

Alan Race's typology accurately represents the three main Christian views of salvation in other religions throughout history. Exclusivism rejects the existence of salvation in non-Christian religions; inclusivism accepts the existence of salvation both in Christian and non-Christian religions, but mediated by Christ alone; pluralism recognizes several independently valid spheres of salvation among the religions without the necessary mediation of Christ (Race 1983).

The problem is that Race's typology cannot be applied to non-Christian religions without somehow imposing upon them Christian concerns and Christian conceptions of what is of ultimate importance, i.e., Christ and salvation. As someone interested in Comparative Theology of Religions and Buddhist-Christian dialogue about what is most important, I find it necessary to expand and redefine Race's typology so that it can be applied across religions without imposing Christian concerns and conceptions of what is most important on other religions.

One cannot just compare the theologies of religions of different religious traditions with a Christian typology because non-Christian religions do not always fit into Race's typology. Similarly, interreligious dialogue while assuming Christian concerns about God and salvation often prevents us from really listening to non-Christians in order to understand their concerns and their alternative conceptions of what is most important. I am not suggesting that Christians should approach interreligious dialogue without being concerned with God and salvation. I am simply saying that Christians should not presuppose that everybody shares their concerns and their understanding of what is most important.

The expanded and redefined version of Alan Race's typology that I propose is intended to facilitate Comparative Theology of Religions and Interreligious Dialogue about the most important reality, truth, or goal. I have developed this new version and applied it to early Buddhism in my book, *The Buddha and Religious Diversity* (Veléz de Cea 2013). In a nutshell, instead of understanding

© KONINKLIJKE BRILL NV, LEIDEN, 2016 | DOI 10.1163/9789004324077_004

the typology exclusivism-inclusivism-pluralism in Christian terms as involving diverse claims about the availability of salvation among the religions, I interpret the typology as representing different degrees of openness to religious diversity. I also interpret theologies of religions as involving a combination of views and attitudes, that is, theoretical claims and practical dispositions.

Before introducing the alternative version of Race's typology that I propose, I discuss other attempts to expand and redefine Race's typology, and explain why I have remained unsatisfied with them. Specifically, I examine the typologies of Perry Schmidt-Leukel, Paul Knitter, and Paul Hedges.

The Need for Another Version of the Typology
Exclusivism-Inclusivism-Pluralism

I never planned to develop a new version of Race's typology but I had to do so because the existing versions of his typology were unable to do justice to the Buddha's way of thinking about other traditions. The new versions of Race's typology developed by Paul Hedges, Paul Knitter, and Perry Schmidt-Leukel helped to understand better Christian theologies of religions, but they were not helpful enough to facilitate comparative theology of religions and interreligious dialogue what is most important.

I chose to expand and redefine Alan Race's typology because despite numerous criticisms (Schmidt-Leukel 2005), the categories exclusivism, inclusivism, pluralism continue to be widely used inside and outside Christianity by theologians and religious scholars engaged in interreligious dialogue. Other typologies that have been proposed have not proven as successful as Race's typology (Hedges 2008b: 23–26).

The first typology that I explored was that of Perry Schmidt-Leukel. He transforms Race's typology into a universally applicable logical framework (Schmidt-Leukel 2005:18 and 1997:65–97). For Schmidt-Leukel, his version of the typology represents all possible logical positions regarding the availability of P among the religions. He defines P as "mediation of a salvific knowledge of ultimate/transcendent reality" (Schmidt-Leukel 2005: 19). According to Schmidt-Leukel, there are only four possible answers to the question of whether P exists among the religions. First, atheism/naturalism: P is not given among the religions; second, exclusivism: P is given among the religions, but only once; third, inclusivism: P is given among the religions more than once, but with only one singular maximum; and fourth, pluralism: P is given among the religions more than once and without a singular maximum. (Schmidt-Leukel 2005: 19). Although I found Perry Schmidt-Leukel's defense of Race's typology persuasive, I could not apply his typology to early Buddhism without continuing to impose Christian concerns and distorting Buddhist conceptions of the most important. Specifically, I found that Schmidt-Leukel's typology was problematic for several reasons.

First, Schmidt-Leukel's conception of P was inapplicable to Buddhism. Buddhists do not define P as necessarily involving the affirmation of an ultimate/transcending reality. For instance, the early Buddhist concept of nirvana can be interpreted in merely psychological terms as a process taking place here and now within one's own mind. Likewise, as Christopher Ives states "Zen thinkers have represented their religious 'experience' not as a perception of a special object of experience, but as a shift in their mode of experience (from a subject-object mode to a "non-dual" mode) through which the discriminating self-conscious experience "drops off," leaving no sense of being a subject over against the experienced object" (Ives 2005:179). Second, even if P were defined by all Buddhists in all contexts as salvific insight into the ultimate nature of reality, such nature is not necessarily interpreted either as an ultimate/absolute entity or as a transcendent reality beyond the universe. For instance, in early Buddhism what constitutes as salvific knowledge is insight into the Dharma in the sense of cosmic order and natural laws of the universe including the four noble truths, the principle of dependent origination, and the three characteristics of reality (impermanence (*anicca*), unsatisfactoriness (*dukkha*), and selflessness/ no-soul (*ānāttā*)). Likewise, Nāgārjuna would reject both that emptiness is an absolute entity and that emptiness is a transcendent reality beyond the universe. These examples show that even if we granted for the sake of argument that Buddhists understand P as mediation of salvific knowledge of an ultimate reality, such ultimate reality need not be conceived by Buddhists as transcendent or absolute.

Third, Schmidt-Leukel's definition of P seems to imply that P must refer to the same thing for all Buddhist traditions, i.e., salvific knowledge of a transcendent reality. However, Buddhist traditions are intrinsically diverse and exhibit multiple understandings of what constitutes salvific knowledge and ultimate reality. For instance, the referent of the perfection of wisdom in Mahayana Buddhism depends on the philosophical views of specific schools. Even if there were a unique referent of salvific knowledge in Mahayana Buddhism as a whole, it would be substantially different from the referent of wisdom in pre-scholastic Buddhism. Similarly, the number of ultimate realities varies across Buddhist schools and there are several conceptions of the ultimate truth/reality (*paramārtha-satya*).

Fourth, the affirmation of a singular maximum is not an adequate criterion to define inclusivism outside Christianity. For instance, the Buddha's dispensation of the Dharma need not be understood as a singular maximum. The Buddha's dispensation can also be interpreted as a particular and historically conditioned representation of the Dharma that is sufficient to attain liberation. Given that the Buddha acknowledges that he did not teach all he knew (*Samyutta Nikāya*.V.438), his teachings cannot be said to exhaust the Dharma and therefore be considered a maximal expression of it. Even if the teaching of the Buddha were a singular maximum in a qualitative sense, for the Buddha that maximum would not be unique because before and after the teaching of Gotama Buddha, there were and there will be other Buddhas with their respective dispensations. That is, the Buddha's teachings can be understood in inclusivist terms without assuming a singular maximum, and even if we assumed one singular maximum in a qualitative sense, the Buddha's teaching would not restrict such singular maximum to his dispensation, i.e., there would be many singular maximums, not just the one exemplified by the Buddha Gotama. This latter position further complicates the matter because then the Buddha would not fit into Schmidt-Leukel's framework. Specifically, the Buddha would not be an inclusivist in Schmidt-Leukel's sense because he would accept many singular maximums, not just one, but he would not be a pluralist either because each of the instances of P would be a singular maximum and pluralists in Schmidt-Leukel's account do not speak about singular maximums. Schmidt-Leukel could perhaps object that the Buddha's position would still be inclusivist because the dispensations of the Buddha Gotama and other Buddhas are instances of the same religion and manifestations of the same singular maximum. But this would be problematic too because there is no historical continuity between Buddhas, and in this sense at least, technically they cannot said to be part of the same tradition. Similarly, self-enlightened beings (*Paccekabuddhas*) are not Buddhists yet they also attain liberation and highest holiness. In other words, the Buddha's position would be in principle compatible with the existence of many independently valid spheres of salvation, each one with their respective singular maximum, a position that would not fit neatly into Schmidt-Leukel's typology.

Fifth, Schmidt-Leukel's typology fails to capture new developments within Christian theology of religions. These new developments do not fit either into inclusivism or pluralism. Specifically, the position that I call pluralistic-inclusivism is a new intermediate position between pluralism and inclusivism. The new and more open pluralistic-inclusivism differs from classical inclusivism on several counts. Pluralistic-inclusivism shows a greater respect not only for differences and particularities, but also for the value of religions, value that is intrinsic, not just instrumental like in classical inclusivism. Pluralistic-inclusivism does not view interreligious dialogue as necessarily subordinated to mission and proclamation. And pluralistic-inclusivism is more open to other religions because it does not assume that they have nothing new or nothing relevant to offer.

Sixth, Schmidt-Leukel's typology does not provide criteria to differentiate pluralism from inclusivist and pluralisitic-inclusivist positions that admit the existence of multiple, independently valid paths to attain salvation or liberation. In other words, claiming that "P is given among the religions more than once and without a singular maximum" is insufficient to characterize the pluralist position. Besides the theology of religions of Mark Heim, Raimundo Panikkar, David Ray Griffin, and John B. Cobb, there are many Hindus, many perennialist philosophers, and many new age seekers who also believe in the existence of many independently valid salvific paths without being pluralists in the sense in which John Hick, Alan Race, and Schmidt-Leukel are. Even inclusivist interpreters of Buddhism could endorse the existence of several instantiations of P without a singular maximum. But this would be best understood as another form of inclusivism, not necessarily a pluralist view. As I explain in the next section, the pluralist view can no longer be equated with the position of those who accept many independently valid spheres of salvation.

Another typology that I considered as a possible framework for my comparative study of the Buddha's 'theology of religions' was that of Paul Knitter. I learned a lot from Knitter's introduction to theologies of religions, which in my view, remains the most accessible, informative, and fair presentation of Christian approaches to religious diversity. Knitter understands Alan Race's categories of exclusivism, inclusivism, and pluralism in terms of models, which he calls replacement, fulfillment, and mutuality models (Knitter 2002: 13 27).

Knitter's typology overlaps to a great extent with Race's typology. The replacement model is similar to exclusivism in that both tend to evaluate other religions negatively. Although moderate forms of exclusivism acknowledge that there is general revelation in other religions, only one religion provides salvation, and eventually it should replace all the other religions. The fulfillment model resembles inclusivism in that both tend to perceive truth and goodness in religions, though only one religion is destined to fulfill the others because it contains or includes within itself the truth and value found in other religions. The mutuality model is akin to pluralism for its tendency to view all religions as equal; this equality is not to be understood in a relativistic sense, but rather in the sense of having similar rights, legitimacy, and independent value.

The main difference between Knitter's and Race's typologies is a new terminology and the addition of a new category, the acceptance model. For Knitter, a great variety of thinkers fall under the category of acceptance: George

Lindbeck, Joseph DiNoia, Paul Griffiths, Mark Heim, Francis Clooney, and James Fredericks among others. What unites all the aforementioned thinkers seems to be their acceptance of religious diversity with emphasis on respect for difference and the particularities of religions. I find Knitter's acceptance model problematic. The main problem is that acceptance of religious diversity in the aforementioned sense does not seem to be unique to just one type of theology of religions. Inclusivists, pluralists, and even exclusivists are also capable of accepting religious diversity, respecting incommensurable difference among religions, and paying careful attention to the particularities of specific traditions. Acceptance of religious diversity as a criterion is also problematic because it does not explain the difference between pluralists and those who object to both classical inclusivism and pluralism, i.e, pluralistic-inclusivists. Both pluralists and pluralistic-inclusivists seem to agree in accepting religious diversity as a matter of principle. What then separates the two? It cannot be openness to interreligious dialogue and comparative theology because many pluralistic-inclusivists including Mark Heim, Jacques Dupuis, James Fredericks, and Francis Clooney are exemplar in their respectful engagement of non-Christians. Are then superiority claims what separates pluralistic-inclusivists from pluralists? I do not think this is a good criterion either because pluralists also make superiority claims, at least about the superiority of the pluralist position.

The last version of Race's typology that I considered was that of Paul Hedges. I sympathize with Hedges' flexible and heuristic understanding of the categories of Race's typology. Like Knitter, Hedges adds a fourth category, which he calls "particularities" (Hedges 2008a). The other three categories of Hedges' typology are exactly the same as Race's typology: exclusivisms, inclusivisms, and pluralisms.

Hedges mentions diverse thinkers under the label 'particularities:' Gavin D'Costa, George Lindbeck, Rowan Williams, Kevin Vanhoozer, Lesslie Newbigin, Joseph DiNoia, John Milbank, Alister McGrath, Paul Griffiths, and with some reservations Mark Heim. What all these thinkers seem to have in common is their postliberal outlook and their postmodern criticism of universal categories and metanarratives. These thinkers reject the rationalistic and egalitarian tendencies of pluralism, which they tend to perceive as a modern, pseudo-religious metanarrative contrary to the Christian self-understanding. Thus, behind the call for respect for differences and attention to the particularities of religions, there is a common interest in safeguarding the uniqueness of Christianity, which for them cannot be understood as one religion among others without simultaneously undermining fundamental Christian claims.

I find Hedges' characterization of theological particularism insightful but insufficient to differentiate among contemporary theologies of religions. Particularism seems to be more akin to exclusivism than to inclusivism and pluralism. At least in practice, the theological position of particularists leads to the 'exclusion' of other religions. This new and intellectually more sophisticated form of exclusivism is not necessarily rooted in arrogance, disrespect, and ignorance of other religions, but rather on humility, respect, and awareness of differences. If it is the case that particularists are best understood as advocating a subtle form of exclusivism, then it would be a good idea to reserve the term 'particularisms' for those who in their theological practice 'exclude' other religions. From my perspective, particularism in Hedges' sense is a postmodern and post-liberal variation of exclusivism rather than a third position between inclusivism and pluralism. It is for this reason that I prefer to keep a clear distinction between exclusivist particularism and pluralistic-inclusivism, which refers to the position of those who in their theological practice actually engage religious diversity with a level of openness that goes beyond inclusivism but does not go as far as pluralism. Whereas particularism remains confined within the borders of exclusivism, the term pluralistic-inclusivism refers to a third distinct position between inclusivism and pluralism. I also find the category particularism confusing because besides exclusivists with a postmodern outlook, there are pluralists and pluralistic-inclusivists with a postmodern outlook. One does not have to be a postmodern exclusivist to emphasize respect for difference and attention to the particularities of traditions. Among pluralistic-inclusivists who emphasize respect for difference and attention to the particularities of traditions I would include not only Paul Griffiths, Gavin D'Costa, and Mark Heim (whom Hedges considers particularists), but also Jaques Dupuis, Francis Clooney, and James Fredericks (whom Hedges considers inclusivists rather than particularists). Similarly, there are pluralists who emphasize respect for difference and attention to the particularities of traditions including Raimundo Panikkar, David Ray Griffin, John B. Cobb, and even Paul Knitter. Given that there are exclusivists, pluralists and pluralistic-inclusivists with a somewhat postmodern outlook, all of them insisting in respecting differences and paying attention to the particularities of traditions, I fail to see the usefulness of the category particularisms/particularities.

Unlike Schmidt-Leukel, Hedges and Knitter do not attempt to redefine Race's typology so that it becomes a comprehensive logical framework applicable to all religions. Hedges and Knitter simply try to provide a faithful account of Christian theologies of religions today. Also unlike Schmidt-Leukel, Hedges and Knitter expand Race's typology with a fourth category (acceptance model, particularities) in order to take into account recent developments within Christian theology of religions.

Given that Hedges and Knitter do not attempt to expand and redefine Race's typology in order to apply the categories exclusivism, inclusivism, and pluralism beyond Christianity, it would be unfair to criticize them for failing to provide a typology that facilitates comparative theology of religions and interreligious dialogue about what is most important. Instead, my criticism of Hedges and Knitter is simply that the fourth category they add to Race's typology does not provide an adequate criterion to distinguish between pluralists and pluralistic-inclusivists, at least among those who accept incommensurable differences between the religions and pay close attention to the particularities of traditions.

Theologies of Religions as Different Degrees of Openness

Some people may insist on defining pluralism as accepting the existence of several independently valid spheres of salvation without the necessary mediation of Christ. This is the conception of pluralism that prevails among Christian theologians due primarily to the influence of John Hick, Paul Knitter, and Alan Race. However, this prevalent understanding of pluralism is problematic for several reasons.

First, the prevalent conception of pluralism conflates one particular form of pluralism, i.e., convergent or identist pluralism, with pluralism in general.[1] However, there are also non-convergent or deep forms of pluralism. For instance, Raimundo Panikkar, David Ray Griffin, and John B. Cobb are pluralists yet they do not assume that all religions lead to the same goal through independently valid venues. For instance, for Panikkar there are several ultimate religious experiences, i.e., ultimate goals, yet they are all mediated by the symbol Christ, which is understood in pluralistic terms. That is, unlike inclusivist readings of Christ, Panikkar's reading admits that other religions need not use the name Christ to designate what for them mediates the ultimate goal, and rejects what he calls crypto-Kantianism, which consists in assuming that underlying all the different names for Christ there must be a universal essence or common thing in itself to which all names point out.

Second, the prevalent conception of pluralism does not provide a clear criterion to differentiate pluralists from pluralistic-inclusivists like Mark Heim. Heim accepts the existence of many salvations without the necessary

---

1 For a discussion on the varieties of pluralisms, see Griffin (2005) and Hedges (2010: 115–18).

mediation of Christ. Heim accuses Hick and other identist or convergent pluralists of not being pluralistic enough. While Heim admits the existence of many independently valid religions, that is, with paths leading to alternative and distinct salvations, Hick and other convergent pluralists only admit one salvation attainable through several independently valid religions. With the prevalent conception of pluralism, there is no way to determine whether Heim's theology of religions is in fact a more pluralistic form of pluralism or rather a form of pluralistic-inclusivism. Heim's model is a form of inclusivism because salvations are understood as alternative and valid relationships with diverse aspects of the Christian Trinity. This inclusivism is pluralistic because it allows for soteriologically significant learning from other religions, that is, the relationships that people establish through other religions with diverse persons of the Christian Trinity may have something new to offer to Christians, not just the same thing. Nevertheless, Heim sees non-Christian 'salvations' as inferior to Christian salvation.

Third, the prevalent conception of pluralism seems to assume that in order to have several independently valid spheres of salvation it is necessary to deny the existence of a universal mediator, i.e., Christ. However, what the theologies of religions of non-convergent pluralists and pluralistic-inclusivists like Heim demonstrate is that it is possible to affirm independently valid spheres of salvation without having to deny a universal mediator. In other words, it is possible to conceive a universal mediator (Christ, the Triune God, the Dharma, the Eightfold Noble Path, Buddha-nature) without having to deny the existence of multiple and independently valid spheres of human fulfillment (salvation, liberation, Buddhahood, sainthood). And if that is the case, pluralism can no longer be defined in terms of accepting several independently valid spheres of salvation without further qualification. For pluralists in Race's sense, all the spheres of salvation are independent and not necessarily mediated by Christ, but they are nevertheless interrelated in some way. What interrelates the different spheres of salvation in Hick and other convergent pluralists is a path from self-centeredness to Real-centeredness, a path that cut across religious traditions. This path, at least in practice, functions as a universal mediator of salvation for the diverse religions. This universal path to holiness is not conceived in exactly the same way across religions but it is not utterly different in each religion either. But one can also say the same thing about Panikkar's conception of Christ, namely, that Christ across the religions is neither exactly the same nor utterly different. Similarly, possible Buddhist names for a universal mediator of ultimate human fulfillment across religions (Buddha's teachings, Dharma, Eightfold Noble Path, Buddha-Nature, etc.,) can also be understood as being neither exactly the same nor utterly different. Hick and other identist pluralists simply substitute one universal mediator (Christ) by another (the path from self-centeredness to Real centeredness). But this is not strictly necessary if Christ were understood in pluralistic terms.

The key to determine whether a theology of religions is pluralist, pluralistic-inclusivist, inclusivist, or exclusivist, is not the name we give to the universal mediator of ultimate human fulfillment but rather the way in which such a mediator is understood. If the universal mediator is understood as being the monopoly of one tradition then we have an exclusivist view of religions. If the universal mediator is understood in a monolithic way as being always the same across traditions, then we have an inclusivist view. But if the universal mediator is understood as being neither exactly the same nor utterly different, then it gets complicated because that view can be either pluralist or pluralistic-inclusivist. How do we differentiate the two views? Well, my contention is that we do not differentiate the two by counting the number of salvations that someone accepts nor by counting the number of mediators that someone posits. In my account, the difference between pluralists and pluralistic-inclusivists is best understood as having to do with distinct types of openness. The expanded and redefined version of Race's typology that I propose distinguishes among two types of openness: openness in practice and openness in theory. Openness in theory refers to views or claims about the existence of OTMIX among the religions.

The acronym OTMIX stands for "our tradition most important X." X is defined in non-essentialist terms as "that which functions as the most important reality, value, goal, or truth in a given context and for a particular tradition or set of traditions" (Veléz de Cea, 2013). X may refer to different things in different contexts, and this can be the case even within a single religious tradition. For instance, among Christian traditions, the most common referent of X is salvation, but in some contexts X may also refer to God, grace, truth, goodness, love, justice, and so on. Similarly, the most common referent of X in Buddhist traditions is the Dharma, but in certain contexts X may refer to liberation or Nirvana, highest holiness or Buddhahood, ultimate truth or Emptiness, compassion, mindfulness, and so on.

X is defined in non-essentialist terms because we cannot assume that all traditions share similar concerns and conceptions of the most important reality, truth, goal, value, good, etc. Likewise, we cannot presuppose that the referents of X do not evolve over time, or that conceptions of X in all traditions are monolithic, and therefore, definable once and for all. If it is true that religious traditions evolve, and if it is the case that such traditions are intrinsically diverse, then X is best understood in non-essentialist terms, i.e., as that which functions as the most important. While a non-essentialist reading of

X allows for multiple referents of X and is more consistent with the dynamism and complexity of religions, an essentialist reading allows only for one universal referent of X.

I have identified four main types of theoretical openness, that is, views or claims about the existence of OTMIX among the religions: tradition-specific openness (exclusivism), openness to what is similar (inclusivism), openness to similar and different instances of OTMIX, but with non-negotiable, dogmatic constraints (pluralistic-inclusivism), and openness to similar and different instances of OTMIX, but without non-negotiable, dogmatic constraints (pluralism). In other words, the exclusivist view is open to the existence of OTMIX but only in one's own religious tradition. Needless to say, the exclusivist does not necessarily accept everything that comes from other members of the same tradition. The inclusivist view is open to the existence of OTMIX in other traditions as long as X outside one's own tradition is similar to X in one's own tradition. That is, those holding inclusivists views are open only to similar instances of X in other traditions; the underlying assumption is that other religions have nothing new or nothing substantially different to offer with regard to OTMIX. The pluralistic-inclusivist is open to the existence of similar and different instances of OTMIX in other traditions. However, new or different instances of X in other traditions must be compatible with the instances of X found in one's own tradition. That is, the new instances of X cannot contradict the nonnegotiable doctrinal or practical standards of one's own tradition. The pluralist view is also open to the existence of similar and different instances of OTMIX in other religious traditions. However, unlike pluralistic-inclusivist views, pluralist views do not assume that X in other traditions cannot contradict X in one's own tradition. That is, the pluralist view does not confine the reality of X with *a priori* nonnegotiable, dogmatic assumptions. Pluralists admit, at least as a possibility, that instances of X found in other traditions may challenge, contradict, and even supersede X in one's own tradition. I am indebted to Raimon Panikkar for this conception of pluralism as openness to other religions without *a priori* nonnegotiable, dogmatic constraints (Panikkar 1995: 79). It is not a coincidence that the beginning of Panikkar's "Sermon on the Mount of Intrareligious Dialogue," which is in the first page of his book *Intrareligious Dialogue*, reads: "When you enter into an intrareligious dialogue, do not think beforehand what you have to believe" (Panikkar 1999: 1). The openness characteristic of pluralism, however, does not mean that pluralists lack normative criteria and deeply held convictions, it simply means that they do not consider such criteria and convictions absolute and unchangeable by definition, i.e., dogmatically. Again, Panikkar's "Sermon on the Mount of Intrareligious Dialogue" captures the commitment to one's own tradition that is characteristic of pluralism: "Blessed are you when you do not give up your convictions, and yet you do not set them up as absolute norms" (Panikkar 1999: 1). Needless to say, Panikkar does not advocate relativism but rather intellectual humility and awareness of the incommensurability of ultimate human attitudes, cosmologies and religions. Lacking dogmatic constraints does not mean lacking doctrines, contentions or absence of roots in specific traditions.

Pluralism cannot be a super system or universal theory of religions precisely because of the aforementioned incommensurability of ultimate systems. This also means that pluralism as a theology of religions cannot be reduced to a mere view or theoretical claim about OTMIX. Besides views, theologies of religions also involve specific attitudes or practical dispositions toward the religious Other. I am also indebted to Panikkar for this understanding of theologies of religions as involving both views and attitudes, that is, theoretical claims and practical dispositions. In fact, Panikkar understands pluralism primarily as an attitude, the attitude of keeping the dialogue and the quest for truth always open.

The expanded and redefined version of Race's typology that I propose distinguishes among three main attitudes or types of openness in practice (exclusivistic, inclusivistic, and pluralistic). Specifically, openness in practice refers to attitudes or dispositions to accept, respect and interact with people and elements from other religions.

Exclusivistic attitudes display the lowest degree of acceptance, respect, and interaction with other traditions. At best, exclusivist attitudes tolerate rather than accept doctrines and practices of other religions; exercise restraint and political correctness rather than genuine respect for their members; and lead to segregation and mutual neglect rather than interaction. At worst, lack of acceptance may lead to confrontation, lack of respect to discrimination, and lack of interaction to prejudices and even systematic attempts to eliminate the religious Other or at least their teachings and practices.

Inclusivistic attitudes display an intermediate level of acceptance, respect, and interaction with other religions. The existence of other religions is accepted but their validity is understood instrumentally, that is, other religions are stepping stones or mere preparations for the most important teaching, reality, goal, or truth found in one's own tradition. People with inclusivistic attitudes genuinely respect other religions and their members but they tend to do so in a condescending way, more interested in teaching than learning, more concerned with preaching than listening. Inclusivistic attitudes presuppose that other religions are acceptable and respectable to some extent and for the time being, but ultimately incomplete and in need of fulfillment by one's own tradition. Inclusivistic attitudes do not discourage interactions with people and teachings from other religious traditions but they tend to perceive such inter-actions as not really necessary, as the monopoly of experts and representatives of religions, and as subordinated to mission and proclamation.

Pluralistic attitudes represent the highest degree of acceptance, respect and interaction with other religions. Pluralistic attitudes tend to perceive diversity in positive terms, for instance, as a blessing, as an opportunity for mu-tual enrichment, or as part of God's will. Religions are accepted and respected as a matter of principle. Religions have intrinsic value, not just instrumental value. Religions are often compared to flowers in a beautiful garden; people may prefer the color, shape, and fragrance of one flower over others, but this preference does not imply that they cannot enjoy other flowers. Each flower is unique and deserves respect and appreciation in its own terms. This does not mean that people with pluralistic attitudes accept and respect everything that exists in other religions. Rather, what people with pluralistic attitudes do is to acknowledge that religions may have something important to offer. Pluralis-tic attitudes assume that interactions with people and teachings from other religions are indispensable and beneficial for everybody, not just for experts and representatives of religions. We interact with other religions not only to promote friendship and harmony but also because we cannot do otherwise: we are dialogical beings, i.e., persons, the commandment to love our neighbor requires us to practice interreligious dialogue, and we are all interconnected. Interreligious dialogue may serve practical goals but it is never reduced to a mere means to attain ulterior goals. Dialogue for dialogue sake and building bridges of communication and mutual understanding among the religions make perfect sense even if it does not lead to agreement or to the achievement of any practical goal. In sum, according to the expanded and redefined version of Race's typology that I advocate, theologies of religions involve a combina-tion of a view or claim about what may be found in other traditions (openness in theory), and an attitude or set of dispositions to accept, respect and interact with people and elements from other religions (openness in practice).

None of the great world religions is reducible to a single theology of religions. There are many possible combinations of views and attitudes, and many of these combinations can be identified at some point in the history of all the great world religions and perhaps in the biography of many individu-als. Even today, it seems possible to detect instances of exclusivist, inclusivist, pluralistic-inclusivist, and pluralist views combined with exclusivistic, inclu-sivistic, and pluralistic attitudes in many religions. Nevertheless, despite the aforementioned multiplicity of combinations, it seems also possible to gen-eralize to some extent and speak about the theology of religions that prevails in one religious tradition. For instance, Buddhist traditions tend to combine an exclusivist view of highest holiness or liberation with inclusivistic attitudes that genuinely accept, respect, and interact with people and elements of other traditions. Similarly, official Catholicism and mainline Protestant churches tend to combine an inclusivist view of salvation with inclusivistic attitudes. No doubt there are pluralist views and pluralistic attitudes among Buddhists and Christians, but they seem to be a minority position. The same can be said about exclusivist views and exclusivistic attitudes.

The new interpretation of Alan Race's typology that I propose is intended to facilitate comparative theology of religions and interreligious dialogue about what is most important, but without presupposing any value judgment about which view or attitude is better. For exclusivists and inclusivists, the pluralist openness will be excessive, and for pluralists and inclusivists, the exclusivist openness will be insufficient. One can only judge other types of openness as better or worse from the perspective of another type of openness. The typology does not favor the perspective of any particular type of openness and, therefore, is axiologically neutral. The only assumption behind the new version of Race's typology is that theologies of religions can be understood in terms of openness to religious diversity, and that openness involves not only a theoretical stand but also a set of practical dispositions. The validity of the framework does not depend on the terminology we use. If someone feels that the categories exclusivism, inclusivism, and pluralism are misleading or no longer helpful, then it is possible to change the terminology and talk simply about levels of theoretical and practical openness. For instance, instead of speaking about 'exclusivist view' and 'exclusivistic attitude,' we can say 'theoretical openness level one' and 'practical openness level one.' Similarly, instead of talking about the 'inclusivist view' and 'inclusivistic attitude' we could speak of 'theoretical openness level two' and 'practical openness level two.' The 'pluralistic-inclusivist view' would be 'theoretical openness level three' and the 'pluralist view' and the 'pluralistic attitude' would be respectively 'theoretical openness level four' and 'practical openness level three.' The substance of the typology does not change after changing the terminology. There are four main types of openness in theory (views levels 1, 2, 3, 4) and three main types of openness in practice (attitudes levels 1, 2, 3). The typology does not exhaust all possible responses to religious diversity and it is in principle open-ended. That is, further subdivisions can be made and new types of openness to religious diversity can be added if necessary. The number of three attitudes, like the number of four views, is not to be understood as unchangeable.

Understanding theologies of religions in terms of openness provides clear criteria not only to distinguish among the most common views of religious diversity across religions but more specifically to differentiate the position of pluralists and pluralistic-inclusivists within Christian theology of religions.

The pluralist position can be formulated as a view that involves three statements: first, 'there are multiple instances of OTMIX in other religions,' second, 'such instances are sometimes similar and sometimes different from the instances of OTMIX found in my religion,' and third, 'the different instances of OTMIX found in other religions are not constrained by nonnegotiable doctrinal claims found in my religion.' The first statement separates pluralistic-inclusivism from exclusivism, the second statement marks the difference between inclusivism and pluralistic-inclusivism, and the third statement distinguishes pluralism from pluralistic-inclusivism. Combining the three statements, the pluralistic-inclusivist view can be summarized as follows: 'there are multiple similar and different instances of OTMIX in other religions, but they are not constrained by nonnegotiable doctrinal claims found in any religion.'

This new definition of pluralism in terms of openness without nonnegotiable, dogmatic constraints helps to appreciate the fundamental distinction that exists between pluralistic-inclusivists and pluralists. Like pluralistic-inclusivists, pluralists accept the existence of new instances of OTMIX in other religions. However, unlike pluralistic-inclusivists, pluralists do not think that the new instances of OTMIX found in other traditions are necessarily constrained by nonnegotiable doctrinal claims, those of one's own religion. Pluralists understand and evaluate the new instances of OTMIX found in other traditions with the standards and doctrinal claims of their own traditions. This is unavoidable. However, unlike pluralistic-inclusivists, pluralists do not consider such standards and doctrinal claims unchangeable dogmas, i.e., nonnegotiable.

Both pluralists and pluralistic-inclusivists are open to the existence of OTMIX in other religions in a limited and critical way, that is, both presuppose standards and doctrinal claims by which other instances of OTMIX are measured. This is important because the stereotype about pluralists as being uncritically open to other religions to the point of lacking standards and falling into relativism needs to be revised. Pluralists do have normative criteria and make doctrinal claims like anybody else. In this regard, pluralists are no different from exclusivists, inclusivists, and pluralistic-inclusivists. What does distinguish pluralists from others is that they do not understand their standards and doctrinal claims as nonnegotiable, that is, as dogmas that can never be challenged and contradicted. Pluralists are not dogmatically constrained; they can reinterpret their doctrinal claims and modify their normative criteria if necessary, even the most sacrosanct ones, provided that they discover new evidence that requires them to do so. Thus, pluralism is not defined by openness to the existence of new instances of OTMIX in other religions, which is something that pluralists have in common with pluralistic-inclusivists. Rather, what defines pluralism is a non-dogmatic openness, the absence of nonnegotiable constrains. Pluralism is open to the existence of new instances of OTMIX in other religions, but with a qualifier: OTMIX is not necessarily constrained by nonnegotiable doctrinal claims and normative criteria.

By providing a clear demarcation between diverse theologies of religions, the new version of Race's typology facilitates comparative theology of religions and interreligious dialogue about the most important. The categories 'openness in theory' and 'openness in practice' can be applied beyond the borders of Christianity without imposing Christian concerns and assumptions. Coupled with the acronym OTMIX, the expanded and redefined version of Race's typology becomes a truly cross-cultural and interreligious framework that can be used successfully to compare views and attitudes toward religious diversity, and in that way, foster authentic dialogue about what religions deem the most important.

Bibliography

Griffin, D.R. (2005). "Religious Pluralism: Generic, Identist, and Deep." In: D.R. Griffin (ed). *Deep Religious Pluralism*. Louisville, KN: John Knox Press. pp. 3–38.

Hedges, P. (2008a). "Particularities." In: P. Hedges and A. Race (eds.). *Christian Approaches to other Faiths*. London: SCM Press. pp. 112–35.

———. (2008b). "A Reflection on Typologies: Negotiating a Fast-Moving Discussion." In: P. Hedges and A. Race (eds.). *Christian Approaches to other Faiths*. London: SCM Press. pp. 17–33.

———. (2010). *Controversies in Interreligious Dialogue and the Theology of Religions*. London: SCM.

Ives, C. (2005). "Liberating Truth: A Buddhist Approach to Religious Pluralism." In: D.R. Griffin (ed.). *Deep Religious Pluralism*. Louisville, KY: Westminster John Knox Press. pp. 178–92.

Knitter, P. (2002). *Introducing Theologies of Religions*. Maryknoll, NY: Orbis Books.

Panikkar, R. (1995). *Invisible Harmony: Essays on Contemplation & Responsibility*. Minneapolis, MN. Fortress Press.

———. (1999). *The Intrareligious Dialogue*. New York, NY: Paulist Press.

Race, A. (1983). *Race, Christians and Religious Pluralism*. Maryknoll, NY: Orbis Books.

Schmidt-Leukel, P. (1997). *Theologie der Religionen: Probleme, Optionen, Argumente*. Ars Una: Neuried.

Schmidt-Leukel, P. (2005). "Exclusivism, Inclusivism, Pluralism: The Tripolar Typology— Clarified and Reaffirmed." In: P. Knitter (ed.). *The Myth of Religious Superiority: A Multifaith Exploration*. Maryknoll, NY: Orbis Books. pp. 13–27.

Veléz de Cea, A. (2013). *The Buddha and Religious Diversity*. London: Routledge.

CHAPTER 3

The Typology and Theological Education: Towards a Practical Theology of Inter Faith Engagement

Ray Gaston

Introduction

It is often remarked upon that the typology on different Christian theologies of religious diversity is a well-worn path and has long lived out its sell by date (D'Costa 2005: 637). However, this chapter will argue that, although the typology has had a long track record in academic theology of religions, it is not particularly well known within the church. My experience of working with ordinands at an ecumenical theological college and amongst congregations in the Methodist District of Birmingham is that the vast majority have never encountered the typology and are unaware of its categories. However, many come to the college module on 'Christianity and Inter Faith Engagement' and church courses on interreligious encounter with real experience of engaging with people of other faith traditions. The typology therefore, it will be argued, is a useful pedagogical tool to enable reflection on attitudes to other faith traditions and can be used to encourage intra-Christian theological engagement. I will seek to counter the claim that the typology necessarily has a pluralist bias, showing that, although Race's original presentation (1983) had such a focus, others have used the typology to assert the positive nature of exclusivisms and inclusivisms alike. However, the critique of the typology that it encourages the construction of fixed positions that drive an unhelpful theological contestation over the possibility of constructive theological dialogue will be taken more seriously. Drawing upon a brief comment by Michael Barnes in his *Theology and the Dialogue of Religions* (2002) I will outline how I have encouraged using the typology as a way for Christians to explore their practice in relation to other faith traditions and how this practice orientated reflection encourages an affirmation of the value of each of the typology's categories and the necessity for intra-Christian dialogue. This chapter will therefore argue that using the typology alongside forms of reflective practice, rooted in real experiences of interreligious encounter, can enhance the confidence of Christians to engage constructively with the multifaith reality of our contexts, whilst also encouraging intra-Christian dialogue on religious plurality. This process enables people to express their own theological understandings in light of their practice and to reflect in turn upon where they locate the primary source of accountability for that understanding.

Building upon this primary reflection I will briefly examine more recent developments in the theology of religions that seek to replace the typology with a debate between pluralisms and particularisms (Hedges 2010; Daggers 2013). I will seek to analyze this development using David Tracy's three disciplines of theology (1981: 47–98). I will argue that whilst pluralisms and particularisms represent explorations within theology of religions that are principally influenced by the fundamental and the systematic disciplines respectively, we require a greater concentration on developing what might be termed a theology of interreligious engagement that is principally influenced by the practical discipline of theology—being built upon a closer analysis of how Christians are actually engaging with their multifaith realities.

Presenting the Typology in Theological Education

Initially, any course I run will begin with asking participants to reflect upon a significant encounter with another faith tradition. Participants are encouraged to define 'significant' for themselves. The following are a small selection of responses gathered from ordinands and congregants in the last five years.

Barbara, an 85 year old woman, who attends a church in an area where 80% of the population is Muslim, regularly talks about her faith and in turn learns about the faith of her Muslim taxi drivers. She finds that they often ask her to pray for a personal or family need, as they take her to the weekly Bible study class she attends at her local Methodist Church in inner city Birmingham.

Siperire, a Methodist minister in Coventry, remembers when she worked for a nursing agency being assigned to a 'live in' post with an elderly Orthodox Jewish woman suffering from dementia and having to learn about Kosher practices and finding herself entering into the rhythms of Jewish life.

Roy, who works for a small engineering firm in Solihull, developed a friendship over 12 years with a Muslim colleague Ahmed—they often talked together about God, prayer, and family life. Recently the firm made a number of people redundant. Ahmed lost his job and Roy kept his; this was a difficult experience for them both.

Roberta, a Primary School Teacher in Wolverhampton, tells a story of being challenged by Sikh children in her class because she had placed a Bible on the floor. One of the 10 year old children in the class left her seat, came forward, picked up the book and placed it on her desk. This incident led to a class discussion on how different faith communities treat their 'holy books.' Roberta

further reflected on the role of scripture in Christian tradition and how it differs to that of other faiths.

Mandy, an NHS manager and an Anglican ordinand preparing for a cura-
cy in Stafford, is a member of a reading group of 'professionals' that includes
amongst its members three Hindus and three Christians. Recently, as part of a
project for her training, Mandy asked the group if they would be willing to read
the Book of Daniel. The generosity and interest with which her Hindu friends
approached the book and the insights they gave caused Mandy to reflect upon
how open she would be to reading the scriptures of other faith traditions.

A church from an evangelical tradition in a West Midlands town that has
had a ministry to night clubbers for some time—including serving tea, coffee,
and water—were approached by local Muslims during Ramadan, who wanted
to join with them and offer food to revelers. The church agreed and a continuing relationship developed.

These encounters are by no means unusual particularly for participants who
live in the urban conurbations of the West Midlands and a sharing of them in
the class encourages an understanding that our theological reflecting is done
in the reality of our lived experience. When we reflect on how we relate to the
typology such reflection is done with the stories of encounter with real people
of other faith traditions present with us in the room. From this exploration and
sharing of stories of encounter I move on to present the typology to the class.
The question then becomes—how should it be presented? Race's original
typology was an argument for a pluralist theology of religions and it is claimed
to have an inherently pluralist bias built into its structure (Barnes 2002: 8).
However, if one examines some popular presentations of the typology from
more conservative theological approaches it can be seen that this is not necessarily the case. For instance in her book *The Bible and Other Faiths—What does
the Lord require of us?* Ida Glaser, from a conservative evangelical perspective,
presents the typology arguing that exclusivism is Christocentric, inclusivism is
Theocentric, and pluralism is Reality-centered (Glaser 2005: 28–33). The aim is
clearly to present to her target audience the positive nature for them of the exclusivist position with its supposed unconditional affirmation of Christ. Meanwhile Veli Matti Karkkainen, in an attempt to affirm mainline church inclusivism to a perhaps more conservative audience, chooses to present exclusivism
as Ecclesiocentric, inclusivism as Christocentric, and pluralism as Theocentric
(Karkkainnen 2003: 165–173). The bias in each of these presentations is towards
exclusivisms and inclusivisms respectively. The typology can be presented
therefore in a number of forms which privilege one of the types over another
as the most appropriate, depending upon the audience and their particular
biases as well as that of the authors. My own presentational bias perhaps leans

towards the inclusivist position, not necessarily because I hold to that myself, but because I interpret that as being the position that might be defined as the one closest to official statements of both the Anglican (Doctrine Commission 1995) and Methodist (Methodist Conference 1999) churches who sponsor most of Queen's' students and who make up the membership of most of my classes in local churches. However, although the potential dangers for Christian integrity of the extreme ends of the continuum may be explored, I seek to emphasize that I believe all three positions can be argued for from within the Christian tradition. I also aim to present the typology in varied form, firstly, presenting a number of bullet points for each type and then secondly presenting quotes from representatives of the type that also challenge easy dismissals of one type or another. So a quote from Barth is used which reads as a strong exclusivist statement, but then Barth's possible universalism is also mentioned (Greggs 2009). A quote from Rahner that presents the anonymous Christian position is presented but then his later interview about mutual inclusivity is also raised (D'Costa 1986: 89–91). Finally a quote from Wilfred Cantwell Smith is used that argues for pluralism on strongly Christian grounds challenging the assumption that pluralism leaves behind the Christian narrative in its presentation of itself.

Having presented the typology participants are asked to identify with one or another of the three positions. The emphasis here is not to commit oneself to one of the positions but to identify which one affirms most closely one's own position acknowledging that the reality may be more complex and considering the engagement with other faith traditions already reflected upon in the start of the class. Participants are encouraged to place themselves on a continuum stretching along the room from conservative exclusivisms at one end to radical pluralisms at the other. The emphasis is on the typology being read as a continuum rather than fixed positions, a continuum on which people may move in different directions in their Christian journey of encounter with other faith traditions. When participants feel they have settled into a position they feel momentarily comfortable with, we take a look at the spread. At Queen's, that is theologically diverse, we usually have a spread of people across the continuum from 'moderate' exclusivisms to 'moderate' pluralisms and everything in between. Students are then encouraged to engage in conversation between the positions to offer to the whole group why they stand where they are, and to question others about their own stance. This often leads to robust defenses and some questioning of exclusivist and pluralist positions especially. Students are encouraged to reflect back to their own sharing of 'significant' encounters, to root their perspectives in the reality of experience of other faith traditions. Students also reflect on how they wish to identify with aspects of the different types within the continuum with some representing this physically by moving back and forth between inclusivisms and exclusivisms, for example, or straddling a perceived 'border' between inclusivisms and pluralisms. The physical representation of a position, the necessity to vocalize and dialogue with other Christians on it and the need to relate it to the experience of engagement with those of other faith traditions allows the complexities of Christian interreligious engagement to arise. Finally students are presented with an alternative way of reading the typology. Michael Barnes argues for a shift in interpreting the typology from a theology of religions to a theology of dialogue:

> Rather than reduce theology to a series of 'isms' … it makes better sense to understand them as each embodying a theological virtue essential to the understanding of the relationship between any faith community and those it perceives as other. 'Exclusivism' witnesses to that faith which speaks of what it knows through the specificity of tradition. 'Inclusivism' looks forward in hope to the fulfillment of all authentically religious truths and values. 'Pluralism' expresses that love which seeks always to affirm those values in the present.
>
> BARNES 2002: 184

Typology as Tool for Reflective Practice

This shift articulated by Barnes is taken further in seeing each of the types as representing the virtues of faith, hope, and love (1 Corinthians 13:13) that are needed to be in dialogue with one another; between faiths, within the community of faith, and also within the individual Christian. Each of these virtues needs expression in the discipleship of the Christian in their engagement with the religious Other in order for that engagement to be true—a balancing of the three virtues in one's continued practice. Students are therefore encouraged to reflect upon the dynamic of faith, hope, and love in their past and future encounters and how the dynamic lives within them in their articulation of their theological perspective on inter faith encounter.

This is further developed by adding to this reflective process the three 'engagements' of inner, intra, and inter—these represent three distinct but interrelated modes of reflection:

Firstly, the inner dialogue of the Christian as they encounter others (inter), paying attention to feelings and internal reactions to encountering difference and reflecting upon the gifts, challenges and questions that one comes away with. A form of what Elaine Graham has called "theology by heart" (Graham,

Walton, and Ward 2005: 18–46). Secondly, the implications of the encounter (inter) for their engagement with the Christian community—the intra
engagement—what resources does the tradition have for enabling the engagement? Does the experience of the inner dialogue raise questions for how
one has understood the tradition or does the tradition pose challenges to how
one has interpreted the encounter? Thirdly, the implications of their engagement with their feelings (inner) and the Christian community (intra) upon
their understanding of their relationship with the other—the inter-religious
engagement.

Students are encouraged to reflect upon how these three relate to each other
in a self-reflective dialogue and to maintain a reflection journal throughout the
course. For instance, do they prioritize the importance of one over the other?
And if so why? Where is God in this dialogue? This is essentially an application
of the pastoral cycle to interreligious engagement.[1]

This dynamic reflective model is introduced in the classroom but as a model
to use in engagement with the Other as opportunities are presented for 'crossing over' (Cousins 1992: 105–15) to other traditions in the course programme.
Options might include amongst others: Qur'anic study groups; Sufi Dhkair;
Langar at the Gurdwara; Aarti at the Mandir; Shabbat in a Jewish home; visiting a Sangha and experiencing Buddhist meditation. These options are where
individuals or small groups of students encounter and engage with people of
different faiths in their own contexts through conversation and experiencing their community in practice. In addition to this students are expected to
engage in a disciplined fashion with the scripture or practice of another tradition during the course through accessible translations and introductions.
All this activity then is reflected upon through the prism of the gifts, challenges, and questions—faith, hope, and love—and inner, intra, inter, modes
of reflection.

There is here then a change of emphasis from a theology of religions through
Barnes' theology of dialogue to a theology of engagement that adopts a model
of theological reflection rooted in contemporary understandings of practical
theology. Barnes' faith, hope and love triad that potentially prioritizes the internal authority of a tradition in reflecting upon the encounter is opened up
through an additional conversation with the inner, intra, inter triad and the reflection upon the direct experience of the engagement in the gifts, challenges,
and questions mode of reflection; neither of the latter assume or exclude the
prioritizing of fidelity to traditional understandings of one's faith tradition.

---

1   Particularly influential here at the interpretations of the pastoral cycle by Larty (2005:
    128–34), and Leach (2007).

The emphasis is upon the individuals' reflection on their practice and where this practice leaves them in their relationship to God and which element (inner, intra, or inter) they consciously prioritize to come to their understanding.

Challenging New Contestations

As was said at the beginning of this chapter, there are many voices that claim the end of the typology for theological understanding; my argument has been for its maintenance as a heuristic and pedagogical tool that appropriately used moves us beyond the old contestations of theology of religions (exclusivisms, inclusivisms, pluralisms), towards a dialogical theology of interreligious engagement. In so doing I want to resist moves to reset the contestation boundaries as between pluralisms and particularisms (Hedges 2010; Daggers 2013). These perspectives seek to construct new contestations or isms initially loosened by Barnes' theology of dialogue. However, perhaps as Barnes sought to read 'behind' the contestation of the three fold typology we might read this new binary somewhat differently too.

In a thorough and extensive article, Richard Sudworth has sought to chart an Anglican theological engagement with Islam over 100 years (Sudworth 2012). From the missionary exclusivisms of the late nineteenth century to the dialogical explorations of the late twentieth century, Sudworth argues for what he terms an "Ecclesial-turn" in Anglican theology in its understanding of interfaith relations in the early part of the present twenty-first century. Drawing heavily upon the document *Generous Love* (NIFCON 2008), Sudworth notes a change in approach:

> Where earlier Anglican documents suggested that the challenge of other faiths might provoke a new scheme of theologies of religions, an "external discourse" shaping the Church's vision, Generous Love begins with God and the consequent nature of the Church within the life of God. What this turn reflects, then, is not a new innovation in theology but a recovery of inherited traditions: a genuine ressourcement.
> SUDWORTH 2012: 91

Here Sudworth notes the influences of fashions in theology of religions upon church exploration. His 'external discourse' refers to what he sees as the influence of the typology upon previous church reports, most notably the Church of England's Towards a Theology for Inter-Faith Dialogue (ACC 1986). This has now been replaced by a theological exploration that, whilst open to engagement with other faith traditions, locates that engagement within a clearly Christian theological framework asserting the importance of the Trinity and the Church for understanding the reality of religious diversity. Here we see charted within Sudworth's exploration of Anglican engagement with Islam the supposed move from the typology to particularism. But it is not a move marked by heavy contestation with what has gone before, indeed it is only through Sudworth's meticulous analysis that the development is charted. In fact there is a strong affirmation in *Generous Love* of the value of theological plurality in interreligious encounter and of what has gone before:

> From every branch of Anglicanism, evangelical, catholic and liberal, missionary scholars, both women and men, contributed alongside local Christians in developing a theology for mission and dialogue through inter faith encounter.
>
> NIFCON 2008: 7

Sudworth perhaps overstates the case of seeing in *Generous Love* a conscious shift from a pluralist influenced typology to a more particularist model. The affirmation of theological plurality does not point in that direction and the shift may be better understood as representing the changing nature of the Anglican Communion and the role of the Church of England within it, an increasing awareness of the international dimensions to dialogue has replaced a model of theological reflection that perhaps privileged local Church of England concerns and its identity as an established church that addresses a wider audience than the committed Christian community.

Jenny Daggers (2013) has recently argued for a move towards particularisms in engagement with religious plurality that seeks to firmly locate this move within a new contestation of theology of religions. For her the combative approach is necessary to free inclusivist and exclusivist theologies from being defined by the pluralist bias she sees in the typology. In her book she casts the net of particularisms widely, drawing into her analysis many theologians particularly from postcolonial contexts who might previously have been claimed by pluralists.[2] In this widely cast net, she also draws into a particularist understanding theologies of dialogue, and comparative and feminist theologies alongside the postcolonial theologies of religion from Asia that allow her to argue for a Eurocentric bias in the typology.

---

2   Daggers presents a very sympathetic reading of both Aloysius Pieris and Stanley Samartha both of whom contributed to the volume that launched the pluralist position onto the international theological stage (Hick and Knitter 1987).

In an earlier book Paul Hedges (2010) also argues for a new division between what he terms pluralisms and particularisms as the new contestation in theology of religions. A little less combative than Daggers, and arguing from a pluralist perspective that claims to learn from and dialogue with particularisms, Hedges charts much of the same territory as she does including postcolonial critiques of Eurocentric understandings of religion, comparative and feminist theologies to argue for a theology of 'radical openness' and 'mutual fulfillment' that maintains 'Christian integrity.' Although essentially a more dialogical argument than that of Daggers, Hedges does stray into the area of strong contestation arguing at one point for reading exclusivisms as fundamentally 'unchristian' and he forcefully argues against the orthodoxy presented by particularist perspectives.

It is into these new contestations that Tracy's categorization of the disciplines of theology might provide a helpful interpretive tool. In his book *The Analogical Imagination* Tracy outlines three disciplines in theology: the Fundamental, the Systematic, and the Practical. He summarizes their particular bias of interest as follows:

> Fundamental theologies will be concerned principally to provide arguments that all reasonable persons, whether "religiously involved" or not, can recognize as reasonable .... Systematic theologies will ordinarily show less concern with such obviously public modes of argument. They will have as their major concern the re-presentation ... of what is assumed to be the ever-present disclosive and transformative power of the particular religious tradition to which the theologian belongs. Practical theologies will ordinarily show less explicit concern with all theories and arguments. They will assume praxis as the proper criterion for the meaning and truth of theology .... (1981: 57)

Using Tracy's categories of disciplines I would want to argue that the pluralist vs. particularist argument is between theologies whose emphasis is on the fundamental and systematic respectively. This can be seen in the changes noted by Sudworth that I would maintain provide a better reference for understanding the shifts in emphasis noticed in *Generous Love*. Daggers recruits to her particularist camp many theologies that seek to engage with religious diversity through the use of Christian language and categories alone, or where dialogue with the other leads to what she says is a Christianity recentered rather than what she perceives as Christianity transcended in pluralist theologies and within the thrust of the typology—even when it is presented in a systematic form as in Race's original book. However, some of those she sees as successfully recentring rather than transcending Christianity are indeed people who have previously been identified with the pluralist theology of religions. How can this be so?

One might argue that the Christianity transcended element within many presentations of the typology and in pluralist theologies of religions points to a stronger influence in such theologies of the fundamental concern to articulate belief beyond the Christian community.[3] Whereas the concern of those engaged in recentering, is to develop a systematics that gives intra-Christian reasons for engaging in dialogue whilst also preserving and reasserting Christian language and symbols as adequately interpretive of religious plurality. This can arguably be done by anyone from the exclusivist to the pluralist.

Hedges (2010) concentrates on a panoramic exploration of theology of religions and religious studies and whilst seeking to articulate in parts a specific Christian narrative for interfaith engagement does so within a framework that might be argued to fit Tracy's fundamental category. For him the exploration of comparative theology moves us not to a recentered systematics but to the possibility of a new fundamental horizon—interreligious theology (Hedges 2010: 252–53). He sees comparative theology as an aspect of the wider theology of religions wherein the religious Other is engaged as a resource for Christian theological thinking (Hedges 2010: 52–55).

It might be argued that free of the polemics of contestation neither Daggers nor Hedges are cavalier in their use of the similar theological and wider resources they recruit to develop their arguments but represent different emphases in their approaches that are systematic and fundamental respectively. A recognition of this difference of approach might allow for a greater dialogue between these positions and hopefully undermine the attempt to construct hardened isms that battle for the loyalty of other theologies—comparative theology for example (Knitter 2012)—that raise questions as to the truth and appropriateness of such fixed articulations and clearly provide resources for the exploration of both. As with the faith, hope and love triad outlined by Barnes, we are not saying here that these theologies are only fundamental or systematic; we are arguing that they emphasize one element over the other. Similarly, using Tracy's disciplines, we might notice the significant absence of

---

3   This is an argument made by Chester Gillis in his defence of Hick's Pluralist Hypothesis which he argues should be read and critiqued as philosophy of religion rather than theology (Gillis in Sugirtharajah 2004: 137–51). I would rather include Hick's hypothesis as a form of Tracy's fundamental theology in its apologetic nature as an argument for the rationality of religious belief (Hick 2004).

theologies engaging with our multifaith reality that emphasize the practical discipline.

Towards a Practical Theology of Interreligious Engagement

A practical theological emphasis brings understandings into the dialogical process as a theological exploration of religious diversity that require a different starting point for the theologian influenced by the more systematic or fundamental mode of reflection. The practical theologian would not give primacy to communication with wider disciplines in the Western academy or to a strong fidelity to the symbols and language of the Christian tradition but to an engagement and examination of the diverse nature in contemporary cultures of the practice of religiosity and spirituality both within but also beyond the confines of official adherence to a faith tradition. It would thus bring that lived human experience into dialogue with the tradition and other reflective disciplines, allowing the findings to shape and inform Christian praxis in our contemporary contexts. A practical theology of interreligious engagement is different from comparative theology that seeks to analyze the texts, spiritual or liturgical practices of a tradition, to bring them into dialogue with the texts and liturgical or spiritual practices of Christian tradition. A practical theology of interreligious engagement would be concerned with gathering quantitative and qualitative data on actual Christian experience in our multi faith world and how particular Christians experience the encounter with other faiths enabling these voices to be more fully represented in theological discussion of interreligious engagement by drawing upon the methods of theological reflection developed in contemporary practical theology. My own reflection here, based upon the way I use the typology alongside encounter based reflection in theological education, is aimed towards such an emphasis.

Bibliography

(ACC) Anglican Consultative Council (1986). *Towards a Theology for Inter-Faith Dialogue*. London: Church House Publishing.

Barnes, M. (2002). *Theology and the Dialogue of Religions*. Cambridge: Cambridge University Press.

Cousins, E. (1992). *Christ in the 21st Century*. Rockport, MA: Element.

Daggers, J. (2013). *Postcolonial Theology of Religions: Particularity and Pluralisms in World Christianity*. London and New York, NY: Routledge.

D'Costa, G. (1986). *Theology and Religious Pluralisms*. Oxford: Blackwell.

———. (2005). "Theology of Religions." In: D. Ford and R. Muers (eds.). *The Modern Theologians: An Introduction to Christian Theology since 1918*. 3rd ed. Oxford: Blackwell. pp. 626–45.

Doctrine Commission (of the Church of England). (1983). *The Mystery of Salvation*. London: Church House Publishing.

Gillis, C. (2012). "John Hick: Theologian or Philosopher of Religion?" In: S. Sugirtharajah (ed.). *Religious Pluralisms and the Modern World: An Ongoing Engagement with John Hick*. Basingstoke: Palgrave. pp. 137–51.

Glaser, I. (2005). *The Bible and Other Faiths: What Does the Lord Require of Us?* Leicester: IVP.

Graham, E. and H. Walton (2005). *Theological Reflection: Methods*. London: SCM.

Hedges, P. (2010). *Controversies in Interreligious Dialogue and the Theology of Religions*. London: SCM.

Hick, J. (2004). *An Interpretation of Religion: Human Responses to the Transcendent*. 2nd ed. Basingstoke: Palgrave.

Hick, J., and P.F. Knitter (eds.). (1987). *The Myth of Christian Uniqueness*. London: SCM.

Knitter, P. (2012). "Virtuous Comparativists are Practicing Pluralists." In: S. Sugirtharajah (ed.). *Religious Pluralisms and the Modern World: An Ongoing Engagement with John Hick*. Basingstoke: Palgrave. pp. 46–57.

Larty, E. (2000). "Practical Theology as a Theological Form." In: W. Woodward and S. Pattison (eds.). *The Blackwell Reader in Pastoral and Practical Theology*. Oxford: Blackwell Publishing.

Leach, J. (2007). "Pastoral Theology as Attention." *Contact: Practical Theology and Pastoral Care* 153: 19–32.

Matti-Karkkainen, V. (2003). *An Introduction to the Theology of Religions: Biblical, Historical and Contemporary Perspectives*. Downers Grove, IL: IVP.

Methodist Conference. (1999). *Called to Love and Praise*. Peterborough: MPH.

NIFCON (Anglican Communion Network for Inter Faith Concerns). (2008). *Generous Love: The Truth of the Gospel and the Call to Dialogue*. London: Church House Publishing.

Race, A. (1983). *Christians and Religious Pluralisms: Patterns in the Christian Theology of Religions*. London: SCM.

Sudworth, R.J. (2012). "Anglicanism and Islam: The Ecclesial-Turn in Interfaith Relations." *Living Stones Yearbook 2012* (LSHLT): 65–105.

Tracy, D. (1981). *The Analogical Imagination: Christian Theology and the Culture of Pluralisms*. London: SCM.

CHAPTER 4

Exclusivism, Inclusivism and Pluralism: A Spatial Perspective

Elizabeth J. Harris

Introduction

'Space' is socially produced and has social meaning. More than a neutral, physical category, it is intimately connected with the way individual and communal identity is expressed. Indeed, it is hardly possible for a community to have a strong identity without this being expressed, in some form, in space, whether through architecture, landscapes or the lines drawn between self and other. Space, therefore, can be shot through with narrative, history and a world view. Yi-Fu Tuan labels the spatial expression of a world view, "mythic space" (Tuan 2008: 86). As Henri Lefebvre has argued, however, this aspect of the production of space can also reinforce power relationships and become a focus for contest (see, for instance Lefebvre 1991). Postmodern geographer, Doreen Massey, therefore, places space alongside concepts such as multiplicity, heterogeneity, relationality, and process (Massey 2005: 9–15). According to Massey, space can lie at the heart of "a complex web of relations of domination and subordination, of solidarity and co-operation" (Massey 1993: 156, quoted in Knott 2010: 36).

In the last two decades, the study of religion has drawn from the engagement of human geographers and philosophers with religion and territory. Kim Knott has been a pioneer of this. She has both drawn attention to the work of human geographers and formulated her own methodology for the spatial study of religion and locality, citing, for instance, the concept of embodiment to evaluate the location of religion in the cultural, political, and economic spaces of multi-cultural Leeds (see Knott 2005, 2009, 2010).

In this chapter, I align myself with scholars such as Massey and Knott, who have stressed the politics, rather than the poetics,[1] of the location of the religions within the spaces that constitute contemporary society. I argue two things: that each of the categories of exclusivism, inclusivism, and pluralism has its own particular spatial dimensions and components; that the

---

1 See Knott (2010), where she refers to two major approaches to place and space: the poetical and the political, citing Kong (2001), and Chidester and Linenthal (1991).

typology itself can aid the understanding of the spatial dimensions of religion. I, therefore, seek to apply human geography not only to religious studies but to the theology of religion. To illustrate my argument, I offer two case studies in which a theology of religion has been expressed through space. The first draws from my current research into the spatial dimensions of evangelical Christian missionary activity in the predominantly Buddhist south of Sri Lanka in the nineteenth century and the impact of this on Buddhist-Christian relations.[2] The second derives from the period when I was national Inter Faith Officer for the Methodist Church in Britain (1996–2007) and concerns the use of Methodist church premises by people of other religious traditions.

When I started to reflect on the relationship between space and the theology of religion, three questions arose in my mind: Do exclusivist perspectives lead to exclusivist or conflict-fuelling uses of space? Do inclusivist perspectives lead to a more inclusivist attitude towards space? Does a pluralist perspective necessarily lead to a conflict-free use of space? These questions lie behind this chapter. My case studies, however, demonstrate that conflict potential arises most potently when different spatial expressions of the typology meet or when the identity-forming specificities of place and space take precedence over theological reflection. Both illustrate this through a clash between exclusivist and inclusivist perspectives.

Missionaries and Buddhists in Nineteenth Century Sri Lanka

Almost without exception, the British Protestant missionaries who travelled, in the nineteenth century, to Sri Lanka, or Ceylon as it was then called, were theological exclusivists. Formed by a theology that encouraged them to anticipate a battle over truth claims between Christianity and the religions of the island, they saw their task as a compassionate and humanitarian one: saving souls from being 'eternally lost.'[3] Spatial images were used to express this. Sri Lanka was a 'field' or a 'stony place' which had to receive seed, or be broken and produce fruit. Buddhism was a 'stronghold'[4] or a citadel that had to be 'swept

---

2 I am currently researching a monograph with the working title of, *Religion, Space and Conflict in colonial and postcolonial Sri Lanka*, forthcoming London & New York: Routledge.

3 Wesleyan Methodist missionary in Sri Lanka, William Harvard, declared that, "to be unsaved by the gospel is to be eternally lost" (Harvard 1833: 23, quoted in Harris. 2012: 279).

4 See for instance, Bishop James Chapman, in a letter to the Headquarters of the Society for the Propagation of the Gospel (SPG) dated 14 February 1846, declared Dondra in the south of Sri Lanka to the "stronghold" of Buddhism (CLR 29, Letters received from Ceylon, SPG Archives).

away' from ground that had to be 'conquered,' occupied[5] or surrounded by the more powerful force of Christianity.

The theology that underpinned this could also be seen in spatial terms. Wesleyan missionary, Thomas Moscrop, could declare in 1891, contesting those Europeans who sought similarities between Christianity and Buddhism:

> Christ can step into no Pantheon except to empty it, and the time will come when the great world teachers will bow, with those whom they have taught, before Him to Whom has been given the Name which is above every Name [Jesus].
>
> MOSCROP 1891: 3394, quoted in HARRIS 2006: 102

Implicit within this vocabulary was a boundary between 'heathen' space and Christianised space. Within the missionary world view, the two were incompatible and irreconcilable, divided on a cosmic as well as a mundane level. On one side lay truth, God, joy and salvation. On the other lay falsehood, idolatry, fear, and eternal damnation (see Harris 2006: 53–61, 101–09, for information about the missionary representation of Buddhist doctrine).

The missionaries met a different attitude towards space within Sri Lankan Buddhists, at least at first. To their astonishment, members of the Buddhist monastic Sangha asked them whether they could use Christian printing presses or Christian buildings for Buddhist purposes (Harris 2006: 193), not seeming to anticipate that the response may be negative. They discovered that lay Buddhists were quite happy to hold together church attendance and Buddhist practices, seeing no religious contradiction in moving between the devotional spaces of Christianity and Buddhism. And when the missionaries visited Buddhist *vihāras* [monasteries/temples], they found, at a distance from structures that housed images of the Buddha, *devālēs*, temples to Hindu gods, who received offerings and appeals for mundane blessings. Within Buddhism, they also discovered, the spatial line between the religious 'self' and the religious 'Other' was drawn differently than in Christianity. As I have argued elsewhere, what they were, in fact, experiencing was a traditional and long-standing Buddhist willingness to honor the religious 'other' with devotion if that 'other' could be subordinated to the Buddha, a form of inclusivism (see for instance, Harris 2013: particularly 88–93).

---

5 For instance see Bishop Claughton to Hawkins at SPG, 17th November, 1862, lamenting the lack of energy in missionary work, pleads for "the endeavour to occupy new ground" (CLR 29, Letters received from Ceylon).

Throughout the first part of the nineteenth century, missionaries expended considerable energy attempting to convince Buddhists that, if they attended church and professed to be Christians, they had to reject 'heathen' space completely. And this had implications for the way they constructed schools and later churches, and the locations they favored for these churches. Of a school at Minuwangoda, near the southern coast of the island, the Wesleyans could, therefore, write:

> [It] stands upon the top of a beautiful hill about a mile from the Fort of Galle, and though it is but a short distance from the public Bazaar, yet its situation is very retired, so that the boys can run from the crowd and noise to this comfortable retreat, to learn the path to happiness and heaven.
>
> HARVARD and CLOUGH 1819: 39

These school rooms contained no images. The missionaries believed these were fearful for children and might remind them, for instance, of the figures within Buddhist shrines or the *devālés*. Any pupils who brought a 'heathen' book into the school risked having it confiscated and removed from Christian space, at least by the more conscientious and Christianized schoolmasters. The same attitude was taken towards churches—and many school rooms doubled as churches in the early decades of the century.

Orphanages and other residential homes were particularly attractive to the missionaries because 'heathens' could be completely separated spatially from their traditional environment, something that could not be achieved in village schools, however far these were away from the Buddhist *vihāra*. As early as 1821, Church Missionary Society missionaries, Lambrick and Browning, in the central hill country town of Kandy, shared with their home committee that they had started a Boys' School with three destitute native boys, whom they provided for, adding, "The advantage of their being entirely withdrawn from the pernicious influence of the native customs, habits and superstitions is too obvious to need pointing out to the observation of the Committee."[6]

The tension between the exclusivist Christian missionary attitude towards space and the inclusivist Buddhist view inevitably led to tension and conflict over space, later in the century. This mirrored the confrontation between the two religions that arose at other levels, for example over missionary representations of and accusations against Buddhism (see Harris 2006; 53–61, 101–09).

---

6   Lambrick & Browning to Pratt & Bickersteth (12 July 1821, CMS Records: Samuel Lambrick).

I have argued elsewhere that Buddhists in Sri Lanka reacted to the Christian missionaries in six major ways in the nineteenth century: offering hospitality and courtesy; demonstrating a willingness to engage in interreligious 'dialogue' and to co-operate if mutual benefit could accrue; showing a polite tolerance that could mask distrust or even contempt; calling for reasoned debates to prove the superiority of Buddhism; engaging in direct confrontation and opposition; taking pragmatic decisions about relationships with Christians in order to survive under imperialism (Harris 2012: 277). The first three, which favored co-existence and inclusivity, were dominant in the first part of the century, and the fourth and fifth, which eschewed co-existence for greater exclusivity and intolerance, towards the end of the century, as a Buddhist revivalism predicated on opposition to Christian missionary work grew.[7]

Examining this from a spatial perspective, confrontation arose particularly in the 1870s, by which time Buddhists were retaliating against Christian missionary exclusivism by themselves adopting an exclusivist attitude towards the religious 'other' that was Christianity. As Christians had condemned Buddhism as atheistic, nihilistic, and pessimistic, so Buddhists were accusing Christians of worshipping a demon-like and violent god.[8] Significantly for this chapter, they used space and sound to reinforce this.

At this point in the century, the Christian missionaries, generally speaking, opted if possible, to build their schools and churches away from Buddhist *vihāras*, not only to separate Christians from a Buddhist environment but also because they feared revivalist Buddhists might use proximity to provoke Christian congregations through sound, street processions, and superior numbers. However, some revivalist Buddhists drew on another Buddhist practice to provoke, even when there was no *vihāra* close to the church—that of constructing temporary preaching halls or *bana maḍuvas*. One of the main Buddhist revivalists at this time was Ven. Mohoṭṭivatté Guṇānanda, a charismatic Buddhist monk with a strident preaching style. According to Wesleyan Methodist minister, David D'Silva, writing in 1871:

---

7   For further information about the nineteenth century Buddhist Revival, see Bond (1988), Somaratne (1996), Blackburn (2010), Harris (2006).

8   A rhetoric that sought to prove that Christians worshipped a demon-like god is particularly evident in the 1873 Buddhist-Christian debate at Panadura, south of Colombo, when Ven. Mohoṭṭivatté Guṇānanda employed a literalist approach to the Bible and the writings of western freethinkers to argue, for instance, that the narrative of Herod's killing of children at the birth of Jesus indicated that Jesus's birth was inauspicious. See Young and Somaratne (1996: 155–80), Capper (1873), Peebles (1994).

> The Buddhist Champion [i.e. Guṇānanda] since entered Colpetty [Kollu-
> pitiya—in Colombo] and continued to deliver his blasphemous lectures
> there in a spacious building erected for that purpose.... The benighted
> and mischief-making people at Wellewatte [a village a few miles south
> of Colombo on the coast] following the example of their neighbours
> erected a poor temporary shed between our Chapel and my residence
> and invited the priest there too. A placard was put a few days previous to
> the effect "that Gunananda Priest of Mohottywatte will deliver a lecture
> showing the fallacy of Christianity and the truth of Buddhism."
>
>   DAVID D'SILVA 1871, Quarterly Letter 11th December 1871, *Extracts from Quarterly*
>   *Letters:* 132–4, 132

Since the chapel and the residence of the minister were very close to each other for purposes of convenience, constructing a preaching 'shed' between the
two could not be seen by D'Silva and his congregation as other than intentionally provocative. There was simply no other way of interpreting it.

Kollupitiya and Wellewatte were not isolated incidents. Paul Rodrigo, another Wesleyan Methodist, also in 1871, claimed that Buddhists had erected a
large, temporary preaching hall not far from the Methodist Church at Angu-
lana, a little further south along the coast, and had continually read *pirit* (Pāli:
paritta), "for eight days" (Paul Rodrigo 1871, Quarterly Letter 22nd December
1871, *Extracts from Quarterly Letters*: 135–38, 136).

It is obvious from the testimonies of D'Silva and Rodrigo that Buddhists
had intentionally placed their temporary preaching halls in locations that
they knew would be provocative and hurtful to Christians, in an attempt to
force Christians to see that their attempts to create exclusivist Christian spaces could be challenged. It was an intentional puncturing of exclusivism, with
the intention to provoke rather than to create a pluralist space where Buddhists and Christians could co-exist. The implicit message was, 'The ground on
which you have built this church belongs to a Buddhist country.' It had both
synchronic and diachronic overtones, pointing both to the contemporary reality Buddhists sought to assert and to the historical continuity of Buddhism in
the island.

About thirty years later, in an atmosphere of continued Buddhist revivalism, another prominent Buddhist revivalist, Välasinha Harischandra, demonstrated that Buddhism could promote as exclusivist a 'theology' of place as
the Christian missionaries had. Harischandra saw his vocation as re-claiming
the ancient Buddhist capital of Anuradhapura for Buddhism. During the nineteenth century, Anuradhapura had become, under the British, a provincial

administrative center, home to Muslims, Hindus, and Christians, as well as Buddhists. Archaeological work, spearheaded by the British but often carried out in co-operation with Buddhists, had done much to clear some of the ancient Buddhist monuments from jungle but these competed in the same space with colonial buildings and commercial enterprise.[9] In 1908, Harischandra published a guide book entitled, *The Sacred City of Anuradhapura*, which demanded a Commission of Inquiry to address the pollution of the city with non-Buddhist elements (Harischandra 1908). He distinguished between the ancient 'political' city and the land given to the Buddhist monastic community by King Devanampiyatissa in 308 B.C.E., which, he argued, had been desecrated with such things as butcher's shops and foreign places of worship. His argument was that the land originally given to the monastic community should be the exclusive possession of Buddhists and should be 'set apart' for the Sinhala Buddhist nation (Harischandra 1908: 15). Places of worship that were not Buddhist, for instance, should not be allowed within it. His dream did not come to fruition under the British. After independence in 1948, however, Anuradhapura was divided into two: the ancient holy city, a place for pilgrims and tourists, and the modern commercial city (Nissan 1989).

My first case study, therefore, illustrates the conflict that can arise when exclusivism, as a theological position, is expressed spatially. The Protestant missionaries were convinced that their exclusivist theology, underpinned by an exclusivist sense of identity, could be reinforced by an exclusivist attitude towards space. Opposing this spatially expressed theology was the inclusivist attitude towards space, and indeed identity, held by many members of the Buddhist monastic community, who would have been happy to co-exist with the missionaries as long as their internal freedom to subordinate Christianity cosmologically to Buddhism was not threatened.[10] The tension between the two led to conflict, when Buddhists realized that the missionaries sought to undermine both this internal freedom and Buddhism itself. Utilizing defensive strategies to protect their Buddhist identity, they, therefore, moved towards a more provocative and exclusivist attitude towards space.

---

9   One chapter in my forthcoming monograph will focus on nineteenth century developments in Anuradhapura. Also see Nissan 1985, 1989.

10   Wesleyan Methodist missionary, Robert Spence Hardy caught sight of this when he wrote with indignation in 1864 that members of the Buddhist monastic Sangha would have had no problem worshipping Jesus if the missionaries would worship the Buddha and accept that the Buddha was 'the best'. See Hardy 1864: 286, quoted in Harris 2006: 193.

The Use of Church Premises by People of Other Faiths

My second case study draws but does not duplicate a paper I wrote in 1999 for a felicitation volume for Wesley Ariarajah, former Director of the Inter Faith Dialogue program of the World Council of Churches (WCC) (Harris 2011). In choosing my topic, I drew inspiration from Ariarajah's book, *Not Without My Neighbour: Issues in Interfaith Relations*, in which he 'gathered up' some of his experiences at the WCC, the painful as well as the positive (1999). In my contribution, I decided to 'gather up' an issue that was important for me during my time as the national Inter Faith Officer for the Methodist Church in Britain between 1996 and 2007: the use of church premises by people of other faiths.

A report on whether people of other religions could pray or worship on Methodist Church Premises was brought to the Conference of the Methodist Church in 1972, in response to a request from the Birmingham Synod in 1969 that the Model Deed for Methodist Trust Premises should be re-examined to see whether it would be "desirable and possible to modify those clauses which at present preclude the offer of the Methodist Trust premises" to "people of non-Christian faiths who may be unable to find any convenient place in which to worship."[11] The Committee that prepared the 1972 report had to take into account: a written Opinion of Counsel gained by the Chapel Department on behalf of the General Purposes and Policy Committee for the 1970 Conference;[12] the responses to this of the Law and Polity Committee and the Faith and Order Committee in 1971; and the doctrinal standards clause of the 1932 Deed of Union—the point where three formerly independent Methodist groupings came together—which referred to "the continued witness of the Church to the realities of the Christian experience of salvation."[13] The Opinion of Counsel, for instance, had stated on the basis of the 1932 Model Deed governing the use of Methodist premises, "No part of trust premises can be let for a meeting which involves the holding of a non-Christian religious service (Clause 6 of the

---

11   Printed at the top of: "Use of Methodist Trust Premises". General Purposes and Policy Committee Report. Representative Session Agenda for the Methodist Conference of 1970: 21–23. In 1971, both the Law and Polity Committee and the Faith and Order Committee reported to conference on the issue, the former concentrating on the legal aspects and the latter on the theological aspects but the Conference was not allowed to approve it.

12   "Use of Methodist Trust Premises." General Purposes and Policy Committee Report. Representative Session Agenda for the Methodist Conference of 1970. Peterborouth: Methodist Publishing House: 21–23.

13   The Methodist Church Union Act of 1929 gave the power to the Uniting Conference of 1932 to adopt the Deed of Union. The Methodist Conference was given the power to amend the Deed, except for the doctrinal standards clause.

Model Deed).["14] It had added, however, that "minor religious acts" such as a grace or blessing at the end of a meeting would not "come within the prohibitions of Clause 6."

Four recommendations within the Committee's report were accepted by the Methodist Conference at this time: that interreligious dialogue was to be encouraged; that people of other faiths should be able to use Methodist premises "for their secular and social activities;" that an "incidental rite" such as a prayer before a meal or "a brief blessing attached to a wedding reception following a religious wedding elsewhere (but not a full wedding service) or an act of individual prayer demanded at a particular hour" was allowed; and that Christians should be encouraged to observe the worship of other faiths sympathetically "for deeper understanding," gladly accepting "whatever experience and communion with God arises in such relationships," whilst avoiding anything that would distort Christian witness or promote syncretism.[15] The following recommendation, which I quote in full, was not accepted:

> The Committee is of the opinion that to give permission to non-Christian communities as an expression of Christian love and the desire to improve relations to hold their worship in Methodist premises does not of itself imply any denial of the uniqueness and finality of Christ or any judgement on the truth of other religions. It therefore recommends that when a non-Christian community seeks permission to use Methodist premises for its worship because no building is immediately available for its use the Superintendent, Minister and Trustees should be given discretion to grant permission as a temporary measure if they are satisfied that the worship will not offend the Christian conscience and that such permission will have the goodwill of the local congregation.[16]

The immediate reason this was rejected was because it would be contrary to "the provisions of the Model Deed, as interpreted by Counsel," the alteration

---

14   "Use of Methodist Trust Premises." General Purposes and Policy Committee Report. Representative Session Agenda for the Methodist Conference of 1970: 21.

15   Part 2, "Reply to Conference (Use of Trust Premises)." Faith and Order Committee Report. Agenda of the Representative Session of the 1973 Methodist Conference. Peterborouth: Methodist Publishing House: 3–4.

16   Part 2, "Reply to Conference (Use of Trust Premises)." Faith and Order Committee Report. Agenda of the Representative Session of the 1973 Methodist Conference: 4, quoted in Harris. 2011. "Hospitality as a Sigh of God's Grace:" 274.

of which "would need an Act of Parliament."[17] The Report had anticipated this and had stated:

> It is not for the Faith and Order Committee to say what should be done when what is held by the Law and Polity Committee to be legally possible is less than what is held by the Faith and Order Committee to be theologically desirable.

The report, therefore, presented the crux of the matter as a tension between legal restrictions and theology. I would argue, however, that failure to accept the last recommendation and proceed to an Act of Parliament was not only due to an unwillingness to pursue legal changes but also to the prevalence of an exclusivist theology in some sectors of the Methodist Church that saw witness to the Christian experience of salvation as antithetical to any accommodation of the worship of people of other faiths within Christianized space. In these sectors, a clear spatial line was drawn between that which was sacred in Christianity and the sacred within other religious traditions. The recommendation that was rejected, however, was not a pluralist one. It was almost classically inclusivist, with its emphasis on potentially allowing only those forms of worship that would not offend Christians, namely only those that were similar enough to Christianity that they could be embraced inclusively. Tension between the exclusivist view that Christianized space could not be used for worship by those of other religions, underpinned by the Opinion of Counsel, and an inclusivist view that the similarities between religions were such that Christian convictions were not compromised by allowing Jews or Hindus, for instance, to worship on Methodist premises continued for the next 35 years and was not resolved by the time I left my post in 2007.

In 1997, a further report was prepared for the Methodist Conference in response to growing interreligious activity among Methodists and an increase in the number of requests coming to Methodist ministers from people of other religions concerning the use of church premises. Its brief was to assess whether any theological reasons existed to change the policy of the Methodist Church through legal statute. By that time the Methodist Church Act of 1976 had been passed. Under this, Model Deed property (i.e. churches) became subject to Model Trusts, and the Methodist Conference was given authority to amend the doctrinal standards clause of the Deed of Union.

---

17   Part 2, "Reply to Conference (Use of Trust Premises)." Faith and Order Committee report. Agenda of the Representative Session of the 1973 Methodist Conference: 3.

The Working Party decided that no reasons existed to change existing policy, the final report affirming two principles:

· It is inappropriate for teachings contrary to Christian doctrine to be proclaimed on Methodist premises.
· It is inappropriate for Methodist premises to be used in any way which will negate (or cause confusion concerning) the distinctiveness of Christian doctrine.[18]

In effect, therefore, it was more conservative and exclusivist than the report of 1972. The distinction between 'informal' and 'formal' acts of worship was nevertheless retained. The 'informal' was permissible but the 'formal' was not. In other words, the report accepted that "the rather loosely-defined view formulated by the Conference in 1972 remains a viable, though still provisional, position."

Significantly, the report appealed to the specificity of sacred space. One member of the working party talked to people from other religions in his own locality in Greater London, and found that almost all of them recognized the formal/informal distinction and agreed that places of worship should be restricted to one faith. This 'contemporary experience' contributed to a statement within the report that "formal gatherings by other faith communities on Methodist premises are not appropriate." A later part of the report examined "Churches as Symbol" and declared, "It may be helpful therefore to speak of the building itself as a symbol of the continued existence of a worshipping community, even though theologically that existence is not dependent on bricks and mortar." To affirm this 'specialness,' the report explained, did not denigrate the worship of people of other faiths but, again, made it inappropriate for that worship to take place in Christian space. A principle of hospitality towards other faiths was encouraged but with an insistence that the special character of Christian buildings helped to mark out how hospitality should be understood.

When the Methodist Committee for Relationships with Other Faiths, of which I was the Secretary, suggested, on seeing a draft, that an exception should be made if another religious community experienced a hate attack on their place of worship and asked for the temporary use of Methodist premises whilst repairs were carried out, for instance an anti-Semitic attack on a synagogue, the suggestion was turned down by the Faith and Order Committee.

18   *The Methodist Church Faith and Order Committee: Use of Methodist Premises by People of Other Faiths: A Report to Conference 1997*. 1998. Peterborough: Methodist Publishing House: 14, quoted in Harris (2011). "Hospitality as a Sigh of God's Grace:" 276.

Even within this context, an exclusivism that drew a non-negotiable spatial line between Christian worship and the formal worship of other faiths was enforced.

The issue did not go away. In 2005, the London North West Synod of the Methodist Church sent a request to the annual Methodist conference that the Methodist Church, in the light of developments such as the "growing number of requests from other faith communities to use Methodist premises for meditation, prayer or worship, as well as for social and community purposes" should explore, "how and in what circumstances other faiths may be granted permission to use our premises for meditation, prayer or worship."[19] In wording, it was similar to that submitted in 1969. Perhaps more than in 1969, however, the proposers wanted change, to reflect a different theology of religion.

Before the 2005 conference, the Trustees for Methodist Church Purposes (TMCP), probably in light of this request, had asked for a further formal legal opinion on the question: "Can the Methodist Property which is held upon the Model Trusts contained in the Methodist Church Act 1976 be used by, or leased to, people of other Faiths (i.e. non-Christian) for their religious purposes?" The question did not distinguish between the 'formal' and the 'informal' and neither did the reply. In fact, the answer Counsel gave threw this distinction into question. Broadly speaking, Counsel concluded that, because of Clause 4 of the Deed of Union (doctrinal standards clause) and the fact that Section 4a of the 1976 Methodist Church Act stated that the purpose of the Methodist Church was "advancement of the Christian faith in accordance with the doctrinal standards and the discipline of the Methodist Church,"[20] it would not be in accordance with the Church's Charitable Trusts for people of other faiths to use Methodist premises for their religious purposes—formal or informal. For this would, in effect, involve the advancement of a non-Christian religion. If the Methodist Church wished for change, it would have to radically revise its doctrinal standards and practice. Key to Counsel's findings, as I quoted in 2011, was paragraph 11:

> Accordingly, in my opinion, although the Conference has power to alter the doctrinal standards of the Church and restate Methodist practice in different terms, nothing less than such a fundamental alteration and

---

19   Memorial 42 (2005) from the London North West Synod. At the Synod, 144 members voted for the memorial and 55 voted against.

20   Methodist Church Act 1976. 1977. London: Her Majesty's Stationary Office: 7.

restatement would permit model trust property to be used for formal worship, or other overtly religious purposes, by people of other, non-Christian faiths.

HARRIS 2011: 278

The 6 member working party that was appointed to write the report in response to the 2005 memorial, including me, wished for change. The representative from the TMCP who was on the working group assured us that legislative change might not be necessary if the Methodist Conference was presented with a compelling enough theological argument that the existing words of the Methodist Church Act, "the advancement of the Christian religion," could include showing a hospitality to people of other faiths that could extend to them worshipping on Methodist premises. In effect he suggested an inclusivist rather than an exclusivist interpretation of this phrase.

The Working Party tried to do this. We argued that there were concepts within the Christian faith such as the universal grace of God and an ethic of radical hospitality that made the opening up of church premises to people of other faiths an imperative in its own right and that this was just as much the 'advancement' of the Christian religion as drawing a non-negotiable spatial line between Christian worship and all other worship. We wrote this, for instance:

2.6. The Opinion of Counsel is that allowing people of other faiths to worship corporately or privately on church premises is not compatible with our existing charitable purpose. The supposition behind this seems to be that Christianity must compete with all other religions for its advancement. For Christianity to advance, other religions must shrink. There are other ways, however, of looking at the advancement of the Christian religion. Christianity is advanced when there is an increased understanding within society of the self-giving love of God that lies at the heart of the Christian gospel. If we give the message to people of other faiths that they cannot pray to God on our premises, they may gain a very different understanding of the God we worship. Christianity may also be advanced if the fruits of the Holy Spirit as seen, for example, in Galatians 5. 22–23 (love, joy, peace, kindness, generosity, faithfulness etc) are encouraged and practised. Since many faiths speak of these qualities, can we speak of an advancement of the Reign of God if people revering these qualities pray on Methodist premises?

At a later point in the report, we wrote:

2.10. In the light of this, the working party would highlight the selectivity of the church welcoming the unchurched, the atheists and the agnostics, who have little cause to respect the sanctity of the space that is being offered them, whilst at the same time denying the opportunity to pray and worship to those who would recognise the extreme generosity of such hospitality as a sign of God's grace. It could easily be interpreted as a lack of confidence—we can only mission in confidence to those who have not yet known anything of religion. But we are not called to offer religion, we are called to offer the gospel and God's grace—to all and for all. Our confidence in God's grace is demonstrated by the diversity of people to whom we are willing to be the means of God's grace. One question that the Methodist Church must consider, therefore, when examining the question of hospitality to people of other faiths or those whose teachings are known to be different from its own is—"How do we respond to requests from such people as co-workers with God such that God's grace abounds?"[21]

The report contained much more than this inclusivist argument. It surveyed changes that had occurred in Britain since the last major report on the use of church premises by people of other faiths and argued for the acceptance of new readings of the meaning of the doctrinal standards clause of the Deed of Union, readings that would then affect the interpretation of the purposes of the Methodist Church as stated in the 1976 Methodist Church Act.

In doing the latter, a previous document accepted by the Methodist Conference was cited, *A Lamp to my Feet*, which had recognized that a variety of approaches to the Bible were present among Methodists. Referring to this, the report stated:

> By adopting this recommendation [that a variety of approaches to the Bible could be recognised], Conference in effect permitted these different interpretations of scripture to exist alongside each other and, whilst some argued at that the time that this ran contrary to Clause Four of the Deed of Union, a precedent was set for the acceptance of a diversity of theologies within Methodism.
>
> HARRIS 2011: 281

---

21   The first report of the working party is available on the website of the Methodist Church in Britain under "Use of Church Premises by People of other Faiths:" www.mwthodistchurch .org.uk.

The report continued, by pointing out that a similar diversity of views existed on interreligious encounter and that, at present:

> those whose theological convictions would persuade them to offer hospitality to people of other faiths or certain other Christian churches, by allowing them to pray, worship or meditate on Methodist premises, are being prevented from doing so by the restrictive way we have been advised to interpret Clause 4.

Appealing to this diversity, the Working Party's recommendation was that any decision on allowing other faith communities to worship formally on Methodist Church premises should be a local decision and that diversity should be recognized. It also set out four options and sought to explain the consequences of each: to leave things as they are; to change the doctrinal standards clause of the Deed of Union (Clause 4); to recognize that the meaning of Clause 4 is interpreted in diverse ways and, therefore, that the purposes of the Methodist Church as stated in the 1976 Act are interpreted in diverse ways; to change the Methodist Church Act of 1976 through an Act of Parliament.

The Report did not cite, but perhaps could have done, a Conference Statement accepted in 1999, *Called to Love and Praise*. Paragraph 3.2.10 to 3.2.16 concentrated on the Church's relationships with people of other faiths. Theologically, these clauses offered an inclusivist position, citing, for instance, a World Council of Churches document that stated that truth, wisdom, love and holiness in other faiths could be accepted as "the gift of the Holy Spirit." The last clause, 3.2.16, stated:

> Christians of all traditions are at the beginning of a long period of growing dialogue with people of other faiths. To refuse opportunities for such dialogue would be a denial of both tolerance and Christian love. To predict, at this point in time, the outcome of such dialogue would be presumptuous or faithless. Christians may enter such dialogues in the faith that God will give them deeper insight into the truth of Christ. People of other faiths can hardly be said to belong to the Church. But the Church has to be understood in a way which does not deny the signs of God in their midst.[22]

---

22   The complete text of the Conference Statement, *Called to Love and Praise* is available on the website of the Methodist Church in Britain: www.methodistchurch.org.uk.

The members of the working party honestly believed that their report could prompt a re-thinking in the Church. It did not. A pluralist argument would have been rejected even more vehemently.

When the Methodist Council debated it in January 2007, they sent it back to the working party for revision, asking it, for instance, to do more work on the four options we presented and to define 'other faiths.' This response was rigorous rather than negative.[23] The Working Party then revised the report. It stressed, for instance, that the biblical imperative to be hospitable was dependent on what we believed, not on what others believed, and questioned further the market-place model that seemed to inform Counsel's Opinion—that the Christian faith could only advance if other faiths declined (Harris 2011: 282, see also pp. 282–83 for a summary of the consequences that the Working Party pointed out if things were left as they are). We also said much more about the four options, for instance what changing the Methodist Church Act of 1976 would entail.

The revised report was sent to the two committees concerned, Law and Polity, and Faith and Order, in March 2007. The Faith and Order Committee concluded that too many issues remained unresolved for the report to go forward to the Methodist Conference of 2007 but, generally speaking, endorsed the report. It envisaged a further re-write and submission in 2008. The Law and Polity Committee, on the other hand, sought Counsel's Opinion again. Counsel's Opinion in 2007 was even more conservative than it had been in 2005: only recourse to Parliament would allow changes to what was currently possible. Section 4(a) of The Methodist Church Act 1976 concerning 'the advancement of the Christian faith' was again cited. This Opinion was brought to the Methodist Conference in a holding report and nothing further was done. As I write in 2014, ministers who would like to respond affirmatively when asked by another faith community whether they could use the church hall for worship are forced to decline. Methodist space is still barred, for instance, from a Sikh community that needs a home whilst repairs are completed on their gurdwara after storm damage or from a Jewish community that suffers an anti-Semitic attack on their synagogue.

Evident from this case study is that a Church that had been willing to endorse formally an inclusivist theological approach to the religious 'other' in 1999 was forced into taking an exclusivist approach to the concept of 'the advancement of the Christian faith' when spatial factors entered, underpinned

---

23   See Harris 2011: 282. I am grateful to Revd Peter Sulston, my line manager within the Methodist Church, for sending me his notes from the meeting of the Methodist Council. I was not present and Peter had presented our report.

with legal restrictions. Key to this were the different Opinions of Counsel that were sought and their increasingly conservative nature, the later ones not even recognizing the distinction between 'minor religious acts' and 'a non-Christian religious service' that had been present in the Opinion of 1970.[24] It could be argued, therefore, that legal considerations simply overwhelmed theological considerations. However, I would suggest that theological considerations were present in the way in which the Opinions of Counsel were received, namely that their exclusivist interpretation of key phrases within the Methodist Church Act and other documents was accepted, by those with power over decision-making, without question.

Conclusion

I have given two case studies of the spatial implications of Christian exclusivism. In each of these, an exclusivist perspective on space was challenged by an inclusivist perspective. In the first, Buddhists offered the inclusivist challenge but it was short-lived. Some Sri Lankan Buddhists, in the face of the strength of Christian exclusivism, developed an exclusivism of their own in order to defend their own identity and security. In my second case study, attempts to move the Methodist Church into a more inclusive theology of space to reflect what had been accepted at a conceptual level was, in effect, seen by some sectors of the Church as an attempt to move it towards a pluralist theology, and was rejected.

I offer the case studies to argue that each of the categories of exclusivism, inclusivism, and pluralism has its own particular spatial dimension. For instance, just as exclusivist lines of non-negotiation can be drawn conceptually between different religious traditions, so they can be drawn in space. My second case study demonstrates, however, that it is too simplistic to assume that an institution or group that endorses one category within the typology at a conceptual level will endorse it at a spatial level. This does not invalidate my point that each category in the typology has a spatial expression or indeed the efficacy of the typology. Rather it illustrates the importance of taking the spatial dimension into account when examining the theologies of religion that are present within different religious communities. Just as the typology can aid an understanding of the spatial dimensions of religion, so the spatial dimension

---

24   'Use of Methodist Trust Premises.' General Purposes and Policy Committee Report. Representative Session Agenda for the Methodist Conference of 1970: 21.

of religion and religious identity can aid an understanding of how theologies of religion are grounded within the religious experience of humankind.

Bibliography

Ariarajah, Wesley. (1999). *Not Without My Neighbour: Issues in Interfaith Relations.* Geneva: World Council of Churches.

Capper, John. (1873). *A Full Account of the Buddhist Controversy, Held at Pantura, in August, 1873, by the Ceylon Times Special Reporter.* Colombo: Ceylon Times.

Chidester, David, and Edward Linenthal (eds.). (1991). *American Sacred Space.* Bloomington and Indianapolis, IN: Indiana University Press.

The Wesleyan Methodist Church in South Ceylon. (1871) *Extracts from Quarterly Letters addressed to the Secretaries of the Wesleyan Missionary Society by Ministers of the South Ceylon District.* Vol. LXXVI. Colombo: Wesleyan Mission Press.

Harischandra, Brahmacari Walisinha. (1908). *The Sacred City of Anuradhapura.* Colombo: Colombo Apothacaries.

Harris, Elizabeth. (2006). *Theravāda Buddhism and the British Encounter: Religious, Missionary and Colonial Experience in Nineteenth Century Sri Lanka.* London and New York, NY: Routledge.

————. (2011). "Hospitality as a Sign of God's Grace: Church Buildings and People of Other Faiths." In: Marshal Fernando and Robert Crusz (eds.). *Theology Beyond Neutrality: Essays to Honour Wesley Ariarajah.* Colombo: The Ecumenical Institute for Study and Dialogue. pp. 273–86.

————. (2012). "Memory, Experience and the Clash of Cosmologies: The Encounter between British Protestant Missionaries and Buddhism in Nineteenth Century Sri Lanka." *Social Sciences and Missions* 25: 265–303.

————. (2013). "Buddhism and the Religious Other." In: David Cheetham, Douglas Pratt and David Thomas (eds.). *Understanding Interreligious Relations.* Oxford: Oxford University Press. pp. 88–117.

Harvard, William (ed.). (1833). *Memoirs of Mrs Elizabeth Harvard, late of the Wesleyan Mission to Ceylon and India with Extracts from her Diary and Correspondence by her Husband.* 2nd ed. London: Printed for the author.

Harvard, William, and Benjamin Clough. (1819). *School Report for 1818: To the Executive Committee in London for the Management of the Wesleyan Missionaries throughout the world.* Colombo: Wesleyan Mission Press.

Knott, Kim. (2005). *The Location of Religion.* London & Oakville: Equinox.

————. (2009). "From Locality to Location and Back Again: A Spatial Journey in the Study of Religion." *Religion* 39: 154–60.

————. (2010). "Religion, Space, and Place: The Spatial Turn in Research on Religion." *Religion and Society: Advances in Research* 1: 29–42.

Kong, Lily. (2001). "Mapping 'New' Geographies of Religion: Politics and Poetics in Modernity." *Progress in Human Geography* 30 March: 211–33.

Lefebvre, Henri. (1991). *The Production of Space*. Transl. Donald Nicholson-Smith. Oxford: Blackwell.

Massey, Doreen. (1993). "Politics and Space/Time." In: M. Keith and S. Pile (eds.). *Place and the Politics of Identity*. London: Routledge. pp. 141–61.

(2005). *For Space*. Los Angeles, London, New Delhi, Singapore & Washington DC: Sage.

Moscrop, Thomas. (1891). "Sir Edwin Arnold's 'Light of the World'." *The Ceylon Friend* October: 360–63.

Nissan, Elizabeth. (1985). *The Sacred City of Anuradhapura: Aspects of Sinhalese Buddhism and Nationhood*. PhD Dissertation, London School of Economics and Political Science.

————. (1989). "History in the Making: Anuradhapura and the Sinhala Buddhist Nation." *Social Analysis* 25 (September): 64–77.

Peebles, J.M. (1994). *Buddhism and Christianity: Being an Oral Debate Held at Panadura between the Rev. Migettuwatte Guananda, a Buddhist Priest, and the Rev. David de Silva, Wesleyan Clergyman*. Repr. Colombo: All Ceylon Buddhist Congress.

The Methodist Church in Britain *Representative Session Agenda for the Methodist Conference of 1970*. (1970). Peterborough: Methodist Publishing House.

The Methodist Church in Britain *Representative Session Agenda for the Methodist Conference of 1973*. (1973). Peterborough: Methodist Publishing House.

Spence Hardy, Robert. (1864). *Jubilee Memorials of the Wesleyan Mission, South Ceylon: 1814–1864*. Colombo: Wesleyan Mission Press.

The Methodist Church in Britain *The Methodist Church Faith and Order Committee: Use of Methodist Premises by People of Other Faiths: A Report to Conference 1997*. (1998). Peterborough: Methodist Publishing House.

Tuan, Yi-Fu. (2008). *Space and Place: the Perspective of Experience*. 6th ed. Minneapolis, MN and London: University of Minnesota.

Young, Richard, and G.P.V. Somaratne. (1996). *Vain Debates: The Buddhist-Christian Controversies in Nineteenth Century Ceylon*. Vienna: De Nobili Research Library.

CHAPTER 5

The Theology of Religions Typology Redefined: Openness and Tendencies

Paul Hedges

Introduction

We live today in a world where it is academically fashionable to be skeptical of typologies, classifications, and grand narratives. We are all, after all, 'post' people, and even if, I expect, most of us would reject the classification 'post-modern' we are nevertheless post-Foucault with regard to his archaeology of knowledge and claims that knowledge is power. We are also post-Lyotard and so are aware that all grand narratives must fail, while things like post-colonialism and the awareness of the Western bias of our systems is something we live with.[1] As such, schemes like the theology of religions typology (hereafter, simply the typology) are naturally subject to suspicion, and even deemed to fail outright before any discussion of them is undertaken. How can a single schema of either three or four categories hope to do justice to such a broad and dynamic area as the theology of religions, and the individual approaches of thousands of churches and theologians, not to mention millions of Christians, with regards to how they understand the religious Other? Defending it sounds like a daunting task, yet to this end I will address a number of potential criticisms of the typology, although as recent works have offered a robust defense, I will not attempt to systematically answer every critique as it would repeat work done elsewhere (see Schmidt-Leukel 2005: 14–18, 23–27; Hedges 2008b: 18–22, Hedges 2010: 18–19). Rather, my aim is to set out something of a vision for what the typology is, and what it can do, in the context of contemporary thinking and developments in the area.

Before proceeding, it is useful to explain what I envisage by the theology of religions. Indicating, I would suggest, the success of the typology in becoming part of the debates, some people associate the theology of religions primarily,

---

[1] A lot of potentially contentious terminology, and conteed issues, are set out here. For some account of how I would see the debates, see Hedges (2010: 165–67), on post-colonialism see Sugirtharajah (2003: 13–16).

if not solely, with the typology. For instance, in calling for a moratorium on the theology of religions in favor of comparative theology, James Fredericks is disavowing attempts to approach religious Others in what may be termed, roughly, broad paintbrush style categorizations which can be termed exclusivist, inclusivist, etc. (Fredericks 1999: 8). Certainly, there seems to be some moves to define comparative theology as a separate discipline. However, I find such approaches quite unhelpful, and am not sure why there needs to be separate spheres within Christian theology for looking at religious Others. Rather, I would contend that theology of religions is a broad term, perhaps within the remit of systematic theology, which looks at the way Christianity approaches and relates to religious diversity; therefore, the typology, comparative theology, even Missiology, all come under its broad arena of operation.[2] It perhaps should be stressed that I do not see it as simply an intra-Christian discussion on its own terms, or as something divorced from other areas of theological thinking. Rather, as contemporary movements within comparative theology are showing, the whole of theology today must engage with religious diversity, reflection upon this, and the fruits of it; comparative theology does not just seek to give a Christian interpretation of the religious Other, but to enthuse Christian theology as a whole with the riches of its exploration (Clooney 2010, Moyaert 2011, Hedges 2010). We may say that the theology of religions is, or should be, marked by intertextuality in its richest sense, as it hermeneutically explores tradition, context, and new landscapes both within and beyond religions, including, it should be mentioned, the secular. It is my contention that the typology also has a broad and diverse application in the wider field of engaging with religious Others. As is generally accepted now, to engage a religious Other requires a theological prejudgment of the variety that the typology defines. While there are certainly good reasons for avoiding it, an overtly stated position may be uncomfortable for dialogue partners—there are sectarian divisions in the labels—such that some theologians wish to bypass it; however, wishing to bypass typological judgments does not mean that they have actually been avoided.[3] Here I hope to open up a vision of the typology that will to some extent overcome such concerns, while also showing the useful application of the typology.

---

2   I have suggested this elsewhere, see Hedges (2010: 15–17, see also 44–55).

3   It has been very convincingly argued that comparative theology needs a typology style decision for it to be operative, see Hedges (2010: 53–54), Schmidt-Leukel (2009: 91–95), Kiblinger (2010). Indeed, other recent work which has suggested it bypasses the typology also actually implicitly engages it, see Cheetham (2013), and my review of it (Hedges, 2014).

Varieties of the Typology

The typology has been used and defined in different ways over the years since Alan Race gave us the so-called classical typology of exclusivisms-inclusivisms-pluralisms, which can be briefly glossed as follows: exclusivists believe only their religion is true; inclusivists that only their religion is ultimately true, others are but stepping stones to it; pluralists that there are, at least potentially, many true religions (Race 1983; for a more recent summary see Hedges 2010: 20–29 and for fuller expositions see Strange 2008, Cheetham 2008, Schmidt-Leukel 2008). However, over the years variations and extensions to this have been offered.

One prominent version is Perry Schmidt-Leukel's typological markers as parameters of all possible soteriological options: the exclusivist suggests all others are not saved; the inclusivist that others may be saved, but via my religion; the pluralist that there may be multiple soteriological paths (2005: 18–23). While this has clarity, and a certain inevitability (in classical Christian terms at least), where people's soteriological fate is fixed depending upon how my tradition conceives truth, it is to my mind too rigid and inflexible. If this is the usage we employed then it would simply be a philosophical definition of options and not particularly useful in helping us look at nuances of meaning and approaches.[4] It also, I would argue, fails to account for those often termed universalist exclusivists who, although seeing no valid religiosity outside of Christianity (exclusivist), believe that God will ultimately save all people due to His omnibenevolence and omnipotence (universalism). Under Schmidt-Leukel's classification such people are inclusivists, but I do not find this a satisfactory classification as it seems to me to blur the distinction between those who do, and do not, see value within the religious life of non-Christian traditions. I also suggest that Schmidt-Leukel's typology has an unhelpful soteriological focus, and various recent discussions have emphasized that there is a tendency to skew discussions in dialogue towards soteriology because of its prominence in Christian thought, aided and abetted by the typology; this is not, of course, to say that such discussions do not have their place.[5] We can usefully mention here criticisms of the typology as a form of meta-narrative, as Schmidt-Leukel's description perhaps comes closest to this, an all-encompassing description

---

4   Having said this, it may be noted that Race himself endorses Schmidt-Leukel's revision of the typology as the most useful way to view it.

5   For an account of why the typology may not be useful see, for instance, Cheetham (2013: 73–80) who particularly discusses Schmidt-Leukel and my own defences and visions of the typology.

where the paradigms sum up the entirety of soteriological options (Schmidt-Leukel 2005: 19). However, I do not believe that Schmidt-Leukel has suggested that all discussion on religious Others should be framed in typological terms, and so such charges are somewhat spurious.

Turning to other variations, Paul Knitter (2002) has given us new terms: the replacement model, the fulfilment model and the mutuality model to stand for Race's initial threefold classification, but he has added a fourth option, the acceptance model. While I would agree with Knitter that we should add a fourth category, we differ on how we define it, I address this in due course. Recently, Gavin D'Costa has also given us a new version in which he further subdivides each option into a variety of types, so we have two types of both exclusivisms (universal-access, and restrictive-access) and inclusivisms (structural and restrictivist), and three types of pluralisms (unitary, pluriform, ethical) (D'Costa 2009: 6–7, 9–33). We need to be aware of this variety, and I think most nuanced explanations of the typology do set out a variety within each category. Indeed, Race and I have adopted plurals for each term (as I do here) to indicate this.[6] Yet I find D'Costa's definitions somewhat problematic especially as he seems to redefine exclusivism to include what everyone else would call inclusivisms, and so when he defines himself as a universal-access exclusivist I see no difference between this and Race's inclusivisms or Knitter's fulfilment model (it crosses over between universalist exclusivism and inclusivisms), while he seems to make what he defines as inclusivism a very narrow category such that even his model for this type, Karl Rahner, seems to me equally, if not better, describable as a universal-access exclusivist (D'Costa 2009: 29–32). It seems, therefore, to simply muddy the waters. Another version is given to us by Abraham Veléz de Cea who has sought, in the pursuit of a Buddhist-Christian comparative theology, to find a version applicable to Buddhism. He suggests we have four terms, but, unlike the four-fold versions of Knitter and Hedges, he does not add something along the lines of a particularist category, but inserts what he terms an inclusivist-pluralist paradigm as a midway point between the two named groups. I will elaborate on his typology further below.

It is worth mentioning that Race's original exposition suggested that the pluralist option was the best, yet it is not, as some critics have suggested, naturally biased this way. As has been argued, the terms do not imply superiority or any derogatory meaning—for instance, in the sense of 'exclusive services,' exclusivism can be seen very positively, and indeed there are those who proudly take the label (see Hedges 2008b: 22; for someone who happily uses and

---

6 Hedges and Race (2008). While the rationale is given in one of my contributions (Hedges 2008b: 27), the suggestion to use plurals was initially Race's.

defends the term 'exclusivism,' see Strange 2008). Also, essentially identical typologies, though with different names, have been propounded which give preference to exclusivist or inclusivist paradigms. Of these that of Veli-Matti Kärkäinen is, probably, the most famous and influential, who uses the terms Ecclesiocentric (exclusivisms), Christocentric (inclusivisms), and Theocentric (pluralisms) (2003).

Amongst this diversity, I will defend a variation of a four-fold revision of Race's classical typology, which gives us exclusivisms-inclusivisms-pluralisms-particularities, and which sees the typology as descriptive and heuristic.[7] This approach aims at simply describing different approaches in a pedagogically useful way, and gives us permeable and multivalent categories that remain loose, a matter I elucidate further below. I suggest that the typology can be seen both as descriptive of specific theological positions, as an act of second order theological reflection, and as representing certain tendencies, which overlap but are not necessarily entirely congruent. In terms of the description of theological positions that encompass exclusivisms-inclusivisms-pluralisms, I follow Race's original classification (see Hedges 2010: 20–27). Space does not allow a full explanation of the particularist position, which is best seen as a post-liberal Christian theological reworking which stresses indeterminacy, that is we do not know the status of other religions, but also challenges the notion that they are in any way comparable to Christianity and claims to respect their difference by not comparing them. However, as has been shown, this claimed pretense at respect for the Other actually hides a Christian triumphalism which it tends to vehemently deny.[8] Moreover, I do not see the typology as simply describing theological positions, but also representing tendencies or tones in the way the religious Other is viewed, and building upon my classification of the paradigms as tendencies (towards *radical discontinuity*, *radical fulfilment*, *radical openness*, and *radical difference*), I will employ Veléz de Cea discussion of the typology as openness to further expand upon this, and also suggest we should disassociate the tendencies from the theological types.

As a heuristic and descriptive typology, I believe it should resist fixed essential types as found, for instance, in Schmidt-Leukel's exposition, where each option is seen as clearly delineated and segregated from the others. While Veléz de Cea certainly sees his own approach as having affinities with my own, and

---

7 I first suggested a four-fold typology in Hedges (2002), and have subsequently expanded and defended this in various ways (2008a, 2008b, 2010). On my view of the typology as descriptive and heuristic, see Hedges (2008b: 26–27).

8 For an account of particularities and the problems with them see Hedges (2002, 2008a, 2010: 146–96).

I will proceed to fleshing out some ways they can both usefully be employed together, nevertheless, he has criticized my approach of seeing the typology as loose and open-ended, suggesting that "Hedges' open and fluid understanding of the typology is compatible with having more accurate definitions .... A more precise working definition ... does not necessarily entail a fixed essence and a single approach as Hedges seems to assume" (2013: 15). While making use of his notion of Openness to help explicate the way that I believe we can most profitably employ the typology, I will nevertheless continue to resist the move towards a more fixed set of definitions, not because they lead to a 'fixed essence,' but rather because it leads to rigid boundaries which are inevitably, depending upon where they are placed, resulting in us leaving some inside or outside them, while being nothing other than arbitrary classifications—to some extent this complaint can, of course, be used of any classification including the typology I am defending, nevertheless, we must always strike a balance between over classifying and drawing too many boundaries, and the reverse impulse to resist all classification which leaves us unable to say anything meaningful about any group of phenomena (and is, of course, a form of meta-classification, the claim that the phenomena are incapable of meaningful classification is a *de facto* classification). Indeed as the typology limits us to three, or four in its modified form, types, these function well in terms of what sociologists call 'ideal types' (the term comes from Max Weber 1978: 19–22). That is to say, they are not set up as actual things which exist in the world in some pure way (although I would say that Schmidt-Leukel's typology does set up distinct things which do exist, i.e. they clearly position people in relation to their views on soteriology), rather they are indicative of a range of positions which may usefully be employed to point towards meaningful patterns, without suggesting that there is a 'pure' thing as an 'inclusivist theology' or any other type. (However, in as far as people adopt these labels they become existing entities, but always in a politically negotiated discourse).

Defining the Typology as Openness: Extending Veléz de Cea's Typology

When we come to think of the typology as tendencies, this can be spoken of in terms of 'openness' to the religious Other, and Veléz de Cea has perhaps most fully explicated this notion in his Buddhist rendition of the typology. Veléz de Cea suggests that we need to distinguish between "two types of openness: openness in practice and openness in theory" (Veléz de Cea 2007: 13). Openness in theory is about openness for "our tradition most important X," for which he uses the acronym OTMIX (Veléz de Cea 2007: 13). He purposely leaves X indeterminate and suggests that even within one tradition it can vary, and notes that in Christianity it could, for example, refer to such diverse things as "God, grace, truth, goodness, love, justice, and so on" (Veléz de Cea 2007: 13). Contrarily to Schmidt-Leukel, whose version of the typology with its soteriological focus he rejects as unsuitable for his Buddhist-Christian comparative theology, he suggests that such indeterminacy is needed as it cannot be supposed that every tradition has the same focus, and certainly suggests that soteriology as relation to ultimate transcendent reality does not work with regards to early Buddhism (Veléz de Cea 2007: 3ff.). Veléz de Cea suggests that we can find four types of theoretical openness which he characterizes as:

> tradition-specific openness (exclusivism), openness to what is similar (inclusivism), openness to similar and different instances of OTMIX, but with non-negotiable, dogmatic constraints (pluralistic-inclusivism), and openness to similar and different instances of OTMIX, but without non-negotiable, dogmatic constraints (pluralism).
>
> VELÉZ DE CEA 2007: 14

In other words, those with tradition-specific openness (exclusivists) are open only to examples of 'X' within their own tradition, inclusivists can find examples of X elsewhere, but only insofar as they exemplify what they see X to be. More openness is found in his pluralistic-inclusivist type, where an openness exists to see what types of ultimate concerns are found elsewhere, but he sees them as in need of mediation or ultimately determined by the home tradition's conceptions. He notes Jacques Dupuis as an example of this, while the pluralist has absolute openness. I would suggest that there is a problem with this definition of pluralisms because part of Hick's hypothesis, at least as I understand it, is that coming from a Christian (or Buddhist, Islamic, etc.) background openness to the Other is not absolute, but implies that what the Other says makes sense in relation to my tradition to at least some degree otherwise the door is opened to relativism, which pluralists disavow. So, for instance, if another religion claims that its deity requires human sacrifice and the slaughter of innocent children, the pluralist would suggest this is not, in Hick's terms, a valid response to the Real. I recognize this is, perhaps, an ethical rather than dogmatic constraint, but there are constraints, and this is one reason why Hick limited his discussion to certain traditions as he felt here we had evidence of them informing cultures throughout time (see Hick 1989: 29–33, 299ff., and 1995: 11–12). As such, while I welcome Veléz de Cea's notion of openness I think we need to be careful how it is expressed, and this is simply a clarification about this.

A significant difference, though, and this picks up themes mentioned above, is the use of the pluralist-inclusivist category, and I will elucidate this issue, with several reasons as to why we should reject this move in terms of developing a typology relating to Christian theological positions.[9] First, if Veléz de Cea wants to include pluralistic-inclusivism at one end of the inclusivisms scale to accommodate those like Dupuis, it is not clear why he does not add exclusivistic-inclusivism at the other end for those like John Nicol Farquhar, for although in many ways he is a typical example of an inclusivist theology, as I have shown elsewhere, his theology has a "negative" tone which I describe as requiring the "death of Hinduism" before it can be reborn as Christianity, making his theology quite exclusivist in its general tendency (Hedges 2001: 293–301, but most especially, 334–40; I briefly discuss this in Hedges 2010: 24–25). I will pick this up further in the third point. Second, it is simply unnecessary to make these kind of distinctions if we think both in terms of the typology giving us classifications and tendencies ("theory" and "practice" openness in Veléz de Cea's terms), as someone like Dupuis has an inclusivist theology but a tendency to radical openness, as I would put it, and often the kind of people that Cea has placed within this category are those with an inclusivist theology who I suggest exemplify a radical openness to the religious Other, like Dupuis and Francis Clooney.[10] Thirdly, if we follow the diversification of different classifications, we will simply find a whole set of competing micro-typologies which broadly agree upon the main typological terms, but draw the boundaries in different places. Certainly, in making his classification, Cea distinguishes his fourth category from that of Knitter, for instance, arguing why some people fit here better than others.[11] They are not alone in seeking to put slightly different borders between the various paradigms nor in drawing specific distinctions, and I have mentioned D'Costa's splitting up into different types; while useful to acknowledge that each is not monolithic I am opposed to the drawing of rigid boundaries—wherever we draw the boundaries, if we see them as rigid and clear, we will always have to draw them so some people fit in one place while others fit somewhere else, which will tend to depend upon the emphasis a particular

---

9   Of course, this does not invalidate the variant typology in the Buddhist context, see Cea (2013: 123ff.).

10 Hedges (2010: 112–13)—though there I do not so clearly demarcate between the theological type of pluralisms and the tendency to radical openness as I do here.

11 Cea (2013: 28ff.). I think to some degree his discussion fails to notice the distinction between Knitter and myself, and he describes those I would term particularists as ultra-particularists, but some like Clooney and Fredericks as particularists which utilizes my terminology but in relation to Knitter's classification which I think is somewhat confusing.

scholar wishes to privilege. As such while Cea has argued that more precise categories are compatible with my heuristic approach, I would argue that part of its strength is that it is loose so we can see where people do not fit neatly into one place or another. Having criticized others for adding a fourth category that effectively competes or sub-divides the other three, I would defend my fourth category of particularism on the grounds that it describes a particular group of post-liberal theologians who seek to provide no assessment of the religious Other in the way that traditional theologies of religion do and so is not simply about drawing another distinction within the typology but adding a descriptive distinction. This is where I think it differs from Knitter's which seems to me to conflate those who support an indeterminacy (i.e. post-liberal particularists) with those who want a more open form of inclusivism (i.e. Clooney) (2002: 173ff.).

Cea's other category of openness is openness in practice, which he associates with "a particular practice" (2013: 16). This he characterizes under the types of exclusivistic, inclusivistic, and pluralistic. The exclusivistic attitude he says does not accept other religions "as a matter of principle" (Cea 2013: 16), which is to say that while the fact of other religions may be acknowledged, the attitude is that such traditions have no legitimacy. The inclusivistic attitude tends to "instrumentalize" the other, which is to say that they are seen as legitimate in as far as they, for instance, act as stepping stones to one's own faith, and always sees the Other as lacking (Cea 2013: 17). Finally, the pluralistic attitude accepts other religions as a matter of principle, with a sense of the genuine worth of the other (Cea 2013: 17). According to Cea, both exclusivists and inclusivists tend not to give full worth to the religious Other on their own grounds, while the inclusivist-pluralist and pluralists do, hence he suggests that both of these are pluralist in practice. I think that an important point is picked up here that helps to clarify a difference between different inclusivists—for instance those on the exclusivist end like Farquhar, and on the pluralist end like Dupuis. However, this further indicates that the inclusivist-pluralist category is not necessary, as the distinction, in Cea's terms, is between inclusivists in theory with an inclusivistic attitude, and inclusivists in theory with a pluralistic attitude.

A Vision of the Typology: Tendencies to Openness

To help elucidate the issue, I would like to take a look at two descriptions of the text *Dominus Iesus* found in Cea and Jeanine Hill Fletcher. Cea argues that revelation outside of Christianity, even "the existence of salvation in Christ outside Christianity," is found in "official Catholicism."[12] However, he says, this does not mean that other religions are accepted as a "matter of principle." Therefore, he says:

> The Catholic declaration *Dominus Iesus*, dated August 6, 2000, when Pope Benedict XVI was known as Cardinal Ratzinger, makes this point clearly when it criticizes "relativistic theories which seek to justify religious pluralism, not only *de facto* but also the *de iure* (or in principle)" (*Dominus Iesus*: 4).
>
> CEA 2013: 30

Here, Cea picks up on some specific language by which *Dominus Iesus* while not departing from the inclusivist theology of Vatican II nevertheless seeks to limit the interpretation of that document to suggest that whatever "light" may exist outside Christianity must not be seen as valuable in and of itself. Meanwhile, Fletcher speaks of tendencies and I have offered the following commentary around her usage of the typological terms:

> The main danger comes when we reify (caricature?) the typology, and suggest that the terms either tell us all we need to know about any one person's theology ... or else see it as something to direct the encounter with those of other religions. Moreover, I think it can be usefully deployed to describe tendencies. This is how Fletcher employs it discussing the recent Roman Catholic document *Dominus Iesus*, which although she notes propounds an inclusivist theology, nevertheless has an exclusivist air: "For example, when the Congregation for the Doctrine of the Faith issued the document *Dominus Iesus*, the argument was not exclusivistic, but the tone of the document often tended to be."
>
> HEDGES 2010: 20, citing Jeanine Hill Fletcher (2005) *Monopoly on Salvation? A Feminist Approach to Religious Pluralism,* London and New York, NY: Continuum: 54

Here she refers to the tone as "exclusivistic," and offers I think, therefore, a similar distinction to that offered by Cea between openness in theory, what she terms "inclusivist theology," and openness in practice, the exclusivistic tone. This is the way that I have, likewise, tried to discuss the description of

---

12   Cea (2013: 30). This claim is somewhat controversial, while it follows a reading that can be found in Paul Knitter, Perry Schmidt-Leukel, and arguably Karl Rahner, it is certainly contested by Gavin D'Costa and I think by Cardinal Ratzinger, later, Pope Benedict XVI (see D'Costa 2011).

the typology in terms of both theological positions and tendencies (or tones in Fletcher's terms), and I think that Cea helps us in seeing the distinction between related, but also distinct aspects: on the one hand a specific theological content, and on the other a practice, or what I would suggest is better expressed as a tendency. To help explicate this, I have previously suggested that each of the classifications can be understood as relating to a tendency. However, I argue here, in agreement with Cea, that a specific theological stance and the tendency while often related are not necessarily linked. Nevertheless, unlike Cea, I think we need to take four tendencies, and as noted I see them better expressed as tones than a practice—although they may well be expressed in practical encounters with the religious Other. The four tendencies, or tones are: *radical discontinuity, radical fulfilment, radical openness*, and *radical difference*, which may also be seen as aspects of openness.[13]

The tendency to radical discontinuity represents a systemic total lack of openness to the religious Other as a system. The stress is upon how non-Christian religions fail to measure up to Christianity, or how revelation contrasts with anything else. In Cea's language it is about the religious Other not being justified as a matter of principle. No matter what their stance, or belief system it is disregarded *a priori*. Much of Karl Barth's writing, for instance of religion as manifesting human sinfulness, typifies this. As a note, theologically I would suggest Barth, in his later works at least, is a universalist exclusivist.

In contrast, the tendency to radical fulfilment wants to integrate the other, where everything (of value) in the Other's religion is explained in relation to my system. Here, no valid truths or knowledge exists unless it ultimately leads to what my tradition claims. There is openness only to anything which fits my system. Again, in Cea's terms, the openness is one of ambiguities where the Other is accepted only where 'similarity' or 'compatibility' with one's own system is found and identified (2013: 224). The fulfilment theology of someone like John Nicol Farquhar is a good example, where for instance the Hindu belief in avatars is explained as a longing for God to be known in human form, a longing only answered by Christianity (see Hedges 2001: 313–22); however, as I have suggested above, he also has an exclusivist tone in stressing how Hinduism fails to measure up to Christianity. As such I believe, while clearly theologically inclusivist (Hinduism is a stepping stone to Christianity), it also has a tendency both to radical fulfilment, all good in Hinduism is only good because it is ultimately transcended in Christianity, and radical discontinuity, in that

---

13   I have previously glossed these in relation to Cea (2007) in Hedges (2014), but expand that
        further herein.

it is only by rejecting Hinduism for an entirely superior system that Farquhar sees it as leading to Christianity; Hinduism 'dies' to become Christianity.

Moving to the tendency to radical openness, we see an attitude wherein we are open to the possibility that truths and knowledge which transcend what my religion says may be known of elsewhere. It means that I should stop defending my own system and insisting I have all the answers and start listening and even boundary crossing in humility to learn of the riches elsewhere. Of course such learning is not indiscriminate, but uses discernment and is embedded within a tradition—we cannot listen from nowhere.[14] In Cea's terms it is about an attitudes that can "genuinely respect" the religious Other without suggesting that there must be agreement, or, he notes, conversion (2013: 17). I would say that the pluralist theology offered by Perry Schmidt-Leukel is a good example, but also that such radical openness is found in figures like Francis Clooney, John Paul II and others who are theologically within inclusivisms (see Hedges 2010: 111–13).

Finally, the tendency to radical difference suggests that we should not compare because we all do different things: Buddhists seek for nirvana, Christians for salvation so we cannot compare chalk and cheese. I see this as a failure to acknowledge openness, and even, perhaps more radically than exclusivisms, to deny openness. In a sense, exclusivists say we are playing the same game but my rules are right whilst the tendency to radical difference is that we are not even in the same ball park. We may even say that it is a failure to see openness, or even to admit that openness is possible.[15] Certainly, in as far as it challenges the typology and its suggestion that we can have different types of openness to the religious Other, this sense of barring or limiting the very conversation of openness is what exemplifies this tendency. John Milbank's writings in the area typify such an approach, though, as I have suggested elsewhere, they exemplify an exclusivist form of particularity theologically (Hedges 2010: 160–61).[16]

Using the typology in this way both moves beyond a focus on soteriology, radical openness is about an attitude of deep respect and learning, grounded

---

14 I have argued, contra those who insist that a Christian pluralist venture is illegitimate because it grounds itself within one tradition to explore religious diversity that this is precisely what makes the pluralist venture possible (Hedges 2010), and a similar case is argued by Cea, who points out that criticizing a pluralist from starting somewhere is simply nonsensical (2013: 25–26).

15 While the particularist stance often vaunts itself as a form of appreciation of the religious Other, and respect for them, that a quite different dynamic is at work can be seen in the critiques of myself (2008b, 2010) and Marianne Moyaert (2010, 2012).

16 More recently, Milbank has adopted what may be termed a more classically inclusivist style in relation to the theology of religions. This is discussed in Hedges (2014b).

from a Christian position in virtues like hospitality.[17] It also helps us to see that the boundaries are much more fluid than any attempt to clearly demarcate and box off each category. Moreover, I believe the tendencies offer a new freedom in the area because, for instance, labelling oneself an exclusivist, pluralist or otherwise immediately positions you in relation to other groups, both in the church and beyond—certainly any declared pluralist is placing themselves outside a boundary that the Catholic Church deems acceptable (see D'Costa's chapter herein). However, as I have suggested, an approach of radical openness is quite orthodox, hence thinking in these ways can help break down divisions and sectarianism in thinking in this area.

Uses and Defenses of the Typology Revisited

Against such an approach most of the typical criticisms of the typology, which are, it must be said, based upon something of a straw man argument, fail. For instance, arguing no one single figure fits neatly into any category, something which Alan's original book certainly noted, is accepted, even in 'paradigmatic' examples like Farquhar. Again, it is not clear why a description of tendencies towards openness limit the real negotiation between religions. Likewise, the claim that it is not useful in actual dialogue misconstrues its role as heuristic and descriptive; it is a bit like complaining that a book on engine mechanics does not help you learn how to drive a car. The analogy is perhaps helpful, just as you could in theory drive a car perfectly well without knowing it needs petrol, or even the role of the clutch in engaging or disengaging the engine, you can dialogue or do theology of religions perfectly well without the typology. However, when we start analyzing what is going on, or how people's attitudes or approaches affect the way they dialogue, it is useful to have a technical manual, and this is what the typology does as a piece of second-order theology, that is reflection upon the process of engagement with the religious Other. Moreover, the typological terms do not define distinct and discrete categories, but rather overlapping spheres or tendencies. As such, to state, for instance, that both Farquhar and Dupuis are inclusivists really tells us very little if we see the typology as giving us fixed categories. However, if we see it as representing varying tendencies, then we get a more nuanced understanding of these two

---

17   The notion of hospitality is a common theme in much writing on the area, see especially in relation to this, Hedges (2010: 231–37, 2014), Cornille (2012: 148–49), and Moyaert (2011b, 2012: 174–76).

theologians. Assessing it as a heuristic and pedagogical tool, therefore, we can see how it can help students think through the issues of defining and categorizing different thinkers into different categories. Indeed, rather than thinking of simply 'categorizing' people, we can see that the typology used in this ways allows us to break down the sense of fixed positions. Understood, as suggested, as 'ideal types,' we recognize that they are not existing categories into which we can place people, rather useful placeholders. The usefulness of the typology in theological education is argued by Ray Gaston from his own practice (see Gaston's chapter herein).

A final issue is whether the typology, as I have argued, is best seen as an act of second order theology, i.e. reflective or analytic work on the business of those actively engaged in the question of how Christians engage with religious Others.[18] First, I would note that while a meaningful distinction can be made, such a distinction is also, in part at least, an artificial construct; as is well known, indeed, it is to some degree a commonplace, interpreters influence those they study and no study is ever objective, neutral or divorced from the reality they observe (Flood 1999). This is especially so in relation to the typology for, indeed, its original exposition by Race was not simply descriptive but was actively engaging in a first order theological argument that a pluralistic position should be favored. Indeed, since then, first order theological positions which describe themselves by one of the terms have arisen, that is to say there are Christian exclusivists (Strange 2008), and the same goes for the other terms.[19] While I have therefore suggested that it is most useful to use the terms in a heuristic and descriptive second order capacity, they inevitably overlap with first order expositions of them. This raises a variety of issues as, for various reasons, theologians may wish to identify themselves with, or distance themselves from, a variety of specific designations.[20] Moreover, I think there can be a sense in which the typology as tendencies could be used in first

---

18   David Cheetham has suggested that while making this distinction I nevertheless violate it in suggesting how to apply the typology (2013: 78) and herein I hope to clarify my usage partly, at least, in relation to this criticism.

19   Perhaps the pluralist designation has been most avidly adopted as a name for a theological party or position by such figures as Hick, Knitter, Schmidt-Leukel, Rosemary Radford Ruether, Kwok Pui-Lan, and others.

20   As we have noted, D'Costa labels himself an exclusivist although his theological stance is what others term inclusivist, while there are problems for Catholic theologians labelling themselves as pluralists as various theologians either fully pluralist or leaning this way have been censured by the magisterium to varying degrees, one can name Dupuis, Peter Phan, Roger Haight, and Schmidt-Leukel as examples.

order terms, if we suggested, for instance, that radical openness was preferable to radical difference as an approach, and I think this could be usefully argued but is not a line I wish to take here.[21] This does not answer our question of the use of the terms within first order theology, but it should help clarify some of the reasons why there is a sense of overlap between the usage of the typology in different variations, and helps to show that these terms are part of the debate and must be looked at and examined, while also making a valuable and worthwhile contribution to the debate.

Bibliography

Cheetham, David. (2008). "Inclusivisms: Honouring Faithfulness and Openness." In: Paul Hedges and Alan Race (eds.). *Christian Approaches to Other Faiths.* Core Textbook Series. London: SCM Press. pp. 63–84.

(2013). *Ways of Meeting and the Theology of Religions.* Farnham and Burlington, VT: Ashgate.

Clooney, Francis X. (2010). *Comparative Theology: Deep Learning Across Religious Borders.* Chichester: Wiley-Blackwell.

Cornille, Catherine. (2012). "Meaning and Truth in the Dialogue between Religions." In: Frederiek Depoortere and Magdalen Lambkin (eds.). *The Question of Theological Truth.* Amsterdam and New York, NY: Rodopi. pp. 137–56.

D'Costa, Gavin. (2011). "Catholicism and World Religions: A Theological and Phenomenological Account." In: Gavin D'Costa (ed.). *The Catholic Church and World Religions.* London and New York, NY: T & T Clark. pp. 1–33.

(2016). "Changing the Typology? Why Pluralism should be Renamed Post-Christian Inclusivism." In: Paul Hedges, Elizabeth Harris, and Shanthikumar Hettiarachchi (eds.). *Twenty-First Century Theologies of Religions: Retrospection and New Frontiers.* Leiden: Brill. pp. 128–41.

Flood, Gavin. (1999). *Beyond Phenomenology: Rethinking the Study of Religion.* London and New York, NY: Cassell.

Fredericks, James. (1999). *Faith among Faiths: Christian Theology and Non-Christian Religions.* New York: Paulist Press.

Gaston, Ray. (2016). "The Typology and Theological Education: Towards a Practical Theology of Inter Faith Engagement." In: Elizabeth Harris, Paul Hedges, and Shanthikumar Hettiarachchi (eds.). *Twenty-First Century Theologies of Religions: Retrospection and New Frontiers.* Leiden: Brill. pp. 45–56.

---

21   For indications of my argument for such a stance, see Hedges (2014a, 2010: 133–45, 228–53).

Hedges, Paul. (2001). *Preparation and Fulfilment: A History and Study of Fulfilment Theology in Modern British Thought in the Indian Context.* Studies in the Intercultural History of Christianity Series. Bern: Peter Lang.

Hedges, Paul (2002). "The Inter-Relationship of Religions: A Critical Examination of the Concept of Particularity." *World Faiths Encounter* 32: 3–13.

———. (2008a). "Particularities: Tradition-Specific Post-modern Perspectives." In: Paul Hedges and Alan Race (eds.). *Christian Approaches to Other Faiths.* Core Textbook Series. London: SCM Press. pp. 112–35.

———. (2008b). "A Reflection on Typologies: Negotiating a Fast Moving Discussion". In: Paul Hedges and Alan Race (eds.). *Christian Approaches to Other Faiths.* Core Textbook Series. London: SCM Press. pp. 17–33.

———. (2010). *Controversies in Interreligious Dialogue and the Theology of Religions.* London: SCM Press.

———. (2014a). "Hospitality, Power and the Theology of Religions: Pluralisms, Particularities, and the Abrahamic Context." In: Douglas Pratt (ed.). *Interreligious Engagement and Theological Reflection: Ecumenical Explorations.* Bern Interreligious Oecumenical Studies, Vol. 1. Berne: Stämpfli A.G. pp. 156–75.

———. (2014b). "The Rhetoric and Reception of John Milbank's Radical Orthodoxy: Privileging Prejudice in Theology?" *Open Theology* 1/1: 24–44.

Hedges, Paul and Alan Race. (eds.). (2008). *Christian Approaches to Other Faiths.* Core Textbook Series. London: SCM Press. pp. 112–35.

Hick, John. (1989). *An Interpretation of Religion: Human Responses to the Transcendent.* Basingstoke: Macmillan.

———. (1995). *The Rainbow of Faiths: Critical Dialogue on Religious Pluralism.* London: SCM Press.

Kärkäinen, Veli-Matti. (2003). *An Introduction to the Theology of Religions: Biblical, Historical and Contemporary Perspectives.* Downers Grove: Intervarsity Press.

Kiblinger, Kristin Beise. (2010). "Relating Theology of Religions and Comparative Theology." In: Francis X. Clooney (ed.). *The New Comparative Theology: Interreligious Insights from the Next Generation.* London and New York, NY: T. & T. Clark. Pp. 21–42.

Knitter, Paul F. (2002). *Introducing Theologies of Religions.* Faith Meets Faith Series. Maryknoll, NY: Orbis.

Moyaert, Marianne. (2010). "Absorption or Hospitality: Two Approaches to the Tension between Identity and Alterity." In: Catherine Cornille and Christopher Conway (eds.). *Interreligious Hermeneutics.* Eugene, OR: Wipf and Stock. pp. 61–88.

———. (2011a). "Comparative Theology in Search of a Hermeneutical Framework." In: David Cheetham, Ulrich Winkler, Oddbjørn Leirvik, and Judith Gruber (eds.). *Interreligious Hermeneutics in Pluralistic Europe: Between People and Texts.* Amsterdam and New York, NY: Rodopi. pp. 161–86.

————. (2011b). *Fragile Identities: Towards a Theology of Interreligious Hospitality*. Amsterdam and New York, NY: Rodopi.

————. (2012). "Lindbeck and Ricoeur on Meaning, Truth, and the Translation of Religions." In: Frederiek Depoortere and Magdalen Lambkin (eds.). *The Question of Theological Truth*. Amsterdam and New York, NY: Rodopi. pp. 157–80.

Schmidt-Leukel, Perry. (2005). "Exclusivism, Inclusivism, Pluralism: The Tripolar Typology—Clarified and Reaffirmed." In: Paul F. Knitter (ed.). *The Myth of Religious Superiority: A Multifaith Exploration*. Faith Meets Faith Series. Maryknoll, NY: Orbis. pp. 13–27.

————. (2008). "Pluralisms: How to Appreciate Religious Diversity Theologically." In: Paul Hedges and Alan Race (eds.). *Christian Approaches to Other Faiths*. Core Textbook Series. London: SCM Press. pp. 85–110.

Strange, Daniel. (2008). "Exclusivisms: 'Indeed Their Rock is Not like Our Rock'." In: Paul Hedges and Alan Race (eds.). *Christian Approaches to Other Faiths*. Core Textbook Series. London: SCM Press. pp. 36–62.

Sugirtharajah, R.S. (2003). *Postcolonial Reconfigurations: An Alternative Way of Reading the Bible and Doing Theology*. London: SCM Press.

Veléz de Cea, Abraham. (2007). "A Cross-Cultural and Buddhist-friendly Interpretation of the Typology Exclusivism-Inclusivism-Pluralism." *Sophia* 46:1: 453–80.

————. (2013). *The Buddha and Religious Diversity*. London and New York, NY: Routledge.

Weber, Max. (1978). *Economy and Society: An Outline of Interpretive Sociology*. Ed. and transl. Guenther Roth and Claus Wittich. Berkeley, CA: University of California Press.

CHAPTER 6

Rethinking the Typology from a Biblical Perspective: Paul, Adam, and the Theology of Religions

Philip Whitehead

A Pauline Contribution to the Theology of Religions Debate

The debate in the theology of religions from the Christian perspective has predominantly focused on the question of the extent of salvation. This is, with respect to the religious faith of the subject, the underpinning of the familiar threefold typology (Race 1983) of 'exclusivists,' 'inclusivists,' and 'pluralists': the extent of salvation excludes those who do not follow the true faith; includes (some/all) others *despite* their other faith; includes (some/all) others *through* their other faith. Given the significance of this question for Christian theology at both the theoretical and practical levels, this focus is understandable. As Dan Strange has demonstrated in his study of inclusivism within Evangelicalism (2002), the question of who may be saved is particularly urgent for Christians for whom the New Testament has a normative theological role. Strange also highlights that the questions posed by the theology of religions intersect not only with the extent and recipients of salvation, but also with many other strands of Christian doctrine, leading to a matrix of responses to pertinent theological questions: whether or not salvation is *solus Christus*; whether conscious faith in Christ is necessary; whether there is an opportunity to respond to the gospel *post mortem*; whether few or many or all will be saved (Strange 2002: 36, 304–31; see also D'Costa 2009: 7). This intersection of theological questions and doctrinal threads is part of what makes the theology of religions a particularly interesting and fecund area of theological study.

Interactions between New Testament scholarship and systematic theological concerns on this issue are, as I shall argue, desirable and mutually beneficial. While different Christian traditions have developed different ways of relating scripture to Christian theology, and theologians since Gabler have grown used to distinguishing between 'biblical studies' and 'dogmatic theology' (Sandys-Wunsch and Eldredge 1980), few would want to rule out interaction between the two sub-disciplines entirely. More recently, the value and propriety of theological interpretation of scripture has been affirmed by many (e.g. Treier 2008) as a way of overcoming this (modern) split between biblical studies and systematic theology.

One criticism it is possible to make about much work in the theology of religions, particularly from some pluralist approaches, is that it relies—usually implicitly—on an optimistic, Enlightenment approach to theological anthropology, as shown in claims about God which imply a privileged epistemological position for the pluralist (Surin 1990: 210), or else collapses into agnosticism in the face of human incapacity to know or speak truly about God (cf. D'Costa 2009: 10–11, 18). As I shall argue, Pauline theological anthropology—along with the biblical tradition more widely—is more cautious and pessimistic concerning human capacities. An appreciation of theological anthropology is key for understanding Paul's theology (Jewett 1971; Moo 1996: 424), and can also pose challenging questions for the theology of religions debate, which may not be obvious when preoccupied with soteriology alone, or when proceeding from a sociological or phenomenological approach to religion.

Why engage with Paul on the issue? Quite apart from the normative status accorded to his writings by large numbers of Christians both historically and now, Paul's theology has been nothing short of formative for the wider Christian theological project and influential upon the Western philosophical tradition. It is hard to disagree with N.T. Wright's appraisal of Paul's significance as an ancient thinker as being comparable to that of Plato or Seneca, in terms of his intellectual stature and influence upon the history of thought (Wright, 2005: 9). Although frequently dichotomous and provocative, Paul is a deep, complex, and nuanced thinker, working to articulate his theology in a religiously plural and politically complex environment. While a simple exercise in proof-texting is to be avoided, a critical but respectful study of Paul brings us into contact with profound theological insights, and holds the possibility of an encounter with 'truth' about God and the world (so Bell 2011: 4, citing Landmesser 1999: 192–94; cf. Tillich 1974: 41). Furthermore, an exegesis of Paul which does not seek to discern his theological contribution is essentially abandoning the hope of finding an argumentative coherence to his thought, and will quickly become either a truncated, bare historical account, or a rapidly fragmenting eisegesis of agenda-driven 'readings.' As such, an exegetically responsible and careful study and analysis of Paul's theology is not only desirable in itself, but also has much to contribute to the theology of religions.[1]

---

1 I adopt the perspective urged, broadly, by Marshall (2004) and Witherington (2010) that New Testament theology must attempt a theological synthesis of the diverse and complementary witnesses in the New Testament, but that the way to do so is first to allow each author to speak clearly through a respectful study of the respective texts.

Objections have been raised against reliance upon Pauline thought by significant voices in the theology of religions debate. Paul Knitter, for example, protests that there is too much disagreement between Pauline scholars on what Paul meant to make much use of him, and that a focus on Paul can 'drown out' other voices in the New Testament witness (1985: 92–94). This concern is misplaced. The recognition that Paul—as Apostle to the Gentiles—is one of the New Testament authors with the most to contribute to the debate is not an invalidation of the other authors; it is the *canon* and not merely the letters of Paul that has been normative for Christian theology.[2] Knitter points to Paul's rejection of justification by 'good works' and the fact that these are seen as "intrinsic to the experience of salvation" in James and the Synoptics (Knitter 1985: 94), hoping that we will infer that we may take or leave Paul. Yet the perspective offered by James and the gospel writers on 'good works' is never that they are a substitute for faith in the God of Israel, and specifically in Jesus Christ.[3] Similarly, the diversity of *interpretations* of Paul in New Testament scholarship is not *a priori* grounds for the conclusion that study of Paul may not contribute to a theology of religions. As much—if not greater—scholarly diversity may be found in the interpretation and application of Karl Barth, or Vatican II, to the theology of religions, without anybody suggesting these sources thereby be ruled out. Another objection, posed by Alan Race (2013: 10) is that the Bible (and hence Paul) knows nothing of contemporary religions. The religion of the Corinthian 'pagans' (τὰ ἔθνη) spoken of by Paul may no longer exist; nor the imperial cult of Rome. Yet Paul's theological response to the Gentiles and (what we would term) their religions relies remarkably little on their specific details—anything which might be thought to present an 'incommensurability' with contemporary world faiths—and is drawn mainly from his Christian gospel and the context and resources of his Jewish background. As I hope to demonstrate in this paper, the category in which he thinks of non-Christians is that of Adam; a category which is inherently universal and which presents no intrinsic obstacle to application to adherents of religions with which Paul had no familiarity.[4]

---

2 One might point here to the twentieth Article of the Church of England, where it is insisted that the church may not "so expound one place of Scripture, that it be repugnant to another".

3 Whatever one thinks about the theological relationship between James and Paul, or the Synoptics and Paul, regarding works, it is clear that all affirm the necessity of faith in Christ, even if 'faith' carries a different meaning for James as for Paul. Given James' strong affirmation of the *Shema* (2:19) and the salvific importance of believing the truth (5:19ff.) he makes as poor a witness for pluralism as Paul. On judgment according to works in Paul, see McFadden (2013).

4 Knitter (1985: 94) also raises, but does not answer, the question of whether Paul's description of human incapability under sin is an ontological state, or something which merely

Adam is the determinative figure for Paul's theology of the human person, and the theological category in which he places those human beings who are not "in Christ." This feature of Paul's anthropology is at once both *universal*, in that it is a way of talking about all humanity and every individual human, and *dichotomous* when placed against Christ as two categories or realms, into one—and only one—of which everyone falls. The anthropological challenge to the theology of religions can be approached via the question: what difference does being a Christian make? Indeed, for Paul, whose own conversion experience bears directly upon his thought and writing (Kim 1981), the question is perhaps better phrased as: What difference does becoming a Christian make? What is involved in the transfer from the realm of Adam to the realm of Christ? Is it an exchange of one set of beliefs, doctrines, sentiments and behaviors for another? Is it a transfer of allegiance from one group to another? Or might it be an altogether deeper matter, one dealing with the very nature of the human being? An analysis of Paul's argument in Romans, and in particular his Adam/Christ language, suggests the latter.

Adam in Romans

As J.D.G. Dunn has said, the importance of Adam for Paul's theology is often understated, although "Adam is a key figure in Paul's attempt to express his understanding both of Christ and of man" (1980: 101). Adam is mentioned by name in Paul's argument in Romans 5, though his significance extends well beyond that in the letter. One of Paul's key concerns in Romans is to address Jewish/Gentile issues within the church, and Adam is employed as a figure with whom both groups[5] have equal solidarity (Moo 1996: 290). In common with Luke in his genealogy of Jesus, and the writer of Jude, Paul undoubtedly took Adam to be a historical figure and the first human being temporally, though his employment of Adam in his theology does not dwell or depend on this. Rather, he employs Adam as a representative figure, even a 'mythic' one in the sense of a figure in whom we participate (Bell 2007: 27, 251). Here, 'mythic' is not to be understood as 'not true,' but to indicate both the trans-empirical manner in which the figure of Adam is deployed by Paul, and the way in which

---

describes first century Gentiles. It is my hope that this study will demonstrate Paul intends the former.

5   That the category of 'Adam' includes Jews in Paul's thought is clear from the appearance of Moses in Romans 5:12–21. Dunn (1988: 284) argues Paul is at pains to demonstrate that "Jews have not escaped the entail of Adam's disobedience by virtue of the law."

RETHINKING THE TYPOLOGY FROM A BIBLICAL PERSPECTIVE

it betokens a claim about the human being at the very deepest level through narrative. As Hans Frei has pointed out (1974: 42f., 124–26) with the opening chapters of Genesis, what we have with Adam is an ascriptive—rather than a descriptive—narrative which really means what it says, but on its own terms. For Paul, the significance of Adam is not genetic or 'scientific,' but rather in the mysterious way humanity is represented in him and bound, with him, to the power of sin.

It is frequently noted that Paul speaks not of ἁμαρτίαι ('sins') plural, but of ἁμαρτία ('sin') as characterizing the human condition. Sin is conceived as an ontological state, as something which:

> affects not only the sinner's actions and behaviour, but reaches into his being and attacks the centre of his person. In the [sinner's] break with God, an irrevocable offence against the very terms of his existence takes place, to live by and for God ... sin is thus determinative for the human being's whole existence; and the sinner is "ungodly" not only in his evil deeds, rather, he is in a state of being comprehensively far from God and hostile towards God. It is of this state of being a sinner—and not merely of a simple misdemeanour or a failure which can be solved by the person themselves—that Paul speaks.
>
> HÖFIUS 1994: 123, my translation.

This state characterizes both Jew and Gentile, as Paul demonstrates in Romans 1:18–3:20, since all alike are under the power of sin (3:9). This 'cosmic' perspective on sin (Gaventer 2004: 229) relates directly to Paul's use of Adam in Romans.

The idea of Adam as a representative of all humanity is one found in the Jewish tradition (Seifrid 2007: 629). Ecclesiastes 7:29 (Hebrew) and Hosea 6:7 make reference to Adam as the first or paradigmatic sinner.[6] The representative motif is developed and elaborated in literature from the Second Temple period and after: for example, the pseudo-epigraphal author of 4 Ezra (7:118,

---

6   While Barr (1992) is quite correct that the Genesis account of Adam as found in the Hebrew Bible is not, on its own, so starkly pessimistic as Paul, and that the radicalisation of sin and representative or participative nature of Adam is found more in Hellenistic Jewish texts, this Hellenistic "anthropological pessimism" is clearly a thought world in which Paul operates (Westerholm, 2006) and, though his interpreting the Hebrew Bible in the light of the Christ event, understands Adam as associated with sin, death, and human incapacity. In other words, Paul clearly believes in a 'Fall' even if one might not reach this conclusion from the Hebrew Bible alone.

transl. Charlesworth 1983) laments: "O Adam, what have you done? For though it was you who sinned, the fall was not yours alone, but ours also who are your descendants." Here the author is reflecting on the enormity of sin in the context of the destruction of the Second Temple, and comes to similar conclusions to Paul regarding the sin of Adam as having radical consequences for humanity after him.[7] Stephen Westerholm has demonstrated similar radicalization of the Genesis Adam material to explain a 'pessimistic' anthropology in (some) sectarian Judaism of Paul's time (2006: 71ff, 93). Anthony Thiselton also demonstrates that this representative view of Adam is found in some Hellenistic Wisdom texts and Philo (2000: 1282). One can point to the 're-writing' of the Adam and Eve material in *Jubilees* as reflecting a belief in Adam as the primordial sinner and origin of sin, though in the Noah testament in *Jubilees* this is seen as radicalized and spread to all humanity via the Watchers story (Cf. Segal 2007: 34, 57–58). Paul's employment of Adam in his argument in Romans is as a counterpoint to Christ, as also in 1 Corinthians 15: 22, 45–49 (Thiselton 2000: 1281–83; Dunn 1973: 127ff.), and is thus more elaborate than those known to us from surviving Second Temple texts.[8] Paul invests Adam with a deeper significance as the (negative) counterpoint to Christ.[9] Adam and Christ form one of Paul's antitheses: each associated respectively with death, sin, and judgement, and life, freedom, and salvation (Höfius 2002a: 65–66).

Romans 1:18–23

The idea of Adam playing a role in Paul's description of human wickedness in Romans 1 is perhaps the most debateable of the Adam allusions in Romans. Morna D. Hooker, among others, has argued that there is a 'remarkable

---

7   Nevertheless, there seems to have been some diversity in the way Adam is interpreted, with the author of 2 Baruch putting forwards the somewhat incompatible idea that "each of us has been the Adam of his own soul" (54:19, transl. Charlesworth 1983, cf. Davies 1970: 53).

8   N.T. Wright argues that there is an established motif of Israel's vocation to be the 'true Adam' in Second Temple literature (1992: 262–68), which Paul then presumably applies to Christ as the 'true Israel'. Whether or not the development of Paul's Christology moved from Adam to Christ directly, or Adam via Israel to Christ, it seems to be the former language he employs most often in his references to Adam.

9   Fitzmyer, who is loath to admit allusion to Adam outside of Romans 5:12–21, thinks Paul invented the doctrine of incorporation into Adam, arguing it "seems to appear for the first time" in 1 Corinthians 15 (1992: 412). While Paul clearly assigns a deeper–as I shall argue, ontological–significance to Adam than other Second Temple writers, this is clearly building upon an understanding of Genesis he gained from his Jewish background.

parallelism' between the language in verses 18–23, and Genesis 1 (Hooker 1990: 77–78; 1960: 297; Hyldahl 1956: 285–88).[10] Dunn also sees an "obviously deliberate echo of the Adam narratives" here (1988: 53), whereby the frustration of the 'thinking' (διαλογισμός) and 'darkening' of the heart (καρδία) in 1:21 is understood to parallel the curse of Adam in Genesis (Dunn 1998: 84).[11] The knowledge of God in Romans 1:18 is thus one that is available to Adam's 'pristine mind' and one in which humanity participates in some manner (Hooker 1960: 300). However, this participation is also a participation in the frustration of Adam's mind due to sin, with the result that humanity now is at an epistemically disadvantaged position when it comes to knowledge of God (Bell 1998: 110; see also Young 2000).

However, not all the details of Romans 1 parallel Adam. In verses 24ff. the Gentiles seem to be in view. For example, Paul's reference to homosexuality and idol-worship is unrelated to the story of Adam (although Wedderburn examines the suggestion that idolatry is associated with Adam's fall in Second Temple Jewish thought, he concludes this is unlikely (1980: 313–19), but very similar to the denouncement of Gentile behavior found in Wisdom 11–15); if Adam's transgression and condition are in mind in this passage, it is likely mixed with humanity's condition in general: a case of Paul using the concept and semantic range of Genesis' Adam story without precise verbal allusion. The fact that there is this mixing and compounding of the fall of Adam and the fallenness of humanity in Paul's language here (Wedderburn 1980: 418; Bell 1998: 24–25) supports the hypothesis that Paul views humanity in solidarity with Adam.

---

10   Fitzmyer counters that Genesis 1 and 2–3 are separate narratives (though presumably not for pre-Wellhausen Paul) and that alleged echoes of Adam in Romans 1:18–23 are "non-existent" (1992: 274). However, the use of γινώσκω in Romans 1:19ff. may be a verbal allusion to the Septuagint of Genesis 3; additionally, allusion and echo is not limited to verbal parallel, but can also encompass semantic domain and concept (cf. Hays 1989: 20–31, 199n.75). Dunn suggests it is "the description of human aspiration for greater knowledge and a position of high regard which actually results in a decline into disadvantage and a position of low regard" which is modelled on and alludes to Adam (1988: 60).

11   The use of these terms seems to indicate the totality of the human being, but dwelling particularly on the corruption of the intellectual aspect of the human person by sin; the 'noetic' effect of sin in obscuring true knowledge of God–so Cranfield: "Paul uses καρδία to denote a man's inward, hidden self as a thinking, willing and feeling subject" (1975: 118). This ambiguity to human knowledge (Moroney 1999; see also Gaffin 1995 on 1 Corinthians 2:6–16) should discourage the appeal to Romans 1:18 as a proof-text for 'natural theology' or the *a priori* validity of non-Christian religious traditions.

Certainly Paul's indictment of the Gentiles in this passage is universal, and encompasses not only their acts of idolatry, and immorality, but asserts that these derive from a corruption of the mind and heart; that is, an ontological 'fallenness' to the whole human being under the power of sin, which he links explicitly to Adam in 5:12.

Romans 5:12–21

In Romans 5, Adam is explicitly described by Paul as a τύπος ('type') of Christ (5:14), though this comparison is not a strict equivalence, and in fact Adam serves largely as a negative image (Cranfield 1975: 273; Dunn 1988: 296–98). My understanding of the progression of Paul's argument here is as follows: Sin, envisaged as a cosmic power, entered the world through Adam's transgression, and death as a consequence of that, with the result that all of humanity following Adam exist under the power of sin and death: to borrow a phrase from Otfried Höfius' study of Romans 7 (2002b: 104ff.), "in the shadow of Adam." Sin exists before the Law and the establishment of Israel, and is thus a feature of all human existence. Adam is a type of Christ, but the negative image of him: their achievements contrast, for Adam's transgression is not like the χάρισμα ('gift' or 'grace') offered by Christ. The result of the one is death and condemnation; that of the other is grace, righteousness, and the covering of many transgressions (Leithart 2008).

The precise understanding of how Adam's transgression causes sin and death to spread to all is controversial, and has been debated since the time of the early church.[12] Pelagius insisted people sin by following Adam's example. However, Paul's use of Adam here would scarcely seem to allow that view: why parallel Adam with Christ in this way if there is no especial significance to Adam? Rather, there seems to be a way by which, in Paul's thought, Adam's transgression has an effect on all human beings. Cranfield suggests (1975: 274–81), and may well be right, that what is inherited from Adam is not shared guilt in his discrete transgression, but a sinful nature or disposition, so that all in Adam are under the power and influence of sin, and inevitably commit transgressions themselves (cf. Höfius 2002a: 82). Thus, it is an ontological condition that is inherited from Adam. I would, however, say that the language and imagery here is that of *participation* in Adam, just as much as the clearly participatory language used to describe Christ in Chapter 6. In some sense human

---

12   A helpful summary of patristic views on this is presented in Greer (1995: 382–94). The exegetical issues involved are covered comprehensively in Johnson (1974: 298–316).

beings are seen to participate in Adam's transgression and its associated consequences, in the same way as Paul considers Christians to participate in Christ's
death: they "have been crucified with Christ" (Galatians 2:20, cf. Romans 6:8).

Romans 7:7–13

Adam also seems to play a role in Paul's argument in Romans 7. There are
well-rehearsed debates over the identity of the 'I' (ἐγώ) in 7:7–25, which
I cannot cover in detail here.[13] Given Paul's language in the preceding chapter
concerning the Christian being "freed from sin and alive to God" (6:22) and of
slavery to sin being a thing of the past (6:17, 20 uses ἦτε, the imperfect of εἰμί,
connoting a continual state of slavery to sin in the past; cf. Wallace 1996: 548)
and the state of freedom described in Chapter 8 strongly suggests that Paul
cannot be describing either his present experience, or the Christian experience in general in 7:7–25.[14] In verses 7–13, however, Adam is a strong candidate
for the 'I.' The description of the 'I' in 7:7–13 as being once 'alive' χωρὶς νόμου
("apart from," or "without the law") has more affinity with Adam than with any
other individual.[15] Paul may be alluding deliberately to the Genesis 3 narrative
of Adam's transgression: There was once a time when Adam was without sin,
and, having been deceived (ἐξαπατάω),[16] sinned, and "died." For Paul, as we

---

13   On the history of interpretation, see Wilckens (1978–1982: 2.101–17) and Reasoner (2005:
     67–84).

14   Though the view that Romans 7:7–25 cannot refer to the Christian is sometimes accused
     of representing an "over-realized eschatology" (Barrett 1991: 137–44) and thus an unrea-
     sonably optimistic view of the Christian experience (Cranfield 1975: 342, 347), it must be
     noted both that Romans 8:10–13, 18–23, 34–36 describes a Christian existence involving
     suffering and death, awaiting eschatological vindication, and thus giving a full expression
     of Paul's 'now-and-not-yet' schema; and that Paul's language in *both* Chapters 7 and 8
     seems to be describing theological and ontological realities for the human being in union
     with Adam or Christ respectively, and not necessarily conscious experience. Even if Paul
     is primarily describing his pre-Christian experience in 7:7ff. we have to reckon with the
     lack of troubled conscience he seemed to have felt as a Pharisee (cf. Philippians 3:6).

15   Schreiner (1998: 361) objects that Adam cannot be meant here as Paul describes a com-
     mandment of the Decalogue, which Adam could not have encountered (also Moo 1996:
     412). However, Paul may use νόμος here not to mean "Law" in the specific sense of the
     Decalogue or Mitzvot, but in a more general sense of God's commandment–specifically
     the Paradise commandment which Adam in fact breaks. Höfius argues persuasively for
     this (2002b: 129, 133–35).

16   On balance this is likely to be a direct verbal allusion to Genesis 3:13. The Septuagint of
     Genesis 3:13 has ἀπατάω, from which ἐξαπατάω is derived. The verb ἐξαπατάω is rare in the

have seen in Romans 5, this is the origin of sin and death in the world, and so, strictly speaking, 7:9 can only refer to Adam. As Ernst Käsemann says of the 'I' of 7:7–13, "[t]here is nothing in our passage which does not fit Adam, and everything fits Adam alone" (1980: 196; cf. Wilckens 1978–1982: 2.79; Sprinkle 2013: 103).

In 7:14ff. more than Adam—most likely the personified general state of the human being under sin—may be in view, but Adam certainly fits the description of one who was once alive and without the law, but who, through the provocation of the commandment, became enslaved to sin, death, and the law. It is hard to make sense of the passage if *only* the Adam of Genesis 2–3 is meant throughout, however, especially given Paul's use of 'I' to describe Adam, who he has referred to in the third-person a few paragraphs ago. The depiction of a historical or literary character in the first-person, known as *prosopoiia*, is a standard feature of Graeco-Roman rhetoric,[17] and could be employed here to stress the identification of Adam with the 'I' Paul writes of here, as Ben Witherington has suggested (2012). I suggest that Paul is using the 'I' to refer to the experience of humanity in general under sin, who are jointly and severally incorporated into Adam. He is thus describing an ontological state of those who are not united to Christ, rather than an historically contingent condition of first century 'pagans.' Sin is, in this passage and for Paul, an enslaving power, and the implications for a theological anthropology of the human being under its power are extensive. Paul's argument in the preceding two chapters has entailed that the human being is either associated with Adam or Christ. To borrow the phrasing of 1 Corinthians 15, the human being is either 'in Adam' (ἐν Ἀδάμ) or 'in Christ' (ἐν Χριστῷ).

This requires more precision, however. If statements such as "I was once alive apart from the law" strictly speaking apply to Adam alone, how then can the 'I' represent humanity in Adam? The difficulty can be resolved if the passage is read in the light of Paul's use of participative language in his Adam-Christ typology. This is recognized in what is often called 'Federal headship' in Reformed theology—the idea that Adam's fall involved a participation of the entire human race, with Adam as their representative head—although I argue Paul goes beyond it in asserting an ontological and anthropological reality to the notion of participation in Adam. Here, perhaps the 'I' is to be understood as Adamic humanity, with the implication that the participation of the human being in Adam is not only legal, but has some ontological basis;

New Testament, occurring only in the Pauline corpus, and explicitly refers to the Genesis 3 narrative in 2 Corinthians 11:3 and 1 Timothy 2:13 (where ἀπατάω is used of Adam and the more intense ἐξαπατάω of Eve!).

17   In which Paul was undoubtedly trained, as demonstrated by Stowers (1994).

just as union with Christ for the Christian is no "legal fiction" but involves a genuine participation (cf. Romans 6:5–11) so too is the non-Christian united to Adam in sin and death. Thus, it is objectively possible for this 'I' to say "I died" in Adam's transgression (Romans 7:10). The condition which follows, for all human beings in Adam, is one characterized by bondage to sin and incapacity to know or relate properly to God. Furthermore, this is how Paul thinks of all non-Christians, and so the relevant consideration for him is not the ethics taught by a particular tradition, but a mission-oriented concern that God effects the conversion of non-Christians, transferring them from the realm of Adam to Christ.

Some Theological Implications

This participative, 'mythic' use of Adam in Paul's theology to describe human beings has a number of implications for a theology of religions following Paul. If we accept Paul's ideas of union with Adam or Christ, we must see these statements as making a far stronger claim than being merely shorthand labels for religious affiliation. It is my contention that Adam provides the central theological category into which non-Christians fall in Paul's thought. There is much here that is mysterious and requires further study. To say someone is 'in Adam,' or 'in Christ' is a claim with a greater ontological significance than we might attach to calling them 'non-Christian' or 'Christian' in everyday language. Paul really does view the actions and fate of Adam as having direct consequences on the very nature of human beings far removed from him in space and time, in the same way that he views Christians as having really been present in Christ's death and resurrection. An aspect of the human being is therefore deeply bound up with either Adam or Christ. This aspect is clearly a non-material and non- or sub-conscious facet of the human being; what Christian theology has traditionally termed the *soul* (cf. Bell 2007). Furthermore, Paul sees this as a genuine dichotomy of belonging to Adam or, and only or, Christ; there is no third option here. His scheme may be summarized fairly as:

> Two great figures stand at the entrances to two worlds: Adam stands at the gate of the old world, Jesus at the gate of the new. Adam's first sin inaugurated the old age and brought sin, death, and condemnation. Now in Jesus a new day of righteousness, life and justification has come (Romans 5:12–21). If we are "in Adam," we are part of the old age and under its sway. But if we are "in Christ," we are part of the age to come and can already experience God's life-giving power.
>
> BARTHOLOMEW and GOHEEN 2004: 189

Paul speaks, too, of conversion meaning a transfer of the human being from the realm of Adam to the realm of Christ. *This* is, beyond the exchange of beliefs, doctrines, and behaviors, the difference that becoming a Christian makes, according to Paul. Conversion involves an ontological change at some level of the human being, and if this is so, we must say that Paul views the Christian as ontologically different to the pre-Christian or the non-Christian. The change is effected by the action of God in transferring the human being from the realm of Adam to the realm of Christ; it cannot be effected by human subjects themselves, who find themselves in a predicament they cannot solve.[18] Human subjects are now united to and participating in Christ, rather than in Adam. A transfer of being and status has taken place, as well as a transfer of religious affiliation. This certainly accounts for Paul's dichotomous language elsewhere concerning Christians and non-Christians, and would support some of the claims made by so-called 'exclusivist' theologians.[19]

As Seifrid points out (2007: 692), Paul's use of Adam in Romans also "clarifies Abraham's place." That is, Paul demonstrates that non-Christian Jew and Gentile alike belong to the realm of Adam, and that the real inheritors of Abraham's blessing are those—both Jew and Gentile—whom God has united with Christ.[20] Both Christ and Adam take priority over Abraham (and Moses) here; with the corollary for Christians engaged in interreligious dialogue that

---

18   This last phrase is borrowed from Judith Butler (2005: 103), who uses it in a different context to describe the human condition.

19   The focus on conversion, however, would add support to a strongly 'missionary' approach which does not write off non-Christians, but seeks their conversion to Christ. Chung (2010: 356–57) urges what he calls a "missional perspective" and objects to 'exclusivism' when it is 'separatist', though he affirms the uniqueness and finality of Christ and refuses to endorse even evangelical 'inclusivism' (370–371). This is an example of one of the major faults of the threefold typology, in that few who affirm core 'exclusivist' beliefs wish to describe themselves as 'exclusivist' as the terminology implies a certain separatism or lack of interest in interreligious dialogue.

20   For Paul this does not erase the history of God's dealings with Israel (Romans 9:4–5; 15:4, 8). Paul seems to be working with the idea, found also in the Hebrew Bible, of the holy 'remnant' (λεῖμμα) within (ethnic) Israel (11:5, 7b) whom he would presumably see as in some way united with Christ, whereas unbelieving/apostate Israel is not (Schreiner shows that Paul's anguish in 9:1–5 can only be explained by his understanding that "many of his [Jewish] contemporaries are unsaved", 1998: 485; cf. Käsemann 1980: 301). Paul never states this explicitly, but his identification of Jesus with the God of Israel in his use of the *shema* formula in 1 Corinthians 8:6 and as having been present with Moses in 1 Corinthians 10:4 leads me to believe his solution to the question of how faithful Israelites who lived before Jesus were saved would be Christological.

it is perhaps not useful to develop a category of the 'Abrahamic religions' over against, for example, Hinduism.

Paul's theological anthropology here poses a strong challenge to the theology of religions debate. If he is correctly understood as claiming that becoming a Christian involves an ontological change in the human being–that Christians and non-Christians are distinct at some level[21]—then a Pauline theology of religion must give due account of this, and will pose challenging questions for the wider debate. Paul alleges differences between Christians and non-Christians at a deep level of the human person. Furthermore, if being in Adam entails a corruption of the intellect, (true) knowledge of God may in fact be inaccessible outside of the gospel, and so claims about God and reality bound to a non-Christian religion cannot be uncritically affirmed by Christian theologians.

Further biblical-theological study is clearly necessary to answer questions about the epistemological necessity of Christ for salvation, especially when evaluating 'inclusivist' perspectives. We see, however, that a study of Paul's theological anthropology suggests the concept of 'union with Christ' is at least as significant as the subject's faith in Christ, which undermines the approaches which are solely focused on the subject's belief. If being 'in Christ' means more than beliefs, behaviors, and affiliation, is it separable from these, or are these necessary manifestations of a transfer from the realm of Adam to the realm of Christ? I would tentatively suggest Paul's theology implies the latter. In any case, the ontological predicament human beings are said to be in without Christ, exemplified by the category of Adam, suggests that phenomenological approaches to the theology of religions are not capable of giving a full account of religious identity and conversion, and nothing short of a theological approach is sufficient for articulating a Christian understanding of those who belong to other faith traditions.

Bibliography

Barr, J. (1992). *The Garden of Eden and the Hope of Immortality*. London: SCM Press.

Barrett, C.K. (1991). *A Commentary on the Epistle to the Romans*. 2nd ed. London: A&C Black.

---

21   I do not think Paul claims that this is precisely knowable from any epistemological position other than God's; that is, it is not possible for us to say with certainty whether a specific person is genuinely united with Christ.

Bartholomew, C.G., and M.W. Goheen. (2004). *The Drama of Scripture*. Grand Rapids, MI: Baker Academic.

Bell, R.H. (1998). *No One Seeks for God: An Exegetical and Theological Study of Romans 1.18–3.20*. Tübingen: Mohr Siebeck.

———. (2007). *Deliver Us From Evil: Interpreting the Redemption from the Power of Satan in New Testament Theology*. Tübingen: Mohr Siebeck.

———. (2011). "Reading Romans with Arthur Schopenhauer: Some First Steps toward a Theology of Mind." *Journal for the Study of Paul and his Letters* 1.1: 41–56.

Butler, J. (2005). *Giving an Account of Oneself*. New York, NY: Fordham University Press.

Charlesworth, J.H. (1983). *The Old Testament Pseudepigrapha*. 1st ed. Garden City, NY.: Doubleday.

Chung, S.W. (2010). "Other Religions." In: G.R. McDermott (ed.). *Oxford Handbook of Evangelical Theology*. Oxford: Oxford University Press. pp. 355–70.

Cranfield, C.E.B. (1975). *A Critical and Exegetical Commentary on the Epistle to the Romans*. Volume I. International Critical Commentary. Edinburgh: T&T Clark.

D'Costa, G. (2009). *Christianity and World Religions: Disputed Questions in the Theology of Religions*. Chichester: Wiley-Blackwell.

Davies, W.D. (1970). *Paul and Rabbinic Judaism: Some Rabbinic Elements in Pauline Theology*. 3rd ed. London. SPCK.

Dunn, J.D.G. (1973). "1 Corinthians 15.45 – Last Adam, Life-Giving Spirit." In: B. Lindars and S. Smalley (eds.). *Christ and Spirit in the New Testament: Studies in Honour of C.F.D Moule*. Cambridge: Cambridge University Press. pp. 127–41.

———. (1980). *Christology in the Making: A New Testament Inquiry into the Origins of the Doctrine of the Incarnation*. Philadelphia, PA: Westminster John Knox Press.

———. (1988). *Romans 1–8*. Word Biblical Commentary 38a. Dallas, TX: Word Books.

———. (1998). *The Theology of Paul the Apostle*. Edinburgh: T&T Clark.

Fitzmyer, J.A. (1992). *Romans: A New Translation with Introduction and Commentary*. Anchor Bible Commentary. New York, NY: Doubleday.

Frei, H.W. (1974). *The Eclipse of Biblical Narrative: A Study in Eighteenth and Nineteenth Century Hermeneutics*. New Haven, CN: Yale University Press.

Gaffin, Jr., R.B. (1995). "Some Epistemological Reflections on 1 Cor 2:6–16." *Westminster Theological Journal* 57:103–24.

Greer, R.A. (1995). "Sinned We All in Adam's Fall?" In: L.M. White and O.L. Yarbrough (eds.). *The Social World of the First Christians: Essays in Honor of Wayne A. Meeks*. Minneapolis, MN: Augsburg Fortress. pp. 382–94.

Hays, R.B. (1989). *Echoes of Scripture in the Letters of Paul*. New Haven, CN: Yale University Press.

Höfius, O. (1960). "Adam in Romans I." *New Testament Studies* 6: 297–306.

———. (1994). "»Rechtfertigung des Gottlosen« als Thema biblischer Theologie." In: O. Höfius, *Paulusstudien*. 2nd ed. Tübingen: Mohr Siebeck. pp. 121–47.

———. (2002a). "Die Adam-Christus-Antithese und das Gesetz." In: O. Höfius. *Paulusstudien II*. Tübingen: Mohr Siebeck. pp. 62–103.

———. (2002b). "Der Mensch im Schatten Adams. Römer 7,7–25a." In: O. Höfius. *Paulusstudien II*. Tübingen: Mohr Siebeck. pp. 104–54.

Hooker, M.D. (1990). *From Adam to Christ: Essays on Paul*. Cambridge: Cambridge University Press.

Jewett, R. (1971). *Paul's Anthropological Terms: A Study of Their Use in Conflict Settings*. Leiden: Brill.

Johnson, Jr., S.L. (1974). "Romans 5:12—An Exercise in Exegesis and Theology." In: R.N. Longenecker and R.C. Tenney (eds). *New Dimensions in New Testament Study*. Grand Rapids, MI: Zondervan. pp. 298–316.

Käsemann, Ernst. (1980). *A Commentary on Romans*. G.W. Bromiley (transl.). 4th ed. Grand Rapids, MI: Eerdmans.

Kim, S. (1981). *The Origin of Paul's Gospel*. Tübingen: Mohr Siebeck.

Knitter, P.F. (1985). *No Other Name? A Critical Survey of Christian Attitudes toward the World Religions*. Maryknoll, NY: Orbis Books.

Landmesser, C. (1999). *Wahrheit als Grundbegriff neutestamentlicher Wissenschaft*. Tübingen: Mohr Siebeck.

Leithart, P.J. (2008). "Adam, Moses, and Jesus: A Reading of Romans 5:12–14." *Calvin Theological Journal* 43/2: 257–73.

Marshall, I.H. (2004). *Beyond the Bible: Moving from Scripture to Theology*. Grand Rapids, MI: Baker Academic.

McFadden, K.W. (2013). *Judgment According to Works in Romans: The Meaning and Function of Divine Judgment in Paul's Most Important Letter*. Minneapolis, MN: Fortress.

Moo, D.J. (1996). *The Epistle to the Romans*. New International Commentary on the New Testament. Grand Rapids, MI: Eerdmans.

Moroney, S.K. (1999). *The Noetic Effects of Sin*. Lanham, MD: Lexington Books.

Race, A. (1983). *Christians and Religious Pluralism: Patterns in the Christian Theology of Religions*. London: SCM Press.

Race, A. (2013). *Making Sense of Religious Pluralism*. London: SPCK.

Reasoner, M. (2005). *Romans in Full Circle: A History of Interpretation*. Philadelphia, PA: Westminster John Knox Press.

Sandys-Wunsch, J., and L. Eldredge. (1980). "J.P. Gabler and the Distinction between Biblical and Dogmatic Theology: Translation, Commentary, and Discussion of His Originality." *Scottish Journal of Theology* 33: 133–58.

Schreiner, T.R. (1998). *Romans*. Baker Exegetical Commentary on the New Testament. Grand Rapids, MI: Baker.

Segal, Michael. (2007). *The Book of Jubilees: Rewritten Bible, Redaction, Ideology, and Theology*. Leiden: Brill.

Seifrid, M.A. (2007). "Romans." In: G.K. Beale and D.A. Carson (eds.). *Commentary on the New Testament Use of the Old Testament.* Nottingham: Apollos. pp. 607–93.

Sprinkle, P.M. (2013). *Paul and Judaism Revisited: A Study of Divine and Human Agency in Salvation.* Downers Grove, IL: IVP Academic.

Stowers, S.K. (1994). *A Rereading of Romans: Justice, Jews, and Gentiles.* New Haven, CN: Yale University Press.

Strange, D. (2002). *The Possibility of Salvation Among the Unevangelised: An Analysis of Inclusivism in Recent Evangelical Theology.* Carlisle: Paternoster.

Surin, K.J. (1990). "A 'Politics of Speech': Religious Pluralism in the Age of the McDonald's Hamburger." In: Gavin D'Costa (ed.). *Christian Uniqueness Reconsidered: The Myth of a Pluralistic Theology of Religions.* Maryknoll, NY: Orbis Books. pp. 192–212.

Thiselton, A.C. (2000). *The First Epistle to the Corinthians: A Commentary on the Greek Text.* New International Greek Testament Commentary. Grand Rapids, MI: Eerdmans.

Tillich, P. (1974). *Systematic Theology.* Vol. 1. Chicago, IL: University of Chicago Press.

Treier, D.J. (2008). *Introducing Theological Interpretation of Scripture: Recovering a Christian Practice.* Nottingham: Apollos.

Wallace, D.B. (1996). *Greek Grammar Beyond the Basics: An Exegetical Syntax of the New Testament.* Grand Rapids, MI: Zondervan.

Wedderburn, A.J.M. (1980). "Adam in Paul's Letter to the Romans." In: Elizabeth A. Livingstone (ed.). *Studia Biblica 1978.* Volume 3. Sheffield: Sheffield Academic Press. pp. 413–30.

Westerholm, S. (2006). "Paul's Anthropological 'Pessimism' in its Jewish Context." In: J.M.G. Barclay and S. Gathercole (eds.). *Divine and Human Agency in Paul and His Cultural Environment.* London: T&T Clark. pp. 71–98.

Wilckens, U. (1978–1982). *Der Brief an die Römer.* Evangelisch-Katholisch Kommentar. 3 Volumes. Neukirchen-Vluyn: Neukirchener Verlag.

Witherington, B. III. (2010). *The Indelible Image: The Theological and Ethical Thought World of the New Testament.* Downers Grove, IL: IVP Academic.

———. (2012). "'But I Would Rather Persuade'…: The Necessity of Understanding Rhetoric for Understanding the Text and Context of the New Testament." Paper presented at the Society of Biblical Literature, Chicago, IL.

Wright, N.T. (1992). *The New Testament and the People of God.* London: SPCK.

———. (2005). *Paul: Fresh Perspectives.* London: SPCK.

Young, R.A. (2000). "The Knowledge of God in Romans 1:18–23: Exegetical and Theological Reflections." *Journal of the Evangelical Theological Society* 43.4: 695–707.

PART 2

Pluralist Voices and Contestation

∵

CHAPTER 7

Race, Religion and Shared Theology

Tony Bayfield

Thirty Years and Still Going Strong

Thirty years ago the late Revd Dr John Bowden handed me a book he had recently published. John was the person who built SCM Press into a major, boundary-stretching, religious publishing house. The book he gave me was *Christians and Religious Pluralism* by an objectionably young man, the Anglican Chaplain at the University of Kent, Alan Race (Race 1983). John said that the book would interest me. He also said that Alan would be ideal for a new kind of dialogue group which the then Executive Director of the Council of Christians and Jews, Marcus Braybrooke, and I were setting up. Alan and I have been dialogue partners ever since.

My thinking and writing about Jewish-Christian dialogue has been characterized by an obsession with Jews and Christians as siblings (Bayfield 2001). Rabbinic Judaism—the Judaism to which I am heir—emerged at the same time and in the same place as Christianity, 2,000 years ago. We are both the children of Abraham and Sarah. We are not, however, twins as the American Jewish scholar, Alan Segal, suggested (Segal 1986), taking the fateful metaphor of Jacob and Esau struggling with each other even in their mother's womb just a touch too literally. But we are siblings.

In that first 'Manor House' Dialogue Group,[1] which Alan and I shared along with John Bowden and Marcus Braybrooke, we were joined by a scholarly, independently-minded Orthodox Rabbi, Dr Norman Solomon. Solomon wrote the concluding chapter to the book that the Manor House Dialogue Group published in 1992 (Solomon 1992). In it he identified a third dialogue partner. Solomon pointed out to us that whenever we met as a group not only were Judaism and Christianity present, but so also was modernity—or post-modernity. This, he explained, was the complex culture within which we had all been brought up and educated, the language of which we spoke (rather than Greek or Hebrew) and within which we lived and breathed. That, argued Rabbi Solomon, is the context which the siblings share and within which they must strive for

---

1 Named after the Jewish Centre in Finchley, NW London at which I was based, later the Sternberg Centre for Judaism.

reconciliation. Alan and I are not just siblings but close friends, filled with mutual respect, in a way that is far from typical of past relationships within the world's most dysfunctional family.[2] But there is no doubt that, whilst we grew up with the same third dialogue partner, we did not grow up in the same house.

In this chapter, I want to explore four areas: our experiences of God; our responses to Absolutism; our commitment to religious pluralism; and our approach to our respective sacred texts. They will, I believe, illustrate what I mean by, 'we did not grow up in the same house' but live as closest of neighbors in the same street.

Different Houses, Different Experiences of God

I am currently engaged in writing a book of personal or synecodotal theology— a systematic account of Judaism but seen through my eyes, drawing on selected episodes in my own life. The working title is, *Challenging God: A Personal Jewish Theology.* At the heart of the book is a chapter entitled "Israel and the Nations."[3] It is deliberately placed at the heart of the book because I believe passionately that relationships between the faiths have moved from the margins to the center. We can, today, only exist authentically in relationship with one another. Collaboration tops the agenda.

My theology is not only personal but idiosyncratic. The entire book will be peppered with brief, argumentative exchanges with God. This quirk notwithstanding, I dared to ask Alan if he would read the first draft of the interreligious chapter. I say 'dared' because opening myself up to criticism from colleagues could be disabling—but Alan I trust. His reaction was kind, positive, and constructive. But he was clearly bothered by the conversations with God. He wondered aloud whether I was being tongue-in-cheek, jokey—a characteristic not unknown. But as soon as he realized I was serious, he said "God's very hard on you, isn't he?"

Alan and I currently occupy the liberal end of a new dialogue group, our present project together. Another member of the group, a most distinguished

---

2 Judaism, Christianity and Islam provide the religious inheritance for over half the world's population. Afghanistan, Belfast, Chechnya, Damascus, Eritrea, or Israel/Pakistan do not suggest a collaborative family contributing to our collective wisdom for the building of a just and peaceful world. Relations within each faith are often as bad as those between the members of the dysfunctional Abrahamic family.

3 Echoing Biblical language. 'Israel' refers to the Jewish people and 'Nations' to the world's faiths, particularly—but only because it's my special interest—Christianity and Islam.

Christian theologian, experiences God as profoundly loving and finds in their relationship what for me is a remarkable degree of joy. My experience is different. In trying to explain that, my starting point is work conducted some decades ago by American Bible scholar, George Mendenhall (Mendenhall 1955). Mendenhall identified a number of forms of political covenant made in the Ancient World between rulers and their subjects or, occasionally, between rulers and rulers. These models of covenant, he argued, were taken over by the authors of the Pentateuch and theologized. They sit side by side, within the text of the Torah, serving as metaphors for the relationship between God and Israel. For me, the idea that there are different models of covenant in Judaism came in equal measure as revelation and relief. There is the Promissory model, exemplified by Abraham and David, in which God, out of love, promises to take care of God's protégé and requires nothing in return except, by implication, love, and fidelity. There is the Suzerainty model characterized by the covenant at Sinai in Exodus, in which a back-breaking weight of obligations are imposed on and accepted by the Children of Israel. God promises nothing in return, except, impliedly, protection and reward for fidelity. Finally, there is the Parity model, based upon Babylonian and Hittite covenants between rulers, which is read by Mendenhall and subsequent scholars into the Deuteronomic account of Sinai (Eisen 1987).[4] Here, extraordinarily, the relationship is one of parity—not parity in the sense of equality but parity in the sense of mutual dependence and need.

   Although this model of the covenantal relationship was not the normative one in classical Rabbinic Judaism, it is nevertheless present—where and when you might expect it to be. Here is a remarkable midrash, a passage of rabbinic interpretation and theological inquiry.[5] It comes from a collection that provides a commentary on the Book of Lamentations, the Lamentations Rabbah, redacted in the fifth century CE. But it is clearly thinking of a later destruction, the destruction and expulsion that took place in the first and second centuries CE. These events provided the disturbing backdrop to the formulation of the

---

4   "The *brit* (covenant) initiated by God, binds Israel to Him .... Deuteronomy's reiteration of the covenant follows the parity form precisely, adopting even the standard six-part structure: preamble, historical prologue, detailed stipulations, provision for deposit and/or reading of the text, invocation of divine witnesses (in this case heaven and earth), and, finally, the recitation of blessings and curses" (Eisen 1987: 108).

5   The word *midrash* is derived from the Hebrew root *dalet-resh-shin* meaning to examine, question, interpret. It gives rise to a huge body of literature but the point I am making is about its methodology–interrogating the text word by word, phrase by phrase. The technique was used equally to develop Aggadah, Theology, and Halakhah, Practice.

theology of Rabbinic Judaism. The text will seem strange to those unfamiliar with classical rabbinic literature and methodology but the king is, of course, God and the consort, Israel, the Jewish people. The passage invokes the tradition that God hawked the Torah round the nations before turning to Israel:

> It may be likened to a king who was enraged with his consort and drove her out of the palace. She went and pressed her face against the pillar. It happened that the king passed, saw her and said to her, "You're acting impudently!" She replied, "My lord king, so it's seemly, right and proper for me to do, seeing that no other woman except me has accepted you." He retorted, "It was I who disqualified all other women [from marriage with Me] for your sake." She said to him, "If that's so, why did you enter such-and-such a side street, such-and-such a court and place; wasn't it on account of a certain woman who rejected you?" Similarly spoke the Holy One, blessed be He, to Israel: "You're acting impudently." They replied: "Lord of the Universe, so it's seemly, right and proper for us to do, seeing that no other nation except us accepted Your Torah." He retorted, "It was I who disqualified all other nations [from accepting it] for your sake." They said to Him, "If that's so, why did You hawk Your Torah round the nations for them to reject?"
>
> LAMENTATIONS RABBAH 3:1

What is so striking is that the relationship between God and Israel has become stressed and reproachful. It stands in the tradition of Abraham and Sodom, where there is a questioning, challenging, querying of God's justice and compassion: "Must not the Judge of all the earth act justly?" (Genesis 18:25). Even more remarkable, God and Israel are now *former* lovers. The text provides a shattering theological precursor to contemporary Jewish questioning of the covenant in the light of the Shoah and the assertion that Jews who affirm their Jewishness today do so on a voluntary basis.[6] But even that is tangential to the point I am making about my own personal experience. I am disturbingly convinced that the 'conversations' I have with God contain—despite the almost overwhelming intrusion of my psyche and intellect—an element of reality, of fleeting engagement with the divine. Those conversations do not come out of love—certainly not on my side—but rather from anger, exasperation

---

6   The Orthodox scholar Rabbi Irving Greenberg argues that the covenant was invalidated by the Shoah and those who today opt in to Judaism do so on a voluntary basis. Reform Theologian, Rabbi Professor Eugene Borowitz says of those Jews who choose to remain Jews that they are 'Renewing the Covenant.'

and an incorrigible refusal to be modest, accepting, and Job-like. I do not love God like my distinguished Christian colleague. I do not experience joy as the predominant product of our relationship. But God will not let me go and I will not let God go. We are bound together in a covenant of mutual challenge and mutual need.

Not all Jews feel as I do—two Jews, three opinions. But there are, thankfully, some who would grant that my experience is not just rooted in intellectual hubris and the peculiarities of my personal psychology and background. It is also rooted in the experience of Judaism and in its texts, as the passage from Lamentations Rabbah illustrates. How we experience God is influenced by the vocabulary of the tradition in which we are brought up. My personal experience of God—if that is what it is—has been affected by the home in which I was raised and have lived for 70 years. Alan, brought up in the large, composite house called the Church of England, experiences God in a different way from me. But neither of us have any doubt that it is—ultimately[7]—the same God whom we both experience.

Different House, Same Street

Alan and I may have been brought up differently and live in different houses but the two houses are in the same street. In fact, we are next door neighbors. One of my teachers, the American Rabbi and theologian, Eugene Borowitz, memorably suggested that one should try to live in creative maladjustment with society. Alan and I seem to live in creative maladjustment with the homes we inhabit and are more creatively maladjusted to our respective traditions and to wider society than we are with each other. For we share one overriding and defining characteristic, we are both pluralists. Alan's pluralism goes back to that first of a number of important books, *Christians and Religious Pluralism*.

In a chapter in a book which he and I co-edited, with a Muslim colleague, Dr Ataullah Siddiqui, published in 2012, Alan defines his pluralism in a distinctive way (Race 2012). He examines religion and violence—he is characteristically familiar with the wealth of contemporary literature. He concludes that violence is a symptom, a consequence, not of religion per se but of religious absolutism. He and I share the view that the rise and rise of religious fundamentalism since the 1960s, in Judaism and Christianity—but not exclusively,

---

7   God 'speaks' to us as the God of Abraham, Isaac, Jacob, Sarah, Rebeccah, Rachel, and Leah or as Christ or Allah but beyond that particular 'voice' lies the *Ein Sof*, the Without End, the Unknowable, the Ground of our Being–the same God.

in Islam and Hinduism as well—is a threat to religion itself. That threat is even greater than the threat of secularism and atheism. The source, not just of religious violence but of woefully insufficient interreligious collaboration, lies in the insistence, however elegantly disguised, on 'my truth' being exclusive or, if not exclusive, 'better than yours.' Being Alan, he eschews diplomatic silences and demonstrates how Archbishop Rowan Williams is not a pluralist (Race 2012: 193). Alan has never put preferment within the Church before the honesty and integrity of his theology.

As a Jew, I am better prepared for pluralism than I would be if I were a Christian. Whereas Christians were fatefully wedded to imperialism, first by Constantine and then by Justinian, their Jewish contemporaries in Babylon were content with their particular technicolor love affair with God. They did not feel the need to be militant about—as they perceived them—the less brilliant, sepia colored love affairs, especially the monotheistic love affairs, around them. Of course, this is not how things are today in the Orthodox Jewish world but nobody expects me, as a Reform Jew, to defer to the authority of Rabbi Lord Sacks or his successor.[8] My opposition to absolutism is far less professionally threatening than Alan's.

My Jewish Pluralism

My personal pluralism has six facets. It is hard—and probably of little importance to anyone other than me—to place them in the order in which I became aware of them. In any event they are neither chronological nor open to prioritization. I will reflect on each.

My Existential Awareness

When I was at Cambridge in the 1960s, a small group of friends, all called David, all historians, and none of them Jewish, introduced me to the great wool churches of the Essex-Suffolk border. I had those churches in mind when, a decade or two later, I gave a paper to that first dialogue group, which Alan and I shared. I said:

> I look up to the roof soaring above me heavenwards. And around at the empty pews. The prayers prayed in this place for centuries are almost

---

8 Less than half the 270,000 Jews of Britain belong to synagogues which accept the authority of the 'Chief Rabbi.' Individual Chief Rabbis such as Rabbi Lord Sacks are, however, widely admired and felt to be 'good' for the British Jewish community.

tangible. Real prayers, honest prayers, true prayers, prayers which are heard. People reach out to God here, just as I strive to reach out to God in synagogue. And if they reach out to God, God comes to meet them here. The smell, the flavour, the accoutrements may not be of my home, but God is as at home here as God is at my house.

BAYFIELD and BRAYBROOKE 1992: 4–5

That existential statement, that articulation of a powerful intuitive sense, has not changed over the subsequent decades. Although Judaism and Christianity are different faiths, configured differently, with distinctive insights and emphases, Christians and Jews are both people of faith, no better and no worse than each other, no more and no less misguided.

At roughly the same time I expressed it in a way that some of my Christian friends and rabbinic colleagues found unacceptable. I said that I looked at Alan (or Marcus Braybrooke or John Bowden or Richard Harries or any other of the Christian members of that group) and I looked at myself (or Michael Hilton or Albert Friedlander or Julia Neuberger) and asked, "How does God feel about us?" Does God want the Christians to give up their Christianity and return to the faith from which they parted company 1,800 years ago?[9] Does God want the Jews to throw in the towel and finally recognize the road they have stubbornly refused to take for two millennia? I am clear about my answer, 'no.' Some, mostly Christians, are upset by my *chutzpah*, declaring it shocking to claim to know the mind of God. Although God is used to my arrogance and impudence by now, I can understand the response. But I cannot deny the deep feeling, first that God has far greater concerns about us than the choice between church or synagogue and second, that the authentic existence of one faith does not preclude or invalidate the existence of the other.

The Consequence of Genuine Respect

In the 1970s and early 80s I was a congregational rabbi, a Jewish teacher to a small community in Surrey. Unlike North West London, Surrey has never been a place where significant numbers of Jews have chosen to live. An important function of my role as Rabbi of the North West Surrey Synagogue was deemed to be providing the Home Counties with an image of the Jew that was other than a throwback to eighteenth century Poland or an evil Christ killer. After some years, I wanted to do more than PR for today's Jews, however necessary.

---

9   '1,800 years ago' acknowledges how relatively late what James D.G. Dunn called the partings of the ways was completed.

I wanted to help Jews and Christians to meet in mutual respect—the necessary precursor to a meaningful collaboration.

Down in Surrey, quite a lot of meeting had taken place, quite a lot of cups of tea had been drunk and many encouraging words spoken, particularly by the Christians. The Jews found it hard to let down their defenses and pretended to a lack of interest.[10] But even at their best, warmest and frankest, I sensed unspoken reservations. The Christians said how much they admired Jewish communal life, the strength of the family and institutions like Friday night but maintained the unspoken qualification: 'Pity you're missing out on the greatest Truth of all.' The Jews could be fulsome about Christian architecture, self-sacrificing lives and a remarkable history of founding hospitals and other caring institutions. But, equally unspoken, they maintained incomprehension about Christian doctrine, particularly the idea that Jesus was the son of God. 'All founded on a mistake' was the phrase not used. For me such 'respect' is not respect at all. If Jews and Christians are to be reconciled then they have to move beyond 'Pity you're missing out' and 'All founded on a mistake' to a fuller acceptance of the other.

The Good Parent Does Not Have Favorites

I have already referred to Alan Segal and his very important observation that Christianity and Judaism both emerged at the same time, in the same place and with a common ancestry. Not twins but siblings. One of the motifs of the book of Genesis is the favoring of one child over another, whether it is Abraham over Ishmael, Jacob over Esau or Ephraim over Menasseh, something I have always found unappealing. There is a strong personal element here. I have three children, each one very different from the other two but each equally loved by me and my late wife. The four of us are able to joke about it because the children know that I love them equally. I now have six grandchildren and I love them equally. As Martin Luther once said, in a rather different context, *Ich kann nicht anders*, "I can't do anything else."[11] I cannot help it. If God is the Good Parent, I cannot conceive of God showing favoritism as between Judaism, Christianity or Islam. That does not mean that God, as it were, does not have some pretty trenchant criticisms of each of us but God is surely incapable

---

10   Many also felt, having gone through the English school system of the 1950s, 60s and 70s, that they know all about Christianity–from Nativity plays in Primary School to singing Hymns at Assembly!

11   Martin Luther, Speech at the Diet of Worms, 1521. Martin Luther was, of course, a major anti-Semite–hence the irony.

of anything but equal favor, however wretchedly we may have exercised our role in the partnership with God (and God with us!).

Do Not Reify Symbols

In the chapter on "Israel and the Nations" in *Challenging God* I have a section in which I, as a Jew, explore my congenital alienation from the symbol of Christ on the cross. The alienation is deeply rooted in the suffering Christians have inflicted on Jews over the past 1,800 years and in what I interpreted as a glorification of suffering and the claim to have overcome it. A few years ago I decided to try to move beyond those feelings—and see where I got. It did not turn out to be as difficult as I had anticipated. I sat, looked, saw a Jew nailed to the cross and heard his words: *Eli Eli l'ma sh'vaktani?* "My God, My God why have You forsaken me?" Not only are those words the Aramaic translation of the Hebrew of the first line of Psalm 22 but I heard a quintessentially Jewish question: "Here I am, God, suffering horribly. Where are You?" For me, the Jew, the answer is "I'm here with you. But I can't pluck you down and save you in the nick of time—any more than I can pluck innocent children from under the wheels of speeding cars. That's not Who I am." In the book chapter, I went on to say that my response was, of course, inadequate because Christians believe that, though Christ was not plucked from the cross, he was, literally, resurrected. Alan's major criticism of my chapter was expressed in one word: "symbolism." "Many of us," he said, "believe that all we have are symbols"— and he referred me to Wilfred Cantwell Smith. We do not have to read each other's symbols in the same way to appreciate and respect them and find value in each other's interpretation. Back to that first dialogue group once more, I remember a paper given by the late Rabbi Dr Albert Friedlander on "The Suffering God in Rabbinic Tradition." The cry of recognition and empathy from Richard Harries, then Dean of King's College, London, later Bishop of Oxford and Chair of the Council of Christians and Jews, reverberated for many of us for years.

As a footnote to this section, I have been to Rome on a number of occasions but recently went there on holiday. My partner and I took the tourist trail to St Peter's and I wandered over to Michelangelo's Pieta. I was utterly transfixed. The body of Christ was the ultimate expression of human vulnerability and the sculptor's compassion made the compassion of God tangible. I remarked on this at a Jewish-Christian gathering and a charming, sensitive, Orthodox Rabbi said to me: "That was an aesthetic response wasn't it?" "No," I replied after a moment's thought, "It was a religious response." "But it could have been a response to any piece of sculpture, couldn't it?" "No," I said with growing confidence, "it was the religious symbolism that was decisive."

Mythtory

My approach to Torah is a modernist one. At some time, at some place, an encounter took place between God and the Jewish people. Who initiated that encounter, God or the Children of Israel, who knows? People spoke about the experience and those oral traditions were passed on—male traditions rather than female traditions, I should add. At some point or points the traditions were written down. Forgive me for the rather cutesy term, the moment of encounter, the point at which God and history touch, I call mythtory. The text is a human record of that mythtory. It is not in itself the word of God, as the founders of Rabbinic Judaism held, but divine fingerprints are to be found on it. I would say as much, but no more, about the Christian experience. I refer to it as the mythtory of Golgotha, spoken about and then written down in the New Testament. I know that, for Christians, Christ is central rather than the New Testament text but I do not think that my understanding of the Christian mythtory in any way fails to recognize that fact. I would say essentially the same thing about Muhammad's experience of Allah and the Qur'an.

I must add what some may see as a qualification. In an extremely powerful and significant book recently published with the sanction of the Catholic Church, *Christ Jesus and the Jewish People Today*, the American Scholar, Professor Mary Boys challenges the stance whereby the text is secondary to the theology (Boys 2011). She insists that the text of the New Testament has to be seen in the context of its times, and that doctrine must be revised to follow new understandings of the polemic against the Jews which it contains. That point will be central to the final section of this essay, in which I want to consider the way I approach the text of the Hebrew Bible and its remarkable interpretative tradition in the light of questions on which Alan, ever probing, insists. Here it should be clear that despite explanations, which some would regard as qualifications, I insist that the Hebrew Bible and the New Testament are both accounts of revelations, separate but connected.

Humility, Ownership, and Truth

Both Judaism and Christianity are big on humility. In reality I am very dubious about how humble we actually are—certainly when it comes to theology and intellectual pretentions. Just how humble is it to suggest that God bestowed the whole of God's truth on our ancestors—and therefore on us—3,250[12] or 2,000 years ago? Is it not ridiculous—as well as the height of hubris—to

---

12   A very rough and rounded figure but one which accepts the Exodus as an historical event
      which occurred in the 13th century BCE.

think that we, never mind we alone, can grasp more than tiny fragments of the divine? If we go back to Alan's contention that religious violence stems from absolutist claims, is it not abundantly clear that the assertion of a monopoly on God's favor and understanding of God's will for humanity is not only overweening pride but a horribly dangerous absurdity? The history of the last fifty years, so deeply scarred by the rise of religious fundamentalism, reinforces what we should have learned long ago. Absolutist convictions readily tip over into knowing what is in everyone else's best interests and then to imposing it by force when the objects of our zealotry resist what is good for them. As Cromwell said, "I beseech you, in the bowels of Christ think it possible that you may be mistaken." And we often are, Christians, Jews, and Muslims alike.

One of the characteristics of post-modernity is an emphasis on complexity and uncertainty. Even Stephen Hawking has renounced the search for the grand theory of everything, which he modestly termed "Knowing the mind of God" (Hawking 1988). He finally bowed to the Austrian mathematician, Kurt Gödel's ineluctable demonstration of indeterminacy. But that has not stopped the mountebanks of political, economic, and psychological theory—not to mention evolutionary biologists and neuroscientists—from pedaling 'the truth.' Too many religious leaders also pander to the supposed needs for simplicity, clarity, and conviction by claiming a hotline to God. Truth, with a capital T, belongs only to God. All we have are fragments of truth with a lowercase t and our post-modernist sense of complexity and uncertainty should make us much more humble in the claims we make for our particular mythtory than it actually does. There is a Hasidic aphorism which I would love to pin up at the entrance of every synagogue and which I know Alan would readily print— never mind the number of copies needed, that never phased Alan—for every church: "Take care of your own soul and another person's body but not of your own body and another person's soul."[13]

Moses famously asked God for God's name in Exodus 3:14. God replied: "I am who I am." The lesson could not be more relevant today. "You've got it wrong, Moses. You're used to naming god because names characterize and control. Name the genie and it will appear. Guess my name and you'll have control over me. But I'm not a god in that sense. I am Who I am—the Unnameable, Unpossessable Ground of Being. You can't capture me in a text, however sacred and you can't control me in doctrines or rulebooks." Humility is the knowledge that no faith owns God.

---

13 Menachem Mendl of Kotzk, quoted in Newman (1963: 451).

So these are my six indicators of Jewish pluralism. I suspect they could be dressed up as existential, historical, metaphorical, textual, linguistic, and ontological. Whatever. They are fundamental to my personal theology and explain why I began this essay with John Bowden's remark: "*Christians and Religious Pluralism* may interest you, Tony." It was a very British understatement.

Scriptures and Integrity

Not long ago, Alan and I were at a dialogue meeting at which two papers were read, one by a Christian, the other by a Jew, on the 'Legacy of Our Scriptures.' They demonstrated the power of the text to live in contemporary interpretation and dialogue. I was full of admiration for both papers, though I had a reservation. I whispered to Alan, "The papers were brilliant—as far as they went." Alan was much more bothered than me, as he muttered to me over lunch and in subsequent discussion. We both recalled our mentor John Bowden, and his repeated criticism of doctrines built on false understandings of the text or of the limitations of the text itself. For me as a Jew, it is much easier to see the Christian problematic. Central to the New Testament is a polemic against the Jews, a polemic which equates Jews with the Scribes and Pharisees out of whom Rabbinic Judaism emerged, over against Christians, the Jews out of whom Christianity emerged. For me, one of the most helpful of all scholars in this regard is Mary Boys, Professor of Theology at Union Theological Seminary in New York. In her essay in *Christ, Jesus and the Jewish People Today*, to which I have already referred (Boys 2011), Boys takes Pope Benedict XVI to task for subordinating the text to doctrine—these are our doctrines and the text has to be read to support them. Mary Boys asks, "If Jesus was crucified as seditious by the power of the Roman Empire, why do the Gospels shift blame to Jews?" and insists that "precisely because of the terrible consequences for Jews ... the complexity of the passion narratives become a pastoral priority for the church." She concludes, "The New Testament's polemic against Jews should be classified as a rhetorical strategy of the Hellenistic world that does not have authority for Christians of our time" (Boys 2001: 61–2). Many Christians today would still prefer to contextualize or explain the words of the Gospel writers or Paul rather than acknowledge the unholiness of the words themselves. Not Alan. Unsurprisingly, then, Alan challenges me about the integrity of the Jewish interpretive process. John Bowden's objection to teachings based on false understandings of the text cannot be evaded. The last part of this essay is my attempt to maintain the Torah text with honesty to God, John and Alan.

The revolution that was Rabbinic Judaism was every bit as radical as the revolution which produced Christianity. The Temple was replaced by dozens of *batei midrash*, houses of inquiry, in which teachers (not priests) interrogated the Torah text.[14] The overriding purpose was to turn that which was set in a much earlier, agrarian society into a comprehensive, portable way of life—distinctively ritualized but ethically focused—that would sustain Jews whatever might happen to them in the Roman and Persian Empires. The enterprise found authority in the formative Rabbinic doctrine of the dual Torah.[15] God gave the Torah at Sinai—God's very words, unmediated by human hand—and also provided Moses with an oral, interpretative 'Torah,' which was handed on to the Rabbis in their houses of inquiry. Rabbinic Judaism is unique in having at its core intellectual debate, discussion, and frequent disagreement.[16] It also had, *ab initio*, a stunning attitude to the Torah text. Let me give one example. Hillel was an older contemporary of Jesus. He would have been called Rabbi but the title had not then emerged. The Jewish world of Hillel's day was confronted with a major problem. The biblical text describes the institution known as the sabbatical year.[17] Every seventh year the land was to lie fallow and loans were rendered null and void. The loan provision was made explicitly to help the poor from falling deeper and deeper into poverty. Yet, in the Greco-Roman world, the provision had come to have precisely the opposite effect. In anticipation of the sabbatical year, loans dried up leaving the rural poor without any means of getting through a particularly difficult period. Hillel and his colleagues adopted a legal device known as the *prosbul*,[18] which enabled lending to continue. What is remarkable about this by no means isolated occurrence is that even an express provision of the Torah could be neutralized, subverted in the interests of advancing the main thrust of the values of Torah.

From the very beginning of Rabbinic Judaism, the Torah spoke through interpretation and that body of interpretation—midrash—is vast. It became both the heart and the mind of Judaism, the source of ethical and ritual development, theology, and practice. It enabled classical Rabbinic Judaism to respond humanely to the frequent provision of the death penalty in Torah and to

---

14   *Batei* means 'houses of,' *midrash* we have already met. The Hebrew equivalent of the Greek 'synagogue' is *beit* (house; *batei,* houses of) *knesset* (meeting). Houses of meeting were buildings not, as the Temple, sited in a special place. People met there, prayed there and it was there the rabbis taught, debated–and disagreed.

15   The term 'dual Torah' is used by the American scholar Jacob Neusner. See Neusner (1990).

16   The Talmud is crammed full of debate, differing opinions and unresolved issues.

17   See Leviticus 25 and Deuteronomy 15.

18   Significantly a word of Greek derivation.

develop the Sabbath as a joyful, sustaining institution. But it had, for me, one limitation, highlighted by modernity.

From at least the early Middle Ages, there were Jewish scholars who were bothered by the Rabbinic doctrine that the Torah had come directly from God and Moses had merely acted as stenographer, as infallible secretary. What of the description of Moses' death? The Spanish-Jewish Bible commentator, Abraham ibn Ezra (1089–1164), went considerably further and gave ten instances of apparent anachronisms in the Torah. But it was in the mid-nineteenth century that the doctrine was challenged head on. The challenge came from non-Jewish German scholars who, as is widely known, developed Higher Criticism, subjecting the text of the Torah to historical and critical analysis. The newly emergent[19] Orthodox school within Judaism felt goaded into taking a stand and its greatest Rabbinic figure, Samson Raphael Hirsch (1808–88), identified the issue as an irreconcilable difference between Rabbinic Judaism and Modernity. Modernity, he said, was wrong and the Rabbinic doctrine was right.[20] A hundred and thirty years later, the then Chief Rabbi Jonathan Sacks emphatically and unequivocally reiterated the position Hirsch had taken (Sacks 1992).[21] Sacks saw the issue as one between Judaism, on the one hand, and secular, often anti-Semitic scholarship on the other. But I would argue that this is a limited, polemical view. It is quite possible for a faithful Jew to see the Torah as their ancestors' account of the mythtory at Sinai, whilst understanding that the Torah text is neither extra-historical (a term used by Sacks), nor inerrant (a term used by Sacks' Predecessor the late Chief Rabbi Lord Jacobovits).

What is not only decisive but liberating for me is that I do not have to follow the tradition of interpretation which limits and minimizes the meaning of, for instance, verses that call upon the Israelites to wipe out the inhabitants of Canaan, such as those found in Deuteronomy 7:1–11 and the commentaries on

---

19   Denominations in Judaism begin in the early nineteenth century as varying responses to being freed from the ghetto and allowed to live in wider society. Orthodoxy is as much a response to modernity as Reform.

20   "Let us not deceive ourselves. The whole question is simply this. Is the statement 'And God spoke to Moses saying', with which all the laws of the Jewish Bible commence, true or not true? Do we not really and truly believe that God, the Omnipotent and Holy, spoke thus to Moses?.... If this is to be no mere lip-service, no mere rhetorical flourish, then we must keep and carry out this Torah without omission and without carping, in all circumstances and all times. This word of God must be our eternal rule superior to all human judgement, the rule to which all our actions must at all times conform; and instead of complaining that it is no longer suitable to the times, our only complaint must be that the times are no longer suitable to it."

21   Sacks (1992: Chapter 7 "Judaism and its Texts").

it. I can and do say more straightforwardly: this is a text which does not reveal the fingerprints of God, merely the limitations and retrospective musings[22] of fallible human beings. The terrible words that John 8:44 places in the mouth of Jesus, "Your father is the devil and you choose to carry out your father's desires," say everything about his sense of rejection by his fellow Jews but nothing of Christ. The equally terrible injunction in Deuteronomy 7:16 to devour the nations of Canaan and spare none of them says everything about the post-settlement fear of syncretism of the authors of Deuteronomy and nothing about the God of Abraham and Sarah.

But Alan's challenge implies a further question. The Rabbis inquired of the meaning of the text. They developed at least four categories of interpretation: Plain; Allusive; Metaphorical; and Mystical. In a large number of instances, their interpretations develop Jewish theology and ethics. In many of those instances, the interpretation reveals more about the interpreter than about the *sitz im leben* of the text. In addition, the interpretations are based on an understanding of the nature of the text we no longer share, namely that God's very words are unmediated by human beings. They also employ a hermeneutic[23] founded on a doctrine—that of the dual Torah—in which most Jews today no longer believe. Does that invalidate the interpretation? I think not. The Hebrew Bible and the New Testament are not the same as the Odyssey or Macbeth. They are both accounts of a mythtory. They are religious rather than literary texts. In one respect at least, I agree with Derrida and the post-modernists: the texts have a life of their own, independent of their human transmitters, authors, and redactors and each generation engages in dialogue with the text. We hear it from where we are, personally, subjectively, open both to persuasion and seduction. The choice of how to hear it—with humility or arrogance, ethically or wickedly is ours. But hasn't it always been?

Let me give classical Rabbinic commentary the last word:

> Scripture says: "The voice of the Lord is with power" (Psalm 29:4). Not "with *His* power" but with power, that is to say, according to the capacity of each individual, even to pregnant women according to their power. Thus to each person it was according to their power [their capacity to hear and grasp]. Rabbi Jose ben Hanina says, "If you are doubtful of this, then think of the manna that descended with a taste varying according

---

22   It has been argued that wiping out the Canaanites was retrospectively interjected into the text on the basis of "if only that's what we'd done, we wouldn't be having defection to their cults now."

23   Rules of interpretation which were laid down by the Oral Torah.

to the taste of each individual Israelite. The young men eating it as bread; the old as wafers made with honey; to the babies it tasted like rich breast milk; to the sick, it was like fine flour mingled with honey; while to the heathen, its taste was bitter and like coriander seed. Now if the manna, which is all of one kind, became converted into so many kinds to suit the capacity of each individual, was it not even more possible for the Voice, which had power, to vary according to the capacity of each individual that no harm should come to him?"

EXODUS RABBAH V:9

There is mythtory. There are texts. There is experience of God. But we hear, experience, intuit God as ourselves—Jews and Christians alike. That permits us to value our own particular insights but debars us from claiming that our insights, our understandings, are the only Truth. I thank Alan for sharing that understanding so deeply.

Bibliography

Bayfield, T. (1992). "Introduction." In: T. Bayfield and M. Braybrooke (eds.). *Dialogue with a Difference: The Manor House Group Experience*. London: SCM.

———. (2001). "Partnership in Covenant." In T. Bayfield, S. Brichto, and E. Fisher (eds.). *He Kissed Him and They Wept*. London: SCM. pp. 25–40.

Boys, M. (2011). "Facing History: The Church and its Teaching on the Death of Jesus." In P.T. Cunningham et al. (eds). *Christ Jesus and the Jewish People Today: New Explorations of Theological Interrelationships*. Grand Rapids, MI: Gregorian and Biblical Press.

Eisen, A. (1987) "Covenant." In A.A. Cohen and P. Mendes-Flohr (eds.). *Contemporary Jewish Religious Thought*. New York: The Free Press. pp. 107–12.

Hawking, S. (1988). *A Brief History of Time*. New York, NY: Bantam Dell.

Mendenhall, G.E. (1955). *Law and Covenant in Israel and the Ancient Near East*. Pittsburgh, PA: The Bible Colloquium.

Neusner, J. (1990). *Torah Through the Ages*. London: SCM.

Newman, L. (1963). *Hasidic Anthology*. New York, NY: Schocken.

Race, A. (1983). *Christians and Religious Pluralism: Patterns in the Christian Theology of Religions*. London: SCM.

———. (2012). "Religious Absolutism, Violence and the Public Square." In: T. Bayfield, A. Race, and A. Siddiqui (eds.). *Beyond the Dysfunctional Family: Jews, Christians and Muslims in Dialogue with Each Other and with Britain*. London: Manor House Abrahamic Dialogue Group.

Sacks, J. (1992). *Crisis and Covenant: Jewish Thought after the Holocaust*. Manchester: Manchester University Press.

Segal, A.F. (1986). *Rebecca's Children: Judaism and Christianity in the Roman World*. Cambridge, MA: Harvard University Press.

Solomon, N. (1992). "The Third Presence: Reflections on the Dialogue." In T. Bayfield and M. Braybrooke (eds.). *Dialogue with a Difference: The Manor House Group Experience*. London: SCM. pp. 147–62.

CHAPTER 8

Changing the Typology? Why Pluralism Should be Renamed Post-Christian Inclusivism

Gavin D'Costa

Since Alan Race's development of the threefold typology in his important book *Christians and Religious Pluralism* (1983), this threefold manner of examining the Christian theology of religions in the literature has proven helpful, illuminative, and stimulating. Since Race's book there have been many attempts to expand that typology (Knitter 2002) and to give it very careful nuance (for example Hedges 2010; Hedges and Race 2009; Race 2013; Schmidt-Leukel 2005a, 2005b), as well as an interesting attempt to argue that the whole enterprise of theology of religions should now come to an end, to make space for a new birth: comparative theology (Fredericks 1999). Fredericks has argued that it is time to call a moratorium on the theology of religions and move into the practice of theology in engagement with a particular religion as opposed to theologizing about all religions without any real interaction with them. Some of the concerns of Fredericks and the comparativists are legitimate: that religions are complex, historically variable traditions and histories; and that their interaction can only be understood within this contextual historicized process. However, the attempt to stifle the discipline of theology of religions, which deals with legitimate theological doctrinal questions that undergird different particular encounters, seems unnecessarily constraining. Many would argue that theology of religions can actually fruitfully illuminate comparative theology and vice versa (see for example: Biesbrouck, 2013: 29–44; D'Costa 2009: 37–44).

In this essay I want to return to a criticism of pluralism that I made some years ago (D'Costa 1996) that requires more development. It certainly requires more development on the grounds that John Hick's initial reaction to it was that this criticism amounted to either a purely "trivial" linguistic point, or it entailed a confusion between theological confessional language and philosophical language (Hick 1997: 162–63). I should confess that others thought this a knock down argument against pluralism! But Hick is too good a scholar to ignore and I need to return to the point. I shall have another go at getting it right or hopefully presenting a more plausible case this time. In what follows I wish to argue that the classical third option in the Christian theology of religions, 'pluralism,' should be renamed 'post-Christian inclusivism.' This is not just a matter of semantics, but a concern that has theological, epistemological,

© KONINKLIJKE BRILL NV, LEIDEN, 2016 | DOI 10.1163/9789004324077_010

and ontological implications. It is also a matter of helping a new generation of students and scholars to correctly theorize the field, and to understand and appreciate certain parameters if the field is to be called a 'Christian' theology of religions.

Let me begin with the theological arguments that pluralism should be re-named post-Christian inclusivism. Significantly, the World Council of Church-es, the Roman Catholic Church and the Orthodox Churches all insist that the criterion for the proper deployment of the word 'Christian' is a profession of faith in the incarnation and the Trinity. The criterion of practice that denotes a 'Christian' is baptism and entrance into the Christian community. Clearly, there may be an internal tension between these two: not all baptized Chris-tians profess the trinity and incarnation, but the point is that according to these ecclesial communities, they should confess the Trinity and incarnation, for that is what defines 'Christian' as opposed to those sets of beliefs that can be termed 'non-Christian' (non-pejoratively).

My focus in this chapter will be on the first matter: beliefs that constitute being 'Christian.' In practice, pastoral discretion operates on this matter and, on the ground, heresy abounds along with orthodoxy. That has always been the case. But for the sake of theological clarity, some definition that is employed by the actual Christian churches must be sought to make sense of what le-gitimately constitutes a Christian, or in this case, a 'post-Christian' position. Currently the mainstream churches have agreed that the thought patterns and philosophies that do not hold to some form of the traditional belief in the incarnation as God's unique and definitive self-revelation in history in the person of Jesus Christ cannot legitimately be called Christian? Clearly in our market culture, no one actually controls or owns the term 'Christian' and in the unregulated markets of academy, the term means whatever those who publish on the term want it to mean. I am here addressing the accountable and com-munal form of "Christian theology" that is called ecclesial Christian theology. This is not to engage in or underwrite witch hunts of any sort against theolo-gians and religious intellectuals, but rather a criteriological matter concerning what constitutes Christian theology and what may constitute para- or post-Christian theologies.

As I am a Roman Catholic theologian, let me briefly substantiate these com-ments with attention to the Second Vatican Council, most formally in *The Dog-matic Constitution on the Church*, 1964 (Latin: *Lumen Gentium*), paragraphs 8, 14–5. Paragraph 14 is pivotal in bringing together the juridical, hierarchal, sac-ramental, and theological traditions of the church in defining what belonging to the Catholic Church entails. The profession of faith is deeply Christocentric, Trinitarian, and ecclesial. I cite it in full:

14. This Sacred Council wishes to turn its attention firstly to the Catholic faithful. Basing itself upon Sacred Scripture and Tradition, it teaches that the Church, now sojourning on earth as an exile, is necessary for salvation. Christ, present to us in His Body, which is the Church, is the one Mediator and the unique way of salvation. In explicit terms He Himself affirmed the necessity of faith and baptism (see Mk 16.16; Jn 3, 5) and thereby affirmed also the necessity of the Church, for through baptism as through a door men enter the Church. Whosoever, therefore, knowing that the Catholic Church was made necessary by Christ, would refuse to enter or to remain in it, could not be saved.

This and the other three paragraphs establish the basics of Catholic Christianity: that it is founded on faith in Jesus Christ as the saviour of the world who uniquely and singularly is the cause of our salvation. The importance of faith is expressed in the orthodox ancient creeds which hold to the full humanity and divinity of Christ and to the Trinitarian nature of God. It also claims that the one God in the action of Jesus Christ founded and 'subsists' within the Roman Catholic Church and that baptism and the profession of faith are required to be fully incorporated into the 'body of Christ.' The Council makes it very clear in paragraph 15 that other Christians (non-Roman Catholics) share in this salvific grace and that their Churches or ecclesial communities contain elements that are found within the Roman Catholic Church. In the next paragraph 16, it also indicates the way in which non-Christian religions are oriented (*ordinatur*) towards the Roman Catholic Church. In this sense, by the Catholic Church's own self-definition at a full ecumenical Council, belief in the full humanity and divinity of Christ is a prerequisite for membership both within the Roman Catholic Church and from the Catholic viewpoint, membership within a church or ecclesiastical body that can be deemed 'Christian.' To repeat the point made earlier: I am not concerned to reject people, to exclude anyone, or to finger-point, but rather to establish clear criteriological grounds for the term Christian. Likewise, in determining what would constitute full voting membership of the World Council of Churches, the vast majority of Christian Churches together felt that the minimum requirement was profession of the creedal teachings of the full humanity and divinity of Christ and the Trinitarian nature of God. None of this is to deny that there are very sincere and deeply impressive people in minority groups that call themselves 'Christians' (such as Quakers and Salvation Army members). This is a theological argument and agreement, not an argument from numbers. Many Christians once believed in slavery, but that did not make it true or right.

If the above is generally accepted—and in one sense it is a straight forward descriptive claim as well as an ecclesial theological claim, then something important follows in relation to 'pluralism.' One of the major 'achievements' of pluralism over the last thirty years has been to argue and defend the position that Christian Scripture and tradition can be harmonized with the belief that God did not become exclusively and uniquely incarnate in the person of Jesus Christ. Sometimes that position has advanced a further step. It has suggested that tradition got it plain wrong in its incarnational and Trinitarian claims. It has also been one of the major 'landmarks' of pluralism to have argued that the belief in Jesus Christ as the unique and exclusive incarnation of God is the major stumbling block to having good relationships and positive attitudes towards non-Christian religions. The leading pluralist of the last thirty years, John Hick, propounded all these claims. Interestingly, he started off as a Presbyterian ordained minister and eventually became a Quaker because it was within that particular tradition that Hick found a home for his non-incarnational and non-Trinitarian theology and his still profoundly spiritual and moral sensibility. The point I am making is that Hick's long pilgrimage from exclusivist to inclusivist to pluralist with an agnostic spirituality and a deep moral sensibility was a pilgrimage from a high Christology and Trinitarian belief to one with a non-incarnational Christology and a trans-theistic belief. As a human person I would not dream of denying Hick the title Christian if he wished to use it. As a theologian, I am raising a legitimate question about applying 'Christian' to the outcome of his religious thinking, given its move outside the communal norm for the word 'Christian.' It should be noted that pluralists such as Schmidt-Leukel and Roger Haight (1999) claim to hold an orthodox high Christology. While their own self-description here needs to be carefully addressed, elsewhere I have questioned whether their Christology meets these specifications (see D'Costa 1994). I would argue that they employ traditional terminology but deny that Jesus is the unique and normative self-revelation of God.

The most influential defenses of pluralism have all recognized the difficulties of a purely theistic form of pluralism. Again Hick's pilgrimage typifies the problem. He initially wanted to argue that all religions lead towards the God of love (Hick 1977). However, Hick then faced the criticism that, while this God-centered pluralism successfully removed the incarnational exclusivity that Hick was keen to dismantle, it still favored "God" to the exclusion of non-theistic religions such as Buddhism, Taoism, forms of Hinduism, Confucianism and so on. To address these difficulties, Hick (1989) argued that the divine reality was beyond both theistic and personal understandings of 'God' and also beyond non-theistic and non-personal or transpersonal understandings of the

'Ultimate.' Hick called this reality behind both personal and non-personal images, the 'Real,' a Reality that was beyond any phenomenal images, to use Kantian conceptuality. This move distinguished Hick from theistic pluralists. Variations of theistic pluralism have been defended by writers like Alan Race, Stanley Samartha, Wilfred Cantwell Smith, and Rosemary Ruether to name only a few. However, Hick's more radical solution to the problem of theistic exclusivism has had vigorous defense by thinkers like Perry Schmidt-Leukel (2005b), and Kenneth Rose (2013). I would argue that both groups, 'theistic' pluralists and transcending theism pluralists, had actually begun to move in a post-Christian direction.

In a criteriological sense, it would be possible and legitimate to see pluralism as a post-Christian phenomenon with two forms: theistic and beyond theism, both sharing the common attribute of moving beyond unique incarnational claims that Jesus is uniquely and exclusively the one God-Man. I submit that pluralism is not a Christian option if one accepts the commonly defined sense of being Christian by the majority of current Christians. However, I argued earlier that 'pluralism' should be renamed as a post-Christian 'inclusivism' and not just a post-Christian option called pluralism. This requires another step.

This step in the argument requires two moves. The first one is a logical and criteriological one. The second requires the employment of the history of ideas.

The first step runs something like this: no position can logically affirm all religions, because in all religions we find elements of doctrinal error, if viewed through the lens of ecclesial Christian theology, and in all religions we find practices that sometimes appear to an outsider (and some insiders) as unacceptable and unjustifiable. What we find is that every form of 'pluralism' affirms only certain forms of religions, and only certain formulations within those religions, and only certain types of practices within those religions—and all, I would strongly argue, from a viewpoint outside of those religions' self-understanding. Where that viewpoint can be located is a matter I take up in my second move.

For example, John Hick was forced to argue, as he clarified his position, that he did not accept every phenomenon that named itself 'religion' and certainly did not accept religious claims that formulated an exclusivist insight into the nature of truth (that Jesus is the unique incarnation of God, that Muhammad is the final prophet and the Qur'an is the Word of God, that becoming a *dGelug* Buddhist monk is the prerequisite for final release, and so on). Hick's baseline was that one could only accept a religion as authentic if it taught its adherents a movement away from self-centeredness towards others-centeredness, in Christian terms promoted 'love,' in Buddhist terms, promoted *karunā* (compassion) and so on. What we see from Hick's grappling with the question is that even the most radical forms of pluralism must exclude all that is in disagreement with its own truth criteria and only include those forms within religion that are in agreement with its own truth criteria. This has been accepted by most pluralists, but they argue that this does not compromise their claim to a pluralism of soteriological traditions.

This inevitable reliance on some notion of truth as a ground for discerning between true and false forms within religion meant that logically pluralism was always a type of inclusivism. The claim that true pluralism lay in affirming multiple religions as being soteriological and not in acknowledging limited inclusive truth criteria will not work. It will not work because it must discount all those accounts of 'release,' 'salvation,' 'liberation' that conflict with its truth claims. For example, the Dalai Lama must be wrong when he claims that only *dGelug* monks gain final liberation (see D'Costa 2000: 72–98 for a close analysis of translated texts from the Dalai Lama). But his understanding of final liberation requires this and cannot be divorced from it. Hence, when pluralists claim that *dGelug* Buddhism leads to the 'Real,' it must be despite the authorized teacher and leader of the *dGelug* Buddhists. The pluralists may be right, but the point is that they are not affirming soteriocentric pluralism except in so much as it conforms to what they deem acceptable. This is not a terminological quibble but a serious claim that pluralism always operates in the same manner as inclusivism: by only accepting otherness when it conforms to criteria that are established and accepted either within one's own religion (religious inclusivism) or within some non-religious tradition (non-religious inclusivism) or, in this instance, a post-Christian tradition.

The logic of my criticism was fully grasped by the American Roman Catholic theologian, Paul Knitter. Knitter argued that there was too much focus on beliefs, doctrines, and metaphysics in pluralism. Instead he employed a 'liberationist' approach, drawing on liberation theology that emphasized liberative social and political praxis (Knitter 2005, 2011). Knitter is confident that this move also avoids the imperialism of imposing some 'divine reality' on the other religions despite their own self-understanding. He is rightly critical of Hick on this point. Knitter argues that all religions are to be judged as to their truthfulness, their real responsiveness to 'God,' in so far as they promote the 'kingdom.' Knitter calls this new emphasis soteriocentrism which is, according to him, a move beyond the doctrinal impositions regarding ecclesiocentricism and theocentricism. While recognizing that the terms 'kingdom' and 'God' are derived from his own Christian tradition, Knitter is confident that the reality denoted by the kingdom is not an exclusive Christian possession or derived exclusively from Christ or God (Knitter 1987). The kingdom is a life style characterized by justice and peace in both personal relations, and social and economic structures. Hence, when religions promote the oppression of women in whatever way, they are to be judged as being against the kingdom. When they tackle the marginalization and exploitation of the poor and the weak, they promote the kingdom. No religion is better than another except by these criteria and under these criteria they are all in need of reform and mutual help.

Knitter has developed an influential theology of religions which has drawn heavily from Asian theologians and also influenced other Asian and European theologians. Some of these Asian theologians emphasize the imperialist and colonial patterns of exclusivism and inclusivism, but their fundamental position is similar to Knitter's in being basically that of liberation theologians (see for example Aloysius Pieris 1988; Samuel Rayan, 1990). What does Knitter's main liberative-praxis orientation amount to? It amounts to freeing the poor and marginalized. Knitter is aware that he is once again being selective and exclusive, but finds 'imperialism' on behalf of the poor and marginalized more acceptable than one that affirms correct doctrine. Such a view is allegedly more satisfactory as it "does not impose its own views of God or the Ultimate on other traditions" (Knitter 1987: 187)—even if it does impose its views on who are the marginal and poor and how they should be redeemed politically.

Knitter's proposals arise from his undialectical promotion of liberating practice without attention to the theological justification for doing so, or the theological implications embedded in any understanding of "liberation." Because he is striving for a common place where differences of doctrine are bypassed, he fails to account for the way in which the paradigmatic and normative sources of a tradition shape their understanding of what the human condition is, and what it ought to be, and what constitutes "liberative" actions. Hence, *promoting human welfare* is an unhelpful common denominator as it specifies nothing in particular until each tradition addresses itself to what is meant by "human" and "welfare." There is no way in which theory can be ultimately bypassed by praxis for they are always in mutual interaction. And if theory cannot be bypassed, then Knitter has not escaped the problem he found so intractable.

Furthermore, Knitter's emphasis on ethics is reminiscent of the Kantian ethical golden rule employed by Hick, which is typical of the strategy employed in modernity's attempt to engage with ethics: since we cannot agree on religious truths, let us be content to agree on universally held moral truths (see the depiction of 'modernity's narrative' that I am drawing on here in MacIntyre 1985; Milbank 1993). The assumption is that universally held moral truths are easy to establish and that religious truths are deeply contested. However, this relies on two faulty presuppositions. The first, as I have argued above, is that there is such a "thing" as praxis without theory. This is a misunderstanding of

Marx who instead argued that theories derived from the social material conditions of societies, not that there were no theories. Marx himself helps us to locate how the cultural tradition of modernity, which generates pluralism (see Surin 1990), is best understood. The second is that ethics is about identifying the right causes we should fight for and then acting on behalf of those causes. This view of ethics is called into question from an Aristotelian virtue-ethics approach in which the relationship of action, theory, and goods is very differently construed. In its Christian iteration, identifying ethical issues and knowing how to act come from a world view in which one is trained to inhabit the world as God's gift and to build up a community that is Christ-like. Here, the *telos* of action is understood in terms of the goods that are internal to particular types of activity, not in their outcome (consequentialism and pragmatism). In Aquinas' utilization of Aristotle, this *telos* is fundamentally part of the human-divine drama, not prior to it, for there could be no 'prior.' This *telos* is about becoming like Christ, being divinized, and participating in the trinity in a state of beatitude.

Some pluralists regard this alternative approach as inevitably leading to incommensurability in both religion and ethics. Can there really be no shared ethics? I think the answer is simple. Christians and Muslims have come together to collectively campaign on issues of reproductive health, and Christians and Buddhists have come together to collectively campaign against nuclear weapons. These shared ethical goals allow for social cooperation. But they do not and need not imply a shared soteriological end nor do they imply a shared intentionality. When a Christian opposes nuclear weapons this might be on quite different grounds to a Buddhist opposition to nuclear weapons and its relation to soteriology may also be very differently construed. This is highlighted most starkly in the intra-Christian difference regarding justification by faith versus justification by faith and works.

Knitter's liberative action, as Milbank (1990) so well pointed out, is an under-theorized exaltation of modern liberalism. The fact that Knitter argues that his ethical approach is grounded in liberation theology cannot hide the truth that his theology has truth claims that are finally based on recognizable liberal practices such as 'equality' and 'freedom.' This is not to decry such values, but to note that they are only properly located within a wider narrative that grounds them and gives them their meaning. Christian 'freedom,' for example, requires slavery, as Saint Paul provocatively and thoughtfully put it, and submission to truth. Modernity's 'freedom' meant autonomy for the individual who should submit to no heteronymous authority. For Kant and Rousseau before him, this was a matter of dogma. However, being good means nothing until we have given some theoretical flesh to 'being good.' Presumably the

Taliban think they are 'being good' Muslims in denying education to women, and the good Catholic thinks he or she is 'being good' in denying a civic right to people in democratic societies to murder unborn children if those children are not desired, and the good Jew is 'being good' in refusing to eat with someone who is not a Jew, and the good Muslim is 'being good' in believing that usury is not a good practice. Being good means 'nothing' without thick description and thick description helps us locate the overarching narrative that constitutes 'being good.' There are other forms of advancing pluralism based on an allegedly moral universalism (see D'Costa 2001).

We are now able to find a clearing in the forests whereby we can see the true nature of the post-Christian form of inclusivism that is being propounded under the name of pluralism. Modernity's towering attempt to ground ethics without any metaphysics is to be found in the Kantian project, despite the fact that Kant was Christian and certainly did not see his project as hostile to true Christianity (rather than revealed priestly Christianity). Kant famously wished to remove any emphasis away from historical particular revelation, because locating truth in such a parochial and contingent manner was inadmissible. Rather, he had to locate God in a universal and the universal ethical imperative provided a most suitable location, because it was universal, not particular. Kant argued that ethics was the presupposition of God. We could arrive at God through ethics, a universal, not through revelation, a particular. In the universal moral law found in the heart of each and every person, every person was connected to God. This move bypassed contingent revelation. In so much as pluralism is a child of the nineteenth century, we find the Enlightenment project as the driving motor when we provide a genealogical account of pluralism—such as I have loosely sketched above. It is not the Christian narrative but a modern 'secular' narrative or worldview that is at the heart of pluralism. I put 'secular' in quotations, because it is an ethics that is trans-religious or better, non-religious. Secular fundamentalists pushed it as non-religious and principled secularists saw it as trans-religious (see further on this D'Costa 2009:107–119).

I am aware that there are forms of postmodern pluralism to be found in the works of Henrique Pinto (2003), S. Mark Heim (2001), and Jeannine Hill Fletcher (2005). If Knitter, Hick, Schmidt-Leukel, Race, Rose, and the likes are grounded in modernity for their version of ethics-based pluralism, these postmodern forms have different genealogies. In the case of Pinto, we find that Michel Foucault provides the non-metaphysical and critical function for Pinto's view of religions, not the actual religions. The Christocentric and Trinitarian element are entirely subservient to the Foucaultian frame. In Fletcher, we find a mixture of cultural studies critique and liberal feminism determining the criteria for pluralism. In Heim, as in the process theologian, John B. Cobb (1992), we find the problematic notion that contradictory ultimate realities are somehow compatible. But they can only be compatible on the basis of some non-contradictory, ultimate synthesizing point or on the basis that rationality has no role in explaining the ultimate. Heim's pluralism seems to eventually fall into a form of inclusivism as he allows the 'ultimates' only a provisional reality as in the end, the Christian 'end' is judged by him as being the most comprehensive and full truth. One would require much closer textual study of the many pluralists I have mentioned above (see in more detail, D'Costa 2010), for 'pluralism' is Hydra-like in its growth.

I could at this point stop for I have achieved the goal set in the title: to show that Christian theological pluralism is best characterized as post-Christian inclusivism. However, there are also epistemological and ontological grounds to support my thesis. Before turning to these further arguments, I should mention the interesting phenomenon whereby a new position called 'inclusivist pluralism' has been advanced, initially and most forcefully by Jacques Dupuis (1977). In one sense, Dupuis is exploring how far one could go and remain a Christian theologian. His basically Rahnerian type position is Christocentric and Trinitarian. From that basis, Dupuis then argues for the legitimate God-given role of other religions. They serve to convey and express God's grace, which is found most fully and explicitly in Jesus Christ. Dupuis still maintains at the heart of his work an orthodox Christological and Trinitarian position, even if his approach has been criticized by some Catholic theologians as departing from the indivisible relationship between the Church as Christ's body and the saving atonement of Christ (for a good summary see Terence Merrigan 1988). Dupuis' position is not unlike traditional forms of Protestant inclusivism in removing the conditional necessity of the church for salvation as the appropriate historical unique mediated form of God's grace. This is not the place to discuss Dupuis work, but to note that the new category of inclusivist pluralism is helpful in indicating the furthest legitimate parameters open to Christians (not post-Christians) theologizing on the matter.

Let me briefly conclude by looking at the ontological and epistemological grounds for characterizing pluralisms as a post-Christian form of inclusivism. In the history of Christian thought, there has been much debate about the difficulty and even impossibility of speaking about God. It may be argued, to simplify, that there have been three patterns of Christian language about God over the long period of Christian history. The first is to claim that certain language about God is univocal and refers to God literally, and that when those same terms are applied to created realities this is done only indirectly or analogically. This is the position held by Duns Scotus. This approach has the benefit of affirming the dependence of all creation upon the one God who makes Himself known in creation. The second approach is characterized by recognizing language about God to be analogical and not univocal, but rather, equivocal. Here, language about created things is applied to God, but it is understood to analogically apply rather than literally apply. This approach has the benefit of affirming both the mystery of God and the reality that God has made Himself known to his creation through created realities. This is the approach of Thomas Aquinas. In many forms of Christian theology, the language of analogy has also been wedded to the apophatic or *via negativa* approach, my third pattern, which emphasizes God as utter and transcendent mystery that cannot be known by the mind. This is almost the reverse side of the first approach, the univocal. It is rare to find this approach used entirely on its own, but it is often used to chasten those who speak too easily about God. The Greek tradition especially is profoundly apophatic, but this has never stopped a decisive theological underwriting of the economic trinity in terms of God's Spirit proceeding from the Father alone (in the work of Vladimir Lossky for example). Apophaticism is used to safeguard the truth of divine revelation, not to say that nothing at all can be said about that revelation. What we uniquely find amongst pluralist theologians is the sole deployment of the apophatic or *via negativa* approach. Sometimes, this is deployed drawing upon Buddhism for that fits well into the model of interreligious dialogue: establishing the truth of the divine based on dialogue. This is the position of Scott Steinkerchner (2011). Hick (1989: 239–40) falsely attributes this position to Aquinas, but also rightly attributes it to Kant.

In the other sophisticated proponents of pluralism such as John Hick, Perry Schmidt-Leukel, and Kenneth Rose we find a defense of the unknowability of the divine reality based on the assumption that the divine reality cannot be adequately described by any language. This indicates a clear divide between theistic forms of pluralism and what I call agnostic forms of pluralism. Theistic forms of pluralism cannot pass the test of properly accommodating non-theistic religions and makes manifest its more inclusive theistic character. Agnostic forms of pluralism pass the test on their own account because they underwrite both theistic and non-theistic forms of religion. Their account of the divine reality, in their own eyes, is able to explain why there are different accounts and why their account makes sense of the different accounts—and it provides an overarching theory of language and the divine to explain why the differences were generated.

However, from within the different religions there may well be serious protests. Here we come to another fork in the pluralist road. On one side of the fork, there could conceivably be pluralists who would be concerned that their solution is not accepted by the religions that it is supposed to explain and account for. It is actually very difficult to name thinkers who stand on this side of the fork in the road, although one should allow for its possibility. What we do find on the other side of the fork in the road are those thinkers who simply preach reform to those in the different religions who criticize this account of language and the divine reality. Curiously, this second position is hardly endorsing religious pluralism but arguing that there would not really be problems if all religions accepted this agnosticism as the final statement on the nature of reality. The answer to religious disagreement is to accept the pluralist solution and then the disagreement would dissolve. This is akin to asking everyone to convert to Christianity and then the problems of different religious truth claims would dissolve.

In this chapter I have tried to show that the third category of the typology, 'pluralism,' in the Christian theology of religions is a pretender to the throne, a Trojan Horse smuggled into the 'Christian' camp. Or to change the metaphor, it is a self-proclaimed emperor not wearing Christian clothes and someone needs to shout out that this is the case. The shouting is not an act of hostility, but an attempt to be truthful to the meaning and practice of Christian theology. Since the incarnation and the Trinity are no longer the normative source of theologizing, these forms of pluralism are best described as post-Christian forms of inclusivism. After that is said, it should also be noted that there are many differences within pluralism. However, these differences do not negate the main claim of my argument. I doubt whether adherents of the traditional religions are attracted by transcendental agnosticism grounded in modern liberal ethics—the main thrust of pluralism. One finds this option taken mainly by modernists who have developed traditional religion into their new forms. Admittedly, this claim has to be eventually settled and tested empirically. However, for the moment, my conclusion seems secure: pluralism is a form of post-Christian inclusivism.

Bibliography

Biesbrouk, W. (2013). *Wrestling with Angels: Catholic & Evangelical Tradition-Specific Approaches to Theology of Religions*. PhD diss. Leuven: University of Leuven.

Cobb, J. (1982). *Beyond Dialogue: Towards a Mutual Transformation of Christianity and Buddhism*. Philadelphia, PA: Fortress Press.

D'Costa, G. (1994). "Response to Father Haight's essay." *Discovery* 5: 25–32.

———. (1996). "The Impossibility of a Pluralist View of Religions." *Religious Studies* 32: 232–32.

————. (2000), *The Meeting of Religions and the Trinity*. Maryknoll, NY: Orbis.

————. (2001). "Other Faiths and Christian Ethics." In: R. Gill (ed.). *The Cambridge Companion to Christian Ethics*. Cambridge: Cambridge University Press. pp. 154–67.

————. (2009). *Christianity and World Religions: Disputed Questions in the Theology of Religions*. Oxford: Blackwell.

———— (2010). "Pluralist Arguments: Prominent Tendencies and Methods." In: Karl J. Becker and I. Morali (eds.). *Catholic Engagement with World Religions*. Maryknoll, NY: Orbis Books. pp. 329–44.

Dupuis, J. (1977). *Towards a Christian Theology of Religious Pluralism*. Maryknoll, NY: Orbis Books.

Fletcher, J. Hill. (2005). *Monopoly on Salvation? A Feminist Approach to Religious Pluralism*. New York, NY: Continuum.

Fredericks, J. (1999). *Faith Among Faiths: Christian Theology and Non-Christian Religions*. New York: Paulist Press.

Haight, R. (1999). *Jesus the Symbol of God*. Maryknoll, NY: Orbis Books.

Hedges, P. (2010). *Controversies in Contextual Theology Series: Controversies in Interreligious Dialogue and the Theology of Religions*. London: SCM Press.

Hedges, P., and A. Race (eds.). (2009). *Christian Approaches to Other Faiths: A Reader*. London: SCM Press.

Heim, S.M. (2001). *The Depth of the Riches: A Trinitarian Theology of Religious Ends*. Grand Rapids, MI: William B. Eerdmans.

Hick, J. (1977). *God and the Universe of Faiths*. London: Collins.

————. (1989). *An Interpretation of Religion*. London: Macmillan.

————. (1997). "The Possibility of Religious Pluralism: A Reply to Gavin D'Costa." *Religious Studies* 33: 161–66.

Knitter, P. (1987). "Towards a Liberation Theology of Religions." In: J. Hick and P. Knitter (eds.). *The Myth of Christian Uniqueness: Towards a Pluralistic Theology of Religions*. Maryknoll, NY: Orbis Books. pp. 178–200.

————. (2002). *Introducing Theologies of Religions*. Maryknoll: Orbis.

————. (2005). *The Myth of Religious Superiority: A Multi-Faith Exploration*. Maryknoll, NY: Orbis.

Knitter, P., G. D'Costa, and D. Strange. (2011). *Only One Way?* London: SCM Press.

Macintyre, A. (1985). *After Virtue*. 2nd ed. London: Duckworth.

Merrigan, T. (1988). "Exploring the Frontiers: Jacques Dupuis and the Movement 'Toward a Christian Theology of Religious Pluralism'." *Louvain Studies* 23: 338–59.

Milbank, J. (1990). "The End of Dialogue." In: G. D'Costa (ed.). *Christian Uniqueness Reconsidered*. Maryknoll, NY: Orbis. pp 174–91.

Milbank, J. (1993). *Theology and Social Theory: Beyond Secular Reason*. Oxford: Blackwell.

Pieris, A. (1988). *Love Meets Wisdom: A Christian Experience of Buddhism.* Maryknoll, NY: Orbis Books.

Pinto, H. (2003). *Foucault, Christianity and Interfaith Dialogue.* London: Routledge.

Race, A. (1983). *Christians and Religious Pluralism.* London: SCM Press.

———. (2013). *Making Sense of Religious Pluralism. Shaping Theology of Religion for our Times.* London: SPCK.

Rayan, S. (1990). "Religions, Salvation, Mission." In: P. Mojzes and L. Swidler (eds.). *Christian Mission and Interreligious Dialogue.* Lewiston: Edwin Mellen Press. pp. 126–39.

Rose, K. (2013). *Pluralism: The Future of Religion.* London: Bloomsbury.

Schmidt-Leukel, P. (2005a). "Exclusivism, Inclusivism, Pluralism: The Tripolar Typology—Clarified and Reaffirmed." In: P. Knitter (ed.). *The Myth of Religious Superiority: A Multi-Ffaith Exploration.* Maryknoll, NY: Orbis Books. pp. 13–27.

———. (2005b). *Gott ohne Grenzen: eine christliche und pluralistische Theologie der Religionen.* Gütersloh: Gütersloher Verlaghaus.

Steinkerchner, S. (2011). *Beyond Agreement: Interreligious Dialogue amid Persistent Differences.* Lanham, MD: Rowman & Littlefield.

Surin, K. (1990). "A Politics of Speech: Religious Pluralism in the Age of the Macdonald's Hamburger." In: G. D'Costa (ed.). *Christian Uniqueness Reconsidered.* Maryknoll, NY: Orbis. pp. 192–212.

Vatican II. *Dogmatic Constitution on the Church.* http://www.vatican.va/archive/hist_councils/ii_vatican_council/documents/vat-ii_const_19641121_lumen-gentium_en.html (accessed October 2013).

CHAPTER 9

The Pluralist Path: Where We've been and Where We're Going

Paul F. Knitter

Introduction

In this chapter, I am to offer some help in reflecting on 'the Pluralist Path'—where it has been and where it is going (or can go). The word 'path' is much too modest for what we are talking about. This 'pluralist path,' I would boldly claim, is really a *Pluralist Reformation*—a call for reform not only for Christians but for all men and women who want to describe themselves as religious, or spiritual. I use the word 'reformation' perhaps somewhat audaciously, but I do believe, appropriately. It is a call to clarify, correct, re-appropriate and so deepen what it means to call oneself spiritual or religious in this incredibly advanced and incredibly threatened twenty-first century world of ours.

This 'Pluralist Reformation,' I believe we can say, was, to a great extent, born and nurtured here on this beloved island of saints and scholars—and scoundrels. It is, largely, another reformation 'made in England.' The names of John Hick and Alan Race figure primarily among the early pluralist explorers and reformers. This chapter looks back on what Hick and Race started. In particular, I want to identify how this reformational pluralistic theology of religions developed through dialogue with its critics.

Let me begin with a procedure that I learned way back during my years of study in Rome at the Gregorian University, from 1962 to 1968. We began every thesis or new lecture with a *definitio terminorum* (definition of terms). I think that practice is particularly important for our topic, since many of the current descriptions of a pluralistic theology of religions that one finds in both the academic and popular media in no way fit most of the pluralists I hang around with. So let me make bold to offer six defining characteristics of the theology that mainstream pluralist theologians like Hick and Race are proposing:

1.   *Pluralists affirm that many religions can be valid.* This means that many religions can offer human beings different ways of apprehending what is real and true and of living in harmony with what is real and true.
2.   *Pluralists acknowledge and affirm that there are real, sometimes incorrigible differences between the religions.* But as pluralists, they want to not only recognize such stubborn differences but also to engage them.

3. *Pluralists affirm—or better, they trust—that no matter how different reli-gions are, there is that which connects them all and thus makes it possible that they can understand each other and challenge each other.* This is not to affirm a 'common ground' or a 'shared essence' for all religions. But it does affirm that if we want to have any kind of a conversation between religions that will enable them to learn from each other, we have to have what Raimon Panikkar called a "cosmic trust" that there is a Mystery that connects them all (1985: 118–53).[1]

4. *The primary (though not only) criteria that pluralists invoke in order to 'grade' religions or to adjudicate the veracity of their claims are ethical rather than philosophical or theological.* This of course, does not deny the necessary role of philosophical and theological reasoning.

5. *Pluralists warn that no religion can hold itself up as containing the only or the superior or the final truth over all other religions.*

6. *Finally, a pluralist theology of religions seeks to lay the groundwork for a more authentic and life-giving dialogue among the religions.* It seeks to promote not just the plurality of religions but the mutuality of religions. Its final goal is not tolerance but engagement.

Vatican II: The Seedbed for a Pluralistic Theology

So, where and when did this Pluralistic Reformation begin to take shape? I offer an answer that may be surprising in itself, but not so surprising in that it comes from a Roman Catholic theologian: the seeds of a pluralistic theology of religions were already planted in the fertile soil of the Second Vatican Council. But these seeds were sown by bishops who, as Karl Rahner has argued, did not fully realize what they were doing (1979). Let me explain.

While Vatican II clearly and boldly moved beyond the exclusivist theology that for the most part animated and guided the Catholic Church's approach to other religions through most of its history, the Council still clearly remained within the borders of an inclusivist perspective. As never before in the history of Christianity, the value of other religions was recognized, especially in *Nostra Aetate*. But that value, in the end, was designated a *"praeparatio evangelica"* (preparation for the gospel), a stepping stone toward fulfillment in Christ and

---

1   Or as Catherine Cornille has more recently expressed it: we have to trust that there is a connector behind or within the splendid, stunning differences among religions (2008: Chapter 3).

the Church. Now, I agree with historians of Vatican II that the Council documents did not themselves offer a developed theology of religions, especially regarding their salvific role. But the Council did open the door and extend an invitation for theologians to take up that task. And the principal, though probably unintended, means by which the Council inspired the task of developing a more adequate theology of religions is contained in the last paragraph of Part 2 of *Nostra Aetate:* "The Church therefore, urges her sons [and daughters] to enter with prudence and charity into dialogue and collaboration with members of other religious."[2] The Council was calling for a *praxis* that would eventually demand a more adequate theory. The praxis of dialogue with other religions would require a sustaining theology of other religions. Authentic dialogue, especially as it was further elaborated in the Vatican's 1992 document *Dialogue and Proclamation*, calls for new ways of understanding the role of other religions—and that means, new ways of understanding the role of Christianity and of Christ. More precisely and uncomfortably, pluralistic theologians argue that authentic dialogue requires something like a pluralistic theology of religions. They hold that a pluralistic theology of religions is but the fruit of an authentic dialogue of religions.[3]

So let me now try to describe the first appearances of this new pluralistic fruit in the Church's theological garden.

The Birth of a Pluralistic Theology of Religions

If we want to identify 'the father of a pluralistic theology of religions'—or the first successful gardener in the new plot of pluralism—all hands would, I suspect, point to John Hick. His *God and the Universe of Faiths*, in 1973, jolted many of us when it sounded the call for a 'Copernican revolution' in Christianity's understanding of other religions and, consequently, in its understanding of itself. Christians would be more faithful both to the God of Jesus and to the God of philosophers, Hick argued, if they no longer placed Christianity, or even Christ, in the center of the universe of truth and revelation, for that center belongs to God alone. If the Church had moved from ecclesiocentrism

---

2   Filios suos igitur hortatur, ut cum prudentia et caritate per colloquia et collaborationem cum asseclis aliarum religionum....

3   I should add that the growth of such fruit was also prepared by the World Council of Churches; it soon followed the good example of Vatican II and in the early 70s increased its calls for interreligious dialogue under the leadership of Stanley Samartha and the sub-unit 'Dialogue with Peoples of Living Faiths and Ideologies.'

to Christocentrism in Vatican II, it was now time to complete the move to theo-centrism (or, as he put it, the Council built a bridge over the Rubicon, but the Church has still to cross it!).

To further that move and to confront its Christological implications, Hick edited what became, he once said, the foremost of his many theological best-sellers: *The Myth of God Incarnate* (Hick 1989b). (John had a philosopher's delight in provocation!). Throughout his long career, especially in his monu-mental Gifford Lectures, *An Interpretation of Religion* (Hick 1989a), he con-tinued as a gentle but persistent proponent of this Copernican Revolution or Pluralistic Reformation. Though he boldly took up the theological implications of his revolution, he remained essentially a philosopher—but what I might call a pastoral philosopher. On a leisurely drive from Birmingham to Oxford back in the mid-90s, after he gently warned me that I might be slipping away from my pluralist commitments, he concluded that he was "John, apostle to the un-churched," while I was "Paul, apostle to the churched."

If Hick was the philosopher who drew theological conclusions, Raimon Pan-ikkar was the theologian who built his theology on multi-cultural philosophy and history. Both Hick and Panikkar laid the first foundations of a pluralistic theology of religions. Foremost, Panikkar was a practitioner of dialogue, both in his engagement with multiple faiths through study and conversation and in his own personal spirituality; he was a 'double' or 'multiple' religious belon-ger long before the term became current (see Drew 2014). In his widely pro-vocative *The Intra-religious Dialogue* of 1978, he laid out the promise *and* the demands of dialogue: what is 'inter' must begin and end with 'intra.' To truly engage the otherness of the other, Raimon insisted, will, in most cases, require one to discover the otherness and the newness in one's own religious tradi-tion and identity. We can take the religious Other seriously, he insisted, only if we truly believe that the other has truth to offer us. And when multi-religious truths engage each other, there will be what he called 'mutual fecundation.' But in this dialogical engagement, he also insisted, *Pneuma* or Spirit will always be two steps ahead of, and therefore never fully grasped by, *Logos* or Word. Or dif-ferently expressed: *mythos* will always be there to tease and elude *ratio*. Panik-kar was profoundly a mystic.

And though Panikkar always smilingly and teasingly avoided identifying himself with any particular theological camp, he did draw clear theological conclusions in the revised 1981 edition of his *The Unknown Christ of Hinduism*. The first 1964 edition had clearly identified the Christ with Jesus and held up Christianity as "the end and plenitude of every religion:" but the revised edition boldly announced that the Christ—or the revealing, saving nexus between the Infinite and the finite—cannot be limited to Jesus (1964: 24; 1981: 14, 27). And so, in 1986, he joined the assembly of first generation pluralist theologians that produced *The Myth of Christian Uniqueness* (Panikkar 1987). Although Panikkar reminded his fellow pluralists that they must cherish what are sometimes the incorrigible and incommensurable differences among the religions, he also called for a cosmic trust that there is that which enables multiple religious believers to bridge their incommensurabilities and learn from and challenge each other in genuine dialogue (1987: 110). Such cosmic trust was for Panikkar grounded in what he called the cosmotheandric Mystery of non-dualistic unity between divinity-humanity-matter that pervades all reality and that he so brilliantly and inspiringly presents in his final publication, his Gifford lectures published some 22 years after they were delivered, and just one year before he left us, *The Rhythm of Being*.

Alan Race must be noted as a key contributor to the first generation of pluralists mainly because it was he who first made the case for the threefold models of exclusivism, inclusivism, and pluralism in his *Christians and Religious Pluralism* (1983). In that bold book, and in many that have followed, Race remains firmly planted in what might be called the far-left wing of the pluralist camp. A functioning Anglican pastor, he preaches a thoroughly historically-grounded, culturally-relativized, but pastorally engaging Christology. And his trinity of models, though attacked and rejected, have, I believe, stood the test of time. Even those who renounce them keep using them! Although it is difficult, and perhaps improper, to assess oneself, I feel a certain obligation to do so in this essay. In my 1985 *No Other Name?* I was, as Hick later identified me, "Paul, apostle to the churches." In that book, I wanted to convince myself and my fellow-Christians that one could be both a disciple of Christ and a pluralist. I cautiously but heartily endorsed Hick's theocentrism and tried to show its compatibility with a revised Christology that drew on New Testament scholarship on the historical Jesus, on Rahner's transcendental Christology, on process theology, and especially on liberation theology. And after its abbreviated translation into German (with the unapproved and inappropriate title *Ein Gott—viele Religionen: Gegen den Absolutheitsanspruch des Christentums* [Knitter 1988]) it prompted an attempt of the Congregation of the Doctrine of the Faith (CDF) to have me removed from Xavier University.

So in an effort to show that Hick and I were not 'loose cannons' on the ecclesial ship but that, on the contrary, the ranks of pluralists were respectable and growing, I immediately agreed when Hick asked me to help him organize a conference that would bring together an international, multi-confessional, and gender-balanced band of pluralists from around the world. The fruit of that gathering was collected in our co-edited: *The Myth of Christian Uniqueness: Toward a Pluralistic Theology of Religions*, which Orbis Books, and the

Maryknoll Fathers and Brothers, published in 1987 (and within two years received a warning from the CDF).

Criticisms and Response: Round One—The Critics

The mounting criticisms of a pluralistic theology during the 80s and 90s fell into two different, but harmonious, camps: the philosophers and the theologians.

The Philosophers: Pluralism Leads to Imperialism/Exclusivism: The first coordinated response to the new pluralist threat came from Gavin D'Costa. He gathered together an equally impressive assembly of international opponents to the pluralists (though they did not meet in a conference); their response to *The Myth of Christian Uniqueness* was the resounding and defiant *Christian Uniqueness Reconsidered: The Myth of a Pluralistic Theology of Religions*, also published by Orbis Books, (and served to assuage the CDF!). Though the cast was theological, a sound portion of their response was philosophical. Essentially, it was a postmodern criticism: they variously made their case that the new pluralists, with their shift toward theocentrism and with their appeal to a universal, saving message in varying religious containers, were, contrary to their intentions and noble aspirations, turning out to be imperialists and exclusivists.

When we pluralists announced that it is God, not Jesus, who is at the center of the salvific universe, these critics responded resolutely and somewhat disdainfully: "Whose God are you talking about?" There are no universals, they reminded us, available outside the course and limitations of history by which we have a 'bird's eye' view of all religious history. Every view is perched on a particular cultural tree. To claim to have this Godlike, universal overview is, unavoidably if unknowingly, to substitute one's own view for God's view. And that is to impose one's own view on others, in the name of God. Which comes close to the definition of imperialism, or Eurocentrism, or as Kenneth Surin put it, it becomes part of the McDonaldization of the world (Surin 1990).

The Theologians: Pluralism Betrays Christian Identity: The theological critics, speaking not just out of a concern for orthodoxy but from a pastoral concern for the health of the Christian communities, delivered a less complex but also more sobering criticism of the new pluralistic theology: to question the uniquely salvific role of Jesus is to put oneself outside the Christian community. As then Bishop Tarcisio Bertone, assistant to Cardinal Josef Ratzinger at the CDF, wrote to my bishop in Cincinnati in the 80s: I can be considered an orthodox Catholic theologian at Xavier University only if I "clearly and unambiguously affirm the exclusive role of Jesus as mediator of all salvation."[4] If such Magisterial criticisms were unsettling, even more so were those coming from fellow theologians such as Hans Küng, Monika Hellwig, Gregory Baum, Karl Josef Kuschel—all of whom, from different angles, warned that the pluralists' decentralizing of Christ would work havoc among the faithful, or that it would dull liberation theology's prophetic call for justice. These were sobering challenges. Pluralist theologians are theologians; they have an abiding responsibility to their communities of believers.[5]

Criticisms and Response: Round One—Pluralists' Response

I must admit, together with many of my pluralist colleagues, that such criticisms were, to a great extent, merited. As with any new growth in the theological garden of the church, this new attempt to engage 'the signs of the times' needed not just fertilizer but pruning. Its critics provided the occasion for both. In response, pluralists pruned their proposal in two ways—again, one more philosophical, the other, theological and scriptural.

Philosophically: John Hick led the response to critics by becoming, if I may put it this way, *more mystical*. Indirectly admitting that his language, and his thinking, were indeed too Eurocentric and Christian, he abandoned his talk of *Theos* as the center or ground of the religious universe and, instead, began to speak of *the Real*. In a personal conversation with me, he spoke of how important the Sufi mystic, Ibn Arabi, was for his own spiritual life; and Ibn Arabi talks much about 'the Real.' In designating the ground and goal of humanity's spiritual quest as 'the Real,' Hick was offering a symbol that reflects what all religions—yes, all—clearly recognize in their teachings if they do not always follow it in their practice: that the Reality that they have discovered or that has been revealed to them always remains more than the human mind can ever comprehend (even when they declare their revelation to be full and final). To recognize, as all religions in their better moments do, that what they are talking about remains incorrigibly and mysteriously 'more than' the human capacity to know is to recognize, implicitly but necessarily, that all religious claims are limited, relative, non-absolute. This recognition and affirmation is at the heart of the pluralists' position.

Theologically: a variety of pluralist reformers tried to respond to these sobering criticisms by showing that the pluralist move can be justified, perhaps

---

4   In an official communication to Archbishop Daniel Pilarczyk, available in the archives of Union Theological Seminary.

5   These critiques are summarized in Knitter 2002: 164–69.

required, by contemporary interpretations of both scripture and tradition. And for this, they turned to liberation theology. In my case, with the help of my mentor and friend, Aloysius Pieris, I came to recognize that the 'many religions' and the 'many poor' are in need of each other. An effective liberation from global structures of oppression calls for a pluralistic collaboration of all religious communities. And a theology or dialogue of religions that ignores the suffering of the poor and oppressed becomes an opium by which theologians can peacefully pursue their academic discourse on mountain tops while in the valley there is no peace.

So if Hick preferred to speak of 'the Real' rather than 'Theos,' my preference was for *Soteria*. Though the term is Christian and drawn from the New Testament, I felt that it could analogously represent, not the essence of all religions, but the goal of all religious strivings—to promote the *salus*, or the well-being and flourishing, of all humans (and as we clearly and uncomfortably realize today, the *salus* of humanity is impossible without the *salus* of the planet). So in my contribution to *The Myth of Christian Uniqueness*, I rather boldly urged that if Christian theology of religions has undergone an evolution from ecclesiocentrism to Christocentrism to theocentrism, it could now take a further step to *soteriocentrism*—to well-being-centeredness. But such a move would imply not just a shift of theological perspective but also one of methodology. All our theologizing about other religions, or even our explicitly religious dialogue with other believers, would be, as liberation theologians put it, a *second act*. Theology and dialogue would follow the *first act* of the praxis of multi-religious collaboration in trying to promote greater wellbeing, greater justice, greater compassion among peoples. Dialogue would come after *dia-praxis*. Theological reflection would follow ethical collaboration.

Criticisms and Response: Round Two—The Critics

What I am calling 'round two' in the conversations between pluralist theologians and their critics has been, again, an opportunity to both prune and fertilize and so bring new growth to the pluralist reformation. Roughly and broadly, between the 90s and the present, I note five major criticisms that not only reprimand but seek to replace a pluralistic theology of religions.

Particularism: with the publication of his *The Nature of Doctrine: Religion and Theology in a Postliberal Age*, George Lindbeck provided the blueprint for what has become a fourth model for a theology of religions (Lindbeck 1984). In addition to—or better, in replacement of—the other models of exclusivism, inclusivism, pluralism, we now have *particularism*. Working with Lindbeck's essentially postmodern insistence that religious experience does not precede language/culture but is determined by it, other theologians such as Paul Griffiths, Gavin D'Costa, Joseph DiNoia (now a mitered-member of the Vatican) have developed a theological model for religious diversity that affirms the *dominance of diversity*, or the *preference for particularity*. Simply stated: religions are more different than they are similar. Indeed, at their heart, they are incommensurable. Therefore, to try to identify 'what all religions have in common' is purely and simply impossible, either because it does not exist, or if it does, we will never find it. In the face of Hick's 'Real,' or Knitter's 'Soteria,' the particularists respond, echoing Alisdair MacIntyre: Whose Real? Whose Soteria? Whose Justice? Whatever is declared to be 'in common' to all religions will inevitably be imposed by one religion (MacIntyre 1989; Heim 2000: 71–98; D'Costa 2000: 30–39; DiNoia 1990).

Deep Pluralists: the cultural-linguistic particularists like Lindbeck and Griffiths prepared the way for what we might call the theological or ontological particularists such as S. Mark Heim, David Griffin, and even John Cobb—all of whom proclaim the radical diversity of both salvation and of ultimate reality. S. Mark Heim has elaborated what is perhaps the most elaborate and well-crafted case for particularism in his argument, both phenomenological and theological, that each religion is pursuing its own end, its own goal. The many religions therefore are not different paths to the same mountaintop. Each is making its way up its own mountain. For Heim this is the case both presently and eschatologically. Heaven will not be a plain where all can gather but a series of mountains from which each can look at the other.[6]

David Griffin and John Cobb agree with Heim but go an ontological step further. Not just many salvations, but many Ultimates. In opposition to what Griffin calls "identist pluralists" like Hick or Race or myself, who affirm diversity but see it originating from and heading towards the same (*idem*) Ultimate, he proposes a *deep pluralism* that recognizes a plurality not only of religions and salvations, but of Ultimate Realities. Cobb even makes bold to identify the characteristics of three such Ultimates: the theistic, the acosmic, and the cosmic (Griffin 2005: 3–38; Cobb 1999: 184–86).

Comparative Theology: the most vigorous and, I must admit, the most successful counter-proposal to a pluralistic theology of religions has come from what has become the new movement of comparative theology. Claiming that the pluralists have created nothing but a theological traffic jam in which the

---

6   Although for Heim, the Christian mountain provides the fullest and the most authentic view of the God who is personal and Trinitarian. Eschatologically, Heim ends up more an inclusivist than a particularist (2000: 256–69).

various models just keep beeping their horns at each other but never move, the comparativists, under the founding leadership of Francis x. Clooney and James Fredericks, have called for a moratorium on all theologies of religions. Their battle-cry, as it were, has become: "Just do it!" Just jump into the study of, or the dialogue with, other religions without having to have all your theological models nicely assembled. Let theology follow dialogue; let theory follow practice. Pluralist theologians, the comparativists claim, resemble arm-chair anthropologists who draw sweeping claims about other cultures without ever having visited them (Clooney 2010; Fredericks 1999).

Feminists: fewer in numbers but representing a much bigger constituency, feminist theologians remind pluralists—as well as all theologians of religions—that the whole Christian debate about religious diversity so far has been unrepresentative, if not intentionally exclusive, of the experience and perspectives of half of the world's religious population. That is the basic feminist criticism of the pluralists—that what is true of the life of religious communities in general is true of the new theologies of religions in particular: the voices of women are not heard. What those voices have to contribute specifically to the conversation about religious pluralism cannot be predicted clearly until they are actually heard (O'Neill 2007; Egnell 2006; Gross 1996). One of these feminist critical voices is being heard—that of Jeannine Hill-Fletcher. She places in question what all the models for a theology of religions take for granted: religious identity. There is no such thing, Hill-Fletcher and other feminists admonish, as a given, definable, solid religious identity from which engagement with other religions is carried on. What is true of all human identities is true of religious identities: we are not purebreds. We are, rather, hybrids! Our identities are both multiple and in process. And both the multiplicity and the changeability of our identities is caused and required by the essential relationality of every being that qualifies as human. Knowing this and practicing this will put into question the presuppositions and procedures of all of the current models for a theology of religions (Hill-Fletcher 2005: 82–101).

The Vatican: the clearest, the strongest, and for many Catholic theologians, the most restricting criticism of a pluralistic theology of religions has come from the Vatican, under the theological tutelage of Josef Ratzinger. Already back in 1996, Ratzinger, from his desk at the CDF, warned that the new pluralistic theology of religions and its inherent relativism were replacing liberation theology as the most menacing threat to the well-being of the church. In particular, he singled out John Hick and myself as the primary menacers (Ratzinger 1996). But the sharpest and broadest censure of any form of a pluralistic theology of religions was delivered in the CDF's *Dominus Iesus* in 2000. Whether, as many Catholic theologians contend, it was a reversal, or a flat-out contradiction, of both the direction and the theological content of *Nostra Aetate* and of *Dialogue and Proclamation* (and even of John Paul II's Encyclical *Redemptoris Missio*), it was a thundering insistence that Catholic theologians are obliged to affirm the absolute salvific *unicitas* of Jesus Christ. To question whether Jesus is the one and only savior is to place oneself outside the Catholic community. Or more accurately, it is to run the risk of *being placed* outside the Catholic community. Today, just about all Catholic theologians who, as a priest or a nun, are questioning the "*unicitas Jesu*" have been censured or forbidden to teach. Examples include: Roger Haight, S.J., Jacques Dupuis, S.J., Jon Sobrino,S.J., Peter Phan, Tissa Balassuriya, and, I believe we can add, Sister Elizabeth Johnson. (Perry Schmidt-Leukel is the unique layperson, as far as I know, to have been given a place on this list).

Criticisms and Response: Round Two—Pluralists' Response

Again, I would like to show, as briefly and clearly as I can, how this second round of criticisms has provided pluralists with the further opportunity to clarify or correct their project.

Responding to the Particularists: The particularists have reminded many of us pluralists that although we call ourselves pluralists, we are also, unavoidably, *inclusivists*. The only way we can approach and bring into view the religious Other is through our own religious perspective. We cannot, as it were, climb out of our own religious skins in order to engage the religious Other. Pluralists forget this at their own peril, and even more so, at the peril of their dialogue partners. To forget that we always begin as inclusivists is to allow ourselves to grow into imperialists. Also, the particularists' insistence that the diversity of religions dominates and prevents any inherent commonality, even though it is too absolute (and too universal!) for most pluralists, still contains a necessary admonition for the pluralist project. Pluralist theologians like John Hick, Lenard Swidler, Alan Race, and myself have to do a better job of balancing our universal assessments with diverse realities. The pluralist desire to determine 'what is in common' among religions must be held in better tension with 'what is diverse.' Indeed, as soon as universality jeopardizes diversity it must be suspect. To lose or diminish the diversity of religions is, perhaps, a greater loss than the gain of establishing commonality. I do believe that the next generation of declared or concerned pluralists are much more aware of this danger, and of this challenge, than we old timers have been.[7]

---

7   I am thinking for instance of Paul Hedges (2010: 228–53) and John Thatamanil (2011).

But to lose the possibility of commonality and universality is also a loss that our threatened global world cannot afford. If Hans Küng is right that there will be no peace among nations without peace among the religions, then interreligious dialogue and cooperation are a moral imperative facing us all. And this is where the particularist model seems to break down. As Catherine Cornille has convincingly argued in her *The im-Possibility of Interreligious Dialogue*, if the religious traditions of the world, despite their incorrigible diversity, do not have anything that *interconnects* them, they will be ships passing in the night (we hope nonviolently!) (Cornille 2010: 95–135). The criticism of the particularists have enabled pluralists, therefore, to clarify their goals: not simply to establish the validity of diverse religions but to promote the dialogue of diverse religions. The particularists have also provided me, and others, with an uncomfortable but needed nudge to be more accurate about what we think interconnects the many religions. I had made an earlier shift, or correction, from proposing a theocentric engagement of religions to one that is soteriocentric. And at the core of this *soteria*, or human flourishing, that I thought all religions are pursuing, I placed *justice*. But sobered by MacInyre's incisive question 'Whose Justice?' and, more so, by the reminders from D'Costa and Heim that justice, while a pivotal concern for the monotheistic religions, does not seem to play much of a role at all in religions like Buddhism and Daoism, I have proposed a concern that I think is prior to justice and that can be found in all, or most, religious teachings. Before they might gather together to promote justice, I believe followers from different traditions are already united in their response to *unnecessary human and environmental suffering*. Solidarity with the suffering ones of this earth, and with the suffering earth itself, can provide the starting point and the stage for a new praxis-initiated interreligious dialogue. I can hope for this because I see it already happening (Knitter 1995).

Responding to the Deep Pluralists: As we saw, the deep pluralists extend the particularists' insistence on the dominance of diversity into the very nature of the Divine. For them, God, or the Ultimate, is not simply one. God is also many. Pluralists respond by noting that these deep pluralists seem to put limits on how deep they are willing to go. After Heim, Griffin, and Cobb insist that salvations and Ultimates are many, they go on to affirm the necessity of conversation, or real relationships, between these many Ultimates. In other words, the many Ultimates, are not *incommensurable*. Although remaining forever many, they are also called to unity. Here Heim and others would do well to extend his use of Trinitarian theology. Amid the irremovable diversity of religions, there is something that connects them all—something 'more ultimate' than the diversity, something like 'the divine nature' that unites the diversity of 'Persons' in the Trinity. Such a picture of religious diversity sure looks like the pluralist model that John Hick and his colleagues have been trying to promote and clarify. The deep pluralists, however, are, in a sense, reminding the rest of us pluralists that we have to be more careful in the way we talk about what religions have in common. Our search for the commonality or unity of religions can succeed only by acknowledging and fostering the diversity of religions. Pluralists' goal should not be *Ex pluribus, unum* (from many, one) but *Ex pluribus, unitas* (from many, unity). The *unitas* (unity) does not exclude, indeed it requires, the *plures* (many).

Responding to the Comparative Theologians: Comparative theologians remind us pluralists of something that even Karl Rahner humbly recognized way back in the days when the theology of religions was in its early stages: that no proposal for a theological assessment of other religions is complete until it is tested, as it were, through the actual study of and dialogue with other religious believers. Admitting this, Rahner also admitted that he was not up to the task (Rahner 1966). Comparativists like Clooney and Fredericks, however, will applaud Rahner but push his followers further: a theology of religions must not simply be tested by but must be fashioned within a comparative engagement with other religions. And there are pluralist theologians who, as trained scholar of religions, have been doing just that![8]

But if we pluralists have much to learn from the comparativists, we also have our respectful counter-criticism. Yes, one cannot be a theologian of religions without being a comparative theologian. But—and here is the critical response—this is not a matter of 'first this, then that,' but, rather, of 'both this and that at the same time.' To make a chronological separation between the work of a theologian of religions and that of a comparativist is both dangerous and impossible. Hugh Nicholson shows clearly how it is dangerous. Himself a member of the new generation of Comparative Theologians, he has recently published a book that makes a convincing case that comparativists who declare a moratorium on theology in their study of other religions are like people in therapy who suppress thoughts or feelings only to have to face them in sublimated or redressed forms (Nicholson 2011: 14, 36–37). Our theological convictions are like the cultural or existential skin that we cannot climb out of. They are present, coloring what we see in other religions, whether we realize it or not.

Responding to the Feminists: the pluralists response to feminist critiques are similar to their response to the comparativists: the issues feminists like Jeannine Hill-Fletcher raise are complementary to, rather than, contradictory of,

---

8   Some examples are Perry Schmidt Leukel, Judith Berling, Diana Eck and of course the late Raimon Panikkar.

the pluralist project. To accept and live out our hybrid religious and theological identities is to affirm and put into practice the basic guidelines of a pluralistic theology of religions: hybrids, like pluralists, recognize that no religious identity can be held up as absolute, superior, final over all others, and that whatever my religious identity is now in this moment, it won't be able to live on unless it is exposed to the identities of others. Pluralism provides the theoretical framework for living out hybridity. This is evidently why the few feminist theologians who have over the past decades taken up the issue of religious diversity are pluralists.[9]

Responding to the Magisterium: when the Magisterium insists that one cannot question the absolute *unicitas* of Jesus and still call oneself a Roman Catholic Christian, I feel impelled to ask if that is indeed the case. I must do that carefully, respectfully, humbly. But I must do that. Why? Not only because, personally and existentially, I cannot free myself from that question. But also, and more pressingly, because of pastoral reasons, because of my responsibility as a Christian theologian: this is an issue that perturbs many Christians, a question which, because they do not find satisfactory answers from the pulpit or from the *cathedra* of Peter, many are leaving the Church.

So, as a Roman Catholic Christian theologian I have the responsibility, the obligation, to explore how we can understand and live a commitment to the uniqueness—I prefer, distinctiveness—of Jesus and at the same time maintain an openness to the uniqueness of other religious figures and traditions. I strongly believe that we can develop a dialogical Christology, based on a kenotic and prophetic Christology, in which, as Krister Stendahl put it, "... I can sing my song to Jesus fully and with abandon without feeling it necessary to belittle the faith of others?" (Stendahl 1984: 133).[10]

Conclusion

This challenge that Krister Stendahl holds up to Christians is really the challenge that the Pluralist Reformation poses for all religious communities: how to sing one's own religious songs, fully and with abandon, without belittling the faith of others—without preventing the dialogue and cooperation among religions that our present world so sorely and urgently needs.

---

9   I am thinking of: Rosemary Radford Ruether, Marjorie Suchocki, Ursula King, Maura O'Neill.

10   I try to develop such a kenotic and prophetical dialogical Christology in Knitter 2011.

Amid all its excesses and mistakes, this Pluralist Reformation, launched by people like John Hick and Alan Race, is a source of hope that such an interreligious and inter-cultural dialogue is indeed possible.

Bibliography

Clooney, F.X. (2010). *Comparative Theology: Deep Learning across Religious Borders.* New York, NY: Wiley-Blackwell.

Cobb. J.B., Jr. (1999). *Transforming Christianity and the World: A Way beyond Absolutism and Relativism.* Maryknoll, NY: Orbis Books.

Cornille, C. (2008). *The Im-possibility of Interreligious Dialogue.* New York: Crossroad.

D'Costa, G. (2000). *The Meeting of Religions and the Trinity.* Maryknoll, NY: Orbis Books.

DiNoia, J.A. (1990). "Pluralist Theology of Religions: Pluralistic or Non-Pluralistic." In: Gavin D'Costa (ed.). *Christian Uniqueness Reconsidered: The Myth of a Pluralistic Theology of Religions.* Maryknoll, NY: Orbis Books. pp. 119–34.

Drew, Rose. (2014). "Christian and Hindu, Jewish and Buddhist: Can You Have a Multiple Religious Identity?" In: Paul Hedges (ed.). *Controversies in Contemporary Religion.* Volume 1. Santa Barbara, CA: Praeger. pp. 247–72.

Egnell, H. (2006). *Other Voices: A Study of Christian Feminist Approaches to Religious Plurality East and West.* Uppsala: Swedish Institute of Mission Research.

Fredericks, J. (1999). *Faith among Faiths: Christian Theology and Non-Christian Religions.* New York, NY: Paulist Press.

Griffin, D.R. (2005). "Religious Pluralism: Generic, Identist, and Deep." In: David Ray Griffin (ed.). *Deep Religious Pluralism.* Louisville, KY: Westminster/John Knox Press. pp. 3–38.

Gross, R. (1996). *Feminism and Religion.* Boston, MA: Beacon Press.

Hedges, Paul. (2010) *Controversies in Interreligious Dialogue and the Theology of Religions.* London: SCM Press.

Heim, S.M. (1995). *Salvations: Truth and Difference in Religion.* Maryknoll, NY: Orbis Books.

Heim, S.M. (2000). *The Depth of Riches: A Trinitarian Theology of Religious Ends.* Grand Rapids, MI: Eerdmans.

Hick, J. (1973). *God and the Universe of Faiths.* London: Macmillan.

———. (1989a). *An Interpretation of Religion: Human Responses to the Transcendent.* New Haven, CN: Yale University Press.

——— (ed.). (1989b). *The Myth of God Incarnate.* London: SCM Press.

Hick, J., and Paul F. Knitter (eds.). (1987). *The Myth of Christian Uniqueness: Toward a Pluralistic Theology of Religions.* Maryknoll, NY: Orbis Books.

Hill-Fletcher, J. (2005). *Monopoly on Salvation? Feminist Approaches to Religious Plural-ism*. New York, NY: Crossroads.

Knitter, P.F. (1987). "Toward a Liberation Theology of Religions." In: J. Hick and P. Knit-ter (eds.). *The Myth of Christian Uniqueness: Toward a Pluralistic Theology of Reli-gions*. Maryknoll, NY: Orbis Books. pp. 178–200.

Knitter, P.F. (1988). *Ein Gott—viele Religionen: Gegen den Absolutheitsanspruch des Christentums*. Munich: Kösel Verlag.

———. (1995). *One Earth Many Religions: Multifaith Dialogue and Global Responsibil-ity*. Maryknoll, NY: Orbis Books.

———. (2002). *Introducing Theologies of Religions*. Maryknoll, NY: Orbis Books.

———. (2011). "Christianity and the Religions: A Zero-Sum Game? Reclaiming 'The Path Not Taken' and the Legacy of Krister Stendahl." *Journal of Ecumenical Studies* 46: 5–21.

Lindbeck, G. (1984). *The Nature of Doctrine: Religion and Theology in a Postliberal Age*. Louisville, KY: Westminster/John Knox Press.

MacIntyre, A. (1989). *Whose Justice? Which Rationality?* South Bend, IN: Notre Dame Press.

Nicholson H. (2011). *Comparative Theology and the Problem of Religious Rivalry*. New York: Oxford University Press.

O'Neill, M. (2007). *Mending a Torn World: Women in Interreligious Dialogue*. Maryknoll, NY: Orbis Books.

Panikkar, R. (1964) *The Unknown Christ of Hinduism*. London: Darton, Longman and Todd.

———. (1981). *The Unknown Christ of Hinduism*. Maryknoll, NY: Orbis Books.

——— (1985) "The Invisible Harmony: A Universal Theory of Religion or a Cosmic Confidence in Reality?" In: L. Swidler (ed.). *Toward a Universal Theology of Religion*. Maryknoll, NY: Orbis Books. pp. 118–53.

———. (1987). "The Jordan, the Tiber, and the Ganges: Three Kairological Moments of Christic Self-Consciousness." In: J. Hick and P. Knitter (eds.). *The Myth of Christian Uniqueness: Toward a Pluralistic Theology of Religions*. Maryknoll, NY: Orbis Books: 89–116.

———. (2010). *The Rhythm of Being*. Maryknoll, NY: Orbis Books.

Race. A. (1983). *Christians and Religious Pluralism: Patterns in the Christian Theology of Religions*. Maryknoll, NY: Orbis Books.

———. (2001). *Interfaith Encounter: The Twin Tracks of Theology and Dialogue*. London: SCM Press.

Rahner, K. (1966). "Christianity and the Non-Christian Religions," In: *Theological Inves-tigations, Vol. 5*. Baltimore: Helicon Press. pp. 115–34.

———. (1979). "Toward a Fundamental Interpretation of Vatican II." *Theological Stud-ies* 40: 716–27.

Ratzinger, J. (1996). "Relativism: The Central Problem for Faith Today." Available at http://www.ewtn.com/library/CURIA/RATZRELA.HTM (accessed 18 January 2013).

Stendahl, K. (1984). *Meanings: The Bible as Document and as Guide.* Philadelphia, PA: Fortress Press.

Surin, Kenneth. (1990). "A 'Politics of Speech': Religious Pluralism in the Age of the McDonald's Hamburger." In: Gavin D'Costa (ed.). *Christian Uniqueness Reconsidered: The Myth of a Pluralistic Theology of Religions.* Maryknoll, NY: Orbis Books. pp. 192–212.

Thatamanil, John. (2011) "Comparative Theology after 'Religion'." In: Stephen D Moore, Mayra Rivera (eds.). *Planetary Loves: Spivak, Postcoloniality and Theology.* New York, NY: Fordham University Press. pp. 238–57.

CHAPTER 10

Pluralist Approaches in Some Major Non-Christian Religions

Perry Schmidt-Leukel

Introduction

Alan Race's classic *Christians and Religious Pluralism* focused entirely on what its subtitle indicates: patterns in the *Christian* theology of religions (1983). Being aware that the issue of making sense of the religious Other is not only a problem for Christians, Race mentions in passing that "[t]he other faiths will have their own approach to the problem" (Race 1983: 5). He does not, however, comment any further on what these approaches might be, although at one point in his final chapter, he hints at some Hindu approaches to other faiths which "could be viewed as comparable with the inclusivist claims of some Christians" (1983:143). Perhaps, one might take this remark as an early indication that his typology of exclusivism, inclusivism and pluralism would also apply to the way other faiths approach religious diversity. In his later book *Interfaith Encounter. The Twin Tracks of Theology,* Race speculates more explicitly about "a struggle that is taking place in religious living and believing across the traditions" (2001: 165). "The problem," he writes, "for a religious understanding which clings to self-sufficiency is how to explain the impressive fruits of religious commitment that are manifest, often in strange guises, elsewhere" (Race 2011: viii). Here it is evident that he does not consider this to be an exclusively Christian problem, though he does not actually pursue the question whether his typology might also work for non-Christian attitudes to other faiths.

In 1987 a group of Christian theologians published the volume *The Myth of Christian Uniqueness. Toward a Pluralistic Theology of Religions* (Hick and Knitter 1987). This book emerged from a conference which had taken place one year earlier in Claremont, California, and entered the history of contemporary theology under the name of the "Rubicon Conference." In accordance with the analysis of Christian attitudes to other faiths by John Hick (1922–2012), Alan Race, Paul Knitter, and others, this conference drew a decisive line between exclusivist and inclusivist approaches on the one hand and pluralist approaches on the other. The explicit aim of the conference was to cross the Rubicon of Christian claims to absoluteness, regardless of whether these take the form of *exclusivism*, claiming the exclusive truth and validity of the Christian faith, or *inclusivism*, claiming a unique superiority of the Christian faith. Neither of

these two positions—so the central argument goes—permits a positive evaluation of religious diversity. According to theological exclusivism other faiths
are false *because* they are different. According to theological inclusivism other
faiths are inferior or insufficient *to the extent* that they are different. Hence
in both of these approaches religious difference or diversity is perceived as
something negative. It was therefore the aim of the Rubicon Conference, as
Langdon Gilkey expressed it, to combine the perception of religious diversity
with the notion of theological parity (1987: 37). Thus, the main goal of pluralist
approaches is to find ways which, from a Christian perspective, permit one to
see at least some other religions (not necessarily all of them) despite their otherness as equally valid in some crucial theological respect. Usually this means
to see them as different, yet equally valid, paths of salvation.

If this, however, is not an exclusively Christian problem, what will it mean
for other religions to develop a similarly pluralist view of their relation to other faiths? How can they arrive at a position that combines the awareness of
religious diversity with the notion of religious parity? Which forms do exclusivist and inclusivist superiority claims take within the doctrinal framework
of religions such as Judaism, Islam, Hinduism, or Buddhism? Do they harbor
a theological potential that allows them to cross their own Rubicon of absoluteness? These questions were at the center of a follow-up conference held
in Birmingham in 2004, which showed that the discussion about reaching a
religious understanding of religious diversity is indeed a vital issue in all the
major faiths.[1] In this chapter, I will briefly introduce some of the main theological movements towards a pluralist position as we find them in the four above
mentioned traditions.

One important insight is that each of these religions has traditionally
held its own exclusivist or inclusivist superiority claims and has done so in
tradition-specific ways. This implies that any kind of pluralist approach will
also need to be developed in ways specific to the religious tradition in question. Pluralist approaches are not only characterized by their joint vision of a
legitimate diversity of equally valid paths of salvation. They need to give this
vision plausibility against the particular background of their respective religious heritage. For the pluralists it is therefore, on the one hand, essential to
demonstrate some continuity between the pluralist approach and their own
religion. On the other hand, pluralists will also have to be critical of those elements within their respective traditions that support the traditional claims to

---

1   Knitter (2005). See also my own contribution to this volume (Schmidt-Leukel 2005) which
    offers a reinterpretation of Race's typology that makes it, in principle, applicable to other
    faiths.

an either exclusivist or inclusivist type of superiority. In this double sense of being faithful to and being critical of one's own tradition, pluralist approaches have to be tradition-specific through and through. Pluralism is not, as so many among its critics hold, a meta-theory beyond and independent of the real religious traditions.[2] On the contrary, pluralism can only exist as Christian pluralism, Jewish pluralism, Muslim pluralism, etc. It is these tradition-specific features on which I will focus in the following and only towards the end I will suggest some more general conclusions.

Pluralist Approaches in Judaism

After World War II, Jewish theology was preoccupied with two subjects: Reflection on the holocaust and its theological implications and the establishment of the modern state of Israel.[3] Over the past three decades, however, there has been a significant increase in voices addressing the question of how Judaism should see other religions and understand itself in relation to them. A crucial role was naturally played by the Jewish interest and participation in Christian theological attempts to overcome Christian anti-Judaism. As one can see from the Jewish declaration *Dabru Emet* (issued in 2000), this also evoked the reverse question of how Judaism sees Christianity. Already in *Dabru Emet* the outlines of a pluralist or perhaps proto-pluralist position can be discerned, for it not only states that "Jews and Christians worship the same God," but further that: "Christians know and serve God through Jesus Christ and the Christian tradition. Jews know and serve God through Torah and the Jewish tradition."[4] Quite obviously two different media of revelation, i.e., Jesus

---

2 This was also affirmed by Alan Race in "Ten Years Later: Surveying the Scene," a chapter he added to the second enlarged issue of *Christians and Religious Pluralism* (1993: 149–80), where he says that pluralism "is not so much a meta-position as a tradition-position which has opened itself sideways, as it were, to accept the validity of the other" (162) This view does not conflict with John Hick's presentation of religious pluralism as "a religious but not confessional interpretation of religion" (1989:1). For as Hick explains on the subsequent page: "A genuinely pluralistic hypothesis will thus inevitably call... for further development within each of the traditions" (1989: 2).

3 Lubarsky 2005. See also Lubarsky 1990, which deals primarily with modern predecessors of a Jewish Pluralism. Many features of a Jewish and pluralist theology of religions are anticipated in Abraham Joshua Heschel's important and influential lecture "No Religion is an Island" from Nov 10th, 1965 (the date given in Kasimow and Sherwin 1991: 4, is mistaken), reprinted with a number of contributions appreciating Heschel's work in: Kasimow, Sherwin 1991.

4 The text of the document is found at http://www.jcrelations.net/Dabru+Emet+-+A+Jewish+Statement+on+Christians+and+Christianity.2395.0.html?L=3.

Christ and the Torah, plus the two traditions based upon them, are presented in strict parallelism without ranking one above the other.

Today Jewish theologians increasingly feel the necessity to comment also on the relation to other religions, for example, Islam, Hinduism, and Buddhism.[5] They often emphasize that Judaism is in principle in a better position to arrive at a positive valuation of other religions than is Christianity or Islam, because, in contrast to them, Judaism never saw itself as a religion destined for all humanity. Nevertheless, the Jewish position too has been traditionally either exclusivist or inclusivist. The Jewish theologian Ruth Langer summarizes succinctly that from the perspective of biblical Judaism all other peoples were seen as "uniformly idolatrous," and hence as "theologically... all total outsiders, uniform in their failure to recognize Israel's God" (2003: 64). A more positive perspective was offered by the rabbinic teaching of the Noahide Laws, first testified to in the 3rd century CE.[6] According to this doctrine God's covenant with Noah comprises all peoples in the world, provided that they honor seven laws of abstinence from (1) idolatry, (2) murder, (3) robbery, (4) sexual immorality (including incest and adultery), (5) blasphemy, and (6) from eating from a living animal, and (7) that they should have just laws and "an effective judiciary to enforce the preceding laws" (Brill 2010: 51). Those among the non-Jews who live up to these commandments will have their "share in the world to come" (Langer 2003: 271; Brill 2010: 41).

But do non-Jews actually comply with these laws? As far as the moral laws are concerned, i.e., abstention from sexual immorality, murder, theft, and vivisection, the rabbis recognized that non-Jewish nations usually do have respective legal regulations and that non-Jewish individuals often keep these commandments. Far more difficult was their assessment in relation to the prohibition of idolatry and blasphemy. Are not all non-Jewish religions clearly idolatrous? As long as non-Jews are uniformly perceived as idolaters, rabbinic teaching on the Noahide Laws does not overcome Jewish exclusivism. However, at a relatively early stage some rabbis introduced the argument that what constitutes idolatry and blasphemy in an objective sense (to them, for example, the classical Roman cult), does not necessarily count as idolatry subjectively. Thus, a religious practice or doctrine that would clearly be idolatrous and blasphemous if observed or held by a Jew could be innocent for a Gentile

---

5   For brief overviews see: Langer (2003), Ravitzky (2006). A very detailed survey of traditional and contemporary elements and models of Jewish theologies of religions is offered by Brill (2010), and of Jewish relations to Christianity, Islam, Hinduism, and Buddhism by Brill (2012). See also the contributions to Goshen-Gottstein and Korn (2012).

6   *Sanhedrin* 56a; *Tosefta Avodah Zarah* 8:4; later understood in relation to *Gen* 2:16 and 9:4. See Langer (2003: 266ff.), and Brill (2010: 51ff.).

if he or she subjectively intends to worship the true God. Later on some rabbis were inclined to extend such considerations to Christians and Muslims (Langer 2003: 268ff).

This approach clearly reflects an inclusivist form of the superiority claim. The superior nature of the Jewish religion is not questioned and has its foundation in its belief in the particular election of the Jewish people. At the same time it is affirmed that some salvific elements are found in other religions as well and can contribute to the eschatological well-being of their members. Particularly in modern times, but with roots already in the work of Maimonides (1138–1204), the concept was even expanded to the idea that Christianity and Islam are divinely ordained ways of preparing Gentiles for the final messianic revelation of Israel's God as the only true God allowing righteous non-Jews to participate in the messianic world (Langer 2003: 270; Brill 2010: 67ff.).

Jewish pluralists of today relate to these traditional ideas in continuity and critique. The teaching of the Noahide Laws is often regarded as a step in the right direction, but as insufficient in not doing justice to the specific form or *gestalt* of the other religions. This instruction is therefore seen as in need of contemporary reinterpretation.[7] The pluralists tend to interpret the Noahide Laws as a theological expression of a divine covenant that comprises all humankind, Jews and non-Jews alike, and involves essential spiritual and moral values binding for all human beings. Yet on the basis of this general covenant and in addition to it there exist a range of special covenants between God and specific peoples. These special covenants find their expression in the different religions including Judaism. Thus, Judaism does have a special election, but a special election is nothing unique. Other peoples too have their own special election and therefore no Jewish superiority claim can be based on it (Langer 2003: 269f.). As Michael Kogan puts it: "Instead of being *the* chosen people, my people begin to see themselves as *a* chosen people" (2005: 114). The official declaration of the "First Jewish-Hindu Leadership Summit" (Delhi, February 5–6, 2007), for example, could thus affirm that both traditions "teach faith in one supreme being who is the ultimate reality, who has created the world and its blessed diversity and who has communicated divine ways of action for humanity for different peoples in different times and places."[8]

---

7 Langer (2003: 267). See also Kogan (2005: 112): "We must now apply it in ways we never have before, dealing for the first time with the specific claims of other faiths and their followers rather than simply lumping them all together as 'Gentiles'."

8 The Summit was jointly convened by a delegation of the Chief Rabbinate of Israel and a group of leaders of various Hindu branches. The text of the declaration and various other documents are found at: http://www.millenniumpeacesummit.com/Hindu-Jewish_Summit _Information.pdf.

Within the theological framework of multiple covenants and elections, Jewish pluralists argue for a legitimate diversity of ways in which human beings know God or transcendent Reality. They differ, however, on how this is to be understood in more detail. Theologians belonging to a more liberal tradition, as for example Dan Cohn-Sherbok (1994), focus primarily on the human side. The teachings of the various religions are seen as being rooted in different, but equally legitimate and authentic human experiences of a divine mystery which exceeds all human forms of expression (Cohn-Sherbok 2005: 125f.). The majority of Jewish pluralists, however, belong to the more conservative strand, for example Jonathan Sacks,[9] Michael Kogan (2008), David Hartman (1931–2013) (1990), Norman Solomon (1991, 1996, 2005), Raphael Jospe (2007, enlarged and revised as 2012), Eliott Dorff (1982, 1996), and Irving Greenberg (2000, 2004, 2006). They tend to emphasize that the different human experiences of transcendence are the result of different divine activities. God-self (him-, her-, it-) addresses different peoples via different revelations and thus, in a way, speaks different languages. In that sense Michael Kogan asks: If the apostle Paul says in the first Letter to the Corinthians (9:22) that he became "all things to all people so that by all means some might be saved", then "why cannot God do the same thing?" (2005: 118). Yet none of these revelations substantiates any religious superiority and this is for two reasons: First, none of these revelations is meant to be universal but has its validity and meaning within God's particular dealings with a specific people. And second, no revelation is capable of expressing in human terms the infinite nature of God.

Pluralist Approaches in Islam

The point from which Islam departs is significantly different from Judaism.[10] For, similar to Christianity but different from Judaism, Islam traditionally enters the scene bearing a universal claim and sees itself as the one religion

---

9   See in particular Sacks (2002). It is on the basis of this edition that A. Brill—I think
     rightly—puts Sacks in the pluralist camp (2010: 144ff.). Though being Chief Rabbi of the
     United Kingdom from 1991–2013, Sacks was nevertheless accused of heresy and hence pub-
     lished in 2003 a revised second edition in which many of the more pluralist statements
     were softened or deleted.

10   For a detailed survey of Islam's relation to other faiths in past and present see Waarden-
     burg (2003); an extensive collection of essays is offered in Ridgeon (2012); a number of
     divergent contemporary views is found in Khalil (2013). Muslim self-understanding in the
     context of interreligious dialogue is the topic of Boase (2005), and Ridgeon and Schmidt-
     Leukel (2007).

destined by God for all. To be sure, the Qur'an repeatedly emphasizes that God has sent his messengers to all peoples so that there is a plurality of authentic revelations (Q. 5:19; 5:48; 10:47; 14:4; 35:24). At the same time, however, Muhammad is presented as the seal of the prophets (Q. 33:40). According to traditional interpretation this does not just mean that the revelation brought by Muhammad serves as the decisive criterion in assessing and confirming all other valid revelations. Being the seal is further understood as implying that God's sending of prophets ended with the appearance of Muhammad. Even more important, the majority of thinkers in the Islamic tradition understood the sending of Muhammad, his transmission of the Qur'an and the resulting foundation of Islam in such a way that all other religions, based on earlier revelations, are thereby surpassed and superseded or in Muslim terminology, 'abrogated.' In other words, after Muhammad, Islam is the one and only religion destined for all people, while the validity of all other religions has expired. "So the understanding for centuries within the mainstream Islamic tradition was that, in order to be saved and to experience salvation with God, one must be Muslim" (Ramadan 2013: x). It is here where Muslim pluralists start with their criticism.

One crucial feature in the arguments of Muslim pluralists is *firstly* the distinction between *islām* in its literal meaning of submission to the will of God, that is, *islām* with a small 'i,' and Islam with capital 'I' as the designation of a socio-cultural phenomenon, i.e., of the religion of Islam. According to pluralists, qur'anic verses which apparently affirm the universal and exclusive validity of Islam as a religion, speak in fact of *islām* with lower case 'i', that is to say a personal existential attitude. For examples they adduce suras such as "The Religion (*din*) before Allah is Islam/islam"[11] (Q. 3:19) or "If anyone desires a religion other than Islam/islam, never will it be accepted of him; and in the Hereafter he will be in the ranks of those who have lost" (Q. 3:85). According to the pluralists these verses do not refer to the institutionalized religion called 'Islam' but to the religious attitude of '*islām*' as submission to God. The realization of this inner religious attitude is by no means confined exclusively to Islam (see also Q. 42:13). Hence the different religions "can be appreciated as being, at their origins, so many modes of 'submission' to God" (Shah-Kazemi 2012: 98).

Muslim pluralists such as Mahmut Aydin (2000, 2001, 2005, 2007), Mahmoud Ayoub (1997, 2007), Asghar Ali Engineer (2005, 2007), Farid Esack (1997),

---

11   All quotations from the Qur'an are taken from the translation by 'Abdullah Yūsuf 'Alī (1999).

and Abdulaziz Sachedina (2001) base their interpretation on a number of detailed exegetical elaborations. Frequently their discussion centers on Sura 2:62, which reads: "Those who believe and those who follow the Jewish and the Christians and the Sabeans—any who believe in Allah and the Last Day, and work righteousness, shall have their reward with the Lord: on them shall be no fear, nor shall they grieve." This is taken as evidence that after Muhammad other faiths can still be valid paths of salvation. Against the traditional view that this verse is abrogated by verses like those cited above (Q. 3:19 and 3:85), according to which the only religion acceptable to God is Islam, the pluralists produce two weighty arguments: Firstly, verse 2:62 expresses a divine promise and not a legal directive. While legal directives can be abrogated, divine promises cannot. Secondly, verse 2:62 is repeated in almost identical words in verse 5:69, that is in one of the last suras of the Medinan period and thus dating back to the end of Muhammad's prophetic ministry, which is also clear evidence against its supposed abrogation (see Aydin 2007: 48f; Esack 1997: 162ff; Sachedina 2001: 32ff.).

In addition to their view that a salvific attitude is not confined to Islam as a religion, Muslim pluralists point out *secondly* that the Qur'an affirms diversity, including religious diversity, as something that God wills. At least in part, this diversity is explained by the qur'anic statement that all prophets were sent to teach in the language of their people (Q. 14:4). Referring to suras such as 2:148, 5:48, and others the pluralists hold that the divine purpose and meaning of religious diversity is to encourage one another in good works and moreover— as it is said in Sura 49:13—to "know each other" both in one's differences and in one's commonalities. In this sense, Muslim pluralists often emphasize the need of overcoming traditional prejudices about the religious Other and of taking the other seriously in his or her own self-understanding; that is, understanding the other from his or her own religious sources.[12]

Muslim pluralists, however, do not go so far as to reject any universal claims of Islam. Instead they reinterpret such claims as confirming religious pluralism. Muhammad has indeed a mission and a message for all human beings, but this must not be misunderstood in an exclusivist sense. On the contrary,

---

12   In the recently published books Atay (2014) and Lamptey (2014) the intra-Muslim discussion about the precise understanding of the divine intention regarding religious diversity plays a prominent role. While Atay argues that religious diversity is the result of both, different human interpretations and different divine revelations, Lamptey is critical of any concepts of diversity in terms of "clear and static boundaries" (2014: 4); Inspired by feminist Christian theologies she argues for seeing religious diversity in terms of "relational complexity" (12), as a divinely willed challenge of fixed boundaries (252f.).

part of his prophetic mission is precisely to warn everyone against exclusivist attitudes. If, for example, Sura 2:111ff and Sura 5:18 reprimand Jews and Christians because of their exclusivist claims, then Muslims have to take care of not making the same mistake (see Aydin 2007: 37, 41; Esack 1997: 18ff; Ayoub 1997: 112). Farid Esack understands Muhammad's prophetic mission in terms of two primary functions: on the one hand, it entails a critical challenge for people of other religions to remain faithful to the revealed essence of their own faith and not to distort it. On the other hand, it entails the call to *islām* in the sense of submission to God's will, which can either be lived out within the context of one of the existing revelations or on the basis of the qur'anic revelation, that is within the context of Islam as an institutionalized religion (see Easack 1997: 172ff.).

In a similar vein, Mahmut Aydin argues that God's revelation in the Qur'an is "universal, decisive and indispensable" but not "full, definitive and unsurpassable" (borrowing the terms from Paul Knitter's designation of the universal role of Christ, see 1997: 3–16). This means, the essential statements of the Qur'an on the relationship between humans and God are universally valid and relevant, they are normative and they are 'indispensable' in the sense that they can enrich and transform the life of everyone. But they cannot exhaust the fullness of God's truth, they do not exclude the existence of "other norms for the divine truth outside" the Qur'an; and they do not entail "that God could not reveal Himself in other ways apart from the Qur'an at other times" (see Aydin 1997: 49f.). This is in line with the approach of Mohammed Arkoun (1928–2010) (see 2002: especially 66–125; see also 1988, 1999) who bases his own version of pluralism on a hermeneutical theory of revelation emphasizing that the infinite Word of God becomes inevitably contextual, fragmented and final as soon as it is "sent down to the earth" (2002: 74). Muslim pluralists recall that the limitation of the qur'anic revelation is taught by the Qur'an itself when it says, as in Sura 31:27: "And if all the trees on the earth were pens and the ocean (were ink), with seven Oceans behind it to add to its (supply), yet would not the Words of Allah be exhausted...."

The latter touches upon a *third* central motif of Muslim pluralists: the insight, emphasized primarily in Islamic mysticism (Sufism), that no finite medium can encompass divine infinity. Therefore it is only God who alone is absolute, but never anything finite, limited or created—including religions. In this sense, Hasan Askari (1932–2008) states "that all religions... are relative to the Absolute Truth" (1985: 191; see also 1977, 1991). Each religion, says Askari, may be in danger from the tendency "to equate one's own religious doctrine with the Transcendent" (1985: 196). Referring to Sura 3:67 Askari holds that true *islām* as submission to God implies not absolutizing one's own faith:

"by 'islam' (primordial and universal) the particular and the historical Islam is abolished. But what is *in principle* abolished is not in historical fact annulled: the abolition of the particular by the universal has to be enacted within the practice of the particular...." (Askari 1985: 199).[13] Religious diversity is therefore seen as a spiritually important fact: it can make each religion aware of its own limitations and relativity while at the same time all religions can enrich and fertilize each other through their encounter and exchange (1985: 204f.). Abdol-karim Soroush (2000, 2009) who also draws strongly on Sufism (in particular on Rumi and Hafez) understands the relativity of religions primarily in terms of hermeneutics: it reflects the inevitable and legitimate diversity of both meaning and interpretation as involved in religious experience[14]: "God has appeared to each person in a particular light and each person has interpreted this appearance in a different way...." (2009: 130). Understanding the religions as reservoirs of valid but nevertheless diverse and multifaceted meaning is also the key idea in Tariq Ramadan's attempt at "Developing a Philosophy of Pluralism" (2010).

A particular strand in Muslim pluralism is formed by the so-called *perennialist* or *traditional school*, with Frithjof Schuon (1907–1998) (Schuon 1953, 1963, Nasr 1991) and Seyyed Hossein Nasr (1989)[15] as the, probably, best-known representatives. The school is deeply rooted in Islamic mysticism. It is particularly keen on emphasizing that religious pluralism is not religious relativism. Taken on its own, says Nasr following Schuon, each religion which is based on genuine revelation has absolute validity because it owes its existence to the absolute reality of God and is able to relate humans to the Divine. Therefore the religions are "relatively absolute". That is, they are "not the Absolute as such" but are "relatively absolute within a particular religious universe" (Nasr 1999: 171). Other Muslim pluralists also distance themselves from relativism and draw on the Qur'an in order to formulate universal criteria by which valid religions can be identified, yet criteria which are at the same time universalizable—criteria that focus on a religion's relation to transcendence (that is, 'monotheism' in an expanded sense) and on its promotion of justice (see,

---

13   Shah-Kazemi repeatedly quotes the first part of this statement in order to criticize Askari (e.g. Shah-Kazemi 2006: 252). But if one looks at the whole quotation one wonders whether it is really that different from what Shah-Kazemi proposes as the alternative: "universal Islam transcends particular Islam whilst simultaneously affirming it" (2006: 259).

14   See also "Religious Pluralism: Kadivar, Soroush Debate" at http://www.drsoroush.com/ English/By_DrSoroush/E-CMB-19980409-Religious_Pluralism-Kadivar-Soroush_Debate .html.

15   For a comparison of Nasr's pluralism with that of John Hick see Aslan (1998).

for example, Ayoub 1997: 110; Esack 1997: 175). Today, the basic tenets of the *traditional school* are creatively developed by Reza Shah-Kazemi (2006a). Shah-Kazemi, however, hovers between an inclusivist and a pluralist attitude.[16] On the one hand, he thinks it is justified to claim "Islam as the best religion, because it recognizes and respects all religions" (2013: 98). On the other hand, he understands the difference between revealed religions as "the results of different combinations of the specific divine qualities which lie at the roots of each of the religions" (Shah-Kazemi 2012: 110)—a position which will hardly allow for the idea that one such combination is better than the others. Shah-Kazemi has also produced significant contributions to a Muslim understanding of Hinduism (2006b) and Buddhism (2010). These are the faiths to which I will now turn.

Pluralist Approaches in Hinduism

Contrary to public opinion, widespread in the West, Hinduism is by no means traditionally pluralistic. What we find is rather a mixture of exclusivist and inclusivist attitudes (for an overview see Clooney 2003; Halbfass 1991: 51–85). Somewhat simplifying one can say that those Indian traditions which based themselves on the Vedas tended to take an exclusivist attitude towards non-Indic religions and towards those Indian traditions which like the Buddhists or Jains rejected the revelatory authority of the Vedas, while they often related to each other in an inclusivist manner.[17] The latter approach is prefigured in a well-known passage from the Bhagavad Gītā (7:22) where Krishna—or better, the highest God Vishnu manifest as Krishna—speaks about someone who venerates other gods:

---

16   Shah-Kazemi is critical of John Hick and Muslim Pluralists like Arkoun, Esack, Sachedina, and Askari, while it is rather questionable whether his objection that they are sacrificing the particular of religions to the universal is justified. In distancing Nasr's pluralism from Hick's, Shah-Kazemi follows closely Nasr's critique of Hick as found in his *Knowledge and the Sacred* (cp. Nasr 1989: 287–97, with Shah-Kazemi 2006: 166f, 249ff.). While in *The Other in the Light of the One* and elsewhere in his writings Shah-Kazemi shows some sympathy for the "attitude of superiority" (2006: 244), he is far more critical of superiority claims in his later work *The Spirit of Tolerance in Islam* (2012: 102–07).

17   It was the German Indologist Paul Hacker who introduced the term "inclusivism" in 1957 to demarcate this particular line of Indian thinking. See Halbfass (1988: 403–18). The lecture of 1977 in which Hacker stated his position most succinctly is posthumously published in Oberhammer (1983: 11–28).

Firm established in that faith,
He seeks to reverence that (god),
And thence he gains all he desires,
Though it is I who am the true dispenser.

GOODALL 1996: 242

However, the subsequent verse hastens to affirm that the reward obtained in those improper ways of worship is finite while those who venerate Krishna/ Vishnu, the true God, attain to ultimate salvation (see also Bhagavad Gītā 9:23f.). We find in traditional Hinduism the belief in an inner unity of different religious paths. But usually this is linked to the hierarchical concept of *adhikāra-bheda* ("differences in abilities") according to which religious diversity reflects and corresponds to the different stages in the spiritual development of human beings (see Halbfass 1991: 72f.). This influential concept is closely intertwined with belief in karma and reincarnation: as one can improve one's caste status via reincarnation and the accumulation of good karma, one can also achieve a higher spiritual level (and, by implication, the corresponding higher religion) not only via conversion in this life but also via reincarnation in one's subsequent life.

When we look at the attitudes of contemporary Hindus towards other religions, what is of particular importance are, apart from the traditional heritage, those developments of the nineteenth and twentieth century which are generally referred to as neo-Hinduism (see Coward 1987a; Halbfass 1988: 334–48). Here, again, the general Western perception tends to be distorted. Usually neo-Hinduism is identified with people like the mystic Ramakrishna (1836–1886), his charismatic disciple Vivekananda (1863–1902) and the eminent scholar and statesman Radhakrishnan (1888–1975). It is often overlooked that neo-Hinduism also involved influential movements like the Arya Samaj whose founder Dayananda Saraswati (1824–83) displayed an extremely polemical and aggressive form of exclusivism, directed not only against all non-Hindu religions but also against all other forms of Hinduism if they were not entirely in line with his own ideas.[18]

However, in the teachings of the triumvirate Ramakrishna, Vivekananda, and Radhakrishnan we encounter not merely a positive evaluation of religious diversity but also numerous statements pointing in a pluralist direction. Nevertheless, it is dubitable whether their ideas are unambiguously

18   See in particular Dayananda's main work *The Light of Truth* (*Satyarth Prakash*). See also Coward (1987b).

pluralist. Especially in the writings of Vivekananda one can identify two strategies through which a Hindu superiority claim is still maintained. *First*, the traditional idea of *adhikāra-bheda* is extended to include the non-Hindu religious traditions.[19] That is, religious diversity is legitimate and desirable but in terms of a hierarchy of higher and lower religions reflecting different levels of spiritual development of their devotees,[20] while Vivekananda's favorite faith—Advaita-Vedānta—is on top of the ladder.[21] For people who are spiritually less developed other religions are more suitable and may contribute to their further advancement. Given that there will always be people on different spiritual levels, there has to be a range of different religions. But this does not entail denying that only one is the most developed. One is in an objective sense superior to all others.[22] *Second*, Vivekananda seems to presuppose that only Hinduism—and within Hinduism primarily the school of Advaita-Vedānta—obtains the philosophical-theological concepts necessary for a proper understanding and acknowledgement of religious diversity. Other religions, particularly Christianity and Islam, lack these conceptual requirements. It is therefore the global and universal mission of Hinduism to challenge the absolutist religions and help them through Hindu wisdom in overcoming their own exclusivist claims (see in particular "The Mission of the Vedanta" in Vivekananda 1989, vol. 3: 176–99, and 251f.).

While the first tendency, assuming that there are more or less advanced religions, clearly displays an inclusivist matrix, the second one, claiming that only Advaita Vedānta can properly understand the nature and value of religious diversity, is at best something like a *primus-inter-pares* pluralism. To paraphrase

---

19   This process already begins with the *sant*-movements that integrated various Hindus and Indian Muslims. See Raghavan (1966: 76) who explicitly mentions the significance of the concept of *adhikāra-bheda* in this process.

20   Cf. the following statement Ramakrishna, Vivekananda's teacher: "God Himself has provided different forms of worship. He who is the Lord of the Universe has arranged all these forms to suit different men in different stages of knowledge" Nikhilananda (1958: 126).

21   Cf. the following statement: "Would to God that the whole world were Advaitins tomorrow, not only in theory but in realisations. But if this cannot be, let us do the next best thing; let us take the ignorant by the hand, lead them always step by step just as they can go, and know that every step in all religious growth in India has been progressive. It is not from bad to good, but from good to better" Vivekananda (1989, vol. 3: 424).

22   "To the Hindu... all the religions, from the lowest fetishism to the highest absolutism, mean so many attempts of the human soul to grasp and realise the Infinite, each determined by the conditions of its birth and association, and each of these marks a stage of progress...." Vivekananda (1989, vol. 1: 17).

George Orwell: All religions are equal but one is more equal in that it alone is able to recognize and affirm their equality without self-contradiction. The quasi-pluralism of Vivekananda and various other neo-Hindu reformers is thus based on a reinterpretation of three traditional ideas: first, the unity of reality through participation in one ultimate divine source—a principle now reinterpreted as including some positive validation of non-Vedic faiths; second, a hierarchical order of diversity—traditionally rooted in the caste (or better: *varna*) system—now transferred, by way of extending the notion of *adhikāra-bheda*, to non-Hindu faith; and, third the idea of progressive spiritual development across numerous lives through reincarnation—now expanded to include adherence to other religions as different stages in one's overall spiritual progress.

Today, the quasi-pluralism of neo-Hinduism has almost become mainstream Hinduism, and even entered jurisdiction when the Supreme Court of India declared in 1995 that the "Features of Hindu religion" include "the realisation that truth was many-sided" and the "recognition of the fact that the means or ways to salvation are many".[23] But the problematic aspects of such *primus-inter-pares* pluralism are now apparent in the so-called *Hindutva*-movement, which supports a highly intolerant politics towards Christianity and Islam. One of their most influential ideologist, M.S. Golwalkar (1906–1973), who had been a monk in Vivekananda's Ramakrishna order for some years, argues like Vivekananda that only Hinduism is able to recognize the unity and legitimate diversity of religions: "it is," says Golwalkar, "the grand world-unifying thought of Hindus alone that can supply the abiding basis for human brotherhood...." This insight is so precious and important for the future of humanity, that it is—for the sake of the world—a "sacred duty" to keep Hinduism "in sound condition" (Golwalkar 1996: 6), which means, among other things, protecting it against the absolutist religions of Christianity and Islam. In India, these religions should therefore never have the same rights as Hinduism (Klostermaier 2000: 145). An intolerant politics of religion is thus justified in the name of a kind of pluralism.

Is it possible for Hinduism to overcome such forms of *primus-inter-pares* pluralism? In this respect the inner development of Mahatma Gandhi (1869–1948) might be instructive. Gandhi initially shared the view that Hinduism is superior to all other religions because only Hinduism is able to value all other religions positively (Jordans 1978: 10). From 1930 onwards, however, Gandhi was keen on developing a conception, which permitted a more consistent

---

23   See: "Bramchari Sidheswar Bhai & Ors. etc. vs. State of West Bengal etc." (Supreme Court 1995 AIR 2089).

recognition of the religions' equality, including Hinduism. In order to achieve this he drew on two interconnected elements: on the one hand, the conviction that truth ultimately transcends all words. All doctrines and doctrinal systems are thus inevitably imperfect, including religions. Truth in its ultimate sense cannot be identified with any one among them, and Hinduism is no exception. On the other hand, the essence of religion can be realized only through practice. While Gandhi initially taught that "God is truth," he now reversed the sentence and held that "truth is God"—that kind of truth which can never become one's doctrinal possession but can only be authentically pursued in religious, particularly non-violent practice. On that practical level, however, the superiority of one religion above others is hard to maintain. The ideal of non-violent practice is rather equally available to all of them (see Rao 2005: 51ff.).[24]

These rather fragmentary considerations are taken up by the contemporary American Hindu Jeffery Long who explicitly relates his own approach to Gandhi (see 2007: especially 101–70; for his reference to Gandhi see 135f; see also 2005). The Hindu claim to superiority, says Long, can only be overcome if Hindus affirm unambiguously that "eternal truth" (*sanatana dharma*) is not equivalent to any specific historical or linguistic articulation of truth, not even to Hinduism. In the case of Long, this position is on the one hand directed against the *Hindutva* ideology and on the other hand intended as a basis for a genuinely pluralist approach. In the end, however, it might not go far enough. In order to overcome the *primus-inter-pares* variant of a Hindu superiority claim, Hindus would have to acknowledge that the capacity of relativizing one's own conditioned expressions of truth in light of its ultimate transcendent nature is not the exclusive property of Hinduism but something that is possible for other religions as well on the basis and within the framework of their own religious insights. Radhakrishnan did at times express the view "that every religion has possibilities of such a transformation" (Radhakrishnan 1956: 204),[25] but usually he too follows the *primus-inter-pares* paradigm.

Pluralist Approaches in Buddhism

Like Hinduism, Buddhism's attitude to other religions is traditionally either exclusivist or inclusivist, exclusivist in relation to other religious traditions (with

---

24   For a comparison of Gandhi and John Hick see Sugirtharajah (2012). For John Hick's own
      views on Gandhi see Hick and Hempel (1989: 21–3, 85–9); Hick (2008).

25   He also uses the image of different colleges and speculates that rather than changing college
      it is more important to improve the standard of all colleges "with the result that each
      college enables us to attain the same goal" Radhakrishnan, 1974, 35.

some notable exceptions in relation to the Chinese religions) and inclusivist in relation to other forms or schools of Buddhism.[26]

Within Theravada Buddhism, Buddhist superiority claims are based upon two crucial tenets: first, the belief that, as explicitly stated in the Dhammapada (273f.), only the Four Noble Truths and the Noble Eightfold Path as taught by the Buddha leads to salvation or liberation. This view is underlined by the teaching that all Buddhas (Buddhas in the full sense) always invariably teach these two doctrines (the Noble Eightfold Path being of course part of the Four Truths). The second is the belief that in each world system there cannot be more than one Buddha, in the full sense, at the same time (cf. Aṅguttaranikāya 1:15:10; Milindapañha 4:6:6), that is, only one who shows the path to liberation and establishes the salvific community, the Sangha, which safeguards and teaches the Dharma for the sake of gods and men. These two beliefs make it extremely difficult for Theravadins to adopt a pluralist position.[27] As far as I am aware, the only Theravada thinker who nevertheless attempted this was the

---

26   For an overview see Kiblinger (2005), Schmidt-Leukel (2008a). A collection of essays on Buddhist attitudes to specific other faiths and to religious diversity as such is offered in Schmidt-Leukel (2013).

27   J. Abraham Veléz de Cea, a scholar of Buddhism, has recently offered an interpretation of some crucial statements in the Pāli Nikāyas which strongly questions the standard exclusivist exegesis found in the Theravada tradition (Veléz de Cea 2013). Most importantly, he understands the affirmation of *pratyekabuddhas* (Pāli: *paccekabuddhas*), i.e. people who achieve enlightenment without having met the Buddhist teaching in their present lives, as strong evidence against Buddhist exclusivism. Unfortunately, he takes no notice of the inner-Theravada debate of whether or not non-Buddhist religious teachings may have any positive role in a *pratyekabuddha's* achievement (see on this Schmidt-Leukel 2013, vol. 4: 88–129). More importantly, he does not reflect on the tension between the acknowledgement of a positive salvific role of other faiths and the Theravāda doctrine that there can be only one Buddha in the full sense (one who, different from a *pratyekabuddha*, teaches the path to liberation) at the same time per world system (though he mentions this doctrine on pp. 100ff.). If one accepts his non-exclusivist exegesis of Dīghanikāya 16:5:27 (Veléz de Cea 2013: 67–77) so that there are possibly *arhats* (enlightened saints of the highest degree) in other schools, this would imply that the founders of these schools have the status of a Buddha in the full sense (*samyaksaṃbuddha*) and hence contradict the aforementioned teaching. Of particular relevance to the development of Buddhist pluralism is his discussion on whether the Dharma allows for diverse forms of representation, so that Buddhists could be open to the possibility of discovering different representations in the teachings and practices of other faiths (Veléz de Cea 2013: 145–56). In this he contrasts the doctrinal narrowness, which regards the Four Noble Truths and the Noble Eightfold Path as the only form of salvifically relevant knowledge with the more open-minded attitude of critical investigation that is also displayed in the canon.

Thai reformer Bhikkhu Buddhadāsa (1906–1993). He argued that the three fundamental principles of the Noble Eightfold Path, wisdom, morality, and contemplation (*paññā*, *sīla*, *samādhi*), are equally present in Christianity, Islam, Hinduism, and Buddhism, though with different emphases and in different forms, which Buddhadāsa explained by their exposure to different cultural influences (Buddhadāsa 1967: 12ff, 24f, 38f.).[28] Even "the few pages of the Sermon on the Mount," said Buddhadāsa, are "far more than enough and complete for practice to attain emancipation" (1967: 29). Accordingly, Buddhadāsa referred to Jesus as a Buddha (1967: 105f.).[29] Yet this implicitly negates the teaching of not more than one Buddha at the same time and Buddhādasa could only do so because of the strong Mahayana influence on his thought.[30]

Mahayana Buddhism certainly offers better conditions for the development of a pluralist position. In at least some forms it has weakened the belief that there can be only one Buddha per world, and in its later forms it generally assumes that all sentient beings participate in a common Buddha-Nature. At times Buddha-Nature is not only identified as the true self but also with ultimate reality. Moreover, Mahayana Buddhism developed the widespread view that there are 84,000 different gates of the Dharma, the true teaching, corresponding to the vast variety of different individual dispositions. This relative openness to diversity is intrinsically connected to two central Mahayana concepts: first, the notion of 'two truths,' that is, the distinction between 'conventional' or 'relative truth' (*saṃvṛti satya*) and 'ultimate' or 'absolute truth' (*paramārtha satya*); and, second, the notion of 'skilful means' (*upāyakauśalya*). While 'absolute truth' is beyond thought and expression, 'relative truth' employs ordinary conceptual schemes and is seen as instrumental in finally achieving the meta-conceptual understanding of 'absolute truth.' For this reason 'relative truth' is often identified with the various 'skilful means' adapted to the different spiritual needs of the people and used by a Buddha or Bodhisattva in guiding them on their way to Enlightenment. Traditionally, various Mahayana schools conceived their own teachings as comprising the best understanding of the two truths and as providing the highest or most suitable means for achieving Enlightenment. Other Buddhist schools were interpreted as less advanced and non-Buddhist teachings and practices as either being outright false and misleading or at best

---

28   It is remarkable that Buddhadāsa, in order to make this point, draws on the qur'anic statement that there is a messenger for each nation (Q. 10: 47); see (1967: 8).

29   See also p. 98, where he speaks of Jesus as a 'victor' (*jina*), that is, using one of the titles of a Buddha.

30   For the Mahayana influence on Buddhadāsa see Jackson (2003: 69–99, 129–200).

as preparatory for Buddhism.[31] Hence in order to develop a Mahayana pluralism it would not suffice to simply expand the conceptual tools of 'two truths'
and 'skilful means' to include non-Buddhist faiths, but to overcome the deep-
seated inclination of hierarchical ranking, which always sees one's own tradition as supreme.[32] So far, however, this has been done only rarely and in initial
or rudimentary ways.

The most prominent example is the 14th Dalai Lama. In his writings we find
statements, which, at first sight, sound rather pluralistic. For example: "We cannot say that there is only one religion and that one religion is the best, or that
a particular religion is the best" (Gyatso 1995: 26). Or, in his most recent book,
Towards the True Kinship of Faiths he states: "The challenge before religious
believers is to genuinely accept the full worth of faith traditions other than
their own. This is to embrace the spirit of religious pluralism" (Gyatso 2010: xi).
But do the Dalai Lama's own ideas meet this standard? This is rather dubious.
He defines 'pluralism' as according 'validity' to other faiths, not as according
equal validity (Gyatso 2010: 147). Being a religious pluralist, would—according
to the Dalai Lama—not exclude maintaining the doctrines of one's own faith
"as representing the definitive truth" (Gyatso 2010: 157). In the end, his version
of pluralism amounts to the identification of a basic equality and 'full worth'
only in terms of the moral potential of the major religions. Apart from that,
he holds the traditional view that a diversity of religions is necessary because
the different mental dispositions of people require different spiritual means
(Gyatso 2010: 154–61). Yet these are apparently still interpreted hierarchically,
as he did when he wrote forty years ago: "Therefore, other teachers, their doctrines, and practitioners can be refuges, but not final refuges" (Gyatso 1977: 35).
He still seems to assume that the religion which is in an objective sense closest
to the truth and hence most adequate to the highest levels of spiritual progress

---

31   In China too, Confucian, Daoist, and Buddhist thinkers employed the concept of the 'har-
      mony of the three teachings' (*sanjiao heyi*) usually in an inclusivist, hierarchical interpre-
      tation, as, for example, in the case of the Buddhist Hanshan Deqing (1546–1623) who
      assessed Confucianism, Daoism, and Buddhism in terms of three stages: "from dealing
      with the world, to forgetting the world, to transcending the world" (Brook: 2013: 298f.). See
      also Gentz and Schmidt-Leukel (2013).

32   The problem is not critical ranking as such but the idea that difference can only be ex-
      plained hierarchically which excludes the possibility of combining difference with parity.
      In this respect I agree with Rita Gross (2014: 86, 93). Yet this kind of ranking did not only
      happen 'sometimes' in Buddhism (2014: 93 fn. 4), nor even 'extensively' (as she admits on
      the same page) but was standard.

is his own version of tantric Buddhism (Gyatso 2010: 159f.). As in Hinduism, the key to this way of understanding religious diversity is the belief that via reincarnation people can gradually advance through different forms of religions until they finally become fit for the ultimate truth as it is only taught in one's own school or sect.[33]

According to the Tibetan-Buddhist Lama and Professor of Indo-Tibetan Buddhism, John Makransky, the similarities in ethical and spiritual qualities produced within the major religions is sufficient evidence to suppose that they are all rooted in the same ultimate reality (2008: 60f.). Further, one should not assume that some type of Mahayana Buddhism possesses the most adequate picture of this reality, for the crucial insight of Mahayana philosophy is that no religious doctrine, not even Buddhist ones, should be taken as absolute truth or as truth in the highest sense (*paramārtha satya*), for this is beyond human words and concepts. However, according to Makransky, Buddhist philosophy offers the best foundation for this insight and provides the best technical means to achieve it. Other religions tend to absolutize their notions of the ultimate and cling to them, so that Buddhism is clearly superior in this regard (see Makransky 2008: 61f., and 2003a: 358ff.). Here Makransky's inclusivism displays a similar structure as the *primus-inter-pares* pluralism of some neo-Hindus. Yet at the same time, he wants to open up this inclusivist approach as much as possible, allowing even for the possibility that non-Buddhists have realized some aspects of ultimate reality "more deeply through their modes of understanding and practice than I have yet as a Buddhist because they are not Buddhists" (Makransky 2011: 131). He reinterprets the notion of 'skilful means' in terms of the socio-historical conditionedness of all religious teachings and communities (Makransky 2003b). When he admits that his own Buddhist position, including its non-dual understanding of the "fullest spiritual fulfilment," is also part of a "historically conditioned tradition" so that, in the end, he cannot "step out of my own conditioned perspective to fully understand and *rank* the possible fulfilments of other world religions (or even other Buddhist traditions)" (Makransky 2011: 130), he is about to transgress the limits of inclusivism toward a pluralist position. For this admission seems to imply at least the possibility of other religions being equally salvific.

Another move toward pluralism has been made by Masao Abe (1915–2006) during the later years of his life. He reinterprets the *dharmakāya*, a traditional

---

33   See on this Williams (1991: 519f.), and the analysis of the Dalai Lama's position in D'Costa (2000: 72–92).

Buddhist designation of ultimate reality, in a characteristically Zen-Buddhist manner as 'boundless openness' and 'formless emptiness,' claiming that each religion, whether based on a personal God or on an impersonal absolute, "must go beyond its substantial, self-identical principle and awaken to the dynamic, self-negating 'Boundless Openness' as the ultimate Ground" (Abe 1985: 187). He insists that this must not be misunderstood as a new form of "Buddhist imperialism" (1985: 189), but points to the necessity and, by implication, capacity of all the major faiths to transcend their own doctrinal fixation (1985: 187f.). Abe, whose views had been informed by many years of intensive dialogue with Christianity, regarded such openness as a sound basis for mutual understanding and transformation (1985: 187f.): Buddhism could help Christianity in liquefying its hard dogmatic ideas while Christianity could help Buddhism in gaining a better perception of the reality of history and its ethical challenges (Abe 1995).

Some creative approaches towards a Buddhist and pluralist interpretation of religious diversity have been developed by Pure-Land Buddhists. For Alfred Bloom, the different personal or impersonal concepts of the religions all point to a reality beyond words and concepts, but legitimately and inevitably the religions refer to this ineffable reality with their tradition specific concepts, which from the perspective of Pure-Land Buddhism can be read as compassionate means by which the ultimate itself, seen in his tradition as Amida Buddha, enables different people in different contexts to achieve final liberation (see Bloom 2013). An analogous structure underlies the pluralist approach of the Pure-Land Buddhist John Shunji Yokota. He identifies the "religious ultimate" as a reality not remaining in itself but "going forth and actualizing itself in our concrete, everyday lives" (Yokota 2005: 92). This encourages him not only to identify Amida Buddha with the 'Christ' who was incarnate in Jesus, but also to call for a multi-religious process of mutual transformation in order to arrive at "a fuller and truer vision of reality" through which each tradition achieves a more adequate understanding of itself (Yokota 2005: 91, see also his contribution to Hirota 2000). Slightly more tentative are the approaches of Kenneth Tanaka and Ryūsei Takeda. Though Tanaka is unambiguous in rejecting the traditional Buddhist approach of hierarchizing the various religious teachings and affirms the *possibility* of different religions being equally valid paths of salvation according to the ultimate goals of their traditions, he refrains from specifying how these different goals might be ultimately related to each other (Tanaka 2008: 69–84). For Takeda's sort of open pluralism this is precisely the kind of question to which an answer must not be preconceived but should be expected as emerging from dialogue itself (2013: 261f.).

Conclusion

Comparing the *development of pluralist approaches* in the four religious traditions, one gets the impression that in Judaism and Islam (and Christianity, see
Schmidt-Leukel 2008b, 2010) pluralist positions are not only proposed more often, in terms of numbers of theologians endorsing them, but also appear more
determined. This finding may come as a surprise, given the widespread cliché
of Hinduism and Buddhism as naturally pluralist religions. Perhaps one might
say that in the Abrahamic religions, for pluralist theologians the point of departure is further removed from their goal than it is the case in the Eastern religions. Although one should not underestimate the extent to which exclusivist
positions existed and still exist in Hinduism and Buddhism, both traditions
had a stronger and more continuous inclusivist tradition than can be found
in the Abrahamic faiths. However, in terms of the point of destination (that is,
the appreciation of other faiths as being as genuine and as salvific as one's own
faith, despite their being different from it), many contemporary theologians in
the Abrahamic religions seem to have come significantly closer to the pluralist
goal than their counterparts in the East. The implication is that pluralists in the
Abrahamic religions are further ahead of (or remote from) the religious mainstream than is apparently the case with the often quasi-pluralist approaches of
the Eastern faiths. One major reason for this difference, between the Abrahamic faiths on the one hand and the Eastern faiths on the other hand, seems to
be the doctrine of reincarnation. Within Hinduism and Buddhism it enables
a limited appreciation of religious diversity as serving in different degrees the
needs of those who are regarded as spiritually underdeveloped. Religions that
are different from one's own faith are thus interpreted as being helpful (at least
in some cases) for the spiritually immature who, once they have made spiritual
progress, will enter (via conversion or rebirth) a higher and finally the highest
faith, i.e., one's own religion. This version of inclusivism has not been available
to most parts of the Abrahamic religions.[34]

As far as the *theoretical foundations of a pluralist option* are concerned,
there seem to be at least two significant commonalities which can be identified across the religion-specific particularities. First, this is the affirmation,
found in all major religions, that ultimate reality transcends human words and
concepts. It is the key presupposition from which pluralists infer the need of

---

34   Although belief in reincarnation has not been entirely absent from the Abrahamic reli-
       gions (and is found in early Christian gnosis and in some branches of Judaism and Islam)
       it was never a mainstream position.

a religious self-relativization, that is, of relativizing any absolutist doctrinal claims. And second, it is the widespread conviction that the exclusivist and inclusivist attitudes of the past are not sufficiently doing justice to the actual reality of other religions and their adherents as encountered today, whereas the pluralist option is in a much better position to do so.

How *sound* this conviction really is, is something that might be assessed only in the course of the future development of interreligious encounter and dialogue. At least it seems to be feasible that pluralists of different religious backgrounds can agree on a pluralist interpretation of religious diversity, even if the specific features of this pluralist view inevitably vary within each of the traditions. In this regard, religious pluralism differs decisively from exclusivism and inclusivism. An exclusivist or an inclusivist of a particular religion could never agree with the exclusivist or inclusivist claims of another faith (though he or she may readily accept, as a matter of fact, that such claims are made), while pluralists can agree with at least some versions of pluralism as affirmed in other faiths. To me it appears rather unlikely that in the long run one of the tradition-specific versions of an exclusivist or inclusivist interpretation of religious diversity would become the globally dominant and more or less generally accepted view. For this would imply that one particular religious perspective would prove to be overall most convincing. The on-going rivalry of conflicting mutual superiority claims may undermine the credibility of each one of them. In contrast, religious pluralism offers an interpretation and appreciation of religious diversity which can be shared, though in different, tradition-specific ways, by several religions. In any way, from the perspective of the history of religions and the theology of all the major religious traditions, we live in extraordinarily exciting times because the rise of pluralist approaches in all major religions may eventually turn out as initial evidence of a gradual process of massive transformation in the religions' self-understanding, as the sociologist Thomas McFaul recently dared to prognosticate (2011: 159–74).

Bibliography

'Alī, 'Abdullah Yūsuf. (1999). *The Meaning of The Holy Qur'ān*. New Edition with Qur'anic Text (Arabic), Revised Translation, Commentary and Newly Compiled Comprehensive Index. Beltsville: Amana Publications.

Abe, Masao. (1985). "A Dynamic Unity in Religious Pluralism: A Proposal from the *Buddhist* Point of View." In: J. Hick and H. Askari (eds.). *The Experience of Religious Diversity*. Aldershot: Gower. pp. 163–90.

———. (1995). "Buddhist-Christian Dialogue: Its Significance and Future Task." In: Masao Abe. *Buddhism and Interfaith Dialogue*. Ed. by S. Heine. Basingstoke: Macmillan. pp. 3–16.

Arkoun, Mohammed. (1989). "New Perspectives for Jewish-Christian-Muslim Dialogue." *Journal of Ecumenical Studies* 26: 523–29.

———. (1998). "From Inter-Religious Dialogue to the Recognition of the Religious Phenomenon." *Diogenes* 46.2: 123–51.

———. (2002). *The Unthought in Contemporary Islamic Thought*. London: Saqi Books.

Askari, Hasan. (1977). *Inter-Religion*. Aligarh: Printwell Publications.

———. (1985). "Within and Beyond the Experience of Religious Diversity." In: J. Hick and H. Askari (eds.). *The Experience of Religious Diversity*. Aldershot: Gower 1985. pp. 191–218.

———. (1991). *Spiritual Quest: An Inter-Religious Dimension*. Pudsey: Seven Mirrors.

Aslan, Adnan. (1998). *Religious Pluralism in Christian and Islamic Philosophy: The Thought of John Hick and Seyyed Hossein Nasr*. Richmond: Curzon.

Atay, Rifat. (2014). *Religious Pluralism and Islam: A Critical Reading of John Hick's Pluralistic Hypothesis*. Saarbrücken: Scholar's Press.

Aydin, Mahmut. (2000). "Is There Only One Way to God? A Muslim View." *Studies in Interreligious Dialogue* 10: 148–59.

———. (2001). "Religious Pluralism: A Challenge for Muslims: A Theological Evaluation." *Journal of Ecumenical Studies* 38: 330–52.

———. (2005). "A Muslim Pluralist: Jalaluddin Rūmī." In: P. Knitter (ed.). *The Myth of Religious Superiority: Multifaith Explorations of Religious Pluralism*. Maryknoll, NY: Orbis. pp. 220–36.

———. (2007). "Islam in a World of Diverse Faiths: A Muslim View." In: Lloyd Ridgeon and Perry Schmidt-Leukel (eds.). *Islam and Inter-Faith Relations*. London: SCM Press. pp. 33–54.

Ayoub, Mahmoud. (1997). "Islam and Pluralism." *Encounters: Journal of Inter-Cultural Perspectives* 3: 101–18.

———. (2007). *A Muslim View of Christianity: Essays on Dialogue by Mahmoud Ayoub*. Ed. by I.A. Omar. Maryknoll, NY: Orbis.

Bloom, Alfred. (2013 [1992]). "Shin Buddhism in Encounter with a Religiously Plural World." *The Pure Land*, NS, 8–9: 17–31; reprinted in: P. Schmidt-Leukel (ed.). *Buddhism and Religious Diversity, Vol 4: Religious Pluralism*. London and New York: Routledge. pp. 297–306.

Boase, Roger (ed.). (2005). *Islam and Global Dialogue: Religious Pluralism and the Pursuit of Peace*. Aldershot: Ashgate.

Brill, Alan. (2010). *Judaism and Other Religions: Models of Understanding*. New York and Basingstoke: Palgrave Macmillan.

———. (2012). *Judaism and World Religions: Encountering Christianity, Islam, and Eastern Traditions*. New York and Basingstoke: Palgrave Macmillan.

Brook, Timothy. (2013). "Rethinking Syncretism: The Unity of the Three Teachings and their Joint Worship in Late-Imperial China." In: P. Schmidt-Leukel (ed.). *Buddhism and Religious Diversity, Vol 1: Eastern Religions*. London and New York: Routledge. pp. 290–317.

Buddhadāsa, Bhikkhu Indapañño. (1967). *Christianity and Buddhism*. Bangkok: Sublime Life Mission.

Clooney, Francis. (2003). "Hindu Views of Religious Others: Implications for Christian Theology." *Theological Studies* 64: 306–33.

Cohn-Sherbok, Dan. (1994). *Judaism and Other Faiths*. New York, NY: St. Martin's Press 1994.

———. (2005). "Judaism and Other Faiths." In: P. Knitter (ed.). *The Myth of Religious Superiority: Multifaith Explorations of Religious Pluralism*. Maryknoll, NY: Orbis. pp. 119–32.

Coward, Harold G. (ed.). (1987a). *Modern Indian Responses to Religious Pluralism*. Albany: SUNY.

———. (1987b). "The Response of the Arya Samaj." In: Harold G. Coward (ed.). *Modern Indian Responses to Religious Pluralism*, Albany: SUNY. pp. 39–64.

D'Costa, Gavin. (2000). *The Meeting of Religions and the Trinity*. Maryknoll, NY: Orbis.

Dorff, Elliott N. (1982). "The Covenant: How Jews Understand Themselves and Others." *Anglican Theological Review* 64.4: 481–501.

———. (1996). "A Jewish Theology of Jewish Relations to Other Peoples." In: H. Ucko (ed.). *People of God, Peoples of God: A Jewish-Christian Conversation in Asia*. Geneva: WCC Publications. pp. 46–66.

Engineer, Ashgar Ali. (2005). "Islam and Pluralism." In: P. Knitter (ed.). *The Myth of Religious Superiority: Multifaith Explorations of Religious Pluralism*. Maryknoll, NY: Orbis. pp. 211–19.

———. (2007). *Islam in Contemporary World*. New Delhi: New Dawn Press.

Esack, Farid. (1997). *The Qur'an, Liberation and Pluralism: An Islamic Perspective of Interreligious Solidarity against Oppression*. Oxford: Oneworld.

Gentz, Joachim, and Perry Schmidt-Leukel (eds.). (2013). *Religious Diversity in Chinese Thought*. Basingstoke: Palgrave Macmillan.

Gilkey, Langdon. (1987). "Plurality and Its Theological Implications." In: J. Hick and P. Knitter (eds.). *The Myth of Christian Uniqueness: Toward a Pluralistic Theology of Religions*. Maryknoll, NY: Orbis. pp. 37–50.

Golwalkar, M.S. (1996). *Bunch of Thoughts*. 3rd ed., rev. and enlarged. Bangalore: Sahitya Sindhu Prakashana.

Goodall, Dominic. (1996). *Hindu Scriptures*. London: Phoenix.

Goshen-Gottstein, Alon, and Eugene Korn (eds.). (2012). *Jewish Theology and World Religions*. Oxford and Portland, OR: The Littman Library of Jewish Civilization.

Greenberg, Irving. (2000). "Judaism and Christianity: Covenants of Redemption." In: T. Frymer-Kensky et al. (eds.). *Christianity in Jewish Terms*. Boulder: Westview Press. pp. 141–58.

———. (2004). *For the Sake of Heaven and Earth: The New Encounter Between Judaism and Christianity*. Philadelphia: Jewish Publication Society.

———. (2006). "Theology after the Shoah: The Transformation of the Core Paradigm." *Modern Judaism* 26:3: 213–39.

Griffin, David R. (ed.). (2005). *Deep Religious Pluralism*. Louisville, KY: Westminster John Knox Press.

Gross, Rita. (2014). *Religious Diversity: What's the Problem? Buddhist Advice for Flourishing with Religious Diversity*. Eugene: Cascade Books.

Gyatso, Tenzin (H.H. the Dalai Lama). (1965). *Universal Responsibility and The Good Heart*. 4th ed. Dharamsala: Library of Tibetan Works and Archives.

———. (1977). "Essence of Tantra." In: Tsong-ka-pa. *Tantra in Tibet: The Great Exposition of Secret Mantra*. Translated and edited by Jeffrey Hopkins. London: Allen and Unwin. pp. 13–79.

———. (2010). *Towards the True Kinship of Faiths: How the World's Religions Can Come Together*. London: Abacus.

Halbfass, Wilhelm. (1988). *India and Europe: An Essay in Understanding*. Albany, NY: State University of New York.

———. (1991). *Tradition and Reflection: Explorations in Indian Thought*. Albany, NY: State University of New York.

Hartman, David. (1990). *Conflicting Visions: Spiritual Possibilities of Modern Israel*. New York: Schocken Books.

Hick, John. (1989). *An Interpretation of Religion: Human Responses to the Transcendent*. Basingstoke: Macmillan.

———. (2008). "Mahatma Gandhi's Significance for Today." In: J. Hick. *Who or What is God? And Other Investigations*. London: SCM Press. pp. 161–78.

Hick, J., and L. Hempel (eds.). (1989). *Gandhi's Significance for Today*. New York: St. Martin's Press.

Hick, John, and Paul Knitter (eds.). (1987). *The Myth of Christian Uniqueness: Toward a Pluralistic Theology of Religions*. Maryknoll, NY: Orbis.

Hirota, Dennis (ed.). (2000). *Toward a Contemporary Understanding of Pure Land Buddhism: Creating a Shin Buddhist Theology in a Religiously Plural World*. Albany, NY: State University of New York.

Jackson, Peter. (2003). *Buddhadāsa: Theravada Buddhism and Modernist Reform in Thailand*. Chiang Mai: Silkworm Books.

Jordans, J.F.T. (1987). "Gandhi and Religious Pluralism." In: H. Coward (ed.). *Modern Indian Responses to Religious Pluralism*. Albany, NY: State University of New York. pp. 3–17.

Jospe, Raphael. (2007). "Pluralism out of the Sources of Judaism: Religious Pluralism without Relativism." *Studies in Christian-Jewish Relations* 2/2: 92–113 (e-journal).

————. (2012). "Pluralism out of the Sources of Judaism: The Quest for Religious Pluralism without Relativism." In: A. Goshen-Gottstein and E. Korn (eds.). *Jewish Theology and World Religions*. Oxford and Portland, OR: The Littman Library of Jewish Civilization. pp. 87–133.

Kasimow, H., and B.L. Sherwin (eds.). (1991). *No Religion Is an Island: Abraham Joshua Heschel and Interreligious Dialogue*. Maryknoll, NY: Orbis.

Khalil, Mohammad Hassan (ed.). (2013). *Between Heaven and Hell: Islam, Salvation, and the Fate of Others*. Oxford: OUP.

Kiblinger, Kristin. (2005). *Buddhist Inclusivism: Attitudes Towards Religious Others*. Aldershot: Ashgate.

Klostermaier, Klaus. (2000). *Hinduism: A Short Introduction*. Oxford: OUP.

Knitter, Paul. (1997). "Five Theses on the Uniqueness of Jesus." In: L. Swidler and P. Mojzes (eds.). *The Uniqueness of Jesus. A Dialogue with Paul F. Knitter*. Maryknoll, NY: Orbis. pp. 3–16.

———— (ed.). (2005). *The Myth of Religious Superiority: Multifaith Explorations of Religious Pluralism*. Maryknoll, NY: Orbis.

Kogan, Michael S. (2005). "Toward a Pluralist Theology of Judaism." In: P. Knitter (ed.). *The Myth of Religious Superiority: Multifaith Explorations of Religious Pluralism*. Maryknoll, NY: Orbis. pp. 105–18.

Kogan, Michael S. (2008). *Opening the Covenant: A Jewish Theology of Christianity*. Oxford: OUP.

Langer, Ruth. (2003). "Jewish Understanding of the Religious Other." *Theological Studies* 64: 255–77.

Lamptey, Jerusha Tanner. (2014). *Never Wholly Other: A* Muslima *Theology of Religious Pluralism*. Oxford/New York: OUP.

Long, Jeffery D. (2005). "Anekanta Vedanta: Toward a Deep Hindu Religious Pluralism." In: D. Griffin (ed.). *Deep Religious Pluralism*. Louisville, KY: Westminster John Knox Press. pp. 130–57.

————. (2007). *A Vision for Hinduism: Beyond Hindu Nationalism*. London and New York: I.B. Tauris.

Lubarsky, Sandra B. (1990). *Tolerance and Transformation: Jewish Approaches to Religious Pluralism*. Cincinnati, OH: Hebrew Union College Press.

Lubarsky, Sandra B. (2005). "Deep Religious Pluralism and Contemporary Jewish Thought." In: D.R. Griffin (ed.). *Deep Religious Pluralism*. Louisville, KY: Westminster John Knox Press. pp. 111–29.

Makransky, John. (2003a). "Buddhist Perspectives on Truth in Other Religions: Past and Present." *Theological Studies* 64: 334–61.

————. (2003b). "Historical Consciousness as an Offering to the Trans-Historical Buddha." In: J. Makransky and R. Jackson (eds.). *Buddhist Theology*. London: Routledge-Curzon. pp. 111–35.

———. (2008). "Buddhist Inclusivism." In P. Schmidt-Leukel (ed.). *Buddhist Attitudes to Other Religions*. St. Ottilien: EOS. pp. 47–84.

———. (2011). "Thoughts on Why, How, and What Buddhists Can Learn from Christian Theologians." *Buddhist Christian Studies* 31: 119–33.

McFaul, Thomas. (2011). *The Future of God in the Global Village: Spirituality in an Age of Terrorism and Beyond*. Bloomington: Author House.

Nasr, Seyyed Hossein. (1989). *Knowledge and the Sacred*. Albany: State University of New York.

——— (ed.). (1991). *The Essential Writings of Frithjof Schuon*. Rockport: Element.

———. (1999). "Religion, Globality, and Universality." In: A. Sharma and K.M. Dugan (eds.). *A Dome of Many Colors: Studies in Religious Pluralism, Identity, and Unity*. Harrisburg: Trinity Press International. pp. 152–78.

Nikhilananda, Swami. (1958). *The Gospel of Sri Ramakrishna*. Abridged edition. New York: Ramakrishna-Vivekananda Center.

Oberhammer, Gerhard (ed.) (1983). *Inklusivismus: Eine indische Denkform*. Vienna: De Nobili Research Library.

Race, Alan. (1983). *Christians and Religious Pluralism: Patterns in the Christian Theology of Religions*. London: SCM Press.

———. (1993). *Christians and Religious Pluralism*. 2nd enlarged ed. London: SCM Press.

———. (2001). *Interfaith Encounter: The Twin Tracks of Theology and Dialogue*. London: SCM Press.

Radhakrishnan, Sarvapepalli. (1956). *Recovery of Faith*. London: Allen & Unwin.

———. (1974 [1927]). *The Hindu View of Life*. 17th imprint. London: Unwin Books.

Raghavan, V. (1966). *The Great Integrators: The Saint-Singers of India*. Delhi: Publications Division, Ministry of Information and Broadcasting.

Ramadan, Tariq. (2010). *The Quest for Meaning: Developing a Philosophy of Pluralism*. London: Alan Lane.

———. (2013). "Foreword. Salvation—the Known and the Unknown." In: M.H. Khalil (ed.). *Between Heaven and Hell. Islam, Salvation, and the Fate of Others*. Oxford: OUP. pp. ix–xiii.

Rao, K.L. Seshagiri. (2005). "Mahatma Gandhi. A Prophet of Pluralism." In: P. Knitter (ed.). *The Myth of Religious Superiority: Multifaith Explorations of Religious Pluralism*. Maryknoll, NY: Orbis. pp. 45–55.

Ravitzky, Aviezer. (2006). "Judaism Views Other Religions." In: J.D. Gort, H. Jansen, H.M. Vroom (eds.). *Religions View Religions: Explorations in Pursuit of Understanding*. Amsterdam and New York: Rodopi. pp. 75–107.

Ridgeon, Lloyd (ed.). (2012). *Islam and Religious Diversity*. 4 vols. London and New York: Routledge.

Ridgeon, Lloyd, and Perry Schmidt-Leukel (eds.). (2007). *Islam and Inter-Faith Relations*. London: SCM Press.

Sachedina, Abdulaziz. (2001). *The Islamic Roots of Democratic Pluralism.* Oxford: OUP.

Sacks, Jonathan. (2002). *The Dignity of Difference: How to Avoid the Clash of Civiliza-tions.* 1st ed. London and New York, NY: Continuum.

Schmidt-Leukel, Perry. (2005). "Exclusivism, Inclusivism, Pluralism: The Tripolar Typology—Clarified and Reaffirmed." In: P. Knitter (ed.). *The Myth of Religious Superiority: Multifaith Explorations of Religious Pluralism.* Maryknoll, NY: Orbis. pp. 13–27.

——— (ed.). (2008a). *Buddhist Attitudes to Other Religions.* St. Ottilien: EOS.

———. (2008b). "Pluralisms: How to Appreciate Religious Diversity Theologically." In: A. Race and P. Hedges (eds.). *Christian Approaches to Other Faiths.* London: SCM. pp. 85–110.

———. (2010). "Pluralist Theologies." *The Expository Times* 122: 54–72.

——— (ed.). (2013). *Buddhism and Religious Diversity.* 4 vols. London and New York: Routledge.

Schuon, Frithjof. (1953). *The Transcendent Unity of Religions.* London: Faber & Faber.

———. (1963). *Understanding Islam.* London: Allen & Unwin.

Shah-Kazemi, Reza. (2006a). *The Other in the Light of the One: The Universality of the Qurʾān and Interfaith Dialogue.* Cambridge: The Islamic Text Society.

———. (2006b). *Paths to Transcendence According to Shankara, Ibn Arabi, and Meister Eckhart.* Bloomington: World Wisdom.

———. (2010). *Common Ground Between Islam and Buddhism.* Louisville, KY: Fons Vitae.

———. (2012). *The Spirit of Tolerance in Islam.* London and New York: I.B. Tauris.

———. (2013). "Beyond Polemics and Pluralism." In: M.H. Khalil (ed.). *Between Heaven and Hell: Islam, Salvation, and the Fate of Others.* Oxford: OUP. pp. 87–105.

Solomon, Normon. (1991). *Judaism and World Religion.* New York: St. Martin's Press.

———. (1996). "Faith in the Midst of Faiths: Traditional Jewish Attitudes." In: H. Ucko (ed.). *People of God, Peoples of God: A Jewish-Christian Conversation in Asia.* Geneva: WCC Publications. pp. 84–99.

———. (2005). "Towards a Jewish Theology of Trilateral Dialogue." In: R. Boase (ed.). *Islam and Global Dialogue: Religious Pluralism and the Pursuit of Peace.* Aldershot: Ashgate. pp. 203–14.

Soroush, Abdolkarim. (2000). *Reason, Freedom, and Democracy in Islam: Essential Writings of Abdolkarim Soroush.* Ed. and transl. M. Sadri and A. Sadri. Oxford: OUP 2000.

———. (2009). *The Expansion of Prophetic Experience: Essays on Historicity, Contingency and Plurality in Religion.* Leiden: Brill.

Sugirtharajah, Sharada. (2012). "The Mahatma and the Philosopher: Mohandas Gandhi and John Hick and their Search for Truth." In: S. Sugirtharajah (ed.). *Religious Pluralism and the Modern World: An Ongoing Engagement with John Hick.* Basingstoke: Palgrave Macmillan. pp. 121–33.

Takeda, Ryūsei. (2013). "Mutual Transformation of Pure Land Buddhism and Christianity." *Bulletin of the Nanzan Institute for Religion and Culture* 22 (1998): 6–40. Reprinted in: P. Schmidt-Leukel (ed.). *Buddhism and Religious Diversity, Vol 2: Christianity.* London and New York: Routledge. pp. 231–64.

Tanaka, Kenneth. (2008). "Buddhist Pluralism: Can Buddhism Accept Other Religions as Equal Ways?" In: P. Schmidt-Leukel (ed.). *Buddhist Attitudes to Other Religions.* St. Ottilien: EOS. pp. 69–84.

Vivekananda, Swami. (1989). *The Complete Works of Swami Vivekananda.* 8 vols. Mayavati Memorial Edition. Calcutta: Advaita Ashrama.

Veléz de Cea, J. Abraham. (2013). *The Buddha and Religious Diversity.* London and New York: Routledge.

Waardenburg, Jacques. (2003). *Muslims and Others: Religions in Context.* Berlin and New York: de Gruyter.

Williams, Paul. (1991). "Some Dimensions of the Recent Work of Raimundo Panikkar: A Buddhist Perspective." *Religious Studies* 27: 511–21.

Yokota, John Shunji. (2005). "Where Beyond Dialogue? Reconsiderations of a Buddhist Pluralist." In: D. Griffin (ed.). *Deep Religious Pluralism.* Louisville, KY: Westminster John Knox Press. pp. 91–107.

PART 3

Beyond the Typology: New Debates, New Vistas

∵

CHAPTER 11

Avowing Religious Identity and the Religious Other: A Postcolonial Perspective

Shanthikumar Hettiarachchi

Introduction

Conversations about religions are often emotionally charged and perhaps uneasy too due to their complex interrelatedness with politics and social mobility, economics and international trade, culture and ethnicity, nationality and land, migration and international relations, family and parenting, and so on. Moreover, religion of late has shown itself to be resurgent, after being subjugated under the Enlightenment narratives, and is now claiming a different space within the sociopolitical matrix of the contemporary world. Arguably, many contemporary issues have some traits or associations with religion, directly or indirectly: the so-called Arab Spring; wishing for democracy and regime change by some of the more powerful states; drone attacks being executed; Israel-Palestine 'mothering' further conflicts; Syria's complicated civil war; Sunni-Shia estrangement as part of political tensions; the Islamic State of Iraq and Syria (ISIS or Daesh) and its crimes against humanity; *Hindutva* ideology accelerated for a Hindu India, even though its political wing, the Bharatiya Janata Party (BJP) now governs the nation; sporadic attacks on the minority Christians in certain areas of Pakistan, Nigeria, and more recently India; a new wave of violence between Muslim and Buddhist citizens of Myanmar and denial of the former's right to vote; and Sri Lanka's nationalist Buddhist groups with their vociferous reaction to Muslims and Evangelical Christian groups. Many of these conflicts make for a litany of serious local concerns with global effects. Signs of new wars fought in these different regions have their own effects in other parts of the world. Electronic media bring video clips competitively designed to have their full impact on viewers across the globe. These images, however, create a mixture of good, bad, and ugly consequences for the masses.

This chapter focuses on the subaltern voices that continue to reclaim their due place in a given context, such that their significance is no longer best considered an 'other' but 'a significant another'. This renewed significance of what was formerly considered 'other' constitutes the core of systemic religious pluralism as well, which has been a key debate in the world of Christian theology over at least three decades. Discussions about both the 'religious other' and related wider questions surrounding religious difference (in particular how these could impact on specific religious dogmas, theology and discipline), is what the postcolonial thinkers theoretically evoked with their rejuvenated language of 'alterity.'[1] This was a conscious re-placement due to a carefully crafted historical dis-placement which had been imposed during the colonial period with its power politics, including the occupation of land and governance. 'Postcolonial' in this discussion does not simply mean a historical periodization: instead, it is used as a critical discursive tool of analysis which emerged as a counter-narrative to other perspectives and scholarship of critical theories. My discussion here will seek to link postcolonial theory and the discussion on theology of religions in the rest of this volume.

The Colonial 'Other'

In his epoch-making text, *Orientalism* (1978), Edward Said embarks critically on a cultural analysis of the 'colonies' from bygone days. His astute reading of the history of colonialism indicates meticulously but controversially a body of material which was up until then unexamined. His exposition revealed cutting-edge issues arising not just from the physical mechanisms of the geo-political colonial industry but more crucially from the perspective of epistemological domination. Said vividly tells us that

> orientalism is premised upon exteriority, that is, on the fact that the Orientalist, poet or scholar, makes the Orient speak, describes the Orient, renders its mysteries plain for and to the West. He is never concerned with the Orient except as the first cause of what he says and writes, by virtue of the fact that it is said or written, is meant to indicate that the Orientalist is outside the Orient, both as an existential and as a moral fact.
>
> SAID 1995: 20−1

---

1   This is the philosophical nuance of 'otherness'; see Levinas (1970). Gayathri Spivak, Ranajit Guha and Dipesh Chakrabarty are key scholars who are part of the subaltern studies group who also focus on alterity but from a 'history told from below' perspective. The term subaltern derives from the 'cultural hegemony' work of Antonio Gramsci, which identified the social groups that are excluded from a society's (othering) established structures for political representation, the means by which people have a voice in their society. I will be using these nuances, alterity, subaltern voices, othering, otherisation, and otherness interchangeably in the text.

This describes a unique narrative of what Said means by 'othering.' 'Othering' is done by the one who has power and authority over the material and the persons he/she investigates. What he calls 'an epistemological foundation' defines 'the other' in order to seek and carve out one's own place in context and in history. This 'other' is in the context of the colony, which was under the colonial regime demarcating what 'East' and 'West' would be. It is like the Cartesian bifurcation: the East, therefore the West. The colonial other was defined with essentializing motifs: "Europe is powerful and articulates; Asia is defeated and distant" (Said 1995: 57). The West describes itself as the 'defining self' in order to prescribe the 'other' who is defeated and distant – the 'defeated other' in terms of fire power with knowledge power, and the 'distant other' in terms of Europe or the West considering itself to be central to global well-being. One thing is sure: the West to this day does not know geographically where it begins and ends. Does it end with Turkey or begin with Ukraine and end with the Iberian Peninsula?

Minimizing the 'other' is the best way to subjugate and rule, which was perfectly performed by colonial administrations. The essentialization of the 'self' and the minimalization of the 'other' created a sociopolitical dynamic that paved the way for a structure between the ruler and the ruled, the donor and the recipient. This continues in East–west sociopolitical interactions even to this day. When the West with its allies becomes involved with issues in different countries, they act quite unilaterally, while they tend to demand that the rest of the world heeds many conventions and the rule of law. They act as if they rule the world, and this is now vehemently detested by the rest. This colonial mindset is abhorred by many as they move into the free world where the information explosion and its technology is now accessible to them as well. The smaller countries feel that the real danger is how the bigger nations will manage their wealth and knowledge. This should be for the benefit of all, rather than a few countries. How accountable and transparent should the bigger nations be, for example, in terms of their callous deployment of lethal warfare, like the drones which have violated international rules of engagement? Violations of human rights and the territorial integrity of sovereign states by the stronger, wealthier, militarily capable countries must be brought under the rule of international law. Such neo-colonial dealings should be enacted in the free world of today. The 'othering' process is the newest way to deal with the ones that one does not like. 'Othering' is an apparently innocent beginning of a very dangerous mode and move to isolate and exterminate very conveniently. The old colonial project cannot be allowed to raise its ugly head through different manifestations whether they be in trade, debt, information technology or diplomacy. Many people around the world, and particularly from the Global

South, feel that these acts are modern soft modes of domination to carry out a certain leverage, remotely controlled from global centers of power.

One such example was the current British prime minister who, with less than adequate knowledge of the on-the-ground realities of the thirty-year-old war in Sri Lanka, visited the northern city of Jaffna, in November 2013[2] and made statements with global implications for which he had to answer to the British public on his return. By his subsequent interventions Cameron obviously portrayed himself as someone who supported the victims of war in Sri Lanka (the 'suffered other'), and the rest felt that he did not support the other 'Other'—the victors in the war in Sri Lanka, although they also suffered. For a former colonial master in the person of this British prime minister, it is crucial that these questions are dealt with first: On what basis is this clear-cut definition made? Whose rights are to be protected, and who is to be alienated? For him, one was a victim (i.e., apparently the Tamils in the North) and the 'other' (the state apparatus), the perpetrator, which is where he made his political blunder. There is a missing link in the Cameron perspective—the Tamil tigers, who were terrorists known worldwide, arguably far worse than the West's security preoccupation—Al Qaeda then, now IS. He should have known that in a conflict nothing is black and white. He already knows about 'his' painful and unwanted incursions that he also supported in Iraq. He did not know then either who decides who is right and wrong in a conflict (Hettiarachchi 2012). In the eyes of the world, the prime minister became a prime suspect for portraying a certain colonial residue in his behavior and perfect 'othering' characteristics.

(Un)holy 'Otherisation'

The vastness of the globe is now known, yet its inhabitants remain so diverse and complex that we have not been able to grasp its richness fully. This complexity itself has driven people with greater power to continue to prescribe, define, name and brand other human beings to this day. Even though

---

2   The British prime minister, David Cameron, participated in the Commonwealth Head of Governments Meeting (CHOGM) in Colombo in November 2013. Even after four months, the Sri Lankan media, both print and digital, did not cease criticising his behaviour while he was touring Sri Lanka. The biggest criticisms were his lack of knowledge, his analysis of the thirty-year-old war, and his cultural insensitivity as an honoured guest of the nation. He was a victim of his own colonial pride, prejudice, and pomp, as suggested by Said and several postcolonial thinkers.

North–south and East–west conversations take place on the level of trade marketing, attitudes and concepts in dealing with human relations and social interaction still remain quite compartmentalized. There could be extensive cordiality while a business deal is in motion. However, once a business plan is agreed and each party is on its own, then what often follows is an interesting conversation about 'the other.' The other is a necessary requirement: nothing can work without the other. Nor can theology work without the other. Even God cannot be God without the other—the created or the devotee. However, it can become an unholy act when a person or a community is 'otherised' to serve one's self understanding. Because 'the other' by its own merit is a 'different other,' wishing, planning and executing to make this different 'other' the 'self' is deeply counterproductive. This is what happens in the entire world of religion. Yet religionists consider it to be an act of faith. But now we know that it can be indecently offensive to embark comfortably upon making the 'other' into the 'self'. This act of faith or duty is identified as unethical conversion to a faith by several religious groups. Examples include religious persuasion, the use of alluring material wealth, other financial deals, or psychological pressure on an individual who is already a man or woman of another faith or religion.

The creation of an East–west divide—Orientalism and Occidentalism[3]— was inevitable, even though what these mean is very different in various periods of history. Although the West desperately needed the East for its own self-understanding, it was not necessarily so that the East needed the West. The West felt fully West when the rest was identified as the East and the East was to be at the beck and call of the West. The West's schizophrenic self-definition lamentably required an 'other' to be itself with meaning. These identities were dampened by the colonial apparatus that operated, as Jonah Raskin (1974: 40) quotes Rudyard Kipling:

> mule, horse, elephant, or bullock, he obeys his driver, and the driver his sergeant, and the sergeant his lieutenant, and the lieutenant his captain, and the captain his major, and the major his colonel, and the colonel his brigadier commanding three regiments, and the brigadier his general, who obeys the Viceroy, who is the servant of the Empress.[4]

---

3 The term *Occidentalism* is probably an inversion of *Orientalism*, Edward Said's label for stereotyped Western views of the East. Alternative views are expressed and argued by Carrier (1995), also see Buruma and Margalit (2004).

4 See Rudyard Kipling, *Her Majesty's Servants*, (Short Story. Full text) available at: http://www .ciudadseva.com/sevacity/stories/en/kipling/her_majestys_servants.htm, last accessed: on 03 Dec 2013.

Raskin's quotation fits also the modern Western diplomatic guru, who keeps to 'his master's voice' in his work and dealings with the East, from Balfour to Kissinger, and John Kerry to William Hague to Samantha Power. Some of their views as expressed and published in the printed and electronic media are quite daunting: "difficult to work with the Chinese"; "Not sure when Africans work"; "Arabs work in conflict"; "South Asians take ages to work"; "Latinos still to know what work is." Said calls this a perfect 'othering' in order to define the 'self.' Some of these generalizations are a bit unkind but could be true, at least partially in some cases. However, what is truer is that all regions function with a sense of essentialism and this was dampened further by the process of colonization. Some try to argue that colonialism is part of the past and those who were formerly ruled must now move on, without being tied to a blame game. What frustrates those governing now is when the same former colonial powers return in different forms to dictate via trade, finance, and human rights from a 'holier than thou' position. This re-enacts the colonial experiment once again right in front of the now globally aware natives. This time around, however, the ruled are ruling, the formerly ruled are enhanced with an identity now willing to resist, revolt, and re-emerge as an alternative power bloc, standing their ground with groundbreaking identity politics.

Religious identity becomes a most powerful tool to display what defines self-worth in order to fight and resist different dictates and forces of power. Hence, future conflicts are more likely to be on a comparatively small scale, but the damage done could as vast as a full-blown war with arms and ammunitions. Such wars may not be officially declared, but intra-religious and intra-ethnic conflicts are bound to flare up. There is already sufficient evidence for these across the globe, from the Middle East, Nigeria, South Sudan, and the Congo to the horn of Africa, and India in the next phase of national politics, and then from the far East all the way to China. Religion and ethnicity, which form the most avowed identity of an individual or a specific community, will set alight an indomitable party line for the simple reason that they feel that their only lifeline is at stake. The core of this battle is the fear of the loss of significance, self-respect, and dignity. For this they will fight, even knowing that it could be unwinnable.

'Otherwardness' and 'the Other'

All religions without exception draw and project their fundamental orientation towards 'the other.' By definition, religion is that which binds people together, both within and without. If it fails then it misses the core of its message: religion must attract followers and make people comfortable, free and connected, an altruism that supersedes all other persuasions. This is recognized in most traditions. In this sense, religion by its own virtue is bent on an 'otherwardness.'

This sense of 'otherwardness' is what makes religion attractive as well as self-focused, and in some cases an ardent competitor and a stubborn crusader. This competitive and crusading attitude is also interpreted as a necessary enthusiasm to win the 'other' into one's own experience. Some condemn this as an unwanted missionary and evangelical proselytization process, while others describe it as sharing one's own religious experience with the 'other,' who perhaps did not have that opportunity previously. The process sociologically is to make the 'far other,' or the 'near other' into an insider. Those engaged in this process often consider that the 'far other' or 'near other' becoming an insider would be the ultimate victory for the fold. It is proven that such magic of conversion has not altogether taken place as expected by the persuader. This is because it is neither the persuader nor the persuasion that finally matters, but the conviction of the 'far other' or the 'near other' that determines the virtue of being an insider. If this were not the case then the whole of Africa and large parts of Asia would never have become significantly either Christian or Islamic. They are neither fully Christian nor fully Islamic. They remain importantly 'One among Many' within very plural societies across Africa and Asia. Hence, the 'otherwardness feeling' of a religious tradition, even though authentic and honest, is yet to be judged by the very *modus operandi* of the tradition and the actors involved in the process. Many are the instances where such conversions have been unproductive, unsustainable, or even unbecoming of the message of the religious founder or the tradition which each celebrates with pomp, vigor, and pride.

'Otherwardness' is foundational for ethical living but is not without its zest for sacrifice and commitment in its summons to social community (*koinonia*). This formation of community is not for 'inwardness' but for total service (*diakonia*), which in fact is to serve the 'other'. This 'otherwardness' is deeply Christian, but must also be able to relate to other religious traditions. It is as if there is 'a prophetic calling' for both one's fellow Christians as well as non-believers and others to return to fundamentals, without being irritatingly evangelical. The sense of 'otherwardness,' as we argue here, is a part of a recovered self-understanding, spiritual maturity, and integrity. Such positioning can only be arrived at when traditions are willing to revisit their roots and gain insight for reading their context courageously.

De-Colonized Reading

When I refer to 'de-colonized' reading, I propose a conscious political reading of everything that was colonial from trade to epistemology, institutional
governance to local rebellion, with little or no exception. It is a hermeneutical
tool or a posture of interpreting what was fundamentally colonial now using a
different set of tools and criteria. It is not a 'politicized reading' but 'a theological comment' on 'political changes' that have impacted on the colony and its
polity where the reader now engages with new realities. The reader comments
contextually on the existing operatives and mechanisms candidly as agents of
change and projects different perspectives into the conversations. This new
reading includes all possibilities for the new reader to read the former reader
and its specific understanding from the current state of affairs. It is not to make
a judgment on the former reading but to understand why it was read differently and the implications of that reading for the present. So the de-colonizing
reading brings the present reading close to home. All critique would ideally be
with no resentment but deployed as objectively, and realistically as possible.

R.S. Sugirtharajah in his *Asian Faces of Jesus* concisely tables a litany of
how the non-Christians, and Christians in the non-Christian context, of South
Asia imagined Jesus they encountered: "Jesus as supreme Guide to human
happiness" (Rajah Ram Mohun Roy); "Jesus as the *Yogi*" (Keshub Chunder
Sen); "Jesus as *Jivanmukta*" (one who attained liberation while alive, Swami
Vivekananda)); "Jesus as Son of Man, seeking the last, least and the lost"
(Rabindranath Tagore); "Jesus as the supreme *Satyagrahi*" (Mahatma Gandhi);
"Jesus as *Advaitin*" (one who realized destiny with Brahman/God, Swami
Akhilananda); "Mystic Christ" (Radhakrishnan); "Jesus as Prajapati" (Lord
of creatures, K.M. Banerjee); "Jesus as *Cit*" (Consciousness, Brahmobabdhav
Upadhyaya); "Jesus as *Avatara*" (Incarnation, A.J. Appasamy and V. Chakka-
rai); "Jesus as *Adi Purusha*" (the first person) and *Shakti* (power/strength,
P. Chenchiah), (Sugirtharajah 1993: 3–4).

I also wish to add a list of Christian theologians from the Global South to
the above collection to make the same point and as an example of the 'decolonized reading' of their key figure in their own tradition: "Jesus as the Covenant
between the poor and Yahweh" (Aloysius Pieris); "Jesus as the Crucified Guru"
(Thomas Thangaraj); "Jesus who is one with the *Minjung*" (Byung Mu Ahn);
"He is *yang* and we are *yin*" (Jung Young Lee); "Jesus as Mother, Woman and
Shaman" (Chung Hyun Kyung); "Jesus as periphery man who pitched his tent
among us" (Kosuke Koyama); "Jesus as Eternal *Om*" (*logos*, S. Jesudasan). These
indicate a sense of rooting their savior figure in the philosophical, cultural,
and symbolic mode and with a perspective 'close to home.' Indeed, these are
postcolonial ways to understand the Jesus of history and the Christ of faith

in their own idiom, language and experience of life and its struggles. A sharp decolonizing reading of the kernel of their theology and catechism led them all to make Christianity truly Asian, which is a more acceptable form of pre-evangelism or primacy of proclamation, as it is termed in the Vatican document, *Dominus Iesus* (2000). Asia, Africa, and Latin America's colonial legacy is a well-known fact. The losses and wasted lives are inestimable and mostly painfully accepted as past. However, the collective memory of that past is not past. The very subjugation and its lessons compel all those who are serious about learning and researching to employ de-colonized reading as a new tool of analysis (known as postcolonial theory). For instance, these three regions were exposed to a particular version of Christianity where the image of Jesus was presented in a 'regal' and victorious formula. This version of Christianity was then linked to loss and pain, just like the experience of the natives of a given country under an occupying force and having to pay homage to a king and royalty in a far-off land.

Particularly in Asia a decolonized reading is a re-reading of the Christian saviour figure. Christian theologians are attempting a re-reading of the theology and doctrine which had been depicted in a regal Christological and theological formula. Their foresight, reading, and interpretation alongside their people will only be tested in history because this Jesus, their saviour figure, must be actively relevant to their contemporary situations. The Jesus of the *eschaton* may be theologically useful but it is metaphorically 'regal.' A judge dispensing judgment on the living and the dead will require a more convincing argument for the struggling masses.

People seem to have renounced the 'regal Jesus' and opted for a Nazarene close to home. A decolonized reading of Christian scripture and the witness of Christians is what makes modern Christianity in Asia appealing:

> It is a witness born out of praxis alongside the 'religious other,' and not a Christology with which Christians could walk any longer over the theological and spiritual thresholds of their religious neighbours. These religious neighbours have consciously ceased to be objects of mission and church expansion, because they are assertively at the centre of a religious discourse, which refuses the exclusive truth claims of "any other", as they too have begun to do the same.
>
> HETTIARACHCHI 2012: 248

Together with fellow theologians of the former colonized region, what I reiterate is that the Christ of Asia is no stranger to their people: they recognize him as a true man of God, decisively close to them in his act of self-emptying (*kenosis*), an incomparable witness to true life. This for them can be the 'decolonized

Jesus of history' who can be their 'Christ of Asia', the Anointed One. John Hick, Paul Knitter, Alan Race, and several other theologians help these Christians provocatively but refreshingly. Hick does so in particular when he writes:

> we want to say of Jesus that he was *totus Deus*, 'wholly God', in the sense that his agape was genuinely the agape of God at work on earth, but not that he was *totum Dei*, 'the whole of God', in the sense that the divine agape was expressed without remainder in each or even in some of his actions.
>
> HICK 1973: 159

None of the three scholars aver that this theological position is a result of a 'decolonized reading'. But in fact, it is the case which I argue in this article. Interestingly, Knitter quotes Hick in a similar context in his *No Other Name* (1985: 152), perhaps agreeing with Hick nearly twenty years later, but Knitter had more exposure to the once colonial world than Hick and several others had.

Postcolonial criticism, as a tool, invokes the decolonized reading of phenomena. For Asian Christians it provides a new avenue to re-describe their tradition, as well as their dogma, catechesis, liturgy, and spirituality. They might agree with St. Anselm's (1033–1109) claim for theology that it is 'faith seeking understanding,'[5] but they add a further step, which is an understanding that faith must be *semper reformanda*—continually opening itself up for revision and reform in the context. Such an approach among the largest population of non-Christians in Asia will certainly stand as an historical corrective in situations where religious annexation, hegemony, and dominance were the hallmark of an era, losing what a religious tradition is meant to be as a catalyst for change and spiritual sustenance. This only can happen when traditions are self-confident and venture out, despite internal bickering and labelling those who plunge into the unknown. Such traditions know that the encounter and dialogue with the 'other', who is different, may also have something unique to offer to the development of ideas, and a mutual growth in spirituality and ethical living.

Dialoging with the 'Other'

Dialogue has become crucially important as communities become plural and complex. The border controls have become stricter across the globe, yet no

---

5   *Fides quaerens intellectum.* See Migliore (2004), for an excellent exposition of Anselm's thesis where the faith and reason debate is assessed.

nation today is mono-cultural. The information explosion has led people to cross those traditional borders and created new 'frontiers' of communication and sharing knowledge and data. These mechanisms evolve and expand on a daily basis; some of them are known, and others have yet to break through. There is bliss and danger for the future as unpredictable circumstances emerge, each finding its own design and plan to divert its energy. Hence, the reason for dialogue with the 'other' is of paramount importance for it is a better way to deal with pluralism and the complexity of issues as the world encounters them.

The typology of exclusivism, inclusivism, and pluralism was decisive in helping Christian theologians grapple with the issue of the plurality of religions and to find a Christian theological response to them (Race 1993). This tool to assess a variety of religions and the truth claims of certain religious traditions, and to make sense of the absolutism of each of their soteriologies, paved the way for many to debate the issues intellectually and from there to adjust, reform, and transform ideas and views while debating and clarifying these theological stand points without malice and prejudice. Three decades of divergent clarifications have pushed the argument in different directions and Christian theologians still wrestle with the fundamentals of the theology of religions. This book itself testifies to the urgency of debates on religious pluralism, something that will not go away. However, each of the theological schools of thought has developed its own theology of religions and operates happily. Less well known is that an Indian theologian in the person of Stanley Samartha asked this pertinent question: "Can it be the will of God that many religions should continue in this world?" (1991:79). Alan Race's observation of Samartha is equally poignant: "Samartha has opened the door to the scandalous possibility that other religions are a product of divine intention rather than human accident—with the consequence that they have a theological right to exist and be heard" (2001: 21). He goes a step further: not only do they justly claim a theological right to be heard, but, by virtue of religious freedom enshrined in human rights, they become equal partners in the spiritual quest of humanity.

These queries and investigations have continued for a long time both within Christian circles and beyond, while the Christian and other religious traditions both pose it as a missiological question, as the Sri Lankan Jesuit theologian Aloysius Pieris (1998) and the Indian theologian Thomas Thangaraj (1994) have shown. Asian religious plurality demands dialogue as mission and as it embarks on the more sensitive area of Christology. Hence, what Christ means to them is integral to their Christian religious identity: mission is that which makes Christ the epicenter of the totality of human salvation. The issue becomes more complicated when the church or churches portray themselves as the custodians of this paradigm, as well as the institutional arm by which this specific religious identity is claimed, justified, and preserved. They fear and detest contamination.

The social anthropologist Mary Douglas provides eloquently in her *Purity and Danger* (1966) an analysis of the concepts of ritual purity and impurity found in different societies and times. These are also equally applicable to religious traditions. This specific text is the key to examine how each religious tradition views the 'other' and wishes to, or wishes not to, dialogue. Her thesis comes alive, when the notion of 'ours' and 'theirs' challenges the architecture of purity and taboo, for, without dialogue, it remains a recipe for conflict and divisive behavior. In one of her later investigations in *Natural Symbols*, Douglas introduces the interrelated concepts of 'group' (defined as an individual's social position as inside or outside a bounded social group) and 'grid' (defined as an individual's social role within networks of social privileges, claims, and obligations). The grid-group pattern was to be refined and redeployed in laying the foundations of a cultural theory (Douglas 1970: 183–254). By way of ideologically rooted religious belief, the 'grid' of an individual creating a single narrative in which one can easily formulate a taboo, and the 'group' further compounds those fundamentals that make 'them' pure and the rest 'impure.' These cultural complexities and normative social stratifications invariably prompt whatever group, more particularly religious groups, to ritualize their behavior and even become impulsive towards the 'religious other.' Hence, dialoguing with an 'other' is filled with suspicion and may become 'a no-go area.' But, without dialogue with the 'religious other,' there can be little meaning to the self-understanding of any institution or agency. Dialogue is not only a necessity but also an imperative for a viable and relevant tradition moving in the modern world. Religions have no choice but to adjust in some measure to cope with the winds of change. A religion may either change its course while in dialogue or be changed while resisting.

Alongside Co-Religionists

Both the established and the evangelical churches are founded on theological foundations, through which they seek meaning for their being as institutions that continue to preach the Gospel. Furthermore, theological development does not necessarily have to entail church expansion, but may become a form of self-understanding in relation to the society in which they are placed, and that includes the co-religionists of that society. The theology and missiology to which each church subscribes controls how each church acts out its mission. There are various theologies which have developed as responses to different religious, social, political and other compelling exigencies. Recent developments such as theologies of religious pluralism and of interreligious dialogue can be seen as progressive approaches to understand and relate to the world of many faiths and saviors. They often sound prescriptive to the outsiders of the particular theological world, for they still dwell on the centrality of Christian dogma while implicitly attempting to walk into other religious traditions which may already have their own profound economy of salvation with revered savior figures. This theological superiority often has in its mind an image of the 'other' that is deficient. It is a colonial construct of 'otherness' (alterity) which remains obstinate and is what co-religionists constantly suspect is a new manifestation of hegemony, ambition, and subjugation in a different form.

I am arguing that even a theological superiority within certain church traditions draws its power from the type of argument which assumes "... the Christian faith will continue to imply a 'fullness' of divine manifestation and revelation in Jesus Christ not realized elsewhere with the same fullness of sacramentality" (Dupuis 1997: 204). This non-negotiable basis of the Christian kerygma (announcement) is understood to be the doctrine of Jesus Christ as the only possible savior in whom salvation is given to human beings. Dupuis does not deny the centrality of Jesus Christ in the Christian project but leaves space for others to interrogate the 'non-negotiability' of the Christian claim to universal salvation. His suggestion for a 'theology of religious pluralism' (his term) may be adequate as a generic approach to the world of many faiths, but it is also equally necessary to develop a theology alongside each tradition of the 'religious other' that Christianity encounters, as this encounter is capable of changing both camps internally. The envisaged change may not be overt but it is inevitable.

Working out an appropriate theology of religions involves a collective search to understand what constitutes the notion of salvation and religious praxis. This has to be seen as real and practical, an endeavor in which churches and people of different faiths become part of a process of self-interrogation in order to create a path for negotiation, consensus and compromise. This is a basic religious provisionalism arrived at through long processes of interaction among traditions at various levels. There are several attempts in this direction; most popular among them are the interreligious dialogue groups of various emphases, with creative designations such as the British model of local interreligious initiatives nationally networked under the Interfaith Network UK, based in London. Others include Sri Lankan and Indian experiment initiatives by academics, spiritual guru led campaigns, and programmes led by study centers, all of which have enabled new relations between groups with divergent beliefs. A second example is the Scriptural Reasoning exercise, begun by the

Abrahamic traditions, more particularly in the UK. Thirdly, comparative theology helps individuals and groups to see at depth the texts which each of them values and to value the same of the other. Fourthly, there is the intertextual reading of the Holy Books, pioneered by the Mar Thoma church groups in Kerala, India. These innovative attempts by co-religionists all have both high and low moments when they are confronted with each other's core beliefs, but they could resolve them amicably if they continue with relationships built on mutual respect—which is what I myself have experienced in all of the above four experiments.

Christian theology has to struggle with the question how it wishes to handle the truth claims of co-religionists. If Christians understand their universality as the extension of their particularity and an expansion of the church at the expense of or even the extinction of other traditions, then it is based on a conquest mindset. If the mission of the church is a triumphalistic proclamation of Jesus Christ over other co-saviors, then it is understood as an absorption of other communities, which is obviously no different to colonial Christianity. This attitude drives co-religionists to be consistently reluctant to initiate conversations or agree to dialogue with their Christian counterparts. The residual fears of colonial subjugation, missionary hegemony, and the political and military capability of their Western counterparts haunt the former colonized global South. As much as there is a particularity of co-religionists, so there is also the same in the case of the Lordship of Christ, whose particularity may be theologically central to Christians but revisable in the light of interreligious encounter. While elucidating Samartha's views on the subject of mission, Wesley Ariarajah states that he felt the question of Christ's Lordship needs re-examination. Ariarajah agrees with Samartha and says: "even though the concept is central to the New Testament, it does not mean that it was faithfully developed in Western theology" (2001: 4). The Christian claim to universality may appeal religiously to co-religionists, but that universality based on a particular Christian soteriology may not be fully admissible to them, as they themselves are familiar with the concept of the savior and another sense of universality. This is what Christian pluralists have helped the churches undertake over the years. However, doing theology alongside co-religionists is neither a denial of each tradition's particular understanding nor an underestimation of their own universal appeal. It may be a community-based praxis that requires religious literacy, multi-cultural competence, community diplomacy, social skills, and the political maturity of all those engaged in this process. Engaging with co-religionists further clarifies what theological commitment the churches have to make in order to 'feel native' alongside other theologies and spiritualities.

This critical engagement is key to devising a theology of mission that respects the dignity and equality of co-religionists.

The twin issues of the displacement of roles and questions of identity in this process become peripheral, not because their resolution is less important but because the engaged parties discover their potential now as co-religionists and not as 'us' and 'them,' which is, as Said reminded us, 'a colonial legacy.' Theology alongside co-religionists is a movement from the 'centre' of a commanding position, to the 'circle' of an inquiring position, where 'dignity of difference,' equality of status, and civic responsibility become the guiding principles.

Conclusion: No 'Self' without the 'Other'

This subtitle for the conclusion to this chapter could sound like yet another absolute position statement which I have been debating ever since I read Said's *Orientalism*. He is also accused of making such absolute statements, especially in that text, and while most of his critics in fact misunderstood Said, alternative explanations did clear matters to some extent. I wish to provide a concluding argument to this position even if the statement is described as either a soft or a hard approach to reality. Let me take an example from the Christian world.

As we know, Evangelicalism is a globalised but nebulous presence of Christianity. Its praxis is wrapped in a spiritual ideology subscribing to a specific brand of theology, passionate about reaching out to those *not* in its fold. It could well be described as its deeply committed 'otherwardness' to which I have referred above. This global Evangelicalism has no centrally accepted leader of its own, but it ardently pursues a mission: that 'others, even including Catholics, must finally become 'us.' The basis of the Evangelical and evangelistic thrust is that the 'other' should one day become like 'us.' This 'theologico-spiritual ideology' and militant thinking about 'seeking souls' is similar to certain development models like trade and financial institutions which function in society and which today have almost become king-makers and custodians of international business. They relentlessly advocate a model and a set of objectives which they think are good, cost-effective, and efficient, growth-promoting and productive. Their position is that 'they' must adopt 'our' economic reasoning in order to develop, prosper, and grow. What I wish to argue is that there is no position of 'self' without the 'other'; it is not in making the 'other' the 'self' that the 'self' achieves its own emancipation or highest good.

It is this ideology which pushes itself and states 'there is no alternative' (TINA) for the finance-led fiscal imperatives manipulating international trade and its market dominance. However, postcolonial critical theory evokes within it a proposition that 'there are several alternatives' (TASA), and different ways of thinking and analysis. This is emancipatory for the 'other' to think and work innovatively. The concept of TINA is perceived and operative as a position where different manifestations of social and cultural intrusions and political and economic hegemonies are pressing the global South to comply unconditionally with the agendas they are reluctant to be part of. These invasive paradigms that wish to pulverize alternatives of the 'other' continue to promote 'self' as the reason for existence. The 'other' battles to hold on to its cultural, religious, even tribal and clannish roots in order to resist the hegemony at all costs; the 'other' refuses the call of the dominant voice.

Acceptance of religious identity by both majorities and minorities is on the same basis, that is, self-preservation, and it may seem normal for each group. However, if a group consciousness compels them to a view of superior self-worth over and above the 'rest,' then survival of the 'other' is under threat. Any resistance then becomes the only means to self-preservation. The 'religious other' insists on their religious identity because it might be the *only* means left for them to express their grievance, contest for their space, display their protest, and pursue a window for dialogue and understanding among other more honest and reasonable interlocutors.

Bibliography

Ariarajah, S.W. (2001). "Some Glimpses into the Theology of Dr. Stanley Samartha." *Current Dialogue* 38: 15–29.

Buruma, I., and Margalit, A. (2004). *Occidentalism: The West in the Eyes of its Enemies*. London and New York, NY: The Penguin Press.

Carrier, J.G. (1995). *Occidentalism: Images of the West*. Oxford: Oxford University Press.

Douglas, M. (1970). *Natural Symbols: Explorations in Cosmology*. London: Barrie & Rockliff.

Douglas, M. (1978). *Cultural Bias*. Occasional Papers of the Royal Anthropological Institute of Great Britain and Ireland. Vol. 35. London: Royal Anthropological Institute.

Hettiarachchi, S. (2012). *Faithing the Native Soil: Dilemmas and Aspirations of Postcolonial Buddhists and Christians in Sri Lanka*. Colombo: Self-published.

Hick, J. (1967). "The World Religions in God's Plan of Salvation." In: J. Neuner (ed.). *Christian Revelation and World Religions*. London: Burns and Oates.

———. (1973). *God and the Universe of Faiths*. New York, NY: St. Martins Press.

Levinas, E. (1969 [1961]). *Totality and Infinity*. Transl. Alphonso Lingis. Pittsburgh, PA: Duquesne University Press.

Levinas, E. (1999 [1970]). *Alterity and Transcendence*. Transl. Michael B. Smith. New York, NY: Columbia University Press.

Migliore, L.D. (2004). *Faith Seeking Understanding: An Introduction to Christian Theology*. Grand Rapids, MI: Wm. B. Eerdmans.

Pieris, A. (1988). *Love Meets Wisdom: A Christian Experience of Buddhism*. Maryknoll, NY: Orbis Books.

Race, A. (1993). *Christians and Religious Pluralism*. Rev. ed. London: SCM Press.

———. (2001). *Interfaith Encounter: The Twin Tracks of Theology and Dialogue*. London: SCM Press.

Raskin, J. (1971). *The Mythology of Imperialism*. New York, NY: Random House.

Said, E. (1995 [1978]). *Orientalism*. London: Penguin Books.

Samartha, S. (1991). *One Christ, Many Religions*. Maryknoll, NY: Orbis Books.

Sugritharajah, R.S. (1993). *Asian Faces of Jesus*. London: SCM Press.

Thangaraj., M.T. (1994). *Crucified Guru: An Experiment in Cross-Cultural Christology*. Nashville, TN: Abingdon Press.

CHAPTER 12

After Deconstruction: A 'Weak' Theology of Religions?

Kristin Beise Kiblinger

Introduction

John D. Caputo is an influential American philosopher and theologian who promotes what he calls 'weak' theology.[1] His work, especially *The Prayers and Tears of Jacques Derrida: Religion without Religion* (1997) and *The Weakness of God: A Theology of the Event* (2006), has generated much interest in the relevance of Derrida's deconstruction for theology and has helped popularize Derrida among the religious studies community.

Caputo's theology has much in common with Alan Race's work. Like Race, Caputo, too:

- thinks that Christianity needs to respond to modern philosophy, science, and historical consciousness;
- is concerned with practical relevance and not just theory;
- stresses ways that every theology and religious language is historically conditioned;
- admits that, because theologies are conditioned by the needs of their times, all theologies are merely provisional (Race 1983: 8);
- argues that "acknowledging the human component and cultural relativity of religion in no way threatens the validity ... of religion," (quoting Rita Gross, Race 2001: 34);
- sees the potential of new interpretations of Jesus to change Christianity's relationship to other religions (Race 1983: 107);
- wants to shift away from literal readings of sacred texts, recognizing the importance of hermeneutics (Race 1983: 147);

---

1 Caputo writes in note 9 on pp. 301–2 of *Weakness of God* that his weak theology is formed "on analogy" to Vattimo's "weak thought," Derrida's notion of a "weak force," and Benjamin's "weak messianic force." It is also used by Jeffrey Robbins, "Weak Theology," *Journal of Cultural and Religious Theory* 5, no. 2 (April 2004) (www.jcrt.org); and Ulrich Engel, O.P., "Religion and Violence: Plea for a Weak Theology *in tempore belli*," *New Blackfriars* 82 (2001): 558–60.

© KONINKLIJKE BRILL NV, LEIDEN, 2016 | DOI 10.1163/9789004324077_014

- establishes religious experience as the best starting point for theology, interested in "follow[ing] through the consequences of philosophical observations about how knowledge comes to human consciousness and then appl[ying] this to religious consciousness," (Race 1983: 139–40; Race 2001: 35);
- approaches the questions raised by religious plurality from the perspective of the transformative purpose of religions (Race 2001: 31);
- defers any final knowledge to the eschaton or future (Race 1983: 146).

However, unlike Race, Caputo does not focus on the theology of religions in particular, and yet his work has important implications for the theology of religions; it is the purpose of this piece to draw them out. In doing so, a key point of difference with Race's view will appear: namely, while Race argues for a pluralist position, Caputo's system achieves the benefits of the pluralist position yet suggests that the debate between inclusivism and pluralism is 'undecidable.' As this essay explains Caputo's thought system, it suggests that perhaps Race's theology should be 'weakened,' à la Caputo.

Caputo's Weak Theology

In Caputo's work, weakness is thematized in two main ways. First, Caputo argues that we should acknowledge the weakness *of our theological discourse.* He champions a "weak" deconstructive theology, saying that the theology he advocates is "somewhat undernourished as opposed to the hearty and robust ones that populate the tradition," which have been too in love with power (2006: 7–8). Confessing the limits of our epistemic situation, Caputo's theology will "not serve up the *Sache selbst* ['the thing itself'] in all its palpable presence ... but only a tearful concession that the *Sache selbst* always slips away" (2006: 7). The theology here is weakened by undecidability and translatability and thus is quite open-ended (2006: 9). Given this, Caputo wants to set aside metaphysics and "strong" onto-theology in favor of hermeneutics, phenomenology, and poetics. All of this means that not only are the goal and yield of his theology "weak" or humble, but also that *we* should be humble *about* our theologies— i.e., vis-à-vis others' thought systems, proceeding with humility and openness rather than with force, dogmatism, or self-righteousness.

Second, Caputo wants to combine this modesty about our theological systems with a modesty about *our conception of God.* He explores envisioning the sacred not as God Almighty, but rather as a "weak" force (2006: 8). The name of God, he says, is the name of a call, not a causality. It is a provocation towards a different future rather than being a determinate presence. It is a specter of a possibility and hence is subject to contingencies. Caputo is after the moment when the order of being is interrupted by something utterly new, when the usual is shocked by something other and economies are disrupted and overcome by a loving excess. His is a theology of this moment or *event*, not of an entity.

It needs to be emphasized from the outset, however, that the weakness of which Caputo speaks is not weakness *simpliciter*, but rather is "provocative and uplifting" (2006: 14); there is, he says, an "existential intensity" to weak theology such that "weak theology does not preclude strong faith" (2006: 11, 121). This kind of weakness or powerlessness, he warns, should not be underestimated, for it can move mountains (2006: 14–5). Thus, for Caputo, weakness is not a loss but a gain. Recognition of it serves a soteriological purpose, and "by untying the name of God from the order of being, it releases the event, setting it free as a vocative force" (2006: 9). This will be explained further below.

Caputo's starting point is the postmodern emphasis on our conditioned existence: we are all historically and culturally situated; we all think within particular linguistic systems; each of us is shaped by our individual experiences. For these sorts of reasons, we are all bound by finite perspectives. There is no way to get outside of our conditioning in order to have a pure meta-view free of such factors. Here down below, until the kingdom comes, until we reach union with *Brahman*, this side of nirvana, etc., this is our predicament. Caputo insists that we must confess this weakness. Our theological discourses, we must admit, are conditioned and thus should have a certain modesty and provisionality in light of this, affecting how we proceed.

When Caputo wants to refer to the *un*conditioned or Absolute, that might be symbolized in endless ways, all of which are conditioned. Using Christian language for now (as Caputo often but not always does[2]), let us refer to the unconditioned as the kingdom. Caputo says that while we hope and pray for the kingdom, meanwhile what we have is the church—i.e., the conditioned. Any kingdom (or unconditioned) that appears, by virtue of its coming, in being received by us thereby becomes conditioned, so that the unconditioned always slips away; it is deferred, ever 'to come.' (This is why Caputo's theology is accurately described as having a messianic or prophetic structure.) The acknowledgement of our conditionedness means that whatever we have, whatever is

---

2 Because it is integral to Caputo's system that no language is final, he deliberately continues
   to mix up his terms, shifting between Christian and non-Christian or between religious and
   non-religious language: kingdom, justice, democracy, gift, prayer, hope, call, etc.

present, we must remember, is merely a church and not the kingdom for which we long.

Once we can admit and accept this situation, then we can see the need for, and value of, deconstruction. Caputo presents deconstruction as the hermeneutics of the kingdom or of the desire for God/the unconditioned. Deconstruction perpetually exposes the conditioned in the name of the unconditioned. It deconstructs out of commitment to that which is not deconstructible. Our laws, for example, are conditioned, limited, imperfect. Therefore, we need to keep deconstructing or re-visiting our laws in order to aspire towards or release justice, which is not conditioned, not able to be captured completely by our conditioned languages and historical forms. The same goes for religion. We need to deconstruct our conditioned religions and theological discourses in the name of the sacred, which can never be adequately grasped by our constrained ways of speaking and symbolizing.

The human tendency, however, is to idolatry. We confuse our conditioned objects with the Absolute. We elevate our church's conditioned words to the status of the kingdom or Truth. We forget that we are human, living in a finite mode. We treat our conditioned things as though they could be unconditioned as a way to puff up ourselves and put down others, defending our place at the top. Claiming access somehow to the unconditioned, in Caputo's view, is either regressing to belief in magic or it is promoting ourselves over others by claiming to have some kind of special access that others lack. This tends to make us dogmatic. It can make us militant. It stems from insecurity, conceit, and similar flaws.

We would do better to stick with the confession of the weakness of our theology and religion. Caputo writes:

> For if there were a Secret Truth, who could we trust with it? Who would not spill blood in its name? It is better that the Secret remain a secret and not be *given* .... If the Secret were given, there would be a terrible fight, a war to the death, over who would get to have it, administer it, interpret it, protect it, speak in its name, rule in and rule out distortions of it. There would surely be a war over which city would be its capital, which language would be the official language, and even over who would have the rights to the T-shirts. If the Secret were given, this gift would quickly turn to poison.
>
> 2003B: 16

For these sorts of reasons, Caputo speaks of a new Enlightenment that is "enlightened about Enlightenment" with a "renewed appreciation for the dark" and for the "dangers of overexposure to the sun" (2006: 291).

Because every earthly answer is conditioned, we would do better to keep questioning and not treat our answers as though they could be more than they are. That is, when it comes to the unconditioned, rather than claiming to know, we should stick to faith. In order to achieve authentic, radical transformation (*metanoia*), we have to put *ourselves* in question, which we cannot do while clinging tightly to our conditioned beliefs and mental habits. To turn to God, we must be willing to be overturned, uprooted, unhinged. (2006: 287) To be open to the unconditioned, Caputo would say, we must deconstruct.

Furthermore, just as 'strong theology' (i.e., theology that does not admit its conditionedness) leads to the above-mentioned problems, likewise divine images of strength tend to cause trouble. Divine images of power spread to and infect human models, leading humans to claim power over other humans, making in-groups and out-groups, and thus tending to cause struggle, oppression, and bloodshed (2006: 78–9).

Process theology has offered a critique of traditional conceptions of God as all-powerful, in part to help with these issues and with the problem of evil (2006: 87). Similarly, weak theology can help with the problem of evil; Caputo says that it is because God is but a weak force that Auschwitzes have been possible (2006: 94). Moreover, in the preface to *Weakness of God*, Caputo reflects on the tsunami that occurred in South Asia at the end of 2004 as he was finishing writing the book. He considers how religious leaders in response to the tragedy spoke of the mystery of God's ways or of God using the tsunami to punish the human race for sin. Caputo imagines telling that to the horrified father who lost his grip on his child and then watched helplessly as the poor babe was carried out to sea. Caputo says that he finds this explanation, this image of God the Powerful, to be blasphemous. This shows, he says, the "bankruptcy of thinking of God as a strong force with the power to intervene upon natural processes like the shifting movements of the crustal plates around the Pacific rim." Weak theology, he asserts, is "an attempt to think of God otherwise" (2006: xi).

Caputo works with imagery far from that of power, strength, certainty, sovereignty, or Being. Instead, he symbolizes our inability to access the unconditioned with the contrasting—much weaker—image of a specter. He says that we need to allow ourselves to be haunted—by questions, other interpretations, other cultural frameworks, remembrance of our limitations, and so on. In addition, for Caputo, the *unconditioned itself* is envisioned weakly as whispery and ghost-like, having an in-between status and occupying a gray area intolerable to metaphysicians but with which hermeneuts and poets are more at home.

On the one hand, any unconditioned that appears would thereby become conditioned, so that the unconditioned always slips away and we are cut off from it. In this sense the unconditioned cannot be here or be grasped. On the other hand, though, the unconditioned prods our conditioned world, its very absence having an experiential impact, inducing an aspiration and dissatisfaction, such as when justice makes us restless and unsatisfied with our conditioned laws, inspiring us to reform. That *is* a kind of presence for justice, although only of an elusive, limited, 'weak' sort. Like a ghost, this is a kind of reality or existence but not the usual kind. Its mode is vocative, not nominative (and, importantly, it puts us in the accusative, summoning us to action). Recognizing our epistemic situation and committed to setting aside metaphysics in favor of phenomenology, Caputo would not exactly want to say that there is a ghost, but rather that something ghostly is happening—i.e. an event is experienced (1997: 144). Events, though, move by haunting and disturbing, by a spirit of inspiration, by an awakening of love, not by brute strength or the strong force of efficient cause (2006: 88). This is why Caputo writes that the name of God is "a promise ... without an army to enforce it, without sovereign power to coerce it" (2006: 90). It is a weak force, yet this is a power of its own kind.

In addition to specters and spirits, another image of weakness upon which Caputo draws is that of something lost. In particular, texts, including sacred texts, never reach a final destination but instead invariably are 'lost.' Caputo understands our inability to know the unconditioned transparently as analogous to our inability ever to settle the meaning of a text. Since all readings are conditioned, none can be the last word. Thus, texts never quite arrive. They are lost when they are understood differently, redacted, translated, misunderstood, applied newly, etc.

Lost items, again like ghosts, have a complicated, betwixt-and-between status. As seekers, we sense that a lost item indeed exists. There is a degree to which we do feel its presence, which is why we feel compelled to seek after it, so that the item has a kind of reality or existence for us, even though the item eludes our grasp. In parallel fashion, Caputo says that his weak theology does not make God graspable or entitative but nor does it reduce God to mere metaphor, projection, or fiction (2006: 123). That is, Caputo insists that with this approach he does not at all mean to diminish God's name; on the contrary, Caputo thinks that this way of theologizing raises God up "beyond entity to the event ... the inner heart or driving force in things" (2006: 123). "My reduction is a magnification," he writes. Moreover: "The name of God is the name of an event ... neither real nor unreal, but not yet real .... The world cannot contain it, and so it makes the world restless until it is brought forth, which never quite happens" (2006: 123). Caputo says that deconstruction is not realism, "not because it is in love with illusion, but because it desires what is more than the real rather than settling for what is less, for the real is always deconstructable" (2007: 79).

As compared to the ghost imagery, the imagery of something lost or elusive adds the important further point that when an item is lost, we seem to long for it all the more. Lost or elusive items elicit a desire in us to pursue them. That desire, at least, *is* here, even if the item itself remains in question because it is out of reach. This is one crucial practical benefit of picturing God, or the unconditioned, this way—namely, motivation to seek and bring the unconditioned increases. In contrast, the unconditioned actually arriving, claiming knowledge of it, or thinking that we have captured it with our words and symbols would instead have the detrimental effect of quelling that urgency and passion.

Additional images or examples of weak forces might be loving enemies, forgiving the unforgivable, mercy transcending the economy of vengeance, or mustering hope in the face of despair (2006: 96). What they all share in common, Caputo explains, is that each represents a passion for the possibility of *the* impossible. Caputo comments that when you go to the possible, you just get more of the same. The only real movement, "the only event," he says, "... is to go to the impossible," i.e., to something more unconditional, to what exceeds the horizon (1997: 50).

Expanding on Derrida's *Given Time*, Caputo unpacks this notion of 'the impossible' with the idea of the gift. The gift is a paradigm for the impossible and helps us see how the unconditional enters our experience. The idea is that pure gifts are impossible, because as soon as something is given, there is an economy that sets in and conditions the gift, even though true gifts are meant to be performed irrespective of any economy. Once a gift is given, inevitably, there is then a debt, such as a debt of gratitude or an expectation of reciprocity, and there is reward, such as feeling generous or now being owed. Although we intend to give purely, the take creeps in. We aim for an excess but are pulled back into economy. The conditioning that always mediates the gift, or the condition in which gifting occurs, makes the pure gift impossible. However—and this part is essential—Caputo is trying to say that *this does not mean that we should not give or that there is no gift* but only that the gift belongs to a different order or mode. The gift is a glimpse, an interruption or breaking out, one that constitutes sacred space and time (2007: 69–72).[3]

---

3 "*The* impossible" refers not to a logical but to a phenomenological impossibility. That there is an unconditional is something of which we can conceive. It does not defy possibility logically. However, that we could ever *know or experience* the unconditional without in the process conditioning it, that is a phenomenological impossibility (2006: 317 n. 1).

The mode or order of the gift is described, therefore, not as nominative but as *vocative*. Analyzing our intimation of the unconditioned, Caputo suggests that our experience of the unconditioned, or the sacred Other, is an experience like that of a *call*. This is yet another 'weak' image. When a distant loved one calls us, to some extent we feel his or her presence, but simultaneously the caller is present in only a limited way. Again, this draws out our longing for fuller presence. Analogously, we do not have—we cannot have—full access to the unconditioned and yet we have some semblance of it because we feel called or solicited by it and yearn for it. This analysis of experience Caputo describes as a peculiar sort of phenomenology because the experience is that of what is *not given*. It is a phenomenology of *anonymity* in that the unconditioned, cut off from us, is anonymous or undecidable (1999: 206–8; 2003b: 2–6).

Thus, it is important to realize that, even though we experience the call of the unconditioned, we cannot know the caller. Caputo wants to suspend "the question of the name or status of the caller" and stick to the phenomenology of the call (2006: 115). Caputo writes: "Whether over and beyond ... the lived experience of the call and of being on call, there is some entitative cause calling, some entity or hyper-entity out there with a proper name, verifiable by a metaphysical argument or certifiable by a divine revelation, is no part of my hypothesis, one way or the other," and "I leave that question to fluctuate in that domain of undecidability wherein all concrete decisions are made, which has the effect of intensifying this decision .... No one has authorized us to settle" the issue (2006: 40). The call originates from "God knows where, from something I know not what" (1997: 113 4).[4] This is why, to be technically correct, when Caputo refers to God or the kingdom/unconditioned, he typically adds "if there is such a thing." The non-knowing is central to this thought system.

Indeed, Caputo's argument is not only that conditioning makes knowing out of reach but that knowing is incompatible with authentic faith and religiosity. To understand, consider the famous story of the call upon Abraham to sacrifice his son. Following typical Christian readings of this story, Caputo argues that if Abraham had known with certainty the existence or nature of the caller asking him to do the unfathomable, it would ruin the power of the story, for then there would have been a cost-benefit analysis on Abraham's part, rather than an impassioned commitment and selfless submission, with all of its inherent risks. If Abraham had *known*, Caputo writes, he "would not be the father of

---

4   Speaking of the call and alluding to Kierkegaard, Caputo writes, "If you do not have the least idea of what that means, you would probably be better served to stop reading and check the stock market page to see how your portfolio is doing" (2006: 113).

faith but of good investments and estate planning" (2003b: 14). Abraham would have remained within an economy rather than transcending it for a moment with an extraordinary, unconditional, impossible obedience and love. The pursuit of the unconditional is about such passion, not knowledge (which, by the way, is why it can go wrong). God is given not to cognition but to desire. Given Kantian limits, we have to say 'yes' on the model of Abraham or, for another example, on the model of Mary at the time of the Annunciation. Theirs are choices with a risk, passions with a fallibility, not a knowledge or something groundable. Caputo reminds us that "religion isn't religious when it's reduced to rewards gained for expenditures made ..." (2006: 248).[5] Connecting this back to weakness and humility versus power and certainty, if Abraham *knew* that there was a God and, moreover, if Abraham's conception of God was *Almighty*, then we have a problem. Abraham's obedience, or Mary's yes, would then be a self-interested, calculated, reasonable, economic bow to the Omnipotent rather than the sort of faith for which they are famous in Christian terms. Theirs would be "an unworthy way to treat God; it is unworthy to think of God in terms of his power to deliver the goods, which is like loving a cow for its milk, as Meister Eckhart says" (2006: 79).

Applying weak theology to sacred texts and stories like that of Abraham, Caputo suggests that we ought to see scriptures neither as divine revelations nor as records of supernatural occurrences from long ago but as calls or appeals about a way to be (2006: 117–8). Their truth is what is trying to come, and this fires our sense of responsibility, moving us to action, to doing the truth (*facere veritatem*). Proceeding phenomenologically and hermeneutically, the starting question is not what there is, what happened long ago, how miracles are possible, or which holy book is *the* book, but instead how does the unconditioned appear in our experience? What *event* do these stories harbor? (2006: 240).[6]

---

5   This is why Caputo asks, "When I pray, am I not also praying that there is someone to hear my prayer?" When he prays, he is praying that his prayer has a prayer, "that there is something to prayer.... The prayer on behalf of prayer itself, is structured into the prayer..." (2003a: 40). This is another way of explaining how and why non-knowing is inherent in religiosity.

6   Speaking of stories, the story of creation is perhaps one of the biggest challenges for Caputo. In trying to reconceive God as a weak force and convince Christians that a weak theology can be a Christian theology, Caputo must address the firmly-rooted image of God as Omnipotent Creator who creates out of nothing (which Caputo describes as a power discourse told by a metaphysician) (2006: 59). Chapters 3 and 4 of *The Weakness of God* take up this task, and, with some help from Catherine Keller's theology of creation, Caputo argues that even in the creation stories of Genesis, there is the possibility of a reading that is compatible with weak theology. Caputo finds in the stories marks of unforeseeability, riskiness, and chance, although the tradition has suppressed them. He finds many instances of indeterminacy and

With strong theology, working from either magic or power, we might read the Passion narrative such that Jesus could have come down from the cross. According to the conventional notion of kenosis [divine self-emptying], weakness was really a demonstration of power, because if weakness is voluntary, then underneath is really strength (2006: 303 n. 24). Instead, Caputo thinks that the divinity is in Jesus' helplessness and powerlessness, which were real, and in how Jesus' death was a protest; the power of it was that it was a call, from which a Spirit rose up (2006: 43–4): "The Romans could extinguish Jesus but not his memory," which constitutes a weak force (2006: 94). Although seemingly impossible, surprisingly, this weak force confounded the reigning powers.

Related to this, in Caputo's estimation, penal atonement theology does not work because it is the world and not God that thinks in terms of paybacks. "The coin of the realm in the kingdom is forgiveness," a weak force, not power to demand punishment or mete out deserved suffering (2006: 232). "When the prodigal son returns and says *metanoo*, I have turned around, the father throws a party. That is how events work. He does not send his son to be crucified as a just repayment" (2006: 233). God is not an accountant, not the Great Power to settle all scores but the weak force of unconditional love and the gift of grace (2006: 44).

Likewise, stories of Jesus' miracles, Caputo thinks, should not be read as magic or demonstrations of supernatural power interrupting natural processes. That would be disincarnation, not incarnation (2006: 239). It would pit the miracle claims of one religious group against those of another and privilege the ones supposedly following the most advanced wizard. Instead, Caputo sees miracles, like gifts, as signifying the event of the impossible within the context of a theology of the event (2006: 238–9). "A miracle," Caputo writes, "has hermeneutical authenticity on the plane of the event by figuring in a purely narratival and imaginative space a transforming experience in our lives …; a miracle is the genuine but weak force of God" (2006: 239). When seen thusly in poetic space, miracle stories of various religious figures no longer need conflict, for they are not about whose god or teacher is most powerful in that sense. In short, Caputo seeks a "phenomenological transcription of Jesus' mighty deeds …. that resists the temptation to turn them into deeds of magic" (2006: 248).

---

sees mutability inscribed in things. He sees God not as bringing beings into being but calling them into life, not making them there but making them stir. Declaring things good becomes in part a promise, enjoining us to keep faith that creation is good (2006: 71). We are asked to say "yes" to second God's "yes" (2006: 74).

To illustrate, in the famous story of Lazarus, Caputo focuses on Jesus' weeping at Lazarus' death (2006: 236–258). *That*, for Caputo, is the key image, which is an image of weakness and finitude, not an image of power to perform a spectacular feat. The Lazarus story, for a weak theologian, is not one of Jesus undoing Lazarus' death. Martha already believes that Lazarus will rise on the last day, so "that is not what she is asking of Jesus" (2006: 252). Furthermore, according to Caputo, "the Johannine contrivance that Jesus purposely stayed away for two days" reflects an "all too human love of displaying power … as if Jesus would be the source of immense human suffering in order to stage a display of divine might" (2006: 258). No, Caputo imagines that Jesus wept because he could not get there in time and Lazarus was gone. The crux of the story is really about what happens with Martha and Mary spiritually, not what happens to Lazarus' body. In Caputo's reading, Jesus "does not effect an entitative change but gives new meaning" (2006: 256). The miracle that Caputo fixes on is that somehow there arose hope and renewal in the midst of death and grief when things seemed hopeless. The hope was not related to an afterlife (which belongs to the compensatory calculations of the world, not the kingdom); the hope was related to relief from present pain and conditions (2006: 251). Caputo sees Jesus letting the loss be a loss but seeking the impossible by trying to comfort. Caputo reads the story as about the transformative, salvific effect— the *event*—of compassion and companionship. The messianic time was not a dramatic, nature-defying miracle of divine power, but more modestly (though powerful in its own right) the sitting up through the night, gently consoling by dividing and sharing the grief with Mary and Martha until somehow they were able to come out from their own tombs of darkness and go on (2006: 250, 258). The miracle, thinks Caputo, is in the compassion: "The divinity is in the weakness," not the power (2006: 258). Just as God is an event of pure forgiveness or grace, not an accountant, so God is an extending of compassion, not a magician (2006: 94). Such weak theology allows us to be both in the role of waiting for the messiah and sometimes to occupy the messianic position ourselves (2006: 252).

Weak Theology and the Theology of Religions

The general direction of this approach to Jesus, it seems to me, has much in common with Race's Christology from his chapter "Incarnation and the Theology of Religions" from *Christians and Religious Pluralism*, where Race writes of seeing Jesus and God as "love in action" rather than in pure ontological terms and where Race asks what effect it has upon theology of religions to call the incarnation a myth rather than understanding it literally (1983: 133). Both Race and Caputo are trying to interpret Christianity in a way that resists pre-judging the relative position of faiths, affirms the tradition's profundity, does justice to its universal intent, and promotes dialogue and cooperation without sliding into syncretism (Race, Alan 1983: 146). Caputo certainly does not advocate that we should blend all religious discourses into a single universal one. This is clear when Caputo discusses the role of particularity in deconstruction. Caputo explains that conditioned laws may be universal or generalized rules but that justice is sensitive to particularities and singularities: "Every time we feel unjustly treated by the law we say, 'But this case is different'" (2007: 65). The event happens, Caputo says, when we suspend a universal law to consider the concrete particularity, such as when Jesus healed on the Sabbath. Singularities and differences are that *in virtue of which* there is deconstruction. They are *why* we deconstruct and translate, why interpretation is necessary and ongoing in changing contexts (2006: 140). Therefore, far from desiring to relativize or diminish differences and singularities, Caputo's system very much respects and works from them.

To head off another potential misunderstanding or danger, when Caputo insists that no interpretation is final, he does not mean that anything goes, religiously speaking. Again like Race, even though Caputo has a pluralistic bent, he wants to allow for the possibility that religious insights may not all be equally adequate, for even if no interpretation can be final, there can still be better and worse interpretations, depending on one's conditioned criteria. Caputo would follow Race in saying that he "has not accepted the view that all faiths are equally true, or of equal value, or are ultimately saying the same thing" (Race 1983: 143). Such claims would require the meta-view that Caputo denies is possible. For both Race and Caputo, the way to evaluate religious discourses is by the kind of living they yield and their adequacy in meeting needs and challenges in particular circumstances. Beyond that, "any verification will be eschatological" (Race 1983: 146).

For all of these reasons, Caputo's work shares much with Race's pluralism. For Caputo, as we have said, the truth of sacred texts is not correspondence but a solicitation, and Caputo holds that the structure of an event of solicitation may stir within the scriptures of numerous religious traditions (2006: 116). "That is why there can be more than one religious discourse," he writes, "and why religions do not compete with one another in a zero-sum game in which the truth of one comes at the cost of the falsity of another. The idea of one true religion or religious discourse or body of religious narratives makes no more sense than the idea of one true poem or one true language or one true culture" (2006: 118).

For Caputo, "no name can be allowed to have a lock on the event" because "the distinction between names is relativized in virtue of the endless semantic translatability and deconstructibility of names as opposed to the undeconstructibility of the event ..." (2006: 267–8). Put differently, if we affirm what cannot be named, then it follows that this is an affirmation that can thus be made under many names, or under many religious discourses.[7] Therefore, Caputo says that "we must be prepared to surrender the name" in order to be faithful to the event (2006: 292). We must "explode the notion that there is a name above all other names" (2006: 296). It is not that we should all throw up our hands and resort to silence. We should still use our names, and of course (because of conditioning) everyone privileges some names over others: "The danger is only to think that your name cannot be translated, that if someone does not use it, they are against you" (1997: 68). Caputo advises, "Profess the name of God while making a confession that what is coming might be called something else ..." (2006: 294).[8]

Names may always be conditioned and thus limited, but this does not mean that we should stop speaking our religious languages and refrain from religious commitment, because names can promise something beyond what they can themselves capture. Consider, Caputo says, what we mean when we speak of something being worthy of the name. This refers, he thinks, to the event called for by the name: "Anyone who hears what is resonating in the word 'democracy' (or 'Christianity') ... knows that no existing democracy [or form of Christianity]... is up to what is called for in that name" (2007: 58–9; brackets, but not parentheses, mine). What is called for is never here but always deferred. Hence weak theology hinges not on particular names, but looks to the events harbored in names. Deconstruction is an effort to release these events. The event delivers us from the search for the name of God while the alternative (i.e., reducing event to name) leads to wars (2006: 298, 296). In sum, the issue, Caputo concludes, "is not so much with what name we are to call God, but what the name of God calls for, what it calls upon us to do" (2006: 39).

---

7   Weak theology is not an exception to its own rule in this respect, trying to trump other theologies. Caputo admits that it, too, is conditioned and thus deconstructible. It is not itself a top position but Caputo sees it rather as a way of treating all positions. This is why Caputo invites analogous versions in other traditions (2006: 303 n. 22) and why he says that his theology is an "interim theology," "a work in progress" (2006: 292). "These are," he says, "at present the least bad names we have, names for the conditioned, empirical counterparts of something unforeseeable, unconditional, and nameless" (2006: 294).

8   Caputo's talk about 'names' is an issue that Paul F. Knitter has also debated. See Knitter (1985) and Knitter (1996). Thanks to Paul Hedges for pointing this out in an email to the author on August 6, 2014.

Applying all of this now to Race's famous heuristic, his three categories within the theology of religions; if we rule out exclusivism because no one religious language can be deemed final and we cannot secure certain knowledge,[9] we are then left to decide between inclusivism and pluralism. This is where Race and Caputo part ways. Race, opting for pluralism, suggests that adherents of various faiths could hold onto their differences and "yet realize that the transcendent reality which is disclosed through the [various] languages is ultimately one" (1983: 147). Caputo, in contrast, does not think that we are in a position to know anything about the transcendent reality, including whether it is one, and thus he wants instead to remain agnostic on this matter. Because we are conditioned and thereby severed from unconditioned Truth, how could we know that our languages refer to the same reality or whether there even is such a thing?[10]

Thus, while Race argues for pluralism, from Caputo's perspective, because we are conditioned, how can we know whether one system has the best language and greatest degree of truth and sits atop a spectrum of lesser traditions, or whether instead there are numerous equally true traditions? Where would we be standing? The choice between inclusivism and pluralism is undecidable. This means that pluralism and relativism are specters, but not dogma (and remember that under this system, such hauntings are necessary to faith, not harmful to it). In any case, if we have no choice but to privilege a discourse but now more adamantly confess its conditionedness, and we confess as well the need to deconstruct our discourses perpetually and be haunted by other religious systems, then the categories of inclusivism and pluralism become less useful, even blur or dissolve.

By ruling out the finality of any particular religious language and by claiming that ideal faith requires non-knowing structurally, a weak theology of the event calls into question the very distinction between believer and unbeliever, or between self and religious other. Since no historically determinate name could ever contain the event or be "uniformly desirable" or "impartially accessible," "who may we now say is in and who is out in the kingdom of God? Has not the whole thing been thrown into a holy undecidability?" (Caputo 2006:

---

9   "Are we to think that life is a gamble in which we had to choose between one name or
     another, a shell game in which we had better make the right guess or regret it for all eter-
     nity?" Caputo asks rhetorically. "Are we to imagine that our prayer is in vain if we cannot
     nail down the Proper Name of its addressee?" (2006: 298).

10   Some pluralists might not agree with Race's move of suggesting that various languages
     refer to the same transcendent reality and may instead pursue different strategies in de-
     veloping their pluralism. However, the question that Caputo's work raises for pluralism
     does not depend upon Race's particular move.

289, 277),[11] where between insider and outsider, "the borders of the kingdom become porous" (Caputo 2006: 269). Let theologians of religion join the Psalms (41:1), Matthew (5:5), and Caputo in affirming, "Blessed are the weak!" (2006: 9).

Bibliography

Caputo, John D. (1997). *The Prayers and Tears of Jacques Derrida: Religion without Religion*. Bloomington, IN: Indiana University Press.

———. (1999). "Apostles of the Impossible: On God and the Gift in Derrida and Marion." In: John D. Caputo and Michael J. Scanlon (eds.). *God, the Gift, and Postmodernism*. Bloomington, IN: Indiana University Press. pp. 185–222.

———. (2003a). "A Game of Jacks: A Response to Derrida." In: Mark Dooley (ed.). *A Passion for the Impossible: John D. Caputo in Focus*. Albany: State University of New York. pp. 34–49.

———. (2003b). "God and Anonymity: Prolegomena to an Ankhoral Religion." In: Mark Dooley (ed.). *A Passion for the Impossible: John D. Caputo in Focus*. Albany: State University of New York. pp. 1–19.

———. (2006). *The Weakness of God: A Theology of the Event*. Bloomington: Indiana University Press.

———. (2007). *What Would Jesus Deconstruct? The Good News of Postmodernism for the Church*. Grand Rapids, MI: Baker Academic.

Derrida, Jacques. (1992). *Given Time: I. Counterfeit Money*. Chicago and London: University of Chicago Press.

Knitter, Paul F. (1985). *No Other Name?: A Critical Survey of Christian Attitudes Toward the World Religions*. Maryknoll, NY: Orbis Books.

———. (1996). *Jesus and the Other Names: Christian Mission and Global Responsibility*. Maryknoll, NY: Orbis Books.

Muers, Rachel, and Mike Higton. (2012). *Modern Theology: A Critical Introduction*. New York and London: Routledge.

Race, Alan. (1983) *Christians and Religious Pluralism. Patterns in the Christian Theology of Religions*. London: SCM Press.

———. (2001). *Interfaith Encounter: The Twin Tracks of Theology and Dialogue*. London: SCM Press.

---

11   Rachel Muers and Mike Higton, in their chapter on postmodernism in *Modern Theology: A Critical Introduction*, discussing the thought of Mark C. Taylor, write that "the loss of a secure and stable decoding includes the loss of any ability to securely and stably define what is mine over and against what is not mine... Taylor insists... that the fruit of the death of the self is not annihilation but compassion, which flows from the realization that the boundary between myself and the other is not an absolute distinction" (2012: 350).

CHAPTER 13

Towards a Relational and Humanizing Theology: A Christian-Muslim Dialogue[1]

Oddbjørn Leirvik

Introduction

The notion of 'theology of religion(s),' as it has been developed in the last decades, commonly refers to the self-reflection of a particular religious tradition (mostly, Christianity) when faced with religious pluralism. Alan Race used the expression 'Christian theology of religions' when in 1983 he introduced the oft-cited triad of exclusivism, inclusivism, and pluralism (*Christians and Religious Pluralism*, 1983). Whereas Jacques Dupuis (1997) aimed at 'a Christian theology of religious pluralism,' Harold Coward (2000) covered six religions when some years later he wrote about *Pluralism in the World Religions*. Paul Knitter moved from critically surveying 'Christian attitudes toward the world religions' (cf. the subtitle of *No Other Name*, 1985) to presenting 'theologies of religions' in a more general sense (*Introducing Theologies of Religions*, 2002—note the double plural).

Theologies of religions are created in response to religious pluralism—either in the form of traditional *plurality* (where different faiths coexist as entities that can be neatly separated) or modern *pluralism* (where the borders are more fluid). In the context of modern pluralism, traditional positions of dominion are challenged by modern ideals of equality and non-discrimination, and inherited stereotypes of the other are challenged by everyday interaction across religious divides and by interreligious friendships. All major religions have their own ways of dealing with traditional plurality. But modern pluralism poses different kinds of challenges, which cut deeper and have potentially more wide-ranging consequences for the religious traditions.

In what follows, I will reflect as a Christian theologian in dialogue with Islam. These two traditions cannot be neatly separated, intertwined as they are in history and contemporary societies. With regard to overarching theological reasoning, 'Christianity' (as an ecumenical whole) is certainly

---

[1] The following text is based on chapter 8 of the author's book *Interreligious Studies: A Relational Approach to Religious Activism and the Study of Religion* (2014), with kind permission from Bloomsbury.

distinctively different from 'Islam.' But in the case of disagreement—be it ethical or theological—the fault lines do not coincide with the boundaries between the two religions.

Abandoning Supersessionist Claims?

Modern pluralism destabilizes traditional perceptions (ecumenical as well as
interreligious ones) of the supremacy of one's faith, reflecting the fact that all
major religions and confessions have been conceived in situations of conflict.
Many theologians claim that, in the context of modern pluralism, traditional
ideas of supremacy and supersession must be abandoned just as—in political
terms—hierarchical models for multi-religious coexistence such as the Islamic *dhimmi* system must be replaced with equal citizenship. In an article from
2007, titled "'My God is Bigger than Your God!' Time for Another Axial Shift
in the History of Religion," Paul Knitter notes that theology is not just about
God—it has also to do with earthly claims of superiority:

> Religious people who make universal claims of superiority believe that
> it is God's will that, if not now then eventually, all people will become
> or should become members of their divinely constituted superior reli-
> gion.... We come to what is for me the most impelling reason why the
> religions are being called to an axial shift regarding claims of superiority:
> the link between claims of religious superiority and privilege and calls to
> religious aggression and violence.
>
> KNITTER 2007: 103, 105

Critically aware of the potentially violent consequences of traditional claims
of supremacy, Knitter calls for a shift from superior truth claims to what
he calls 'the mutuality model,' in which "many true religions [are] called to
dialogue" (Knitter 2002: 109ff.). He strongly believes that such an 'axial shift'
is in fact possible, because of what he calls the mystical and the ethical-
prophetic elements in all religions which—in his terminology—constitute
'bridges' between religious traditions that may otherwise seem to be worlds
apart.

Catherine Cornille, in her book *The Im-Possibility of Interreligious Dialogue*
(2008), expresses a similar view when under the heading of 'Interconnection'
she speaks of ethical issues as 'common external challenges' and mystical
traditions as 'common experience.' It is not clear, however, why Cornille sees
ethical concerns such as sustainable development and alleviation of suffering

as 'external' challenges. In Knitter's reasoning, the ethical bridge seems, rather, to be conceived of as an 'internal' construction built on the religions' strong prophetic traditions. Knitter's solution to the seemingly unsurpassable problem of superlative language in the religious traditions, such as the proclamation of Jesus as the only way, is to see such expressions as a kind of 'love language' meant for internal consumption only. He also calls for a dialogical Christology which—in conjunction with John Cobb—sees Christ as 'the Way which is open to Other Ways' (Knitter 2002: 119–23, 156f.).

Such solutions to modern annoyances with claims of supremacy seem not, however, to be acceptable to other theologians who would otherwise be ready to tread the ethical and mystical bridges between the religions. For instance, in an article from 1999 titled "The Last Trump Card: Islam and the Supersession of Other Faiths," the Islamic theologian Tim Winter (*aka* Abdul-Hakim Murad) criticizes Paul Knitter, John Hick, and Muslim pluralist theologians such as Fazlur Rahman, Farid Esack, and Mahmoud Ayoub for identifying supersessionist claims with confrontation:

> Hick, Knitter and their Muslim travelling-companions are... mistaken in suggesting that foundational claims for the present centrality of one's own community in salvation history ineluctably lead believers towards *hubris*, discord and confrontation.
>
> WINTER 1999: 152

According to Winter, the doctrine of Islam's abrogation (*naskh*) of prior religions is constitutive of Islam itself: "As in its treatment of Judaism, but more sharply, the Muslim revelation deploys arguments against a historically-evolved Christianity in order to justify the latest divine intervention" (Winter 1999: 142). However, Winter does not see Islamic supersessionist claims as a problem in itself for dialogue in modern pluralistic societies: "Supersessionism... has negative implications for dialogue only when read as cause for triumphalism, rather than as a spur to the contrite awareness of a heavy responsibility" (1999: 152).

In Winter's view, "The surest sign of a supersessionism that is humble, and seeks the esteem rather than the alienation of earlier communities, is a commitment to the struggle against oppression and injustice" (1999: 153). With the latter formulation, Winter might seem to join Paul Knitter and Farid Esack (cf. Esack's book: *Qur'an, Liberation and Pluralism. An Islamic Perspective of Interreligious Solidarity Against Oppression*, 1997) in the conviction that joint struggle against oppression and injustice may constitute a firm bridge between people of different religious affiliations. However, as he has also demonstrated in a polemical review of Esack's book (Murad n.d.), Tim Winter sees no need to reconsider theological claims of supersession in the light of modern experiences of interreligious cooperation.

Against Winter, it is hard to see how supersessionist claims could *not* be associated with political claims of supremacy or—at least—heavily colored by established majority/minority constellations. It should be remembered, however, that theological claims of supersession are not always wedded to political power. In minority situations, supremacy claims may function instead as a kind of political protest, quite similar to the way in which both the Jesus movement and Muhammad's prophetic mission initially took shape in opposition to established power structures. But contemporary theological reflection cannot overlook the fact that both religions have historically functioned as religions of power, and that claims of supremacy have generally come to be associated with political majority positions—or ambitions to achieve such power. From this perspective, neither dominion-seeking nor protectionist theologies can meet the contemporary need for dialogue and relationality in theological reasoning.

Toward a Relational Theology in Dialogue with Islam

What is lacking in most theologies of religion, because of their orientation towards self-reflection, is a *relational* perspective like the one implied in Knitter's (2002) "mutuality model." In what follows, I will try out a form of theological reasoning that is *relational* in the sense of seeking meaning and truth in the 'spaces between' the religious traditions. Treading Knitter's 'ethical bridge,' I will also investigate the potential for a joint Christian-Muslim concern for the *humanization of theology*.

In my outline of a relational theology, I will structure my discussion according to a Trinitarian scheme of reasoning. How can essential elements of the Christian belief in the Creator, in Jesus Christ, and in the Holy Spirit be meaningful in a dialogue with Islam? Trying to avoid the imposition of Christian theological models on the conversation, I will formulate my Trinitarian reflections as a response to challenges posed by the Qur'an, a Shi'ite theologian, and a Jewish thinker.

Christian theologians conventionally characterize Trinitarian theology as a relational understanding of divine reality. Trinitarian theology is regularly associated with the mystery of love, reflecting a recognition that the belief that 'God is love' can only be expressed in relational terms—for instance in the image of mutual love between father and son, or in an understanding holy spirit as the power of love that holds everything together. Thus, in his response to the Muslim dialogue initiative *A Common Word between Us and You* (2007), Archbishop Rowan Williams writes:

> Because God exists in this threefold pattern of interdependent action, the relationship between Father, Son and Holy Spirit is one in which there is always a 'giving place' to each other, each standing back so that the other may act. The only human language we have for this is love.
>
> WILLIAMS 2008

The question is how a theological understanding of the relational nature of love can be translated *from* a meditation on the nature of the divine *to* a reflection on how theology can be shaped in living relationships with—or in the sacred space between—believers of different faiths.

Is Religious Plurality Willed by the Creator?

A fundamental challenge posed by the Qur'an to Christians in all times and places is to see religious plurality as something willed by God. As regards the first article of faith, in the Creator, dialogically minded Muslims are still waiting for a Christian response to what they perceive as the Qur'an's acceptance of religious plurality as divinely instituted. Some well-known and oft-cited verses of the fifth sura read as follows:

> To each among you have we prescribed a law (*shir'a*) and an open way (*minhaj*). If Allah had so willed, He would have made you a single people (*umma*), but His plan is to test you in what He hath given you: so strive as in a race in all virtues. The goal of you all is to Allah; it is He that will show you the truth of the matters in which ye dispute.
>
> Q 5: 47F—in Yusuf Ali's translation

In this passage, the historical fact of religious plurality is seen as a divinely-willed test for humanity, in which each people (or community) is seeking to implement the will of God in accordance with the revelation they have received and the path (*shir'a*, a cognate of *shari'a*) to which they have been guided. Sura 49: 13 seems also to associate cultural—and possibly, religious—diversity with something willed by God: "O mankind! We created you from a single (pair) of a male and a female, and made you into nations and tribes, that ye may know each other not that ye may despise (each other)."

There are, however, other passages in the Qur'an that point in a different direction. For instance in sura 2—which for a large part is dedicated to the demarcation between Islam and the People of the Book—differences in religious matters are seen as a result of human selfishness (sura 2: 213). In the most polemical passages, Christians and Jews are chastised as *kafirun* because they are perceived as having 'covered up' some central aspects of God's will.

One may also ask how inclusive the quoted passage from Sura 5 actually is, in light of a different verse in the same literary context: "Oh ye who believe! Take not the Jews and the Christians for your friends and protectors!" (5: 51) Although the latter verse might seem to circumscribe any 'pluralist' implication of the preceding verses, it could also be read as a warning not to blur the distinctions between the three different Abrahamic faiths—as it is precisely the differences ("to each of you we have prescribed a law") that are meant to serve as a divinely constituted fundament for the competition in good works.

The quoted passages from Sura 5 have been subject to quite contrary interpretations by Muslim theologians, ranging from conservative exclusivism to modernist inclusivist or pluralist interpretations (Sirry 2009; Esack 1997: 166ff.). But the question remains of how Christians will respond to the fundamental qur'anic acceptance of religious plurality as a divine *test* and a potential *blessing*.

This has also to do with how we see the other's scriptures. When the Muslim signatories of *A Common Word* quote the Qur'an and the Bible side by side, they implicitly dissociate themselves from cruder versions of the *tahrif* dogma,[2] treating instead central aspects of the Bible as reliable revelation. How do Christians respond to that, with regard to the Qur'an? In the Archbishop of Canterbury's response to *A Common Word* (Williams 2008), which is very rich in biblical references, he also quotes verses from the Qur'an. Implicitly, he treats the holy book of Islam as a divine source of spiritual guidance.

Are Christians ready to pursue this course? The movement known as Scriptural Reasoning (Ford and Pecknold 2006), in which Christians, Jews, and Muslims reflect together on texts from the Bible, the Qur'an, and Hadith, seems to imply a deep acceptance of the meaningfulness of the Others' scriptures. In such practices, a double experience is often felt: a sense of joint blessing, but also a recognition that differences in scriptural interpretation do not necessarily coincide with the boundaries between religions. Although the theological consequences of such experiences remain to be spelled out, it seems that practices of Scriptural Reasoning have the potential of engendering a kind of theology that is as relational as the reading experiences underlying it. In David

---

2 Implying that Jews and Christian have altered their scriptures.

Ford's words, Scriptural Reasoning seeks for meaning "in the interpretative space between the three scriptures ... and in the spiritual space between interpreters of scripture and God" (2006: 12).

In a Trinitarian scheme, the question at stake is whether and how human experiences of deep sharing across religious differences can be interpreted as a sign of divinely-created diversity; that is, as part of the belief in the Creator.

Can Christ be a Common Sign?

For me, the double experience of joint blessings and challenging differences in interreligious encounters resonates with an article that was written by Hasan Askari (an Indian-British Muslim of Shi'ite background) as early as 1972, entitled "The Dialogical Relationship between Christianity and Islam" (Askari 1972, cf. Leirvik 2010: 258f.). The double context of Askari's writings is his experience from multi-religious societies in India and Britain, and his commitment to Muslim-Christian dialogue on the international scene.

In dialogue, existence for Askari means inter-existence: "Each man becomes a neighbor" (Askari 1972: 481). In this inter-existence, neither the living neighbor nor the divine truth can be objectified. Reminiscent of Martin Buber, Askari seems to associate objectification with monological communication. In his reflection on the dialogical relation, Askari warns against the monological tendency in both religions, suggesting that 'the monological trap' can only be escaped if Christians and Muslims engage each other in an open conversation about how to understand the signs of God:

> The truth is that Christianity and Islam constitute one complex of faith, one starting with the Person, and another with the Word. Their separateness does not denote two areas of conflicting truths, but a dialogical necessity.
>
> ASKARI 1972: 485

According to Askari, reading the revealed signs of God in a dialogical (that is, relational) way is different from both objectifying the Word of God in a Book (the potential Muslim fallacy) and identifying it with a particular Person (the corresponding Christian one). Convinced that Christianity and Islam constitute 'a dialogical whole,' Askari speaks of Christ as a common sign of God for Christians and Muslims. Plunging deep into the mystery of dialogue, Askari states that "Unity is had when a religious sign is shared." Since Christ is a common sign for Christians and Muslims, Askari suggests that "Once having known Christ is to belong together" (Askari 1972: 485).

When Askari speaks of Christ as a common sign and divine revelation as essentially dialogical, this has nothing to do with harmonizing away religious differences. Recognizing that Christ is regarded as a divine sign in both religions, but interpreted in painfully different ways, Askari suggests that it belongs to the very nature of a divine sign that it is interpreted in different ways. The fact of conflicting interpretations should not be regarded as a threat but, rather, as a reflection of what a divine sign implies:

> A common religious sign must be differently apprehended. It is the very ambiguity, richness, of the religious sign that gives rise to different and even opposed interpretations and understandings [in this case, of Christ].
>
> ASKARI 1972: 485

On the human level, pain is related to the discovery of the other's irreducible difference: "To drop monologue is to immediately discover the other." However,

> [t]he discovery of the other, of our own being, is both soothing and painful, more the latter. The other is pain, a sting, a bite, but a pain in our very being, of it. It is right in the middle of this pain and anxiety that a Divine Sign is known.
>
> ASKARI 1972: 486

If Christians and Muslims venture a joint reading of the signs of God, in a friendship that is potentially painful, they might experience an even deeper, but shared suffering:

> Thrown in front of God, facing this deep, vast Absolute, Christians and Muslims will undergo the second pain, far acuter, wider and sharper than the first. This is Second Suffering. It is here that God meets man, and man meets Christ. It was in this state that Mohammed heard the Word of God.
>
> ASKARI 1972: 486

This is Askari's way of reasoning about religious plurality before God: the Creator has left signs for the human being the meaning of which (also in my further reflection) should be sought in the spiritual as well as ethical spaces between Christianity and Islam. Can Christians follow Askari in this line of reasoning? Or do they feel that such an open and relational approach to divine signs compromises their Christian faith in Christ?

In my own reflections on Christology in dialogue with Islam (Leirvik 2010), I have suggested that serious theological conversation with Islam may lead to a rethinking of classical formulations of the mystery of the incarnation, divine sonship, and the meaning of the cross. The point is not to take away the difference between Islamic convictions and Christian beliefs about Christ. That would go against Askari's reminder that the divine mystery can only be approached in respect of real differences in how Christ is understood in the two religions.

Nevertheless, there are some unnecessary stumbling blocks that may be removed in order to facilitate an open conversation about the sign of Christ. For instance, Olaf Schuman in his (1988) book *Der Christus der Muslime* ('The Christ of the Muslims') critically examines notions of divine sonship that have been wedded not only to Christian claims of supremacy but also to political power. He advocates instead a Servant Christology that is sensitive to Muslim sensibilities and still true to basic Christian teachings. Admitting that notions like 'Son of God' and 'Lord' had become part of a power language long before the Islamic era, Schumann suggests that the Qur'an might thus have been 'contextually right' in rejecting the notion 'Son of God.' Instead, the Qur'an venerates Jesus as Servant of God.

In his Christian response, Schumann recalls the fact that according to the (synoptic) Gospels, Jesus himself was reluctant to accept the title 'Son of God.' Instead, he refers to himself as 'Son of Man,' and acts as a Servant, not as a Lord. In the early Christian hymn preserved in the Letter to the Philippians 2: 5–11, Jesus is portrayed as the obedient Servant/Slave of God, who, despite his origins in God, chose to be made in human likeness, assuming the nature of a servant/slave, humbling himself to the point of death on a cross. Speaking from within Christian sensibilities, Schumann raises the question of whether the cross can be acceptable to Muslims as the deepest expression of Jesus' humanity and his obedience to God; i.e., not as a failure, but as faithfulness: 'Christ's humility in his service and his obedience to the will of his Father did not stop *before* the cross, but included it.' And maybe even more important for a Muslim awareness: "Only on the cross, through the final submission of will and its ambition 'to be like God' may the always present temptation of '*širk*' be defeated" (Schumann 1988: 178).[3]

Referring to the more mundane conceptions of divine power in Islam, Schumann concludes his reflections by asking the Muslims whether a political understanding of God's rule is really defensible in theological terms. From the Christian side,

---

3 Translations of Schumann are my own.

> Jesus' refusal to identify the Kingdom of God with a political understand-
> ing of society or state ... is not seen as a deficiency. On the contrary, the
> confusion of God's kingdom with society and state is seen as an unholy
> temptation.
>
> SCHUMANN 1988: 179

Would it be thinkable, although at present mostly un-thought, that Christians
and Muslims together might overcome the temptations of absolute power, in
critical awareness of human vulnerability and in a shared confession that ultimate meaning and power rest only with God?

As can be seen from Schumann, rethinking Christology might be good for
more than preaching Christ in more sensitive ways in an Islamic context. It
touches upon questions of general relevance in interreligious dialogue.

Relational Pneumatology

Before pursuing my Christological reflections on power, suffering, and vulnerability by approaching the issue of a humanization of theology, I will briefly
touch upon the question of a relational Pneumatology. What I have in mind is
Martin Buber's philosophy of dialogue which can be taken as a relational way
of understanding the work of the Holy Spirit.

The main ethical point in Buber's philosophy of dialogue is to avoid reducing one another to an object, an 'It.' Like Askari, he associates objectification
with monologue (2002: 22f.). If, instead, in a dialogical relation, we treat each
other as I and Thou, something sacred takes place in the space between. In
an essay on dialogue, Buber speaks of it as 'communion' (2002: 6). He even
characterizes true dialogue as a sacrament, "where unreserve has ruled, even
wordlessly, between men, the word of dialogue has happened sacramentally"
(2002: 5, cf. 21). If in a truly dialogical relation, we treat each other as I and
Thou, the space between us will be filled by Spirit. When in *I and Thou* Buber
speaks of the realm of between, he explicitly refers to it as the place of the
Spirit: "Spirit is not in the I, but between I and Thou.... Man lives in the spirit,
if he is able to respond to his Thou.... Only in virtue of his power to enter into
relation is he able to live in the spirit" (Buber 1987: 57f.). In later writings, Buber
elaborates his relational philosophy and speaks of the 'sphere' or the 'realm'
of between. In Buber's understanding, the *realm of between* is the sphere in
which true dialogue takes place, as a third dimension beyond the individual
and social aspects of existence: On the far side of the subjective, on this side of
the objective, on the narrow ridge, where I and Thou meet, there is the realm
of 'between'" (Buber 2002: 242f.).

Buber's horizon of dialogue was mainly a Jewish-Christian one. Does this kind of relational theology, or Pneumatology, make sense in Christian-Muslim dialogue? I believe it does, because this way of reasoning protects the sanctity of every true encounter, whether it is experienced as a blessing or as a difficult test. It reveals both modes of interreligious encounter as a potential dwelling place of the Holy Spirit.

Toward a Humanization of Theological Ethics?

With its focus on interpersonal, face-to-face relations, my theological reflections on dialogue with Islam can also be read as the expression of an *ethical turn* in contemporary theology. Whereas theologies of religion are often self-centred, in the sense of being focused on how to understand one's own faith in relation to what others believe, ethics (at least in Levinas' sense) is fundamentally oriented towards the human Other. By virtue of its obligation towards the *vulnerable* Other, a Levinasian turn to ethics may also entail a moral critique of the Bible (Leirvik 2011; 2014: 105ff.) or a "moral enrichment" of the Qur'an (Abou El Fadl 2002)—in so far as sacred scriptures might seem to collide with contemporary perceptions of human dignity. What, then, would an ethical, other-directed theology of religions look like? Is it possible—interreligiously—to formulate a theology of religion that is fundamentally relational, oriented toward the vulnerable Other, and open to a humanization of theological ethics?

In terms of systematic theology, Olaf Schumann's Christological reflection on sonship and servanthood, with its critical perspective on power language and its orientation towards vulnerability, can in fact be read as a humanization of Christology. One voice in late modern philosophies of religion, the Jewish philosopher, Emmanuel Levinas, speaks of the face of the Other as an epiphany of God: "The wonderful thing about the face is that it *speaks*, it says need, vulnerability, it asks, begs *me* for help, it makes me responsible.... God, the god, it's a long way there, a road that goes via the Other. Loving God is Loving the Other" (1993: 214f[4]).

The common frame of reference for Levinas and Schumann is the Jewish-Christian tradition, in which the human Other is often seen as an epiphany of God, literally standing between the Self and God. For instance, in Genesis 33:10, when Jacob returns from his exile to meet his brother Esau, whom he had once cunningly cheated, Jacob presents his gift of reconciliation with the following

---

4 My own translation from, not for the Norwegian version of Levinas Cf. Emmanuel Levinas' reflections on the face of the Other as an epiphany of God in his book Of God who comes to mind (1998).

words: "If I have found favour in your eyes, accept this gift from me. For to see your face is like seeing the face of God, now that you have received me favourably." In the New Testament, 1 John 4:20 proclaims that "anyone who does not love his brother, whom he has seen, cannot love God, whom he has not seen." And in the judgment scene of Matthew 25, Jesus is held to foretell that on the Day of Judgment, with reference to the treatment of the hungry, the thirsty, the naked, the sick, the imprisoned and strangers he will say: "Truly I tell you, whatever you did [not do] for one of the least of these brothers and sisters of mine, you did [not do] for me."

In a similar vein, the Muslim dialogue initiative *A Common Word* (2008) suggests that the uniting bond between Muslims and Christians should be the double commandment of love, in which love of God can never be separated from "loving your brother as yourself." Unlike the picture of Muslim theology presented in *A Common Word*, Islam is generally seen as a religion in which the distance between God and the human being is too vast to be bridged by human love. There are, however, other strands in Islamic theology in which the notion of love unites the human and the divine. Islamic mysticism has a long, poetic tradition of obliterating the distinction between human and divine love.

With regard to ethical reasoning, qur'anic ethics seem ultimately aimed at attaining proximity to God. The Qur'an may even speak of the desire for 'God's face' (*wajh Allah*) as the ultimate aim of a righteous life (Sura 2: 272; 6: 52). And with regard to the Jewish-Christian idea of the vulnerable Other standing between oneself and God, a well-known hadith about the merit of visiting the sick in the collection of *Sahih Muslim* comes astonishingly close to the judgment scene in Matthew 25:

> Abu Huraira reported Allah's Messenger (may peace be upon him) as saying: Verily, Allah, the Exalted and Glorious, would say on the Day of Resurrection: O son of Adam, I was sick but you did not visit Me. He would say: O my Lord; how could I visit Thee whereas Thou art the Lord of the worlds? Thereupon He would say: Didn't you know that such and such servant of Mine was sick but you did not visit him and were you not aware of this that if you had visited him, you would have found Me by him (*la-wajadtani 'indahu*)? O son of Adam, I asked food from you but you did not feed Me. He would say: My Lord, how could I feed Thee whereas Thou art the Lord of the worlds? He said: Didn't you know that such and such servant of Mine asked food from you but you did not feed him, and were you not aware that if you had fed him you would have found him by My side (*dhalik 'indi*)? (The Lord would again say:) O son of Adam, I asked drink from you but you did not provide Me. He would say: My Lord, how could I provide Thee whereas Thou art the Lord of

the worlds? Thereupon He would say: Such and such of servant of Mine asked you for a drink but you did not provide him, and had you provided him drink you would have found him near Me (*dhalik 'indi*).

MISLIM 1993: 176

Interestingly, other translations render the expression *dhalik 'indi* ('found him by My side,' 'found him near Me') as 'retrieved it by Me'-in Nora Eggen's Norwegian translation: '... så ville du komme til å se det igjen hos Meg?'—referring probably to a heavenly reward or loss ('it') instead of a vulnerable human ('him') behind whom God is found. But the other reading, in which God intimately identifies himself with the suffering human being, may be just as plausible.

Whether or not the above hadith should be taken as a loan from the New Testament or not, it testifies to the fact that the idea of God standing by the side of the vulnerable human being is a motif shared by Christianity and Islam. When *A Common Word* links love of God and love of the other as intimately as it does, I take this as a possible point of departure for a dialogue on humanization of theology and ethics.

The important question is of course what concrete consequences a humanization of theological ethics might have. In March 2005, Tariq Ramadan called for an immediate moratorium on the death penalty and *hudud* punishments (such as corporeal punishment for theft and for illegitimate sexual relationships) in the Muslim world (2005). The intention behind the call, Ramadan explains, was to address:

> the conscience of each individual, to mobilise ordinary Muslims to call on their governments to place an immediate moratorium on the application of these punishments, and to call for Muslim scholars for the opening of a vast intra-community debate on the matter.
>
> RAMADAN 2009: 165

When reading his call, it struck me that the guiding principle behind it was clearly a theologically-motivated concern for vulnerable human beings. Ramadan realizes that, in an imperfect world with asymmetrical power relations, severe punishments will regularly hit women more than men, and the poorer and weaker members of society more frequently than the wealthy and powerful ones. If we recognize this somber reality, says Ramadan, "it is impossible for us as Muslims to remain silent as irreversible injustice is done to the poorest and weakest members of society in the name of our religion" (2009: 163).

Muslim reactions against the proposed moratorium proved its controversial character, whereas some Western reactions implied that Ramadan should have called for a full abolition of *hudud* punishments and not merely a 'moratorium'. The way Ramadan argues his proposed moratorium, however, gives the impression that his call is really meant for an indefinite period of time, probably until the end of the world as we know it. For, from Ramadan's perspective, how could such punishments ever be justified, as long as human injustice exists?

In my reading, ethical concern for the vulnerable human being is clearly the implied premise for Ramadan's moratorium call. I therefore take his call as a recent example of humanizing theological reasoning in Islam. In Ramadan's case, his application of the humane criterion in theological reasoning leads him to sidestep important aspects of classical Sharia—for the sake of humanity.

A similar line of reasoning was expressed by Arwa al-Tawil, a female member of the Muslim Brotherhood who took an active part in the Tahrir demonstrations in 2011, when commenting upon violent demonstrations in Afghanistan against the burning of the Qur'an by two American pastors: "Life is more sacred than the Qur'an.... A mad pastor burning a Qur'an does not justify killings. A life is more holy than the Qur'an in Islam."[5]

Conclusion: A Shared Concern for the Vulnerable Individual

The cited examples of humanizing readings of the Islamic ethico-theological tradition correspond to parallel tendencies in Christian-Muslim dialogue. In my analysis of joint statements from the official Contact Group between the Church of Norway and the Islamic Council Norway (Leirvik 2014: 33ff, 155ff.), I identify a development from mutual group solidarity to joint protection of the vulnerable individual who may often be threatened by his or her own cultural or religious group. Salient examples are joint declarations on the right to conversion (2007),[6] violence in close relationships (2009),[7] and religious extremism (2011).[8]

Although the language in these secular-style declarations is not explicitly religious, it is nevertheless possible to deduce a certain type of humanizing, theological reasoning underlying them (cf. Terzic 2013). Whatever style of language is used, when in Christian-Muslim dialogue the ethics of vulnerability is given trump over forms of religious ethics that threaten the integrity of

---

5   'Liv er helligere enn Koranen', *Klassekampen* 4 April 2011 (my translation).
6   http://www.gammel.kirken.no/english/news.cfm?artid=149142 [accessed 09.02.2015].
7   http://www.gammel.kirken.no/english/news.cfm?artid=265872 [accessed 09.02.2015].
8   http://www.gammel.kirken.no/english/news.cfm?artid=363357 [accessed 09.02.2015].

the individual, a relational theology of religions expresses itself as humanization of theology.

In humanizing theological ethics, Christians and Muslims are not merely in dialogue with each other but with secular society as well. In the cited declarations, the language is generally 'secular' in that it leans heavily on human rights discourses and a faith-transcending ethical reasoning which I (with reference to Levinas) would characterize as an ethics of vulnerability. Being focused on the vulnerable face of the Other, an ethics of vulnerability is predominantly oriented towards the precarious situation of individuals—whose integrity in many cases is threatened by their own cultural and religious group. An ethics of vulnerability may thus be far more challenging to the religious communities than group-oriented approaches to ethics.

Bibliography

Abou El Fadl, Khaled et al. (2002). *The Place of Tolerance in Islam*. Boston: Beacon Press.

Al-Nawawi. (2008). *De rettvises hager: Al-Nawawis samling av overleveringer om profeten Muhammad*. Transl. Nora S. Eggen. Oslo: Bokklubben.

Askari, Hasan. (1972). "The Dialogical Relationship between Christianity and Islam." *Journal of Ecumenical Studies* 9: 477–87.

Buber, Martin. (1987). *I and Thou*. Edinburgh: T&T Clark.

———. (2002). *Between Man and Man*. With an introduction by Maurice Friedman. London and New York: Routledge.

Cornille, Catherine. (2008). *The Im-Possibility of Interreligious Dialogue*. New York: The Crossroad Publishing Company.

Coward, Harold. (2000). *Pluralism in the World Religions. A Short Introduction*. Oxford: Oneworld.

Dupuis, Jacques. (1997). *Toward a Christian Theology of Religious Pluralism*. New York: Orbis Books.

Esack, Farid. (1997). *Qur'an, Liberation & Pluralism: An Islamic Perspective of Interreligious Solidarity Against Oppression*. Oxford: Oneworld.

Ford, David, and C.C. Pecknold (eds.). (2006). *The Promise of Scriptural Reasoning*. Oxford: Blackwell Publishing.

Knitter, Paul F. (1985). *No Other Name? A Critical Survey of Christian Attitudes Toward the World Religions*. New York: Orbis Books.

Knitter, Paul F. (2002). *Introducing Theologies of Religions*. New York: Orbis Books.

———. (2007). "'My God is Bigger than Your God!' Time for Another Axial Shift in the History of Religions." *Studies in Interreligious Dialogue* 17/1: 100–18.

Leirvik, Oddbjørn. (2010). *Images of Jesus Christ in Islam*. London and New York: Continuum.

———. (2011). "Interreligious Hermeneutics and the Ethical Critique of the Scriptures." In: David Cheetham, Ulrich Winkler, Oddbjørn Leirvik and Judith Gruber (eds.). *Interreligious Hermeneutics in Pluralistic Europe: Between Texts and People*. Amsterdam and New York: Rodopi. pp. 333–53.

———. (2014). *Interreligious Studies: A Relational Approach to Religious Activism and the Study of Religion*. London: Bloomsbury.

Levinas, Emmanuel. (1993). *Den annens humanisme: Oversatt og med innledning, noter og et essay av Asbjørn Aarnes*. Oslo: Aschehoug.

———. (1998). *Of God Who Comes to Mind*. Transl. B. Bergo. Stanford, CA: Stanford University Press.

Murad, Abdul-Hakim. (1997). "Book Review of Farid Esack's *Qur'an, Liberation and Pluralism*. Oxford: Oneworld." Available at: http://www.masud.co.uk/ISLAM/ahm/esack.htm.

Muslim. (1993). *Sahih Muslim*. Transl. Mahmoud Matraji. Beyrouth: Dar El Fiker.

Race, Alan. (1983). *Christians and Religious Pluralism: Patterns in the Christian Theology of Religions*. London: SCM Press.

Ramadan, Tariq. (2005). "An International Call for Moratorium on Corporal Punishment, Stoning and the Death Penalty in the Islamic World." Available at: http://www.tariqramadan.com/spip.php?article264. Accessed 9 February 2015.

———. (2009). "A Call for a Moratorium on Corporeal Punishment—The Debate in Review." In: Kari Vogt, Lena Larsen, and Christian Moe (eds.). *New Directions in Islamic Thought: Exploring Reform and Muslim Tradition*. London: I.B. Tauris.

Schumann, Olaf. (1988). *Der Christus der Muslime: Christologische Aspekte in der arabisch-islamischen Literatur*. Köln and Wien: Böhlau Verlag.

Sirry, Mun'im. (2009). "Compete with One Another in Good Works: Exegesis of Qur'an verse 5: 48 and Contempary Muslim Discourses on Religious Pluralism." *Islam and Christian-Muslim Relations* 20/4: 423–38.

Terzić, Faruk. (2013). "Theological Principles versus Secular Language: An Analysis of Joint Statements of the Council on Ecumenical and International Relations of the Church of Norway and the Islamic Council Norway." *Norsk Tidsskrift for Misjonsvitenskap* 4: 173–85.

Williams, Rowan. (2008). "A Common Word for the Common Good." http://rowanwilliams.archbishopofcanterbury.org/articles.php/1107/a-common-word-for-the-common-good.

Winter, Tim. (1999). "The Last Trump Card: Islam and the Supersession of Other Faiths." *Studies in Interreligious Dialogue* 9/2: 133–55.

CHAPTER 14

Christianity as the Measure of Religion?
Materializing the Theology of Religions

Marianne Moyaert

Introduction

In the aftermath of the decay of European colonialism and in the face of the devastations of the *Shoah*, Christians have come to realize that there is a correlation between their Christologies, soteriologies, and eschatologies on one side and the way adherents of foreign religious traditions are depicted on the other. Answers to theological questions about salvation, revelation, and truth spill over into the practical realm and have concrete repercussions for how Christians approach religious Others (Griffiths 1990: 10). The realization of the unhealthy connection between particular faith convictions and various forms of Christian triumphalism has given rise to a number of theological questions about Christian self-understanding in relation to religious Otherness. Christians are being challenged to reconsider who they say they are in a way that is congruent with tradition while being conscious of the potential hegemonic power of their religious discourse (wcc 2013).[1] In response to this challenge, various theologians have endeavored to develop systematic-theological responses to religious diversity, known as theologies of religions.

In my understanding, the field of the theologies of religions is marked by a deliberate ethical concern for the religious Other and a desire to reach out to those of other faiths. The undergirding assumption is that Christians may only alter their troubled interreligious relations and rectify at least some of the wrongs of the past if they learn to make space for the Other in their theological frameworks. From this perspective, theologians ask if there is a way to overcome supersessionist accounts of religious plurality. Is it possible to avoid exclusivist interpretations of the Christ-event? Can we keep away from triumphalist interpretations of our revelatory truth claims; can we perhaps include the religious Other in our eschatological hopes?[2] Many theologians

---

1 Hegemony has Greek roots: Greek *hēgemonia,* from *hēgemōn* leader, from *hēgeisthai* to lead.
2 These questions show that theology and dialogue—the so-called twin tracks of for Christian engagement with religious diversity—are closely intertwined. See Race (2001).

recognize the ethical dimension of their theological reasonings and accept that it is their responsibility to develop a theology of religions that at least endeavors to overcome Christian dominance while remaining committed to the Christian faith.

Nevertheless, despite good intentions theologies of religions have sometimes reproduced prejudiced patterns of Christian thought. Theologians are not always conscious of just how complex the problem of hegemonic discourse is. It is not merely a surface problem that can be easily removed through some uncomplicated and straightforward measures. Symbolic violence is deeply ingrained in our theological discourse and often exclusionary strategies go unnoticed. As many postcolonial (and feminist) thinkers have pointed out, the problem really is not just about dogmatic claims to absolute truth; hegemonic discourse is far more subtle, and because it has become so deeply implanted in our frames of thought, it is difficult to see it, let alone that we know how to bring about a change in thinking. It seems that any systematic-theological approach may end in a Christianization of other religions, i.e., the explicit or implicit, conscious or unconscious misrepresentation of other religions based on Christian prejudices and assumptions. As a form of *Hineininterpretierung* (misinterpretation due to preconceptions), such a Christianization is problematic, not only because it misconstrues religious Otherness but also because, by doing so, it inhibits nuanced theological responses and constructive interreligious relations. That is why theology continues to require a 'hermeneutics of suspicion' that may expose how one community of faith manipulates or even distorts the tradition of another to meet its needs (Barnes 2011: 390). Ideology critique should be part and parcel of theology.

In this contribution I will sketch the recent history of the theology of religions and I will show how theology has struggled with the problem of religious hegemony. Though this contribution will show how difficult it is to avoid the problem of misrepresentation, I will also establish how the growing awareness of the potential (and real) hegemonic nature of Christian discourse has affected Christian theological self-understanding, such that it institutes at least a feel for the sensitive issues related to religious diversity, and increases theological humility (Cornille 2008). In brief, the ongoing dialogue between Christianity and other traditions has helped to shape and reshape the way Christians understand themselves in relation to others; that too needs to be mentioned.

The first stage that deserves our attention is of course the theology of religions with its threefold typology of exclusivism, inclusivism, and pluralism.

Theology of Religions

The theology of religions is a systematic discipline whose overall aim is to make sense of religious plurality in light of the central tenets of Christian tradition. Many theologians of religions—though not all—developed their understanding of religious plurality in a global context of missionary activity and/or dialogue with adherents of other faiths. The serious and lively interaction with 'non-Christians' often ingrained in them a deep sense of the moral and spiritual richness of these foreign religious traditions and incited a willingness to theologically attend to religious diversity. From the close contact with 'religious Others' a dynamic of growing sensitivity seems to have developed.[3] Not only did it become inadequate to describe adherents of other traditions simply as pagans or in mere negative terms as non-Christians,[4] there was also a growing urge to recognize and name the value of other traditions. Many theologians struggled with the question of how they might theologically express their appreciation for other traditions.

The question of salvation especially has been at the forefront of this theological discussion: How are other religious traditions related to the Christian mystery of salvation? Is it possible for 'non-Christians' to be saved and, if so, how may salvation be mediated to them? In some sense, one could say that the concern for the religious Other was translated into a concern for their soteriological fate. From a Christian perspective this soteriological focus is logical, since the question of salvation is closely interconnected with two traditional axioms that form the heart of Christian faith: (1) God's will for universal salvation and (2) the notion that salvation comes through Christ (Moyaert 2011:14).

Different answers to the question of salvation have been formulated, and these answers are usually classified in the now widespread typology of exclusivism, inclusivism, and pluralism, which was first surveyed by Alan Race (1983). The exclusivist model proposes that only Christians can attain salvation. No matter how interesting other religions may be, no matter how valuable these traditions are as moral guides, no matter how inspiring their narratives or symbolic practices continue to be, they cannot offer salvation. Hence, non-Christians are excluded from salvation. Inclusivism acknowledges that, though it is possible for 'non-Christians' to be saved, Christ is always involved in this soteriological process. The idea is that Christ's salvific outreach mysteriously extends

---

3   See the biographies of J. Hick, M. Heim, and P. Knitter as exemplars of this development.
4   See Ratzinger (1998: 30): "... inadequacy of describing representatives of other religions simply as pagans or else in purely negative terms as non-Christians."

to other religious communities.[5] The pluralist view regards the religious traditions as different expressions of the way human beings in different historical
and cultural contexts have faithfully responded to ultimate reality. Rough parity is the key to this model (Gilkey 1987: 40). This means that the religions are
different yet more or less equal salvific paths towards ultimate reality. Thus,
Christianity is no longer the center of the religious universe but comes to be
regarded as one particular path to salvation, while others are equally valid.

Up until today proponents of these three soteriological options have been
engaged in an ongoing theological debate about which model is most helpful
to Christians as they seek to establish friendly interreligious relationships with
people belonging to other faith traditions.[6] This debate has been a particularly
lively one, probably because it touches upon the soteriological nerve of the
Christian tradition: it affects the self-understanding of Christianity as a religious tradition that is intended to bring 'good news for all' but which has often
brought quite the opposite. An understanding seems to have grown among
Christian theologians that any triumphalist account of Christian salvation is a
contradiction in terms.

I agree with Hugh Nicholson that the theology of religions and its threefold typology of exclusivism, inclusivism, and pluralism can be understood
as successive moments in 'a dialectical process' in which theologians have
sought to overcome various expressions of religious exclusion and antagonism (2011: 27). That also explains why many surveys discuss the threefold
typology in a specific order, starting with the 'least' open, the exclusivist
model, then discuss the 'half-open' inclusivist model, and finally look at the
model that claims to live up to the dialogical virtue of openness, i.e., pluralism

---

5 Today the question is no longer if it is possible for individual non-Christians to be saved
   despite their religion but rather how adherents of different religions can be saved *in* and
   through practicing their faith.

6 This threefold typology is criticized by various authors for various reasons. Perry Schmidt-
   Leukel summarizes the objections: "(1) The typology has an inconsistent structure, because
   the positions are not of the same genre and do not address the same questions (Markham,
   Tilley); (2) the typology is misleading, because it obscures or misses the real issues of a theology of religions (DiNoia); (3) the typology is too narrow (Markham, Ogden); (4) the typology
   is too broad (D'Costa); (5) the typology is too coarse or abstract. It does not do justice to the
   more complex and nuanced reality of real theologies (Ariarajah, Tilley); (6) the typology is
   misleading, because it does not do justice to the radical diversity of the religions (Heim); (7)
   the typology is offensive (Neuhaus); (8) the typology is pointless, because we are not in position to choose any of these options and therefore have to refrain from all of them (Clooney)."
   Schmidt-Leukel himself defends the typology (2005).

(e.g., McCarthy 1998: 101). In retrospect, it seems fair to state that pluralist theologians rapidly had the upper hand in this discussion. Up until the 1990s, pluralists took the lead and successfully argued that the only way to overcome Christian triumphalism and the associated violence against others was to reject all claims to Christian superiority and finality (Knitter 2004). John Hick's so-called 'Copernican revolution' in particular claimed to mark a definite shift within the Christian tradition of absolutism (Hick 1973: 133).

Conscious of the symbolic violence of traditional Christian discourse, Hick argued that it is simply no longer convincing, let alone acceptable, to put Christianity at the center of the religious universe, thereby at once looking down on other religions. History bears witness to the devastating consequences of such a hierarchical outlook on religious plurality. That is why Christian theology is urged to develop an account of Christianity that moves away from unwarranted claims of superiority and finality. Other religions too are faced with the challenge to move beyond absolutist claims. Hick aptly expressed the moral dynamic of this approach in the following quotation:

> We are acutely aware that throughout history almost all human conflicts have been validated and intensified by a religious sanction. God has been claimed to be on both sides of every war. This has been possible because each of the great world faiths has either assumed or asserted its own unique superiority as the one and only true faith and path to the highest good—in familiar Christian terms, to salvation. These exclusive claims to absolute truth have exacerbated the division of the human community into rival groups, and have repeatedly been invoked in support of oppression, slavery, conquest and exploitation. (2004: 253)

Dogmatism, being the bad religion of those who are too confident that they possess the complete, final and superior truth, needs to be overcome (Clatworthy 2010: 48). Especially problematic, according to pluralism, is "the material identification of a particular religion (or form of that religion) with the essence and substance of true universal religion as such" (Pratt 2003: 405). Rejecting any claim to superiority, finality, or exclusivity and building an argument for soteriological parity, pluralism set itself up as the natural partner of interreligious dialogue (Hick 1993: 178). In his book *Introducing Theologies of Religions*, Paul Knitter reinforces this claim by renaming pluralism *the mutuality model*, expressing the pluralist commitment to "foster conversation" among the various religious traditions (2002: 110). Alan Race agrees, stating that pluralism presents the best option for "reciprocity, parity and complementarity which dialogue itself assumes, promotes and develops" (2001: 121). When it comes to promoting interreligious dialogue based on equality and reciprocity, this model really seemed to hold all the winning cards, and the development of the pluralist theory of religion has given a tremendous boost to reflections on interreligious dialogue. No matter what criticism one might formulate against the pluralist's position, there can be no question about their wholehearted commitment to overcoming the hegemonic nature of the Christian tradition.

Pluralism as a Form of Hegemonic Discourse?

The argument for the pluralist approach to interreligious dialogue is strengthened by how pluralist approaches are contrasted with exclusivist and inclusivist ones. On the one side are the 'closed' exclusivists and inclusivists and on the other the 'open' pluralists. The idea is that both exclusivisms and inclusivisms employ an inappropriate starting point in their interpretation of religious diversity. They judge other religions on the basis of their own confession. This is an expression of closure: the other is either excluded from or absorbed into one's own confessional perspective. To do justice to the self-understanding of other religions, the confessional perspective must be transcended. That is why pluralisms can be presented as a supraconfessional, meta-interpretation of religions, claiming that different religions are historically and culturally determined interpretations of the unknowable Real. Religions do not revolve around a church, nor do they revolve around Christ or God. The center of the religious universe is the Real—*that* is the ultimate religious object. In addition, all religions are stamped by the same generic soteriological structure: they attempt the transformation from self-centeredness to Reality-centeredness (Hick 1995: 17). The other religions are not rivals but "fellow travelers to the Ultimate" (Cheetham 2003: 165).

Though this vision of interreligious solidarity between different traditions continues to appeal to many people, critics have since seriously berated the claim that pluralisms succeed in overcoming religious hegemony. I will not repeat the often sharp criticisms formulated against this project; it suffices to mention that pluralists have been accused of being covert proponents of the typical Western and modern world view. This is expressed in the pluralist urge to develop abstract and systematic theories in which universalities, essences, and commonalities are sought. Authors like Gavin D'Costa and John Milbank especially have raised the critique that the pluralist philosophical hypothesis shows itself to be a totalizing form of discourse, reducing plurality to unity (D'Costa 2000; Milbank 1990). Pluralism understands all religious traditions merely as different interpretations of the one and same common ground and as variations on the same soteriological theme. Thus it reduces the plurality of religions to phenomena of the same (Barnes 2000: 9). As such, pluralism forces awkwardly unstable religious realities onto a Procrustean bed of untrammelled homogeneity (Barnes 2002: 10). The pluralist presumption of an *Arché* (origin/source) underlying religious diversity is subtly oppressive. Michael Barnes sums up the critique as follows:

> Indeed particularity becomes subsumed under an "ethic of openness" which quickly becomes rigidly ideological. By defining in advance the canons of acceptable religious value in a multi-faith world, the normative pluralist project has already determined, and therefore controls, the response which the other can make.
>
> BARNES 2000: 13

The pluralistic discourse on openness turns out to be a strategy: it constitutes order and thus gives a sense of comfort because it takes away the interrupting and confronting, indeed, even the discomforting, character of the encounter with the foreign. What is more, the claim that pluralism would be a supra-confessional meta-theory of religious diversity is untenable. As D'Costa puts it, pluralism, like all rationalities, is tradition-dependent and the roots of Hick's pluralist hypothesis are obvious: modern Kantian agnosticism (D'Costa 1996). Pluralisms are an exemplar of a typical liberal understanding of religion exhibiting not only a modern fear of particularities but also a great interest in essences, commonalities, and universal structures. Clearly, pluralists should not be presented as oppressive imperialists or triumphalist exclusivists of some sort. Nevertheless, there is some truth in the charge that they are "well-intentioned liberals who have failed to see that their attempts to include others actually involve subsuming them into their own world view" (Hedges 2010: 130). Though many pluralists have made important adjustments to their approach, they have never been able to completely refute the charge that pluralism is yet another form of a modern Western (hegemonic) discourse resulting in a case of *Hineininterpretierung*.

Theology of Religions without Religion?

The fierce criticism of the pluralistic difficulty in recognizing real otherness has triggered a more fundamental discussion about the very meaningfulness of the endeavor itself to develop theologies of religions. The question has been raised whether this typical Christian approach would ever enable theologians to overcome the problem of hegemony. Indeed, at a deeper level, one could argue that the very approach, the entire setup of the theology of religions and its threefold typology, is problematic and yet another expression of Christians setting the agenda for dialogue and forcing other believers into a mold that does not suit them. Several scholars have pointed out that the problem of Christian hegemony is not simply that of Christians making absolute truth claims. The problem is much more complex and actually relates to the way religion itself has been conceptualized in most theologies of religions. To put it briefly, the basic and obvious category of 'religion' that undergirds and frames the theological discussion turns out to misdirect this discussion before it.

Postcolonial thinkers in particular have shown how most definitions of religion explicitly or implicitly build on Christian assumptions. A great deal of religious scholarship assumed for a long time that one could define religion and its essence by looking at Christianity. It was not seen as wrong to apply Christian categories and experiences to other religions; what is more, the application of Christian schemes to other religious traditions frequently resulted in a hierarchical ordering of religious traditions with Christianity as the most superior or cultivated religion. Of course, the study of religion has developed a critical consciousness of its own (hegemonic) history. Nevertheless, many would argue that the current study of religion still carries traces of a *too* Western (Christian) understanding of religion, an understanding that can also be found in many theologies of religions. It would seem that Christianity has cast a shadow on the study of religion, and it has proven to be very difficult to shake off this Christian legacy. Drawing on postcolonial thinkers such as Talal Asad, Richard King, and Kwok Pui Lan, I will enumerate a number of issues that may (should) provoke theologians of religions to become more attentive to the hegemony of their own discourse. Each of these critiques is driven by a concern for the Other and a wish to theologize in a way that does justice to otherness; and each critique brings to the surface the extent to which Christian discourse continues to dominate (reflections on) interreligious relations.

As indicated, the theology of religions and its threefold typology hinges upon the question of salvation. It is precisely this soteriological focus that has come under heavy criticism. There is a sense that the soteriological focus actually misdirects the discussion and inhibits authentic engagement with the religious Other *as other* because it continues to place him/her in a systematized Christian framework. According to postliberal theologian George Lindbeck, soteriology is "an agenda which is of interest to non-Christians to the extent that they feel threatened by Christianity, but not otherwise" (Lindbeck 1997: 425). Other religions feel obligated, as it were, to go along with the fixation on soteriology, out of fear that the failure of interreligious dialogue would entail the return of Christian proselytism (Lindbeck 1997: 426). Because the theology of religions, and hence the question of salvation, determines the interpretation of religious diversity, Christianity sets the agenda for interreligious relations. The threefold typology asks Christian questions and suggests Christian answers. As a consequence, it tends to address the other religious traditions in its own terms: "either one baptizes the other religions and claims that they are implicit versions of one's own or one develops a philosophical standpoint from which one claims to be able to evaluate all the religions" (Placher 1989: 144). However one looks at it, the religious Other is seen as "a problem to be excluded, included—or more safely—pluralized" (Barnes 2002: 13). By making soteriology the focal point of interreligious learning, Christians actually extend their age-old hegemonic tendencies: Christians set the boundaries of the dialogue (Fredericks 2010: xv). With the best of intentions, this discussion is nevertheless yet another expression of the Christian inclination to dominate otherness.

Beyond the soteriological fixation, there is a more profound problem, namely, that most theologies of religions uphold a rather mentalist approach to religion. This mentalist approach also affects the way systematic theologians tend to approach the phenomenon of religion. They are inclined to focus on *high* tradition, which is discursive and propositional, and fits well with a theological discourse (Tanner 1997). This doctrinal focus does not always match the importance of these doctrinal questions in lived religious life and so can even be said to be reductive. According to David Morgan, this mentalist focus is a remnant of a Christianity that continues to cast a shadow on the way religion is understood. According to him, "focus on 'belief' as a set of teachings derives from the creedal tradition of Christianity, which was intensified by Protestantism" (Morgan 2010a: 1). The general understanding became that

> a religion is what someone believes, which consists of a discrete subjective experience of assent to propositions concerning the origin of the cosmos, the nature of humanity, the existence of deities, or the purpose of life. When seeking to understand religion, scholars have ... tended to ask: what are its teachings?
>
> MORGAN 2010a: 1

Daniel Lopez has questioned the assumption that doctrine is the core business of religious traditions. According to him, "belief appears as a universal category because of the universalist claims of the tradition in which it was most central, Christianity" (Lopez 1998: 33). From this perspective, it becomes understandable that Kwok Pui Lan asserts that "Christianity continues to serve as the prototype of a religion and as the standard for evaluating other wisdom traditions" (Kwok 2005: 189). According to her, theologies and religious studies that do not take into account the ambiguous nature of this notion of religion may even continue some of the imperialistic tendencies that have dominated the attitude of Western Christianity vis-à-vis other religions and cultures.

The mentalist approach to religion has also fostered certain "creedal and dogmatic notions of what 'real religion' is, that is what Christianity, or Judaism or Buddhism or Hinduism is." The underlying assumption is "that such abstractions may be satisfactorily defined by crystallizing their world of belief into clear tenets concerning more or less universal categories of God or gods, afterlife, scriptures, revelation, transcendence, and so forth ..." (Morgan 2010b: xiv). As a consequence, religious traditions are presented as monolithic wholes revolving around core beliefs. Postcolonial and feminist thinkers in particular have indicated that this presentation is far from obvious. They have in fact criticized the understanding that it would be possible to divide the religious world into discrete entities, with more or less clear boundaries. It is important to realize, so they continue, that the religious traditions "as they are usually portrayed are idealized and largely theoretical constructs that bear some relationship to, but are by no means identical with, the actual religious expression of humankind ..." (King 1999: 67). Religious traditions, however particular they may be, are not constituted by sharp boundaries as if they would be fixed wholes. Rather, they are marked by a certain fluidity, permeability, and hybridity, even though this often goes unnoticed. Because their boundaries are more porous than is often acknowledged, religious realities are 'messy,' they simply cannot be contained in neat categories (Egnell, 2011). Religious traditions have always been affected by other wisdom traditions, shifting contexts, and various cultural encounters with intercultural borrowing as the result.

Furthermore, the need for systematization, so typical of the classical theology of religions, and enhanced by the mentalist approach to religion, sometimes endorses generalized statements about other religions that come at the cost of religious particularities. The critique formulated against the theology of religions is that "it may be greatly detailed with respect to the nuances of the home tradition, but most often remains broadly general regarding the traditions that are being talked about" (Clooney 2010: 10). The lack of interest in the concrete and empirical details of what religious communities and their adherents actually tend to believe, value, and practice results in what James Fredericks has called "a domestication of difference" (Fredericks 2010: xiv). From this perspective, I have argued elsewhere that any theology of religions demands an ethical attitude of reticence: a form of 'hesitation' and 'utter cautiousness' that expresses a fear of doing injustice to the other (2012).

If one takes seriously some of the discerning insights from the vast literature on the genealogy of religion, it becomes evident that the problem of hegemony surpasses the problem of dogmatism and absolutism and demands more complex methodological measures. If theologians operate with a one-sided understanding of religion, they limit the possibility of interreligious recognition, and it certainly is a heavy burden on interreligious relations because in the end, Christians, despite good intentions, still set the agenda. That is why any theology of religions must also include a genealogy of religion and should invest in the development of a conceptual framework not overly determined or constrained by Christian categories. Of course, this makes great demands on theologians. Indeed, to avoid the problem of Christianizing other religions, we need theologians who take seriously the messy complexities of trans-religious and cross-cultural transformations, who are unafraid to cross borders and refrain from the tendency towards *a priori* systematization.

Comparative Theology

From the 1990s onwards,[7] comparative theology entered the theological scene, contributing to the debate on religious diversity. Attentive to the above-mentioned criticisms, comparative theologians contest neat distinctions, reject grand narratives and undercut abstract systematizations in the name of difference (Fredericks 2010: xv). Some even argue for "a moratorium on construction of theologies of religion" (Duffy 1999: 105). Instead of spending all their time and energy on elaborating a systematic-theological approach to religious diversity that replaces the real diversity with neat schematic interpretations, comparative theologians devote themselves to the serious study of one or more traditions.[8] To them, serious study is both an ethical and theological

---

7 Since the 1990s, an increasing number of studies explicitly identified as 'comparative theology' have been published. Academic communities and associations under this name have been founded, and professorships as well as postgraduate study and research programs have been established at several, also top ranking, universities (e.g., Harvard). Though most comparative theologians operate in the American academy, in Europe too, scholars are beginning to explore the possibilities of this innovative theological approach.

8 If the theology of religions might be called an exemplar of the modern penchant for big theories, comparative theology rather tallies with a postmodern mindset (see Knitter 2002: 175).

responsibility: it is an ethical responsibility to do justice to the otherness of the Other; and it is a theological responsibility not to a priori limit where God may reveal Godself. Comparative theologians at least try to keep the question of a deep engagement with another religious tradition open in a theological sense. The result is a particular form of doing theology that sets out to reflect on the Christian faith tradition in comparison with one or more other traditions (Hedges 2010: 52). Particular and local comparison becomes an integral part of theology without, however, seeking to develop overall and systematic accounts of religious pluralism.

Comparative theology consists of an intersection of two different disciplines: theology and religious studies. This intersection implies a cross-fertilization between the 'confessional and normative' perspective of theology dedicated to truth-seeking on the one hand and, on the other hand, the 'distanciated, neutral' perspective of the comparative religions approach devoted to an 'objective and fair-minded' representation of the 'Other.' According to Michael Barnes, this double commitment of comparative theology is meant to "avoid the twin pitfalls of imposing particular faith-based categories on other traditions and presuming a neutrality that fails to acknowledge its presuppositions" (Barnes 2011: 393).

Comparative theology shares the intention with comparative religion to understand other religions in the most objective and fair-minded manner possible. This implies, first of all, that the theologian "must achieve a certain distance from his or her own starting point, in order to be able to learn from another tradition by understanding it on its own terms" (Clooney 1990:7). It also implies a detailed consideration of religious traditions that are other than one's own. The focal point of this detailed study is the close and comparative reading of strange and familiar texts, referred to as 'inter-texting.' This theological approach is intellectually demanding: only by becoming deeply and holistically engaged in a tradition does it become possible to understand and evaluate a religious text of another tradition. Learning the language of another religious tradition is a prerequisite to understanding strange religious texts. Clooney also advocates reading religious texts along with their formal traditional commentaries, their related scriptures and in light of normative religious practice (Clooney 1990: 30). It is clear that comparative theology really wants to avoid any form of *Christianizing other religious traditions*. The distanciated and 'objective' perspective of comparative religion is there to preserve the self-understanding of other traditions and to avoid stereotyping them.

Nevertheless, the detailed study of other traditions does happen from a commitment to God. Comparative theology acknowledges its normative and *prejudiced* underpinnings: it does not claim to start *tabula rasa*. Comparison is 'alternated' within the theological reflection of the Christian faith commitment to God. As *fides quaerens intellectum*, comparative theology aims at "knowing a loving God more completely and intelligently" (Clooney 2001: 7). The assumption is that theological reflection and judgments based on shaky or biased knowledge of a foreign tradition leads to bad theology. However, whereas the classical theology of religions seems to be motivated by the conviction that it is both possible and necessary to come to a final and definite soteriological appreciation of religions, comparative theology sees interreligious encounter first and foremost as an ongoing conversational process that can yield preliminary results only. The only way to move forward is to ask questions, to study and learn, to seek understanding, to gain insights that only evoke new questions in search of even more nuanced answers. This question-and-answer approach is set in motion by a comparative reading of religious texts that have the power to challenge, interrupt, and transform their readers. Indeed, Clooney warns:

> If we seek a meta-solution, we may inadvertently deny to texts their particular power, and thereby dissipate textual urgency in the course of an investigation ostensibly dedicated to understanding it. We must, therefore, stay with the particularities of the reading process across religious boundaries and the affective states generated in that process. (2005: 389)

Comparative Theology and Religious Hegemony

If one would ask comparative theologians how they seek to overcome the problem of theological hegemony, they would first draw attention to their empirical and comparative method that rectifies the theological bent for abstraction; next, they would argue that their theological approach remains pre-dogmatic and pre-systematic. They principally reject the 'totalizing perspective' of the theology of religions (Nicholson 2011: 28). Their approach focuses on particularities rather than generalities, and possible theological conclusions retain their preliminary character. What is more, Nicholson rightly points out that,

> by keeping theological reflection closely tied to the careful reading of particular texts, Clooney's comparative theology maintains a healthy critical distance from reified conceptions like 'Buddhism,' and 'Hinduism,' which

... often reflect and embody a history of asymmetrical power relations between the west and other religions and cultures.

NICHOLSON 2011: 58

Third, and connected to the former point, while comparative theologians do seem to presume that the category of religion is a necessary category for their particular project, they are sensitive to some of the concerns formulated by postcolonial thinkers. From this perspective, they reject a reified understanding of religion and operate rather with a hybrid and fluid understanding of tradition. Clooney, for example, emphasizes that religion is not a static entity but that it undergoes transformation in conversation and confrontation with other religions. He emphasizes that one cannot always predict (let alone control) possible change (Denney 2009: 414). Fourth, comparative theologians reject any ideology of purification that implicitly intends to preserve and protect the doctrinal center of (Christian) tradition (Laksana 2010: 4). Rather, their comparative approach happens in a liminal space and acknowledges that creativity often occurs at the margins of tradition (Lee 1995). In this context, Clooney sometimes depicts the comparative theologian as a marginal theologian.

> Comparative study makes the theologian a person inhabiting the border between two worlds, in a space distinguished by a variety of disciplines, traditions, and loyalties. She exists in-between, no longer a sure fit in the world of theology as comfortably imagined within a specific community. She is likely then to remain a marginal figure—albeit of a kind valuable to the religious traditions and also to the wider religiously diverse society.
> (2010: 158)

Instead of trying to 'solve the problem of religious diversity' in a theological meta-narrative, comparative theologians engage in crossing borders, moving back and forth between one's own tradition, and the strangeness of another religious tradition, allowing themselves to be truly immersed in both. Instead of encircling the doctrinal heart of Christian tradition trying to find definitive answers to the theological meaning of religious diversity, comparative theologians practice theology in a marginal space. Instead of trying to protect the tradition from the possibility of contamination that comes with encounter, comparative theologians intentionally move to the borderland of tradition, accepting strange religious texts as sources for theologizing.

> The Christian who first reads and then asks the theology of religions questions will not be asking about what is entirely strange or alien, as if she or he were a gate-keeper who has to decide whether to let the other

in at all; nor will she or he be dealing with what is entirely predictable, once inside. Rather, the basic question will be about how to make sense, as a Christian, of a set of Christian experiences and texts and theologies that now includes certain non-Christian texts that remain vital and creative.

CLOONEY 1990: 36

As go-betweens, comparative theologians invest in learning from the other, accepting that this also entails disturbing experiences of alienation, disenchantment, and friction (Clooney 2001: 165). In this sense, comparative theology seems to be all about leaving the theological comfort zone of the centrist approach to theology. For that reason I have called comparative theology *vulnerable theology* (Moyaert 2012).

The Need for a Certain Vigilance

Comparative theology promises much and at first sight it seems to be successful in its intention to overcome hegemonic theological discourse (Nicholson 2011: 45). Nevertheless, there are reasons to remain vigilant, certainly in light of history. As Hugh Nicholson rightly points out, we know that the problem of religious hegemony is a complex problem that will not simply disappear (Nicholson 2011: 58). Every theological approach has its weaknesses.

In what follows, I want to submit this new theological discipline to a hermeneutics of suspicion in an effort to detect some of its potential blind spots. In particular, I want to examine if the textual focus of comparative theology does not unduly limit this project and does not misconstrue religious Others from the outset. Indeed, I wonder if comparative theology, because it privileges interest in religious texts, does not remain stuck in the typical Western cognitive approach to religion, focusing on comparable beliefs and containable convictions. Is its underlying understanding of religion not too elitist or even intellectualist, and therefore too narrow? Does it really succeed in overcoming some of the problems related to the notion of 'religion' as discussed earlier? To address these questions I turn to Clooney and explore how he justifies the textual focus of comparative theology.

Clooney explicitly states that there is no reason why comparative theology *should be* limited to the study of texts, and he "often tells his students one could (also) do a study of ritual, one could do a study of art or music" (2011: 136). He makes it clear that he does not want his textual approach to become *the model* for what comparative theology should be. Nevertheless, to his mind, the practice of comparative *reading* is the most promising and, as a matter of fact, most comparative theologians have followed his example, focusing on inter-texting. Clooney states:

> In my view, the foremost prospect for a practical comparative theology is
> the *reading* of texts, preferably classical scriptural and theological texts
> that have endured over centuries or millennia and guided communities
> in their understandings of God, self, and other. (2010: 58)

He gives various reasons for the textual focus of comparative theology: apart from his own intellectual curiosity, he argues that sacred books are consti-tutive for the formation of the religious imagination of particular religious communities and that the practice of reading is formative of faith. If we want to access the central (theological) convictions of particular religious commu-nities, we should read and study their religious texts. Reading a "non-Christian" text "initiates an encounter of religions, and involves the reader in hearing and understanding a specific other voice, not just the generic 'world religions'" (Clooney 1990: 34).

Next, he refers to the public accessibility of religious texts (in contrast to, for example, ritual practices and sacred spaces).[9] In our globalized world, re-ligious texts are easily available, whether online or via specialized bookshops and even tourist stands. What is more, there often exist good (authoritative) translations and, together with their present commentaries it becomes fea-sible, according to Clooney, to read and compare religious texts from different traditions (if one is willing to engage in serious study!). It is clear that Clooney is reacting against tribal property claims; it simply makes no sense to him to widely distribute religious texts and then react in anger at those who actually read and study them.[10] The fact, of course, that symbolic practices, rituals, and

---

9   On the sensitivity of rituality in interreligious encounters, see Moyaert (2014).

10 From a hermeneutical perspective, one could argue that comparative theology builds on
    the principle of distanciation, which explains its focus on the universalizability of written
    documents. According to this hermeneutical principle, writing institutes a threefold dis-
    tanciation vis-à-vis the original author, context and public. In straightforward terms, this
    means that the "ideas and ideals conveyed within a written text can no longer be firmly
    tied to their authorial context" (King 1999: 65). What a text may come to mean is at least
    co-determined by the interaction between the text and its contemporary readers. The
    good thing is that religious meanings become more universalizable, and thus accessible
    to a greater public. As Richard King explains, "written texts become disembodied and de-
    contextualized in so far as they can now be separated from their original contexts" (King
    1999: 65). The process of distanciation makes strange texts accessible beyond the borders
    of their cultural, religious, and historical community. As a consequence these scriptures

sacred sites are much more sensitive and often remain off-limits to outsiders, explains why Clooney argues that "a text is surely the easiest and surest site of learning" (2011: 136).

Third, Clooney strongly believes that theology is a human and religious activity common to many wisdom traditions. What is more, "if faith is articulated in reasonable terms and defended reasonably, then that reasoning provides a shared theological ground, and intelligent disagreements become possible in an interreligious context" (2001: 8–9). Of course, if a theological reasoning about beliefs is central to comparative theology, the sacred scriptures of faith communities become the "privileged target" of comparative exploration (Maraldo 2010: 90), for texts have been "central to most theologies."

Again, Clooney does not claim that comparative theology *should* be focused on texts, and he emphasizes more than once that the meaning of religious life cannot be exhausted in textual study. When justifying the textual focus of this theological project, he even downplays its significance at times, as if it could just as well have been different, as if it would not alter comparative theology fundamentally if it were to shift its focus to non-textual dimensions of religious traditions. However, on other occasions, Clooney not only expresses his love for texts but also his firm conviction that they are the privileged locus for comparative theology. In his understanding, a religious text may function as an exponent of an entire religious tradition, rich in wisdom. The strangeness of a religious text, even though it is only a minor part of a larger religious whole, evokes the beauty, vitality, and richness of the religious life of another. It has the strength to catch our eye, precisely because what it expresses, symbolizes, and enacts is so different from the way we try to live our (religious) life. By reading another text one may become subject (also as outsider) to the transformative power of religion. Let me quote him here at length:

> Texts are sites wherein intentional, integral transformation is plotted and promoted in a coherent way. Skilled authors compose in such a way as to transform their intended, attentive readers, to bring their lives into

---

have become "world scriptures" (Leirvik 2011: 337). The idea that 'insiders' would be the only true possessors of their religious texts and hence the only ones authorized to read and interpret them becomes contested. A strange religious text may disclose its meaning to attentive readers, even if they do not belong to the community for which the text was originally meant. In view of interreligious hermeneutics, the importance of the distanciation of the text should not be underestimated. It is actually preconditional to an interreligious hermeneutics (and thus also to comparative theology) which presumes that "one can also understand what one is not, cannot be, or does not want to be" (Mattern 2008: 71). Decontextualization and recontextualization go hand in hand.

conformity with the realities and values their texts describe. Step by step, such texts draw the well-disposed person into a religious reading that is richly multidimensional and productive of affects irreducible to reasons offered in justification. Religious writing itself becomes the locus for further theological reflection: if openings for spiritual commitment and practice are written into a text, and if the text is read across religious boundaries to good effect, then intellectual and spiritual formation may be deepening and intensifying, as it were, line by line.

CLOONEY 1990: 368

By reading the religious texts of another tradition one gains some sort of insider perspective, experiencing something of the richness and wisdom of that tradition in a way that would otherwise be difficult. That is why Clooney claims: "If we wish to learn and be changed by what we learn, in the process of learning and over a longer period of time, we are unlikely to identify any other practice as reliably rich and fruitful as the reading of rich and complex religious classics and their commentaries ...," and he concludes by saying that "reading can be primary even if religion is not lived only or mainly through books, and even if religious learning is not always a matter of book learning" (2010: 58).

I am not sure whether I fully can agree with this conclusion. Indeed, there are various reasons to believe that this textual focus is far less innocent than is often assumed. It could even be argued that Clooney, and this seems to be true for most comparative theologians, is an exponent of what has been called 'textualism,' which precisely has contributed to the construction of world religions as monolithic entities with more or less fixed boundaries. Though this may be putting it too strongly, I do not think it suffices to counter this critique by saying "others may develop a different approach that focuses on art, performance, space or rituality, but I like reading texts," as Clooney sometimes does. If comparative theology is serious about its effort to overcome religious hegemony, it has to scrutinize what has been called the textual *bias* of comparative religion and theology and explore how it will have contributed to the misconstruction of religious Otherness (King 1999: 43).

The Textual Bias of Comparative Theology

The study of religion (and theologians of religions follow this lead) has tended to focus on written documents that can be subjected to various hermeneutical analyses that enable the disclosure of meaning and truth. Religion became associated primarily with the realm of beliefs and convictions, which, in the opinion of most academics, are translatable into doctrinal statements. Scholars like King, Asad, Goody, and Ong have called this literary bias the most important factor in the misrepresentation of religions. They have argued that the importance attached to sacred texts as central to the identity formation of religious communities is typical of a Western Christian understanding of religion that is too cognitive and elitist. It will be difficult to do justice to the particularities of religious traditions if one departs from this textual bias.

According to King, the textual bias of religious studies originates from (liberal) Protestantism:

> The two interrelated factors of the Protestant Reformation and the mass production and distribution of printed texts in Europe since the eighteenth century have both contributed to a high degree of literacy in the West. The Reformation promoted an individualistic approach to religion and the ideal that all Christian should be able to read the bible for themselves. Combined with the growing availability of the printed word, we find a strong academic emphasis upon the text as the locus of religion. (1999: 43)

Indeed, the increased circulation of religious texts as a consequence of printing allowed certain wisdom traditions to spread beyond their original and local context and become world religions (Clooney 2010: 58). In the West, academics have come to regard 'world religions' that have written documents on myth, rite, doctrine, and ethics as models for defining religion.

This textual focus is understandable: when encountering strange cultures and traditions, people always search for something they recognize. This was no different for academics operating in the emerging field of the study of religions; they looked for something that resembled their own tradition (Droogan 2013: 29). They searched for something manageable in the midst of bewildering strangeness. This often resulted in a focus on those wisdom traditions that shared certain Christian characteristics, particularly that of textuality. The outcome is a contested focus on the 'world religions,' which are, by and large, religions that have produced written texts. Religions that do not have written texts are often ignored by religious scholars and this certainly also holds true for theologians. The disregard of non-textual wisdom traditions is significant, if we take into account that "the vast majority of religious expression throughout history has been of a non-literate nature, taking the form of speech, song, performance or iconography" (King 1999: 62).

The problem, however, is not only the disregard for non-scriptural traditions. Even with regard to so-called scriptural traditions, the assumption that religious texts form the heart of religious life is not self-evident. To a certain extent, comparative theology too complies with what John Maraldo has called the "standard understanding of religion and interreligious dialogue;" the latter "takes religion to be primarily a matter of teaching and belief in teachings. It presupposes that teachings are formulated and handed down in texts, or at least that they can be so formulated .... The usual emphasis is on what adherents of the religion believe, on expressible content" (2010: 90). This mentalist approach to religion and, by extension, to interreligious dialogue, has been criticized for being disconnected from *lived enacted religion, everyday ritual, and practice*.[11] Comparative theology, too, is more about what has been written down in canonical texts or authoritative commentaries and less on what people believe and practice in reality:

> Whose religion do idealized doctrinal systems, labeled Hinduism and Christianity represent if they can be said to exist in separation from and, in some instances, in direct opposition to what actual Hindus and Christians believe? What sense does it make to refer to actual beliefs and practices of certain religious people as Hindu and Christian if these phenomena bear little relationship to the doctrines and practices of Hinduism and Christianity.
>
> KING 1999: 69

The importance attached to sacred texts as central to the identity formation of religious communities is overstated. This is especially problematic since comparative theology intends to do justice to the particularities and complexities of the religious traditions it studies.

While any theological discussion about religion will most likely also relate to textual sources such as sacred scriptures and their commentaries, it does not follow that textuality is the most likely locus to describe and interpret religion. One might rightly argue that this approach is reductive and unable to do justice to the particular realities of lived religion. The overemphasis on textuality does not succeed in adequately describing important elements of the religious dynamics. I agree with Peter Kenny who states that

> it is just as important to discuss and interpret its activities, its liturgies, its recommended lifestyles, as well as its sacred texts. The creative interaction between what is textual ... (in religion) and what is non-textual (liturgical rites and/or following a way of life guided by specific practices) is here not properly appreciated. The non-linguistic and non-textual

---

11   See Arbuckle (2010), Tanner (1997), Tanner et al. (2001).

religious expressions may be more difficult to describe and evaluate phil-osophically, yet they are just as real as the textual expressions. (Believers) are formed religiously in a complex nexus of religious experiences that form a way of life that includes sacred texts, but certainly not exclusively an in many cases not primarily. (2004: 103)

Materializing Religion

The critique of textual bias does not mean that one can no longer engage in interreligious hermeneutics or that comparative theologians should give up their commitment to interreligious reading practices. It is clear that religious texts continue to play an important role in religious traditions. Nevertheless, the central place that has been attributed to them should be nuanced. What is more, comparative theologians ought to be aware that this textual bias may function as a blind spot vis-à-vis non-textual practices. To be more specific, I would argue that this textual bias, which has long informed the study of religion, has led especially to an underestimation of the importance of the material dimension of religion.

As explained above, the focus on texts goes hand in hand with a mental-ist understanding of religion, which associates religion primarily with beliefs. The emphasis on the cognitive dimension of religion—on what is believed—can go together with the assumption that the beliefs of one tradition can be thematized, understood, and rationally discussed apart from that tradition's related religious practice.[12] If and when that is the case, beliefs become disembedded and disembodied. They become disconnected from lived reli-gion, and the problem of abstraction resurfaces. This is a real problem since the mentalist approach to religion builds on an antithetical scheme, in which mind and body, belief and ritual, content and form, contemplation and social action, are contrasted. As Birgit Meyer and Dick Houtman have argued, this has even resulted in an antagonism between religion and materiality, accord-ing to which matter may divert from real religion (2012: 1). Religion becomes dematerialized.[13] Authentic religious life comes to presume an emancipation (and Enlightenment) from attachments to concrete and material things and

---

12   In Jewish tradition, for example, beliefs are not that central at all. 'Judaism' does not have
      a creed like Christians do. Of course, Jews do talk about God, but they do so mainly in
      stories that are complex and contradictory.
13   Meyer and Houtman (2012: 8): "The dematerialization of religion points to a semiotic op-
      eration that downplays or overlooks ... materiality, placing it in opposition to spirituality
      and establishing the antagonism between religion and things."

practices (Droogan 2013: 22). True religiosity is an existential or experiential state that may be expressed in more or less reasonable beliefs. These non-material elements of religion, these "experiences, beliefs, philosophies, doctrines, textual history, literature, ethics" (Droogan 2013: 23), have been central to religious studies and theology. The material dimension of religion, however, has been overlooked at worst or underrated at best. As Julian Droogan describes the situation:

> Overwhelmingly, the studies of religion community [sic], and historians of religion especially, have placed material objects and things outside of their usual field of inquiry, or at least shifted them to one side of it. This has resulted in a situation where material objects are perceived (if they are perceived at all) as almost irrelevant, or at best a distraction, from the other more important elements of religion under consideration.
>
> DROOGAN 2013: 23

As is usually the case with such antithetical schemes (religion vs. materiality; mind vs. body; spirit vs. object; belief vs. rite), they are evaluative too, expressing appreciation for so-called de-materialized (read: spiritual and textual) religions and disapproval of the more material religions. Indeed, certainly in nineteenth century studies of religions, this evaluation was often expressed in a genealogical perspective. High traditions were less dependent on material elements than less developed traditions, which revolved around concrete worship practices, religious objects and sacred sites: "Obviously this view echoes typically Protestant critiques of Catholicism and, for that matter, 'Paganism' as 'idol worship,' as being steeped in a magical attitude that falsely attributes a spirit to inanimate matter" (Meyer and Houtman 2012: 10). The textual focus of comparative theology does not testify to a critical consciousness of this critique. It may even reproduce a (Protestant) dematerialized account of religion, which is, to my mind, a one-sided account of religion.

For that reason, I would argue that comparative theology stands in need of what has been called a materialization of religion (King 1999: 72). At stake is the effort to move beyond the antithetical pattern that opposes religion and materiality, and privileges textuality as the locus to understand religion, to instead appreciate matter as the primary dimension of religion. This means:

> asking how religion happens materially, which is not to be confused with asking the much less helpful question of how religion is expressed in material form. A materialized study of religion begins with

the assumption that, their use, their valuation, and their appeal are not something added to a religion, but rather inextricable from it.
MEYER and HOUTMAN 2012: 7

This also means that we must at least begin to consider the possibility that religion is not primarily a theory or a worldview: it is first and foremost a form of life centered on incarnated meanings and embodied practices. What is religiously meaningful is profoundly intertwined with particular words, standard formulas connected to particular rhythms and rhymes, or objects, certain places or moments, specific sounds, chords, etc. The 'material' gives shape to religious meaning. For that reason, to understand religion, one should not focus solely on the 'cognitive' dimension of religion but also take into account those concrete, particular, and 'outer' elements that form the heart of religious life. This demands that we open our eyes to the obvious, namely that religious faith manifests itself in a variety of concrete material forms. Indeed, William Keenan and Elisabeth Arweck are right when they state that in the religious realm matter *matters*:

> Without their material expressions, religions float in theological ether, and spiritualities enter the void, lifeless and deracinated. The human mind and hand, be they refined and delicate or rude and horny, are turned doggedly down the generations to the creation of countless material modes of expressing religious sensibility, identity and belonging. When dealing with the things of the spirit, matter matters inordinately.
> KEENAN and ARWICK 2006: 1

Religious beliefs are embedded and embodied. They are, as I explained elsewhere, incarnated (Moyaert 2014). The point is not simply to discover or uncover deep religious meanings/truths about the divine that lie beneath their material expressions; at stake is rather that we learn to grasp how these material expressions re-present the divine—they make it present in this world. From this perspective they are of primary importance if one wants to understand religion. On the one hand, religious meanings cannot exist apart from their *material embodiment*; on the other hand, they cannot be reduced to it either.:

> What is holy or sacred in a religion is in a special way connected with holy names, places, moments, objects or events in which it is or was once present. The name needs to be pronounced with dignity, written

> in capitals, the places and times dissociated from everyday activity; the
> objects are taboo or to be touched only by ordained people, etc.
>
> DE DIJN 2006: 17

The divine moves in what is tangible and visible, and hence the importance of
concrete religious aspects. The outer religious aspects are "paradoxical ways
in which the transcendent becomes immanent, but without losing its transcendence and without the immanent being a mere, disposable vehicle of
the transcendent" (De Dijn 1999: 373). The 'outer,' the symbol, the ritual performance, the words uttered, "are not the house in which the transcendent
finds a temporary accommodation, not the incarnating envelope that is simply
wrapped around the *incarnatum*, as the body to the soul. They are neither sign
nor expression nor supplement; they sign-ify, in-form, im-press themselves, or
they produce that which one would be mistaken to think they only serve to
supplement" (Visker 2004: 138). These concrete religious elements are *marked*
by the divine, which they incarnate.

Inspired by recent insights from religious scholars, ritualists, and archeol-
ogists, I would argue that material culture may act as one of the important
locales for the study of lived religion. This focus on material culture is not opposed to belief. Rather, one might argue that material religion is how belief
comes into being and becomes real. As David Morgan puts it: "materiality mediates belief ... material objects and practices enable it and enact it. Handling
objects, dressing in a particular way, buying, displaying, and making gifts of
particular commodities, attending certain events are all activities that engage
people in the social relations and forms of sacred imagination that structure
their relations to the divine" (Morgan 2010a: 12). This approach is not about
marginalizing belief, but rather about how belief has been embedded and
embodied in the material features of lived religion (Morgan 2010a: 7).

It is clear that both religious scholars and comparative theologians do not
often relate to the more concrete embodied dimensions of religion—such
as symbols, ritual, and sacred space—possibly because these dimensions do
not seem to lend themselves naturally to systematic reasoning. Nevertheless,
if comparative theology wants to rectify some of the problems related to
the theology of religions, I think this discipline should consider this turn to
materiality and should develop a meta-reflection on how matter matters in
the encounter between religions. This is particularly important, because this
novel approach—comparative theology—really intends to do justice to the
concrete particularities of religious traditions. Its textual bias, however, limits
this. I would argue that the material dimension is indispensable for the formation of beliefs, religious identities, and faith communities and, for that reason,

to bring 'matter' into focus would present a novel and exciting new approach that will do more justice to lived religion.

Conclusion

Looking back at thirty years of theologies of religions, I see subsequent stages in a dialectical process in which theologians—committed to the goal of constructive interreligious relations—have set out to move beyond various forms of Christian triumphalism. I have argued that Christian hegemonic discourse and the accompanying symbolic violence is much more deeply rooted in our theological language than is usually recognized—even by comparative theologians. Though the latter set out to overcome the hegemonic tendencies inherent to Christian discourse, I have showed that this specific approach suffers from a textual bias, which may unduly limit this project and may even lead to a novel misconstruction of religious Others. From this perspective, I have argued that this textual focus of comparative theology needs to be corrected by a *materialization* of religion.

Bibliography

Banki, Judith. (2008). "Praying for the Jews. Two Views on the New Good Friday Prayer." *Commonweal* 14 March: 12.

Barnes, M. (2000). *Traces of the Other: Three Philosophers and Inter-Faith Dialogue*. Chennai: Satya Nilayam Publications.

———. (2002). *Theology and the Dialogue of Religions*. Cambridge Studies in Christian Doctrine Series no. 8. Cambridge: Cambridge University Press.

———. (2011). "Reading Other Religious Texts: Intratextuality and the Logic of Scripture." *Journal of Ecumenical Studies* 46: 389–410.

Cheetham, D. (2003). *John Hick: A Critical Introduction and Reflection*. London: Ashgate.

Clatworthy, J. (2010). "Liberal Theology to Bring Peace or a Sword." *Modern Believing* 51: 44–53.

Clooney, F.X. (1990). "When Religions Become Context." *Theology Today* 37: 30–8.

———. (2001). *Hindu God, Christian God: How Reason Helps to Break Down the Boundaries between Religions*. Oxford: Oxford University Press.

———. (2005). "Passionate Comparison: The Intensification of Affect in Interreligious Reading of Hindu and Christian Texts." *Harvard Theological Review* 98.4: 367–90.

———. (2010). *Comparative Theology. Deep Learning across Religious Borders*. Chichester: Wiley-Blackwell.

———. (2011). "Comparative Theology as Theology." In: D. Cheetham, U. Winkler, O. Leirvik, and J. Gruber (eds.). *Interreligious Hermeneutics in a Pluralistic Europe*. Amsterdam and New York, NY: Rodopi. pp. 131–47.

Cornille, C. (2008). *The Im-Possibility of Interreligious Dialogue*. New York: Crossroad.

D'Costa, G. (1996). "The Impossibility of the Pluralist View of Religions." *Religious Studies* 32: 223–32.

———. (2000). *The Meeting of Religions and the Trinity*. London: Continuum.

De Dijn, H. (1999). "Values and Incarnation." In: Marco Olivetti, Michel Henry & Rolf Kühn (eds.). *Incarnazione*. Padua: Cedam. pp. 371–79.

———. (2006). *Religie in de 21ste eeuw: Kleine handleiding voor voor- en tegenstanders*. Kapellen: Pelckmans.

Denny C. (2009). "Interreligious Reading and Self-Definition for Raimon Panikkar and Francis Clooney." *Journal for Ecumenical Studies* 44: 409–31.

Droogan J. (2013). *Religion, Material Culture and Archeology*. London: Bloomsbury.

Duffy S. (1999). "A Theology of the Religions and/or Comparative Theology." *Horizons* 26: 105–15.

Egnell H. (2001). "Scriptural Reasoning: A Feminist Response." In: D. Cheetham, U. Winkler, O. Leirvik, and J. Gruber (eds.). *Interreligious Hermeneutics in Pluralistic Europe: Between Texts and People*. Amsterdam and New York, NY: Rodopi. pp. 79–82.

Fredericks, J. (2010). "Introduction." In: F. Clooney (ed.). *The New Comparative Theology: Insights from the Next Generation*. London: Continuum. pp. ix–xix.

Gilkey, L. (1987). "Plurality and its Theological Implications." In: J. Hick and P. Knitter (eds.). *The Myth of Christian Uniqueness*. London: SCM Press. pp. 37–52.

Griffiths, P.J. (1990). "Introduction". In: P.J. Griffiths (ed.). *Christianity Through non-Christian Eyes*. Faith Meets Faith Series. Maryknoll, NY: Orbis.

Hedges, P. (2010). *Controversies in Interreligious Dialogue and the Theology of Religions*. Controversies in Contextual Theology Series. London: SCM Press.

Hick, J. (1973). *God and the Universe of Faiths: Essays in the Philosophy of Religion*. London: MacMillan.

———. (1993). *Disputed Questions in Theology and Philosophy*. London: MacMillan.

———. (1995). *Christian Theology of Religions: The Rainbow of Faiths*. London: SCM Press.

———. (2004). "Pluralism Conference." *Buddhist-Christian Studies* 24: 253–55.

Keenan, W.J., and E. Arwick. (2006). "Introduction: Material Varieties of Religious Expression." In E. Arwick and W.J. Keenan (eds.). *Materializing Religion: Expression, Performance and Ritual*. Aldershot: Ashgate.

Kenny P. (2004). "Conviction, Critique and Christian Theology: Some Reflections on Reading Ricoeur." In M. Junker-Kenny (ed.). *Memory, Narrativity, Self and the Challenge to Think God: The Reception Within Theology of the Recent Work of Paul Ricoeur*. Münster: Lit. pp. 92–116.

King R. (1999). *Orientalism and Religion: Postcolonial Theory, India and the 'Mystic East.'* London: Routledge.

Knitter, P. (2002). *Introducing Theologies of Religions.* Faiths Meets Faith Series. Maryknoll, NY: Orbis.

———. (ed.). (2004). *The Myth of Christian Superiority: A Multifaith Exploration.* Maryknoll, NY: Orbis.

Kwok, Pui Lan. (2005, 1989). *Postcolonial Imagination and Feminist Theology.* Louisville, KY: Westminster John Knox.

Laksana, B. (2010). "Comparative Theology Between Identity and Alterity." In: F. Clooney (ed.). *The New Comparative Theology: Insights from the Next Generation.* London: Continuum. pp. 1–20.

Lee, J. Young. (1995). *Marginality: The Key to Multicultural Theology.* Minneapolis: Augsburg Fortress.

Leirvik, O. (2012). "Interreligious Hermeneutics and the Ethical Critique of the Scriptures." In: D. Cheetham, U. Winkler, O. Leirvik, and J. Gruber (eds.). *Interreligious Hermeneutics in Pluralistic Europe: Between Texts and People.* Amsterdam and New York: Rodopi. pp. 333–52.

Lopez, D. (1998). "Belief". In: M.C. Taylor (ed.). *Critical Terms for Religious Studies.* Chicago: University of Chicago Press. pp. 21–35.

Maraldo, J. (2010). "A Call for an Alternative Notion of Understanding in Interreligious Hermeneutics." In: C. Cornille and C. Conway (eds.). *Interreligious Hermeneutics* Interreligious Dialogue Series 2. Eugene, OR: Wipf and Stock. pp. 89–115.

Mattern, J. (2008). *Zwischen kultureller Symbolik und allgemeiner Wahrheit: Paul Ricoeur interkulturell gelesen.* Nordhausen: Traugott Bautz.

McCarthy, K. (1998). "Reckoning with Religious Difference: Models of Interreligious Moral Dialogue." In: S.B. Twiss and B. Grelle (eds.). *Explorations in Global Ethics: Comparative Religions Ethics and Interreligious Dialogue.* Boulder, CO: Westview. pp 73–117.

Meyer, Birgit, and Dick Houtman. (2012). "Introduction: How things Matter." In: Birgit Meyer and Dick Houtman (eds.). *Things: Religion and the Question of Materiality.* New York: Fordham University Press. pp. 1–23.

Milbank, J. (1990). "The End of Dialogue." In: G. D'Costa (ed.). *Christian Uniqueness Reconsidered: The Myth of a Pluralistic Theology of Religions.* Maryknoll, NY: Orbis. pp. 174–91.

Morgan, D. (2010a). "Introduction the Matter of Belief." In D. Morgan (ed.). *Religion and Material Culture: The Matter of Belief.* London: Routledge. pp. 1–20.

———. (2010b). "Preface." In: D. Morgan (ed.). *Religion and Material Culture: The Matter of Belief.* London: Routledge. pp. xiii–xiv.

Moyaert, M. (2011). *Fragile Identities: Towards a Theology of Interreligious Hospitality.* Amsterdam: Rodopi.

————. (2012). "On Vulnerability: Probing after the Ethical Dimensions of Comparative Theology." Special issue on European Perspectives on Comparative Theology. *Religions* 3: 1144–61.

————. (2013). "Interreligious Dialogue." In: D. Cheetam, D. Pratt, and D. Thomas (eds.). *Understanding Inter-religious Relations*. Oxford: Oxford University Press. pp. 193–217.

————. (2014). "Inappropriate Behavior? On the Ritual Core of Religion and its Challenges to Interreligious Hospitality." *Journal for the Academic Study of Religion* 27: 1–21.

Moyaert, M., with D. Pollefeyt. (2010). "Israel and the Church: Fulfillment Beyond Supersessionism?" In M. Moyaert and D. Pollefeyt (eds.). *Never Revoked: Nostra Aetate as Ongoing Challenge for Jewish-Christian Dialogue*. Louvain Theological and Pastoral Monographs, 40. Louvain: Peeters.

Nicholson, H. (2010). "The New Comparative Theology and Theological Hegemonism." In: F. Clooney (ed.). *The New Comparative Theology: Insights from the Next Generation*. London: Continuum. pp. 43–62.

————. (2011). *Comparative Theology and the Problem of Religious Rivalry*. Oxford: Oxford University Press.

Placher, W. (1989). *Unapologetic Theology: A Christian Voice in a Pluralistic Conversation*. Louisville: Westminster.

Pratt, D. (2003). "Contextual Paradigms for Interfaith Relations." *Current Dialogue* 42: 3–9.

Race, A. (2001). *Interfaith Encounter: The Twin Tracks of Theology and Dialogue*. London: SCM Press.

Ratzinger, J. (1998). "Interreligious Dialogue and Jewish-Christian Relations." *Communio* 25: 29–41.

Schmidt-Leukel, P. (2005). "Exclusivism, Inclusivism, Pluralism: The Tripolar Typology—Clarified and Reaffirmed." In: P.F. Knitter (ed.). *The Myth of Christian Superiority: A Multifaith Exploration*. Maryknoll, NY: Orbis. pp. 13–27.

Tanner K. (1997). *Theories of Cultures: A New Agenda for Theology*. Minneapolis: Fortress Press.

Tanner K., et al. (2001). *Converging on Culture: Theologians in Dialogue with Cultural Analysis and Criticism*. Oxford: Oxford University Press.

Visker R. (2004). *The Inhuman Condition: Looking for Difference after Levinas and Heidegger*. London: Kluwer Academic Publishers.

WCC Subunit. (2013). *Who do We Say that We are?—Christian Identity in a Multireligious World*. Geneva: WCC.

CHAPTER 15

Theology of Religions in a Postcolonial Perspective: Epistemological and Ecclesiological Reflections

Sigrid Rettenbacher

Introduction

No judge, if he had before him the worst of criminals, would treat him as most historians and theologians have treated the religions of the world. Every act in the lives of their founders which shows that they were but men, is eagerly seized and judged without mercy; every doctrine that is not carefully guarded is interpreted in the worst sense that it will bear; every act of worship that differs from our own way of serving God is held up to ridicule and contempt. And this is not done by accident but with a purpose, nay, with something of that artificial sense of duty which stimulates the counsel for the defence to see nothing but an angel in his own client, and anything but an angel in the plaintiff on the other side. The result has been—as it could not be otherwise—a complete miscarriage of justice, an utter misapprehension of the real character and purpose of the ancient religions of mankind.

MÜLLER 1873: 221F

Nearly a century after Friedrich Max Müller gave expression to this negative assessment of theologians and their treatment of other religious traditions something happened within the Roman Catholic Church (which is the specific denomination this paper will deal with) that Müller in the context of his colonial times would not have dared to dream of: for the first time in the history of that church the Second Vatican Council (1962–1965) officially appreciated other religions in a positive manner by recognizing elements of truth and holiness inherent in their traditions (*Nostra Aetate* 2). The positive appreciation of other religious traditions was accompanied by an awareness for the church's history of guilt vis-à-vis these traditions, in particular Judaism. While in comparison to the preliminary discussions and drafts this history of guilt is only treated in a cautious and reserved manner in the texts of the council (cf. Siebenrock 2009: 663), it is explicitly dealt with in the confession of guilt that John Paul II made in the name of the church in the year 2000. This confession of sin not only faces misconduct in the church's relation to the people of Israel but in relation to other religious traditions and cultures as well. In straightforward openness it is admitted that:

> Christians have often denied the Gospel; yielding to a mentality of power, they have violated the rights of ethnic groups and peoples, and shown contempt for their cultures and religious traditions.

Thus, they have:

> to repent the words and attitudes caused by pride, by hatred, by the desire to dominate others, by enmity towards members of other religions and towards the weakest groups in society.
>
> JOHN PAUL II 2000: V

In the light of this admission of sin and the development of what came to be called the theology of religions—a direct result of the new definition of the church's relation to other religious traditions at the Second Vatican Council—it might seem that Müller's negative judgment regarding the theological view of other religious traditions no longer holds. However, is a biased and dismissive attitude towards other religious traditions really only a question of the past? Or is this question treated in a more subtle way today—disguised in the seemingly positive acknowledgement of political correctness? Though it will not be possible to answer this question in a generalizing and once-for-all manner, a closer look at the present debate in the theology of religions prevents us from putting this question aside too quickly.[1] Although one cannot deny the positive developments and the more nuanced theological perspectives on other

---

1   *Christianity and the World Religions*, for example, published by the *International Theological Commission* in 1996, is one official document that treats the challenges of theology of religions in a rather nuanced way—even if theology of religions is once again often identified with an undifferentiated view of the pluralist position. In this document the *International Theological Commission* recognizes that—out of theological reasons—theology of religions is an unavoidable undertaking. Still the document sees imperfection and weakness only in other religious traditions and it does not identify weaknesses in one's own ecclesial tradition. Interestingly enough, the document states that "The theology of religions does not yet have a clearly defined epistemological status" (4). This remark indeed seems to be the cause why, in the present debate about theology of religions, the discussions revolve around the same problems without a solution being in sight. Unfortunately, *Christianity and the World Religions* also fails to propound new insights. The problem is stated, but not further elaborated. In this article, an attempt will be made to introduce new epistemological reflections into the

religious traditions, which reflections in the theology of religions have brought about, one aspect of interreligious encounters closely linked to the above cited observation of Müller remains notoriously blanked out in the present debate. Beyond the insight *that* it is necessary to theologically reflect on religious plurality in order to do justice to the present context and the signs of the times, the epistemological and power-related question remains unanswered *in which way* religious plurality is construed by way of discourse and *how* one's own religious identity is discursively constructed in demarcation to other religious identities. These questions of discursive identity constructions, of representation, and power politics are dealt with in postcolonial theories (e.g. Ashcroft et al. 2006; Castle 2001; Castro Varela and Dhawan 2015). While a postcolonial theoretical framework stemming from cultural studies is now taken up in religious studies as well (King 1999; Nehring 2012b; Nehring 2003b; Nehring 2012a), its systematic adoption in the theology of religions is to a large extent still overdue.[2] This is what the German theologian and scholar of religion, Andreas Nehring, has worked out with respect to the Indian context and Christian mission there in the colonial times of the nineteenth and twentieth century:

> While theology reflects this encounter [between Christianity and other cultures in a colonial context] in the hermeneutics of interreligious encounter, cultural studies have adopted another perspective: since two decades they have been focusing on the discourse model which was developed by Edward Said—taking up Michel Foucault and Antonio Gramski—in order to unmask the structures of power underlying Western representations of the Orient in the colonial context. Up to now there has been only little relation between both levels of reflection. Although inner-Christian reflections on interreligious dialogue [i.e., the theology of religions] have critically analysed the pre-conditions of perceiving other religions, and the theological implications of an intercultural hermeneutics—developed within cultural studies—of understanding the stranger have [also] been reflected upon, it has hardly been taken into consideration in interreligious dialogue that the conditions of

---

discussion by integrating thoughts from postcolonial theories into the, especially its ecclesiological foundation.

2 This is most notably true for the German speaking context. In the English speaking debate one finds more differentiated approaches to the theology of religions, including the adoption of insights from postcolonial theories (see, for example, Daggers 2013; Hedges 2010; Hill Fletcher 2005).

understanding are influenced by a hegemonic discourse, which exercises its power in the very fact of representing the stranger.

NEHRING 2003A, 18

In a systematic perspective this chapter intends to integrate these discourse-critical questions from postcolonial theories into the project of the theology of religions. In what way can the theology of religions profit from adopting a postcolonial perspective? What theological insights can be drawn from this non-theological perspective by integrating a critical awareness for discursive representations and questions of hegemonic power relations into the present debate on the theology of religions? The structure of the chapter is tripartite. The first part consists of an analysis of the shortcomings and problems in the present state of debate in theology of religions. The second part concentrates on postcolonial theories and their contribution to the topic of religion and religious identities. In the third part, these two perspectives are brought together with a view to developing a postcolonial approach to theology of religions. This postcolonial approach is situated within the framework of systematic theology especially concentrating on the ecclesiological and epistemological implications of postcolonial theories for the theology of religions.

A Theological Perspective on Other Religious Traditions: The Present State of Debate in the Theology of Religions

The Catholic Church rejects nothing that is true and holy in these [other] religions. She regards with sincere reverence those ways of conduct and of life, those precepts and teachings which, though differing in many aspects from the ones she holds and sets forth, nonetheless often reflect a ray of that Truth which enlightens all men.

NA 2

The importance of this statement of Vatican II for establishing a positive relation to other religious traditions becomes obvious when one compares it to previous statements, such as that issued by the Council of Florence 500 years earlier:

[The Holy Roman Church] firmly believes, professes and preaches that 'no one remaining outside the Catholic Church, not only pagans,' but also Jews, heretics and schismatics, can become partakers of eternal life; but they will go to the 'eternal fire prepared for the devil and its angels' (Mt 25:41), unless before the end of their life they are joined to it.

Without exaggeration one can say that the Second Vatican Council is *the* important milestone in the Catholic tradition for the development of the theology of religions (Dupuis 1997: 2–4, 12). At Vatican II, a new self-concept of the Catholic Church emerged which made a positive appreciation of other religious traditions possible. The important hermeneutical change in perspective that took place at this last council of the church was that attention was not only given to the question of salvation of individual non-Christian believers but equally to the status of other religious traditions as such in God's plan for salvation (Dupuis 1997: 158–70). The ability to recognize truth and salvation outside the church was founded in a new understanding of the ecclesial tradition. The church no longer conceived of itself as a *societas perfecta* independent of all earthly realities. Recollecting qualities of the church in its early biblical and patristic times, the modern Roman Catholic Church began to enter into a dialogue with the contemporary world. Thus, also on a performative level the new developments in the church's relations to other religious traditions were a genuine outcome of the council and its new self-understanding of the church: an appreciation of elements of truth and holiness in other religious traditions was not on the Council's agenda from the very beginning. Only through impetus from without was the church finally able to recognize truth and salvation outside its own reality (Rettenbacher 2011; Batlogg 2003).

When one looks into current approaches to the theology of religions, the Second Vatican Council is generally recognized as the condition that made the development of the theology of religions project possible. However, what present debates do not take into consideration is that the new ecclesiology of the Council was the driving force behind this new theological discipline. This reveals a peculiar ecclesiological ambivalence in the theology of religions. A positive appreciation of other religious traditions only becomes possible because the church is no longer the exclusive indicator for a salvific relation to the divine mystery. The divine reality itself and its mediation through Jesus Christ are at the center of current debates in the theology of religions. This legitimate turn from an ecclesiocentric approach to other religious traditions and their believers to a Christocentric or theocentric approach is due to a long and problematic history of the axiom *Extra ecclesiam nulla salus est* ('there is no salvation outside the church) (Sullivan 1992; Dupuis 1997: 84–109). However, it is exactly the new self-concept of the church as developed by the Second Vatican Council that makes the new approach to religious plurality and thus the development of the theology of religions possible. It is not by chance that it was the first council of the church that was about the church that called the church's attention to other religious traditions as mediators of salvation and truth. Hence, ecclesiology and its relevance for the theology of religions have to be taken into consideration anew. Therefore, some important elements of the new self-concept of the church as it emerged in the Second Vatican Council shall be dealt with in more detail in order to work out some of the shortcomings of the present debate in the theology of religions.

Two important elements of the new self-concept of the Catholic Church as developed in Vatican II have already been mentioned: an openness to religious plurality that goes hand in hand with a new capability of the church, namely the capability to confess guilt for its own ecclesial past. Both capabilities were not restricted to the realm of religious plurality (cf. Rettenbacher 2010b: 341ff.). On the contrary, they were connected to the very identity of the church as represented by Vatican II and could therefore be found in a variety of documents in different contexts. The church was no longer conceived of as a *societas perfecta*, a direct and explicit foundation of the historic Jesus, based on a strong identification between Jesus Christ and the church and resulting in a hierarchically structured institution independent of other realities of the world and immune to all criticism whatsoever (cf. LG 5). At Vatican II, a new ecclesial attitude was performatively enacted and discursively specified: an attitude of self-relativization. Identification and exclusion were no longer the only means of defining the identity of the church.[3] Rather the new self-understanding of the church was based on an acceptance of alterity and differences within and outside the church (cf. Hoff 2011: 117–36). Inside the church, the relation of Christ and the church was no longer described as a pure identification—the church as a prolonged incarnation so to speak, an understanding of the church that marked the concept of *societas perfecta*. The *Dogmatic Constitution on the Church* used the metaphor of the incarnation in a more nuanced way stating that the church was comprised of earthly and heavenly, human and divine elements. Therefore,

> [w]hile Christ, holy, innocent and undefiled knew nothing of sin, but came to expiate only the sins of the people, the Church, embracing in its bosom sinners, at the same time holy and always in need of being purified, always follows the way of penance and renewal.
>
> LG 8

---

3 This can, for example, be observed in a new form of language at the council: Vatican II was the first council that was not based on anathemas but on a positive appreciation of otherness.

This nuanced perspective on the reality of the church corresponds to a new appreciation of the world outside the church, where "many elements of sanctification and of truth" (LG 8) were to be found. Thus, the relation between the church and world with its multiple others, the relation between the gospel and the signs of the times was conceived of as a mutual enrichment. Plurality and the strengths of others could be accepted exactly because one's own weaknesses were no longer denied.

However, this nuanced new self-concept of the church, which made the development of the theology of religions possible, has not been integrated into current approaches to this discipline. When one looks at current debates in the field of the theology of religions, one finds that ecclesiological reflections are completely missing due to the above mentioned axiom *Extra ecclesiam nulla salus est*. Yet, since ecclesiology, as the place of Christian identity construction, is directly connected to a Christian epistemology (the way reality is understood and conceived of), a lack of ecclesiological awareness in the theology of religions (the attempt to understand and make sense of religious plurality) is problematic. This is where I see two of the main shortcomings in the present debate in the theology of religions. First of all, current debates only see the connection between Vatican II and the theology of religions in a historic perspective. The council is valued highly as the central event that made openness towards other religious traditions and thus the development of the theology of religions possible. However, one does not find reflections on how the new openness is rooted in a modified self-understanding of the church. In other words, systematic reflections on ecclesiology as the necessary epistemological requirement for opening oneself towards other religious traditions are totally missing. The second shortcoming in the current debate on the theology of religions concerns Christology. Given the fact that the mystery of Jesus Christ stands in the center of Christian theology, a Christian theology of religions, as a theological enterprise, has to revolve around Christological questions. Christology is the most fundamental challenge in the present theology of religions as it is not clear how belief in Jesus Christ as the unique savior of humankind goes together with a positive acceptance of other religious traditions. Therefore, pluralist theologians have modified the traditional understanding of Jesus Christ, denying his divine nature and stressing his humanness. The impetus behind these pluralist attempts is clear: by stressing that human knowledge of transcendent reality is limited, they seek to overcome an arrogant Christian attitude of superiority vis-à-vis other religious traditions that they see as intricately interwoven with the belief in the divine nature of Christ (Kuschel 1996: 481ff.). In the face of the guilt connected with the Christian Church's

encounter with other religious traditions resulting from this attitude of superiority, the pluralist motivation is more than comprehensible. However, a
closer examination shows that the problem of a Christian history of guilt vis-
à-vis other religious traditions and the challenge of limited human knowledge of transcendent reality cannot be solved in the framework of Christology
(Rettenbacher 2011: 58ff.). A Christian attitude of superiority and a blinding
out of human perspectivity do not lie in the intention of the mystery of Christ.
In Jesus Christ, whose humanity is intricately connected to his historic particularity, God reveals himself as the one who humbles himself and was made
in the likeness of human beings (Philippians 2:5–8), a God who is on the side
of the marginalized.

When one takes the idea of incarnation and kenosis seriously, any Christian
attitude of superiority vis-à-vis other religious traditions is a contradiction in
itself. On the other hand, it does not make sense to speak of kenosis if the
human nature of Christ is emphasized alone—as some pluralist theologians
do in order to avoid any claim of Christian absoluteness. The theological and
soteriological significance of the idea of kenosis is only complete when one
acknowledges the Chalcedonian confession in the divine and human nature
of Christ—without confusion, unchangeably, indivisibly, inseparably. Therefore, any attempt to solve the problem of the church's history of guilt and the
limited nature of human knowledge of transcendent reality on the level of
Christology is prone to failure from the very beginning. One has to shift the
question to another level, namely the level of ecclesiology. The problem of the
history of guilt and the challenge of the limited nature of human knowledge
do not lie in the mystery of Christ. They have to do with the church's mediation of this mystery through time and space. This mediation of the church,
however, even if it is an authentic and authoritative one, remains human and
thus prone to failure. The question not tackled so far is how the church, in its
mediation of Christ, construed its own identity and the identity of others by
way of binary oppositions and whether these identity constructions correlate
with the kenotic character of the Christian faith.

Summing up the two shortcomings of the present debate one can say that
a lack of ecclesiological reflection within the theology of religions goes hand
in hand with a missing epistemological awareness for the role of the church as
the central place of identity construction. There is no theory of identity or the
discursive construction of identities within the theology of religions. This is
exactly where postcolonial theories come in as they offer a critical framework
for analyzing how the way one sees oneself and the way one sees the other are
intricately related.

A Perspective from Cultural Studies: Religious Traditions in a Postcolonial Hermeneutics

In the quotation cited at the beginning of this chapter, Müller claimed that a dismissive interpretation of other religious traditions was not an accidental occurrence but part of a larger strategy, followed by theologians and historians (in a modern context one could probably add atheists or radical secularists) in order to show the superiority of one's own tradition or perspective in comparison to the inferiority of competing others. The non-objectivity observed by Müller in his studies on comparative religion is now—over a century later—developed in a more systematic manner in the field of postcolonial studies. Emerging as an interdisciplinary project at the time of the independence movements within former colonies after the Second World War, postcolonial studies are especially interested in the discursive construction of identities, in questions of power and representation, and in silenced voices. Using theoretical frameworks from poststructuralism, postcolonial theories show in a deconstructive mode of thinking that identities are not fixed entities (see Castro Varela and Dhawan 2015). Rather identities are discursively constructed on the borders between two traditions or cultures. In this process of identity negotiation, however, the power balance is not even. In the contact zones at the borders "disparate cultures meet, clash, grapple with each other, often in highly asymmetrical relations of domination and subordination" (Boyarin 2003: 74). Thus, the demarcation line between two cultures is not clear-cut and predetermined once for all. On the contrary, one has to ask which strategies of representation and which power interests have discursively generated seemingly fixed and independent identities. This is not only true for cultural identities but for religious identities as well. Religious traditions "rather than bounded cultural systems... are intrareligious and interreligious networks of cultural relations" (Chidester 1996: 260). This dynamic system of interrelationships discloses religions as "invented traditions" and "imagined communities" (Chidester et al. 2003: 302) so that—in a genealogical perspective—one has to ask "where and when did this idea [of religion(s)] emerge" (Boyarin 2003: 66). The answer does not surprise: "It is on the borders, at the contact zones, that we find 'religions' being produced" (Boyarin 2003: 66). "It is the 'inter'—the cutting edge of translation and negotiation, the in-between space... —that carries the burden of the meaning of culture" (Bhabha 2006: 157) and religion. Thus, religious traditions, in the process of their formation but also in the context of later encounters, are produced and discursively constructed in a complex network of power-related interreligious relations.

In his concept of third space, the important postcolonial theorist Homi Bhabha has offered a theoretical explanation of the discursive construction of identities taking place at the borders (Bhabha 1994). The third space uses a spatial metaphor to make clear how identity negotiations take place at the borders, in the in-between-space that marks the contact zones between cultures. The spatial concept of the third space thus has significant epistemological implications: there are no immutable meanings and no fixed representations. Rather identity constructions have to be imagined as a liminal process marked by hybridity. The concept of third space thus offers a theoretical explanation for a dynamic and relational understanding of identity. In the discursive construction of identities, the image one has of oneself and the image one has of the other(s) are mutually related:

> The intervention of the Third Space, which makes the structure of meaning and reference an ambivalent process, destroys this mirror of representation in which cultural knowledge is continuously revealed as an integrated, open, expanding code. Such an intervention quite properly challenges our sense of the historical identity of culture as a homogenizing, unifying force, authenticated by the originary Past, kept alive in the national tradition of the People.... It is only when we understand that all cultural statements and systems are constructed in this contradictory and ambivalent space of enunciation, that we begin to understand why hierarchical claims to the inherent originality or 'purity' of cultures are untenable, even before we resort to empirical historical instances that demonstrate their hybridity.... It is that Third Space, though unrepresentable in itself, which constitutes the discursive conditions of enunciation that ensure that the meaning and symbols of culture have no primordial unity or fixity; that even the same signs can be appropriated, translated, rehistoricized, and read anew.
>
> BHABHA 2006: 156F

By deconstructing the idea of apparently immutable and essentialistically given identities and by destabilizing seemingly fixed boundaries, the concept of third space thus offers a subversive potential to critically interrogate dominant discourses of power and representation.

Even if at first glance, it may seem that postcolonial theorists like Homi Bhabha propose a constructivist position by claiming that identities are discursively constructed, their main purpose is not to show that there is no reality outside discourse. Rather they want to draw attention to the insight that there is no possibility of relating to reality outside this power-driven discourse:

Indeed, to 'refer' naively or directly to... an extra-discursive object will always require the prior delimitation of the extra-discursive. And insofar as the extra-discursive is delimited, it is formed by the very discourse from which it seeks to free itself. This delimitation, which often is enacted as an untheorized presupposition in any act of description, marks a boundary that includes and excludes, that decides, as it were, what will and will not be the stuff of the object to which we then refer. This marking off will have some normative force and, indeed, some violence, for it can construct only through erasing; it can bound a thing only through enforcing a certain criterion, a principle of selectivity.

BUTLER 2011: XX

If the only possibility of grasping reality is by way of discourse, a critical awareness has to be developed for the epistemological and hermeneutical perspectives and power interests by which the discourse is formed. Furthermore, an imbalance in power between those who have the power to represent and define and those whose voice is not heard has to be discerned. An awareness of the silenced voices and those aspects that are concealed in the discourse helps to lay open the complex processes of exclusion that are at the basis of every discourse. As a consequence the subalterns and marginalized are not reduced to their status of victims. Rather, their potential for subversive resistance is laid open (see Spivak 1994).

As a deconstructive approach to the question of identity, postcolonial theories cannot be reduced to a mere historic enterprise focusing on (post) colonial issues. Rather, their critical view on discourses and power politics makes postcolonial theories an eminently epistemological enterprise offering insights into a wide range of issues even beyond those immediately connected to colonial times. Even if in the beginning postcolonial studies were very much focused on the question of cultural identities, their scope has been continuously widened so that postcolonial theoretical frameworks have been adopted in different disciplines. Thus, religious identities have been subject to postcolonial investigation as well. Postcolonial scrutiny has not only offered insights into the idea of "religion" as a Western hegemonic concept (Smith 1991) but also into the discursive construction of religious traditions in the encounter with religious Others—be it in the time of their formation (Boyarin 1999; Boyarin 2004; Lieu 2006; Neuwirth 2010), in missionary or colonial encounters (Nehring 2003a; King 1999; Bauer 2011; Sørensen 2007) or in present-day dialogue (Rettenbacher 2013).

If one takes postcolonial insights into representation, power politics, and the discursive construction of identities seriously, one has to put any theological treatment of other religious traditions under a hermeneutics of suspicion—at least at first glance. Even if theological perspectives on other religious traditions are no longer guided by the blunt refusal described by Müller, theological representations of other religious traditions are nevertheless far from being innocent. Thus, the project of the theology of religions and its theological reflection on other religions traditions is severely called into question regarding its material object (the concept of religion and other religious traditions) as well as its formal object (its theological and thus biased perspective). The question is: is a theological perspective on other religious traditions still legitimate? Is it possible to integrate questions of power, identity constructions, and hegemony into theological reflections on other religious traditions in the theology of religions? Based on historical, formal, and material reasons that have to be specified in more detail in the next section one can argue it is.

Ecclesiology as an epistemological concept directly related to identity politics will play a central role in bringing a postcolonial perspective into the theology of religions. For only when ecclesiology is not excluded but actively dealt with can questions of representation, power, and identity politics be tackled in this field. The problematic consequences of the axiom *Extra ecclesiam nulla salus est* should not lead to ignoring ecclesiological questions in the encounter with other religious traditions. A theology of religions allegedly free of ecclesiology, and the questions of identity construction and power associated with it, is all the more prone to be subject to its own claim of power. Only if a theology of religions is done in a postcolonial perspective can a critical awareness of questions of power relations and identity be developed. Thus, a deconstructive mode of thinking in the theology of religions can help to creatively and productively reveal resources in one's own theological tradition that overcome biased perceptions of alterity and difference based on a binary definition of otherness.

Thinking the Two Together: Theology of Religions in a Postcolonial Perspective

Seen in a postcolonial perspective, the question is: is the theology of religions still possible? Based on historical, formal, and material reasons one can argue that it is. However, a new theological epistemology is called for that is able to integrate an insight into the limited nature of human knowledge of transcendent reality with a theory of the discursive construction of identity. This has to be done in an awareness of the history of guilt in the church's encounter with other religious traditions. These epistemological reflections are very much connected to ecclesiological questions, as ecclesiology is the place where Christian identity is constructed and is thus intricately related to the epistemology of the Christian tradition. If one looks into the Christian tradition, one can find many theological resources with the help of which postcolonial challenges for the theology of religions can be encountered. Before these material resources for adopting postcolonial thought into the theology of religions are specified in more detail, historical and formal reasons that justify the use of postcolonial theoretical frameworks in theology will be dealt with.

Even if it is generally not perceived in all clarity, from a historical perspective the theology of religions and postcolonial studies are connected in their origins. Developing in the 1960s, both were an answer to the radical changes that came about in the world after the Second World War. After former colonies had become independent in the wake of the Second World War, the plurality of cultures, of different ways of life, and of religious traditions became apparent. While Vatican II recognized *that* it had to deal with this challenge of plurality in theological terms, postcolonial studies were already one step ahead. They were aware that plurality as such was not the primary concern; the primary concern was the *way in which* or *how* this plurality was construed. They knew that Western representations of other cultures were not innocent and had to be subjected to a hermeneutic of suspicion. Now, half a century after the church opened itself to plurality and cultivated a certain competence in dealing with plurality and alterity, which it had not been able to do before Vatican II, it is time to go one step further and ask how plurality and otherness are constructed within the church. This will help to develop a self-critical awareness for instances where alterity is not appreciated due to binary constructions of otherness. And it is exactly Vatican II that formally justifies an adoption of postcolonial theories within theology, as it was the Council itself that made it part of ecclesial identity to seek dialogue with interlocutors from outside the church. These dialogue partners can help the church to better understand the signs of the times and thus the gospel itself, which has to be read in constant interaction with the challenges of contemporary society. What a concrete dialogue between theology and postcolonial theories can look like will now be examined by taking up two basic postcolonial principles and their respective theological counterparts. The question of the power of discourses is paralleled with a theological epistemology, and the discursive construction of identities is brought into dialogue with ecclesiological questions. This dialogue between postcolonial theories and theology will help to develop criteria for a theology of religions in a postcolonial perspective suitable for current challenges in the field.

Epistemological Insights: The Power of Discourses

One great issue in the field of postcolonial studies is the power of discourse to create reality. What is interesting is the fact that one finds this very insight in the concept of theology itself as well: talk about God. That one can talk about God is not founded in the fact that God is an object of reality like other objects. No, there is no direct access to God. The divine reality can only be grasped through language. Language is the only means to create a certain conception of the divine reality. Three examples will be mentioned very briefly to illustrate the connection between the human conception of the divine reality and language. Revelation is a very apt example. Revelation does not mean that the divine reality is entirely given. Revelation only functions in the grammar of revealed and concealed (Hoff 2007). As one cannot get hold of transcendent reality, language is the only means to apprehend it. Another theological instance of the power of discourses to create reality is Christology. Systematic Christological reflections only started when the historical Jesus was no longer there. Only through language and interpretation could the first Christians grasp what had happened at Easter. The sacraments can also be mentioned as another example of the power of discourses. The well-known formula *Accedit verbum ad elementum et fit sacramentum* ("when the word is added to the element or the natural substance, it becomes a sacrament") directly hints at the power of language to create reality. These examples show that theology as a discursive enterprise is very much concerned with interpretation and it is important not to forget that the boundaries of language and interpretation are not the boundaries of the divine reality itself. For theology this means that one also has to expect to find God in unknown and unexpected places. When talking about postcolonial insights for a theological epistemology one has to ask how far questions of power and representation influence theological discourses and their apprehension of the divine reality. In the field of the theology of religions, the same question has to be applied to theological representations of other religious traditions. Up to now it is not very common to ask questions like these in the field of the theology of religions.

Ecclesiological Insights: The Discursive Construction of Identities

Besides theological epistemology, ecclesiology is another important theological field where the insights of postcolonial theories can be reflected, as ecclesiology is the place where the Christian identity is discursively constructed (Rettenbacher 2010a). Focusing on the discursive construction of identities it must be seen that processes of inclusion and exclusion are unavoidable and necessary for identity construction (Nassehi 2011: 161–90). However, where the boundaries are drawn is contingent. Boundaries are not naturally given, they are historically grown and thus contextually influenced. For the identity of the church and the boundaries on which it is based, this implies a moment of self-relativization (as demonstrated by Vatican II) and an attitude of humility (see Cornille 2008). This has consequences for the concept of church itself: when the church is conceived of as a sign, the sacramental role of the church cannot be understood as a direct correspondence between a signifying element and a signified reality. Rather—following the concept of sign as proposed by Charles Sanders Peirce—it is a three-digit relationship between a signifying element, a signified reality and the context of interpretation. To be understood, a sign has to refer to multiple other signs—a process of an infinite semiosis according to Peirce (Oehler 1993: 60–75, 126–33; Hookway 1992: 118–44). If the interrelationship between signs turns out to be harmful, it can be corrected by introducing other, more fruitful, interrelationships between signs. For the understanding of the church as a sign, this means that the church is always influenced by a certain context and that the church is part of a complex network of interrelationships, which are not free of power politics (Rettenbacher 2010a). So what is called for is a greater awareness in ecclesiology and the theology of religions of the discursive politics on which the identity of the church is based. The identity of the church and its history of guilt have to be seen within the complex network of power relations in which they are embedded.

Consequences for a Theology of Religions in a Postcolonial Perspective

To conclude, one can sum up the thoughts presented in this chapter on the theology of religions and its relation to postcolonial theories as follows: given the limitations on human knowledge of transcendent reality and the absolute claims nevertheless related to it—often resulting in a history of guilt in the encounter with other religious traditions—it is necessary to integrate insights from postcolonial theories into epistemological and ecclesiological reflections within the field of the theology of religions in order to be able to self-critically address questions of power and representation as well as the discursive strategies of identity construction. The discursive and performative construction of identity as represented in ecclesiology is an unescapable process. Still, a critical awareness of questions of power and the systematic exclusion of differences in this process of identity construction is called for. This implies a deconstructive mode of thinking within the theology of religions. The central criterion for such a postcolonial approach to the theology of religions is the question of how far one is able to construct one's own identity and relate to oneself in such a way that there is place for a positive relationship with others. Or to put it another way: is it possible to accept differences in such a way that one's own weaknesses can be accepted as well as the strength of others?

Bibliography

Ashcroft, B., G. Griffiths, and H. Tiffin (eds.). (2006). *The Post-Colonial Studies Reader.* 2nd ed. London and New York: Routledge.

Batlogg, A. (2003). "Christentum und andere Religionen: Die Konzilserklärung *Nostra Aetate.*" *Historicum. Zeitschrift für Geschichte* 73: 16–22.

Bauer, T. (2011). *Die Kultur der Ambiguität. Eine andere Geschichte des Islams.* Berlin: Verlag der Weltreligionen.

Bhabha, H. (1994). *The Location of Culture.* London and New York: Routledge.

———. (2006). "Cultural Diversity and Cultural Differences." In: B. Ashcroft, G. Griffiths, and H. Tiffin (eds.). *The Post-Colonial Studies Reader.* 2nd ed. Oxford and New York: Routledge. Pp. 155–57.

Boyarin, D. (1999). *Dying for God: Martyrdom and the Making of Christianity and Judaism.* Figurae: Reading Medieval Culture. Stanford: Stanford University Press.

———. (2003): "Semantic Differences: Or, 'Judaism'/'Christianity'." In: A. Becker and A. Reed (eds.). *The Ways that Never Parted: Jews and Christians in Late Antiquity and the Early Middle Ages.* Texts and Studies in Ancient Judaism 98. Tübingen: Mohr Siebeck. Pp. 65–85.

———. (2004). *Border Lines: The Partition of Judaeo-Christianity.* Divinations: Rereading Late Ancient Religion. Philadelphia: University of Pennsylvania Press.

Butler, J. (2011). *Bodies That Matter: On the Discursive Limits of "Sex."* Routledge Classics. London and New York: Routledge.

Castle, G. (ed.). (2001). *Postcolonial Discourses: An Anthology.* Oxford: Blackwell.

Castro Varela, M., and N. Dhawan. (2015). *Postkoloniale Theorie. Eine kritische Einführung.* Cultural Studies 36. 2nd rev. ed. Bielefeld: Transcript.

Chidester, D. (1996). *Savage Systems: Colonialism and Comparative Religion in Southern Africa.* Charlottesville: University of Virginia Press.

Chidester, D., A. Hadland, and S. Prosalendis. (2003): "Globalisation, Identity and National Policy in South Africa." In: P. Dexter and G. Wilmot (eds.). *What Holds Us Together: Social Cohesion in South Africa.* Cape Town and Chicago, IL: HSRC Press. Pp. 295–321.

Childs, P., and P. Williams (eds.) (1996). *An Introductory Guide to Post-Colonial Theory.* London: Prentice Hall.

Cornille, C. (2008). *The Im-Possibility of Interreligious Dialogue*. New York, NY: Crossroad Publishing Company.

Daggers, J. (2013). *Postcolonial Theology of Religions: Particularity and Pluralism in World Christianity*. London and New York: Routledge.

Dupuis, J. (1997). *Toward a Christian Theology of Religious Pluralism*. Maryknoll, NY: Orbis Books.

Hedges, P. (2010). *Controversies in Interreligious Dialogue and the Theology of Religions*. Controversies in Contextual Theology Series. London: SCM Press.

Hill Fletcher, J. (2005). *Monopoly on Salvation? A Feminist Approach to Religious Pluralism*. New York, NY: Continuum.

Hoff, G. (2007). *Offenbarungen Gottes? Eine theologische Problemgeschichte*. Regensburg: Pustet.

———. (2011). *Ekklesiologie*. Gegenwärtig glauben denken -Systematische Theologie 6. Paderborn: Schöningh.

Hookway, C. (1992). *Peirce*. The Arguments of the Philosophers. London and New York: Routledge.

John Paul II. (2000). "Confession of Sins and Asking for Forgiveness." Available at: http://www.sacredheart.edu/faithservice/centerforchristianandjewishunderstanding/documentsandstatements/popejohnpauliiasksforforgivenessmarch122000.

King, R. (1999). *Orientalism and Religion: Post-Colonial Theory, India and "The Mystic East."* London and New York: Routledge.

Kuschel, K.-J. (1996). "Christologie und pluralistische Religionstheologie: Die Herausforderung John Hicks und eine theologische Antwort." In G. Riße, H. Sonnemans, and B. Theß (eds.). *Wege der Theologie: An der Schwelle zum dritten Jahrtausend.* Festschrift für Hans Waldenfels zur Vollendung des 65. Lebensjahres. Paderborn: Bonifatius. Pp. 481–93.

Lieu, J. (2006). *Christian Identity in the Jewish and Graeco-Roman World*. Oxford: Oxford University Press.

Moore-Gilbert, B. (1997). *Postcolonial Theory: Contexts, Practices, Politics*. London: Verso.

Müller, F. (1873). *Introduction to the Science of Religion: Four Lectures Delivered at the Royal Institution with Two Essays on False Analogies, and the Philosophy of Mythology*. London: Longmans, Green, and Co.

Nassehi, A. (2011). *Gesellschaft der Gegenwarten: Studien zur Theorie der modernen Gesellschaft II*. Berlin: Suhrkamp.

Nehring, A. (2003a). *Orientalismus und Mission: Die Repräsentation der tamilischen Gesellchaft und Religion durch Leipziger Missionare 1840–1940*. Wiesbaden: Harrassowitz Verlag.

———. (2003b). "Religion, Kultur und Macht: Auswirkungen des kolonialen Blicks auf die Kulturbegegnung am Beispiel Indiens." *ZMR* 87: 200–17.

————. (2012a). "Aneignung von 'Religion': Postkoloniale Konstruktionen des Hinduismus." In: M. Stausberg (ed.). *Religionswissenschaft: Ein Studienbuch*. Berlin and Boston, MA: De Gruyter Studium. Pp. 109–121.

————. (2012b). "Postkoloniale Religionswissenschaft: Geschichte—Diskurse—Alteritäten." In J. Reuter and A. Karentzos (eds.). *Schlüsselwerke der Postcolonial Studies*. Wiesbaden: Verlag für Sozialwissenschaften. Pp. 327–41.

Neuwirth, A. (2010). *Der Koran als Text der Spätantike: Ein europäischer Zugang*. Berlin: Verlag der Weltreligionen.

Oehler, K. (1993). *Charles Sanders Peirce*. Beck'sche Reihe Denker 523. Munich: C.H. Beck.

Quayson, A. (2000). *Postcolonialism: Theory, Practice or Process?* Cambridge: Polity Press.

Rettenbacher, S. (2010a). "Endlich endlich? Vom Überleben der Kirche im Anerkennen ihrer eigenen Endlichkeit." In: G. Hoff (ed.). *Endlich! Leben und Überleben*. Innsbruck and Vienna: Tyrolia-Verlag. Pp. 160–92.

————. (2010b). "WeltReligionen—Die Kirche in der Welt der Religionen von heute." In: F. Gmainer-Pranzl and M. Holztrattner (eds.). *Partnerin der Menschen—Zeugin der Hoffnung. Die Kirche im Licht der Pastoralkonstitution*. Gaudium et spes. Salzburger Theologische Studien 41. Innsbruck and Vienna: Tyrolia-Verlag. Pp. 323–48.

————. (2011). "Christologie und Religonstheologie: Zum gegenwärtigen Stand einer wechselseitigen Herausforderung." *ET Studies* 2: 41–70.

————. (2013). "Interreligiöse Theologie—postkolonial gelesen." In: R. Bernhardt and P. Schmidt-Leukel (eds.). *Interreligiöse Theologie*. Beiträge zu einer Theologie der Religionen. Zürich: Theologischer Verlag Zürich. Pp. 67–111.

Siebenrock, R. (2009). "Theologischer Kommentar zur Erklärung über die Haltung der Kirche zu den nichtchristlichen Religionen *Nostra aetate*." In: P. Hünermann and B. Hilberath (eds.). *Herders Theologischer Kommentar zum Zweiten Vatikanischen Konzil 3*. Freiburg: Herder. Pp. 591–693.

Smith, W. (1991). *The Meaning and End of Religion*. Minneapolis, MN: Fortress Press.

Sørensen, J. (2007). *Missiological Mutilations—Prospective Paralogies: Language and Power in Contemporary Mission Theory*. Studien zur interkulturellen Geschichte des Christentums 141. Frankfurt, New York, and Oxford: Peter Lang.

Spivak, G. (1994). "Can the Subaltern Speak?" In: P. Williams and L. Chrisman (eds.). *Colonial Discourse and Post-Colonial Theory: A Reader*. New York, NY: Columbia University Press. Pp. 66–111.

Sullivan, F. (1992). *Salvation Outside the Church? Tracing the History of the Catholic Response*. New York: Paulist Press.

Williams, P., and L. Chrisman (eds.). (1994). *Colonial Discourse and Post-Colonial Theory: A Reader*. New York, NY: Columbia University Press.

Young, R. (2003). *Postcolonialism: A Very Short Introduction*. Oxford: Oxford University Press.

CHAPTER 16

The Four Chalcedonian Adverbs: A Reflection on Buddhist-Christian Dual Belonging

Janet P. Williams

Introduction

Reflecting on personal experience of practice in the Zen and Christian traditions, I suggest that the four adverbs of the Chalcedonian definition of faith offer a strong and effective framework within which to explore dual religious belonging. Formulated to address the salvific mystery of two natures in one person, the adverbs remind us that religious identity is always performed in a particular way, and therefore wholesale judgments about dual belonging are inevitably too simplistic to gain any real traction; they are apophatic in tone, and therefore not prescriptive; and they are oriented towards the goal of understanding what it might be to be most fully a person, most completely alive.

Scholars including Perry Schmidt-Leukel, Paul Knitter, and Peter Phan have already connected the Chalcedonian definition of the Christian faith with the contemporary discussion of dual religious belonging; rather than offer a detailed critical appreciation of their work here, I intend instead to offer some further thoughts focused on the significance of the adverbs (Knitter 2012; Schmidt-Leukel 2006: 113; Phan 2004: xxi). By way of a very brief (and inevitably rough-hewn) reminder, the Chalcedonian definition was formulated at a mid-fifth century ecumenical council as a means of marking out the boundaries of orthodox Christology, in response to an increasingly acrimonious controversy between two broad schools of thought, the Alexandrian and the Antiochene. The Antiochene approach stressed the full humanity and the full divinity of Christ to such a degree that it was felt to create what we might call a schizophrenic Christ, someone with rather too much going on inside to be capable of integration into a psychological whole. The Alexandrian approach, by contrast, achieved a much more secure sense of Christ as a being in whom divine and human nature were combined in a single individual agent, but appeared to do so at the cost of attributing to him a less than full humanity. The Council of Chalcedon defined Christ as "one person in two natures," with four modifying adverbs (ἀσυγχύτως, ἀτρεπτως, ἀδιαιρετως, ἀχωριστως) usually rendered into English as "without confusion, without change, without division, without separation."

Much more might be related, of course, including the ongoing controversies, the evaluations and re-evaluations of how far the decision favored either side in the debate, and the linguistic-philosophical wrestling that was required to take the Greek vocabulary of *hypostasis* and *ousia*, and craft an understanding of the human person that was new to these cultures. But prima facie, as others have already recognized, there is an intuitive sense that this Chalcedonian formula, addressing as it does the question of how one psychologically healthy and integrated individual can participate in or belong to two modes of life that have hitherto been seen as contradictory, might have something to offer a discussion of dual or even multiple religious belonging. It is the adverbs, though, that fascinate me.

The Point of Adverbs: We Belong after a Fashion

They fascinate me, first, because our discussion of religious belonging could often be greatly improved by the addition of more modifiers.[1] Ascriptions of faith—or culture—identity are often made simply, so that we can focus on the question at hand, as to how one balances primary and secondary belongings, how far these belongings are complementary, how far incommensurate, how far mutually supportive and so on. But none of us belong, say, to the Christian tradition *simpliciter*; all who belong do so after a particular fashion—in an Anglican or a Reformed sort of way; half- or whole-heartedly; consonantly with or dissonantly from the fashion of our own family or social group; critically or unreflectively; more or less joyously. Furthermore, we all need to add at least one cultural, denominational or ideological modifier—we are liberal Episcopalians, Marxist Methodists, Neoplatonist Anglicans, Scottish Calvinists, African-American Baptists, or Polish Catholics.[2] For some practitioners of dual belonging, the second religious tradition can be seen as an adverbial modifier of the first: for instance, some folks are Christian in a (more or less,

---

1 I will speak here of 'dual belonging' rather than of 'dual identity,' partly because of the reminder that this phraseology contains, that there is a concrete praxis and a relationship to community involved, and partly to locate my thoughts in relation to the admirable work of Rose Drew in her (2011) *Buddhist and Christian?*.

2 There is a depth of complexity to this process, as Ama Samy notes: it isn't enough to say that one understand and performs one's Christian identity through an engagement with the mystical tradition—one needs to specify whether it is an Eckhartian mysticism, or an Ignatian, and so on. (2007: 91).

Soto or Rinzai, Kyoto School-influenced or other) Zen way. In other cases, distinct modifiers will be needed to express both how they are Buddhist, and how they are Christian.[3]

At the very least, therefore—and I want to argue that there is much more—but at the very least the Chalcedonian adverbs serve as a reminder that we need to be sensitive not simply to what sorts of identity are involved in cases of complex religious belonging, but also to how these identities are expressed and performed. One of the reasons why the simpler outright statements such as those of Ross Thompson or Paul Knitter, that Christianity needs Buddhism to complete it; or the Pieris-style analysis that has agapeic Christianity a necessary complement to gnostic Buddhism, do not entirely convince, is that they gloss over the crucial issue of how the tradition is accessed and practiced. For a Christian who has only experienced a conservative literalist approach to the biblical texts, any encounter with Buddhism will simply turn out very differently than it will for a Christian who is already aware of a range of possible readings of John 14:6; and whether the encounter is with the True Pure Land school or Sri Lankan Theravada is also likely to make a considerable difference. Someone with a clinging-on-by-their-fingernails Vatican ii—informed residual Catholic spirituality will encounter the Bede Griffiths Sangha quite differently from someone with a whole-hearted African Pentecostal spirituality. More important still is the question of how all this fits—or fails to fit—with other aspects of cultural and political identity: for example, a western liberal exploring dual belonging to Buddhism and Christianity may enjoy a comfortable and accommodating environment a world away from the challenges faced by a community of immigrant Koreans who are still struggling to connect to their new context the Evangelical Christianity which was defined in Korea over against Buddhism, and who carry the memory of tension and even persecution between the Christian and Buddhist communities. In much of the

---

3   Cornille—among others—recognises that in practice there is a range of ways of engaging with more than one religious tradition; but then goes on to assert that the "selective adoption of [complementary or compatible] beliefs and practices from another religious tradition does not constitute double belonging. The question of the possibility of double belonging presents itself when confronted with the totality of religious beliefs and practices, whereupon the encounter with conflicting or incompatible claims to absolute truth becomes unavoidable" (2003: 45). However, even from *within* a singular tradition, no-one surely ever encounters the *totality* of beliefs and practices, while the decision as to *which* beliefs and practices are complementary and which conflicting will itself be relative to the individual's standpoint within the tradition.

literature on dual belonging the world-view represented seems to be that of the academic community and their peers, for whom religious belonging may be largely a matter of choice[4]—and all the more so in some of the particular niches of Christian-Buddhist dual belonging. But for many people who belong in some fashion to more than one faith tradition, the driver is not choice but parentage, or locality, or livelihood, or relationships. The second or secondary faith is not selected from the available range either thoughtfully or on a whim; rather, it is likely to be a response to something encountered, an experience of being addressed, touched, challenged, intrigued, affected by a person, text, idea, or practice. And for some dual or multiple belongers, at least one of their faith identities might be for all sorts of reasons an uncomfortable and contested place, or might simply be hidden or unacknowledged even to the self, such as those who do not recognize the role that a childhood religious identity continues to play in the construction of an apparently distinct adult religious identity.[5]

Further, it is both normal and desirable for the adverbial modifiers of our religious identity to change over time. Even those of us who remain in one and the same spiritual tradition for the whole of our lives rarely perform it in the same way throughout.[6] Moreover, whatever theological reservations the religious traditions have about changing core identities, they do tend to understand that change in these modifiers can be a sign of positive spiritual growth. That, after all, is the whole burden of faith-development theory.

So far, therefore, attention to the Chalcedonian adverbs should discourage us from ever offering a general verdict, as some have attempted, on the theoretical legitimacy or practical efficacy of dual or multiple belonging between any of the faith traditions; always, it would seem, the inquiry would have to come down to adverbial particularities, to an individual at a specific time and place, at a specific cultural map-reference, in such-and-such a manner, and to the vantage-point from which we are asked to make a judgment.

---

4 Once dual or multiple belonging is seen as *chosen* it is then susceptible to the criticisms that it is ego-driven and part of a shallow eclectic pick-and-mix 'spirituality not religion.' I do wonder about this stereotype: I have met it often in books and talks, but never seen an incarnation of it. It is too liable to support a patronising dismissal of spiritual paths that inconvenience religious leaders.

5 For instance, Western converts to Buddhism from Christianity are often effectively constructing a Protestant form of Buddhism that is deeply coloured by Christian assumptions—a good example of this would be attitudes to merit-making among Western converts affected by the Protestant critique of Catholic indulgences (see Bell 1988).

6 Carlson sees this clearly, arguing that tradition is better understood as a verb than a noun, and that all belonging is inevitably dual or multiple (2003: 79).

Apophatic Adverbs

Further, it is not just that those who framed the Chalcedonian definition relied on adverbs, but the particular ones they chose: the four Chalcedonian adverbs are negative in form, each beginning with the alpha-privative. Nomenclature notwithstanding, these adverbs do not so much define the nature of Christ as map out the limits of acceptable variation. You can express the two-natures-in-one-person doctrine in whatever way works in your context, so long as you do not end up with a Christ who is like one of the demigods of classical culture, neither fully divine nor fully human; so long as you do not end up turning divinity or humanity into something else; so long as you do not make Christ a schizophrenic with more than one center of agency unintegrated inside a single skin; so long as you do not divide him up, divine in certain respects but human in others.

These adverbs place the Chalcedonian definition squarely within the Christian apophatic tradition. They do not tell us how to speak about the union between humanity and divinity in Christ, but only how not to speak about it. The force of the adverbs is epistemological, not ontological: they do not so much comment on what his nature was/not, as on how it would not be helpful to conceive of it. Thus the Chalcedonian definition reminds us that the mystery of Christ cannot be flattened out and pinned down for inspection by the application of categories and analysis; that words are merely verbal gestures pointing our attention in a particular direction, like a finger pointing to the moon. It is not so much that one may choose any positive or kataphatic Christology that fits within the boundaries marked out by the definition, but rather that the terrain becomes a space of practice where there are no guarantees given in advance as to what will emerge within it, and where one will repeatedly try moves and patterns of moves that have then to be abandoned or redirected as they come up against the buffer zones. The enterprise of theological practice within these boundaries becomes anagogic, iteratively experimental, a playful or wrestling engagement with the Spirit and the occasion. And all of this is as true of the mystery of dual belonging as it is of the mystery of Christ. From my own conversations and encounters with practitioners in more than one religious tradition, I would say that very few people indeed—if any—can determine in advance what the relation between their two fidelities will be, nor define exactly what it is at any one time, though they can usually say something about where the boundaries are and how the land lies for them at the moment. One of the reasons why so many Christians say they are attracted to Zen[7] is

---

7 And also, I think, for those attracted to Advaita Vedanta—the many Christians inspired by Bede Griffiths or Abhishiktananda.

that it offers a robust and well-developed practice to Western Christians whose own apophatic tradition has become attenuated by neglect—Zen graciously acting as a surrogate parent to an element of the Christian tradition that had become infertile and inaccessible to many.[8] So for those in particular whose practice combines Zen and Christianity, and in general for any whose dual or multiple belonging is informed by one or more of the apophatic traditions, attention to the Chalcedonian adverbs will be an especially fertile stimulus to their developing practice. There is a paradox to be enjoyed here, too: the apophatic traditions move away from speech because they are convinced that the experience towards which our individual spiritual paths tend is not accessed by the discriminative or dualistic consciousness. If the Chalcedonian adverbs provide an apt framework for dual belonging, they should deter any expectation that we will have two beautifully-worked-out sets of words or images to describe our paths and our aspirations; even to have one such language is more than we should expect or desire.

The impression is sometimes given that we can know in advance of experiment, and absent the modifiers discussed earlier, whether or not a certain type of dual or multiple belonging will bear fruit, and of what type—by setting a list of doctrines or texts or practices against each other and measuring them up.[9] But the apophatic tradition denies that this is possible, because religious or spiritual living cannot be thus reduced: it is an activity and a process which cannot be known in advance, which changes through time, which involves vulnerability to events, and surrender to the possibility of a change of heart and mind.[10] As dual or multiple belongers, if we follow the invitation issued by both Jesus and the Buddha to 'come and see,' we have perhaps only to ask ourselves before we start, what are the boundaries to this space of practice? I suggest that the four Chalcedonian adverbs offer a helpful and viable framework: I perform my Christian practice and I perform my Zen practice largely by paying attention to what arises, mindful to avoid four dangers.

First, I practice ἀσυγχύτως. Usually translated 'without confusion,' I suggest in this context 'without fusion.' The image is not about becoming mentally

---

8   This is clear, for example, in Hakan Eilert's description of his encounter with Zen freeing
        him from having been "imprisoned in thinking about God, creating my own images..."
        ("Journey through the Gateless Gate," quoted in Cheetham 2013: 114).

9   Not every comparative reading of Buddhist and Christian doctrines is done simply with
        a view to assessing their commensurability. Knitter (2013) is an impressive example of a
        genuinely exploratory reading.

10   As Geffré says, "Christian identity is always a matter of becoming" (2002: 104).

confused about what we are doing,[11] but about pouring or mixing substances, such as flour and water, creating a new compound which loses some of the characteristics of the ingredients; or in the Dalai Lama's image, it is about putting a yak's head on a sheep's body (His Holiness the Dalai Lama, *The Good Heart: A Buddhist Perspective on the Teachings of Jesus* (Boston: Wisdom Publications, 1996: xii), quoted in Carlson 2003: 78).[12] This is what Ama Samy refers to as "false convergences," creating a synthesis which does not honor the vitality, distinctiveness and sheer complexity of the traditions involved (Samy 2007: 90 et *passim*). Many hybrids in the natural world are infertile, and the same may well prove true of some fused spiritual traditions: while they may form and sustain individual identities, they will lack the generative energy of their original constituents.

Second, I practice ἀτρέπτως. This is usually translated 'without change,' but I suggest 'without alteration.' Although the Middle Platonist metaphysics that dominated at Chalcedon tended to see all spiritual change as decline, we recognize that there is organic change in all religious traditions, as the potential within them develops in response to local conditions, and different elements within them come to dominate at different times. Neo-Darwinist biology shows us exactly why organic change is essential for life, and within spiritual traditions an element of adaptation to changing environments is now usually seen as necessary and good. On the other hand, the kind of change that I mean by 'alteration' is externally-imposed, the deliberate introduction of an alien element. Now given that the point of these spiritual practices is to allow us to break through the delusions of the ego, to find our true selves beyond the 'self' of culture and dualistic consciousness, to begin deliberately modifying our spiritual practice is a risky venture best avoided. Or to put it another way, we do better by adopting the epistemological humility to suppose that it is the self, and not the practice, that is broken and in need of fixing. Both these adverbs (ἀσυγχύτως, ἀτρέπτως) address the Alexandrian style of Christology, and articulate the concerns of the Antiochenes, that in emphasizing the individual integrity of Christ as a living person, the theologians might get divinity and humanity so mixed up that either Christ emerged as a semi-divine hero or that humanity or divinity got changed into something else entirely as a result of the incarnation.[13] Applying them to the practice of dual belonging, we

---

11   Confusion, in any case, is largely a good thing: a precursor to deeper clarity. As Knitter has it, "no confusion, no deepening" (2013).

12   The yak and the sheep, of course, both die in the operation.

13   Of course, there is an *organic* change in human nature that has always been asserted by orthodox theology as a result of the Incarnation—namely its healing or divinisation.

are reminded that even though we are each striving to live one integrated life, to bring together our practices in such a way that they produce harmony and growth in us, we need to do so by honoring their distinctiveness. Practitioners of dual belonging adopt different expedients and make their own judgments in this respect: some will be comfortable, for example, with iconography from both traditions in their practice space, while others have a defined Buddhist space and a defined Christian space, and others still will draw inspiration from art that blends Buddhist with Christian elements; some—such as Corless and Knitter—will be willing to combine Buddhist and Christian approaches in one meditative practice while others like myself prefer to keep them separate. All of us are liable to change and develop our attitudes and behaviors over time.

Third, I live my Christian practice and my Zen practice ἀδιαιρέτως. This is usually translated 'without division,' but I suggest 'without partition.' Whereas division might generate such benign images as cutting up a shared cake, partition evokes the painful memory of a city or province where only the building of a wall will protect citizens from violence. Some degree of division is going to be practically inevitable, but the significance of 'without partition' is that we need to ensure that the two practices are allowed to run up against one another in some way. In Dunne's terminology, we need to be able to cross over from one of these territories to another, and to pass back again. It is this 'without partition' that makes dual belonging such a positive experience for so many of us, as people attest that, for instance, by exploring Zen koans they have acquired new ears for the Sermon on the Mount, or that their practice of Lent has given them new insight into the Buddha's second Noble Truth.

Fourth, I engage in dual belonging ἀχωρίστως. This is usually translated 'without separation,' but I suggest 'without assigning territories.' In David Cheetham's 'architectural' metaphor, drawing on Teresa of Avila's interior castle, the suggestion is that we think of multiple interior spaces (Cheetham 2013: 110–111). There are rich possibilities here to be explored, but I would want to add a word of caution: we come from a tradition in which space is contested, enclosed, and held by authorities under flags. If we begin to assign interior spaces to two or more religious traditions, then the boundary questions naturally arise: where do jurisdictions begin and end? Is there disputed territory, and if so what strategies are employed there—are there skirmishings, fortifications, an intentional and treatied demilitarization, or a no-man's-land littered with ruins and corpses? Perhaps the image we need to complement Teresa's is of territory in those cultures—Australian Aboriginal, native American, and others—where territory is never owned but only wandered, inhabited, graced by the presence of those whom it feeds. This is my sense of the space carved out for practice and contemplation by the four Chalcedonian adverbs. This second pair of Chalcedonian adverbs, ἀδιαιρέτως, ἀχωρίστως were posited to guard against the dangers of an overly Antiochene Christology, to safeguard the core intuition of Alexandria, which is that if all of this conceptualizing does not give us a sense of a living energy, a personality fully alive, fully human and utterly possessed by the activity of divine spirit, wisdom and compassion, then we have not yet got it right. In the same way, if my performance of more than one religious tradition simply divides my energy, makes me half-heartedly Buddhist and half-heartedly Christian, if it is in effect a zero-sum game, then it is not worth the time.[14]

Putting together the two pairs of adverbs, the discipline of observing dual faith-practice without fusion, without alteration, without partition and without assigning territories is intriguingly reminiscent of the Buddhist tetralemma, the strategy of responding to a question by rejecting all possible answers: neither p, nor not-p, nor both p and not-p, nor neither p nor not-p. The phrase 'dual belonging' itself therefore, though it has a functional resonance, does not quite fit the bill: we are neither simply 'of one faith' nor 'of two.' Religious faiths are, as the Buddhist phrase goes, 'neither the same nor other.' Christian apophasis and Buddhist non-dualism both recognize that to say that I have one single religious practice would be only partly true; to say that I have two, also only partly true. As regards the positions taken by scholars of religion, both the pluralist stance of some underlying commensurability, and the particularist insistence on radical difference, are affirmed and denied in the fourfold pattern of negation. One has only to live the question, to become it, shifting gear from the cogitative to the existential, from substantives to modifiers, ceasing to wonder 'what is this?' and beginning to explore 'how is this for me?'

From Natures to Persons, Adverbially

Thus the four Chalcedonian adverbs do not simply address the question of the two natures, marking out a space within which they can come together, to coinhere without fusion or alteration, without partition or assigning of territories. The adverbs also mark the conditions under which something new is brought to birth, where a unique and integrated personality or hypostasis emerges—the mystery of Christ, of God incarnate in whom all humanity is

---

14   This is the issue which concerns Cornille (2003: 49): "Double or multiple religious belonging always implies a certain holding back, an inability to accept fully some form of heteronomy, or an inability to let go of one religion when in heart and mind one has already converted to another."

made anew, united with the divine nature. In Buddhist terms, the Chalcedonian adverbs, like the tetralemma, point to the emptiness which is the womb of Buddha-nature, the Tathagatagarbha.[15]

In all the theological and terminological creativity and debate which led finally to the formula of 'two natures in one person,' the issue of what makes a hypostasis or person comes finally down to the fact that an individual person-ality instantiates its nature in a particular way. To put it crudely, the modifiers are not merely about the relation of the natures, but essential to the formation of one person. Therefore, to pay attention only to the tradition/s to which a person belongs is in a sense only to ask the question about their natures. The more interesting questions, as I argued above, will focus on the manner in which they belong. In the case of dual or multiple belonging or practice, we need to ask not only how the individual belongs to each tradition, but how these belongings relate to one another. There are elements of recent writing about dual belonging that recognize this. Elizabeth Harris has described the developments in Sri Lanka which led from a time when dual belonging was seen as perfectly natural, to a time when "religious identity is asserted through difference," (Harris 2002: 78) on the other hand some—perhaps taking a *perennial philosophy* approach—assert (their own) religious identity through an underlying identity of faith traditions. But the dualism of same/different is inadequate to a discussion of faith practice, as Geffré argues: "religious truth is not necessarily under the sign of the principle of non-contradiction" (2002: 101). The Chalcedonian adverbs encourage us to turn from asking about the identity or difference of the faith traditions, to enquire into how we are with their similarities and their differences—in other words, from a theol-ogy of religions to a theology of encounter—and gives ground for hope that we might encounter the many faiths in others and integrate them in our own practice without partition or assigning territories, but also without fusion or alteration.[16]

---

15   For a detailed treatment of the meaning and significance of Tathagatagarbha, see King (1991).
16   Brian McLaren has recently offered a list of un-Christlike ways to be with a different tradition—a sort of '7 deadly sins' of encounter, namely "Domination (Us over Them); Revolution (Us overthrowing domination by Them); Assimilation (Us absorbing Them); Purification (Us eliminating Them); Competition (Us competing with Them); Victimi-sation/self-preservation (Us oppressed by Them); Isolation (Us apart from Them)." The more Christlike manner of encounter would be, to paraphrase McLaren, *after the fash-ion of creation—in tune with the 'fiat' that blesses diversity and fruitfulness.* McLaren has framed his whole book, we might say, adverbially, beginning not with the question of

In some form or other the meeting with the stranger is essential to Christianity, which is by its very nature a practice of encounter with otherness. Or to put it another way, if the central mystery, the saving mystery, of the Christian faith is the life and work of the divine man Jesus, then reconciliation, integration, and preservation of diversity is at the heart of Christian identity. To practice within a second religious tradition (or more) is therefore both additional, or even in a sense superfluous, to Christian faith and at the same time expressive of its core identity.

And in some form or other the realization of interdependence with the other, and the emptiness or non-self of all beings, is essential to Mahayana Buddhism, which is by its very nature a practice of nondualism. Christian practice is just the way impermanence-Buddha-nature manifests in this time and place; it is one of the 'ten thousand things,' it is Suchness, skilful means, the dharmagate. In discussions of dual belonging, attention is often focused on the two natures, the two faith traditions and argument over their commensurability or incommensurability, and the verdicts on the desirability or legitimacy of dual belonging that would follow from the various positions in the typology. Attention to the Chalcedonian adverbs, finally, may lead us instead to the question of the individual person (or by extension, the particular community) in which these natures are incarnated. What is the manner of their encounter? Are they able to come together in such a way as to create a psychological or psychic whole, an energy marked by compassion and wisdom, or are they scarred by domination or assimilation, competition, partition, fusion or alteration? Perhaps the Christian or Buddhist character of an individual is to be seen, not so much in the tradition to which s/he belongs, as in the manner in which s/he incarnates the multitudes s/he contains. According to the tradition represented by the Chalcedonian definition of faith, salvation was enacted not by the two natures but by the mystery of the one person, the one hypostasis of Christ. Those of us who belong to dual or multiple traditions do not then need to select from them only what is compatible; we do not need to resolve the contradictions; we only need to have faith that when we make room to live in the tension, something gracious and salvific, something distinctive and authentic may manifest even if it is beyond words. One returns to the mystery of an incarnate person living two natures with integrity, perichoretically. Just as the Chalcedonian fathers chose to affirm both the insights of Alexandria and those of Antioch, while cautioning against the excesses of both, so also by applying the four Chalcedonian adverbs to the question of dual religious belonging we

---

what we believe about other religions, but of *how* Jesus would treat the great figures of different traditions (2012:108).

might affirm that together both the approaches which stress the irreducible distinctiveness of faiths (particularism, exclusivism) and those which envisage the possibility of their being united in one person (pluralism, inclusivism) may serve as boundaries within which a space opens up for our spiritual practice and growth together. As Rowan Williams puts it, the task is "Not to make sense, inside the keel of sweating ribs, not to make sense but room."[17]

Bibliography

Bell, S. (1988). "British Theravada Buddhism: Otherworldly Theories and the Theory of Exchange." *Journal of Contemporary Religion* 13.2: 149–70.

Carlson, J. (2003). "[Double Religious Belonging: A Process Approach] Responses." *Buddhist-Christian Studies* 23: 77–83.

Cheetham, D. (2013). *Ways of Meeting and the Theology of Religions.* Farnham: Ashgate.

Cornille, C. (2003). "Double Religious Belonging: Aspects and Questions." *Buddhist-Christian Studies* 23: 43–9.

Drew, R. (2011). *Buddhist and Christian: An Exploration of Dual Belonging.* Abingdon: Routledge.

Geffré, C. (2002). "Double Belonging and the Originality of Christianity as a Religion." In: C. Cornille (ed.). *Many Mansions? Multiple Religious Belonging and Christian Identity.* Eugene, OR: Wipf & Stock. pp. 93–105.

Harris, E.J. (2002). "Double Belonging in Sri Lanka: Illusion or Liberating Path?" In: C. Cornille (ed.). *Many Mansions? Multiple Religious Belonging and Christian Identity.* Eugene, OR: Wipf & Stock. pp. 76–92.

King, Sallie B. (1991). *Buddha Nature.* New York, NY: State University of New York.

Knitter, P. (2012). "A 'Hypostatic Union' of Two Practices but One Person." *Buddhist-Christian Studies* 32.1:19–26.

———. (2013). *Without Buddha I Could not be a Christian.* 2nd ed. Oxford: OneWorld.

McLaren, B. (2012). *Why Did Jesus, Moses, the Buddha and Mohammed Cross the Road? Christian Identity in a Multi-Faith World.* New York, NY: Jericho.

Phan, P. (2004). *Being Religious Interreligiously.* New York: Orbis.

Samy, A. (2007). "Zen and Christians." *The Way* 46.2: 89–102.

Schmidt-Leukel, P. (2006) "Chalcedon Defended: A Pluralistic Re-Reading of the Two Natures Doctrine." *The Expository Times* 118: 113–19.

Williams, R. (2013). *A Silent Action: Engagements with Thomas Merton.* London: SPCK.

---

17   The concluding line from his poem "Thomas Merton: Summer 1966," Williams (2013).

CHAPTER 17

Passion and Fog: The Impact of the Discussion about the Theology of Religions Typology on the Epistemology of Comparative Theology

Ulrich Winkler

Introduction

I must confess that I stopped following the discussion on the typology in the theology of religions many years ago, even working on developing a model of my own that was distinguishable from all the other trees in the forest. Such Olympic sports are widely practiced in the discipline of the theology of religions. Moreover, one can sometimes have the impression that the discussion on typologies is the only issue in the theology of religions and that this discussion is a synonym for the theology of religions. But this is not the case.

If this typology and the theology of religions are to be understood in their own right and according to their distinct purposes, we need to clarify the terms and concepts used. We need to do this not only for the sake of the typology or the theology of religions as such; rather, these clarifications are important with respect to the epistemology of comparative theology. Due to the complicated situation in the field of the theology of religions, there is a tendency on the side of comparative theology's proponents to avoid any relation to and dependence on the theology of religions. But this is not advisable because this decision compromises comparative theology when it tries to make a case for its own project.

Therefore, in this chapter I will argue that looking at the typology's epistemology will encourage a broader discourse in the theology of religions and reinforce comparative theology.

Passion and Fog, or Some Reasons for Discomfort with the Typology

In addition to those who find the typology developed by Alan Race (1983) and reinforced by major representatives such as Wilfred Cantwell Smith, John Hick and Perry Schmidt-Leukel helpful, there has been a wide variety of counter-arguments and further suggestions for going beyond or amplifying this threefold typology. According to a very rough distinction between opponents and supporters of pluralism in the theology of religions, the former try to establish the aporia or dead ends to which the typology leads, whereas the latter want to make a more precise survey of the interreligious field. But both are inclined to work with similar insinuations and misinterpretations.

Inappropriate conceptions can be divided into two groups. The first group is relatively harmless—the misconception sees the typology as a description of the actual relations between religions. Therefore, scholars in this group add many other distinctions within the threefold typology or go beyond it in order to arrive at an exhaustive list. But, drawing on Schmidt-Leukel's ground-breaking work (1993, 1996, 1997, 2005), I argue for a strict logical distinction between exclusivism, inclusivism, and pluralism. The first (i.e., exclusivism) claims truth and salvation for only one—that is, one's own—religion. The second (i.e., inclusivism) claims truth and salvation for more than one, but only one incorporates truth and salvation in the highest degree. The third (i.e., pluralism) claims that truth and salvation can be found at the same level in more than one religion. According to Schmidt-Leukel, this typology entails that one make a decision between them. This is a very uncomfortable situation for someone who wants to avoid making a decision and being classified as belonging to one party. Therefore, one proven remedy for escape is to produce a fog by creating a series of other types. I do not want to imply that this is the sole motivation for all these suggestions, but I suspect this might be true in some cases, especially in situations where the church has spoken out against pluralism. I am not condemning these motivations—they may, after all, create room for freedom.

The second, more popular and always polemical, type is the caricature of the pluralist position as a so-called postmodernist trend that is very tolerant, accepting all the different truth claims of the religions without noting their differences, tensions, and mutual contradictions. Those guilty of such caricatures claim they have looked behind the curtain and discovered the real nature behind pluralism, namely, that pluralism is not concerned with truth and not interested in the truth claims of religions at all. Pluralism is, in fact, indifferent towards truth and assumes all religions to be equal without any differences between them.

One variation on this polemical attitude interprets this apparently tolerant position as not, in fact, tolerant at all but as claiming truth for itself rather exclusively, as Gavin D'Costa argues (1996: 225).[1] Uncovering pluralism (and

---

1   For a response and subsequent discussions, see: D'Costa (2003: 30ff, 2011: 35); D'Costa, Knitter, and Strange (2011: 140); Hick (1997).

in some way inclusivism too) as relativistic and, consequently, as a performative self-contradiction is the well-known standard argument against any type of relativistic, critical, and deconstructive approaches. Beyond the more intellectual approaches, this fixed ascription became popular and widespread among the anti-pluralism advocates. I argue, however, that I do not know a single pluralist who considers all religions strictly equal. In addition to being rude polemics, this kind of critique is based on *an epistemological confusion* of the theology of religions typology. It is therefore essential to clarify the epistemological status of the typology.

The Confusion between Epistemology and Theology of Religions

With respect to the threefold typology, it is to Perry Schmidt-Leukel's merit that he distinguishes between the two disciplines of epistemology and the theology of religions (2005: 72f.). I will set out below three epistemological stances related to the typological terms.

An *exclusivist epistemological position* affirms that 'a' and 'non-a' cannot be true simultaneously. In this sense, anyone who tries to speak comprehensively has to adhere to this rule of logic. Therefore, in an epistemological sense, we are all exclusivist, since we want to be seen as wise and not as fools.

An *inclusive epistemological position* implies that all knowledge and experience is inevitably bound to how our perceptions operate. Epistemological inclusivism underlines the binding of all knowledge to perceptivity. The act of understanding has an inclusivistic nature. There is no pure objective knowledge without, for example, any origin, subject, context, worldview, understanding, perception or comprehension. Everyone speaks from a particular perspective, with presuppositions and pre-understandings; everyone has his or her own epistemological position and constructs the entire surrounding world on the basis of this epistemological starting point.

A *pluralistic epistemological position* changes epistemological exclusivism into its opposite and assumes that all truth claims are valid, even if they are contradictory.

In summary, since we prefer to speak comprehensively and truthfully on an epistemological level, both an epistemological exclusivism and an epistemological inclusivism are needed. In addition and consequently, it is imperative to avoid epistemological pluralism.

I will now look at the consequences of mingling epistemology and the theology of religions, which happens very often within the debate. This mingling is a source of misinterpretations, suppositions, the creation of fog, and, more accurately, as Paul Hedges put it during a conference discussion, a matter of muddying the waters.[2]

The *inclusive epistemological counterargument* against any theology of religions' argument for exclusivism or pluralism is obvious, since the theology of religions sees itself as doing theology, which is faith-based reflection on particular beliefs within a particular faith community; the theology of religions is always from a certain perspective. But, in fact, inclusive epistemological counterarguments like these actually take a position above the theology of religions' discussion, while still claiming that they are involved in the game of the theology of religions. In reality, however, all they are doing is causing confusion.

The same is true of the *exclusive epistemological counterargument* against the theology of religions' positions of inclusivism and pluralism: that everyone, except a fool, wants to be considered an epistemological exclusivist. But this is not a decision within the field of the theology of religions: it is an epistemological one. Exposing theological pluralists as secret exclusivists is nothing more than a methodological juggling trick, or, if I want to be clear, a rude polemic against religious pluralism. In addition, it insinuates that theological pluralism is a nonsensical position when viewed through the lens of epistemological pluralism. This kind of counterargument, however, does not reveal hidden exclusivism within religious pluralism; rather, it reveals the critic's own confusion or his/her malicious intent.

Ideology and the Need to Make a Decision

Aside from these two above-mentioned critiques of the typology, there is a more serious objection to the threefold typology: this critique is uncomfortable with the fact that this typology inevitably calls for a decision. It recognizes the logical nature of the typology and realizes that there is no way out of choosing one of the models. But, for a variety of reasons, it affirms that not everybody is prepared to act at this stage and to reveal his/her position. Furthermore, it argues that the pressure for a decision is framed within an ideology of religious pluralism. In other words, this critique argues that there is an inherent tendency toward the pluralistic model among the supporters of the typology, The

---

2 The comment was made during the "Thirty Years of the Typology of Religions" Conference, University of Winchester, UK, September 2013.

logical distinctions between the types are biased by an affinity for pluralistic theology.[3]

I think this observation is correct and an appropriate account of the typology. And there are many good reasons why a decision in the field of the theology of religions is nevertheless required. I would like to indicate this through comparative theology.

Comparative Theology's Objections to the Meaningfulness of a Theology of Religions Typology Decision

Almost all comparative theology's proponents—except me—are extremely skeptical of the benefits and advantages of reflections on the theology of religions. Some of them consider it impossible to decide on an appropriate type for comparative theology, because the choice, after the exclusion of the exclusivist option—between the inclusivist and the pluralist model is subject to aporia: if one chooses an inclusivist theology of religions, one preserves the identity of one's own faith but compromises other religions. But if one decides for a pluralist theology of religions, one appreciates other religions but jeopardizes one's own.[4] That is why they choose not to take a position within this typology.

A second or supplementary argument by comparative theology's proponents views reflections on the theology of religions as being too theoretical and removed from the particularities of religious traditions (Clooney 2010b: 196). Generalized representations of other religions are simply not helpful for this group. The theology of religions, they argue, lacks competence and real interest in other religions (Fredericks 1999: 167). Therefore, they consider decisions on the models fruitless and superfluous.

This second argument leads to a third. If decisions on particular models within the typology are to be legitimate, they require substantiated and proven knowledge of other religions, but, because the theology of religions cannot provide this, such decisions are far too premature. This argument might admit that, after a hundred years of comparative theology, enough data to evaluate the relationship and hierarchies between different religions might have been

---

3   The more drastic version of this criticism charges the typology with being violent in a subtle way. See Grünschloß (1999: 28).

4   The thesis was first developed by Fredericks (1995, 1999, 2003, 2010: xiv), but also by: Hintersteiner (2001: 319f.); Stosch (2007: 507–12, 2012: 216ff.); Rettenbacher (2005). On the defense: Schmidt-Leukel (2007: 493–505); Hick (2003); Kiblinger (2010); Hedges (2010: 53–54).

gained. It is, therefore, at the end and not at the beginning of comparative theological research that a decision can be made.[5]

In conclusion, almost all try to avoid making a decision. But I think this is an unfortunate position: it endangers *the theological character* and motivation of comparative theology.

An Appropriate Concept of the Pluralistic Model

In addition to these objections by comparative theologians, I assume that a fear of becoming identified with the religious pluralism project also exists. I want to take motivations like this very seriously (Winkler 2012). Comparative theologians can be easily misunderstood as no more than defenders of pluralism and unlimited relativism, abusing the religion's data as a means of proving a problematic presupposition; comparative theology could function as a support for an ideology. However, this need not necessarily be the case if we elaborate on the notion of the theology of religions' pluralist model in a more appropriate way.

The pluralist model of the theology of religions does not claim that the content of all religions are true on an equal level. The pluralist model simply rejects the assumption of the inclusivist model that, prior to any experience, the highest degree of truth and salvation can be found in only one particular religion. Rather, the pluralist model expects more than one equally advanced religion. It considers similarities on as high a level as possible. Therefore, the pluralist model speaks about the *possibility* of equality or superiority. It does not affirm equality between religions as *a priori* fact. This is my next point.

Since the theology of religions participates in the very problematic notion of 'religion',[6] which, among other things, has been driven by external attributions and outsider representations, the theology of religions has to be alert to the fact that diverse traditions, sacred texts, times, cultures, practices, rituals, and regions have been reduced to accord with the concept of one 'religion,' such as Hinduism, Buddhism or Christianity (see Moyaert's chapter in this volume). If we want to be serious about our decisions, we have to identify the points of comparison more adequately. Effective decisions on the hierarchy of religions can be taken only at the level of particular items. So I will try to speak about a pluralist theology in *particular mode* or a *partial* pluralist theology.

---

5 The most prominent proponent of this type is Francis X. Clooney (2008: 183, 2010a: 14ff.).

6 Cf. two major studies: Smith (1963) and Masuzawa (2005). For some discussions see: Auffarth (2005); Bergunder (2011); Feil (2000); Fitzgerald (2000); Hedges (2013); Nehring (2006, 2008); Stausberg (2009); Stietencron (1993).

This definition is consistent with the self-understanding that I mentioned above, that the typology is not a means of description and empirical measurement of the religions but more of a systematic theological tool for evaluating one's own theological position and self-understanding with respect to the claims by another religion concerning salvation and truth. The theology of religions is less appropriate for observing actual religious pluralism or, as Jacques Dupuis puts it, a pluralism *de facto*, rather than claiming to assert a pluralism *de jure* (2005: 208, 312, 386f.).

Theology of Religions as a Precondition of Comparative Theology

In addition to theology, there are several other honorable motivations for inter-religious dialogue and studying other religions such as exoticism, pragmatism, ethics, common action, and philosophical motivations. But they all fall short of giving theological authority within a theological discipline like comparative theology. Why should I deal theologically with other religions if my concern and motivation are only a fascination with the exotic or practical questions, ethics, or philosophy?[7] Therefore, I am convinced that a theological answer to the motivation and starting point of comparative theology is required.

Since one of the most accepted criteria for the idea of comparative theology is its difference to comparative religion, this criterion needs to be applied, even in the field of reasoning within the new theological discipline. For the older discipline, the scholar's subjective fascination and personal openness and curiosity is quite enough, like the scientists' observation of the world's most extraordinary or most common phenomenon. But these scientists do not expect truth, values, and answers to ultimate questions like theologians do. One of comparative theology's aims is to learn about other religions in particular. But why should other religions be viewed as functioning at a theological level as *loci theologici*, as sources of theological insights that become an authority for my own faith? Here I have to give a twofold answer.

---

7   Even though Klaus von Stosch and I collaborate in fostering comparative theology in German-speaking theology, we choose different epistemological and hermeneutical approaches in this respect. Because, in addition to theology, Von Stosch was also trained in philosophy, he relies more on philosophical reasoning than I do. For him, the philosophical argument is also sufficient for comparative theology too in that everyone's worldview encounter with other worldviews is substantial for one's own self-understanding and searching for truth. Theology need not justify an extraordinary theological epistemology to face the challenge of other religious truth claims. Stosch, Klaus von, *Komparative Theologie als Wegweiser in die Welt der Religionen* (Beiträge zur Komparativen Theologie 6), Paderborn u.a. (2012: 220ff.).

The theology of religions argues that there are theological values in other religions. For example, as a Catholic theologian, I draw on the Second Vatican Council and the declaration of *Nostra Aetate*. There are "truth and holiness" and *"bona spiritualia*/good things given by the Holy Spirit" (*NA* 2) in other religions. Furthermore, acceptance of this statement will result in an attitude in practice, an attitude toward other religions. Hence, the Council "exhorts" Catholics not only to tolerate the values of the others but also to "recognize, preserve and promote" (*NA* 2) them. The second and third call for active engagement on behalf of the other's values and goods. This theological reflection on other religions is the major concern of the theology of religions, besides the typology discussion.

What are the qualities of these theological values in other religions? If the level of the realization of these values is *a priori* and automatically higher in my own religion, and other religions are thereby inferior, namely the assumption of the inclusivist model, other religions contain no serious resources or possibilities for learning. If we want to be honest and learn theologically from other religions, we have to make a decision that other religions possibly contain high quality insights. That implies choosing the pluralist model, as I have defined it above. *The decision for a pluralist theology of religions in a potential and particular mode constitutes the precondition for serious comparative theology.*

There has to be a reciprocal exchange between the theology of religions and comparative theology. On the one hand, while I affirm that the theology of religions is a prerequisite for comparative theology, on the other I stress that it is also the result of comparative theology, because the theology of religions continuously becomes more distinguishable and sophisticated through the results of comparative theology. Both are linked to each other within the principle of reciprocal interaction, what Georg Simmel terms the "Prinzip der Wechselwirkung" (2013).

The Authority of Theologically Based Comparative Theology

Again, we have to reflect on the differences between comparative theology and comparative religion, like Arvind Sharma's "Reciprocal Illumination" (Sharma 2005), which is very close and similar to works in comparative theology, as he deals in detail with several theological issues. In short, the criteria for differentiation are the theological truth claims of comparative theology. But, as we can observe, they are not used by comparative theologians primarily to separate other religious traditions, or issues within another religion in particular, into true and false.[8] Moreover, I suggest one significant impact is that we learn and bring the results of dialogue home into the house of our own theology.

Since identities are complex, hybrid, fluid, and negotiated, interreligious dialogue and comparative theology are also about authority. What are the implications of comparative theology on one's own faith community and one's own theology? A comparative theology that is theologically grounded in the theology of religions is able to claim a theological authority at the negotiation table in one's own house of the church, and in theological thinking about one's own identity.

Bibliography

Auffarth, Christoph. (2005). "'Weltreligion' als Leitbegriff der Religionswissenschaft im Imperialismus." In: Ulrich van der Heyden and Holger Stoecker (eds.). *Mission und Macht im Wandel politischer Orientierungen: Europäische Missionsgesellschaften in politischen Spannungsfeldern in Afrika und Asien zwischen 1800 und 1945*. Missionsgeschichtliches Archiv 10. Stuttgart: F. Steiner. pp. 17–36.

Bergunder, Michael. (2011). "Was ist Religion? Kulturwissenschaftliche Überlegungen zum Gegenstand der Religionswissenschaft." *Zeitschrift für Religionswissenschaft* 19: 3–55.

Bernhardt, Reinhold. (2012). "Comparative Theology: Between Theology and Religious Studies." *Religions* 3: 964–72.

Clooney, Francis X. (2008). *The Truth, the Way, the Life: Christian Commentary on the Three Holy Mantras of the Śrīvaiṣṇava Hindus*. Christian Commentaries on non-Christian Sacred Texts Series. Leuven and Grand Rapids, MI: Peeters and William B. Eerdmans.

———. (2010a). *Comparative Theology: Deep Learning Across Religious Borders*. Chichester: Wiley-Blackwell.

———. (2010b). "Response." In: Francis X. Clooney (ed.). *The New Comparative Theology: Interreligious Insights from the Next Generation*. New York: Continuum. pp. 191–200.

D'Costa, Gavin. (1996). "The Impossibility of a Pluralist View of Religions." *Religious Studies* 32/2: 223–32.

———. (2000). *The Meeting of Religions and the Trinity*. Faith Meets Faith Series. Maryknoll, NY: Orbis.

---

8 While Gavin D'Costa shares some sympathy with Comparative theology he criticizes the lack of this judgment within it (2009: 40ff.); cf. Bernhardt (2012).

———. (2009). *Christianity and World Religions: Disputed Questions in the Theology of Religions*. Chichester: Wiley-Blackwell.

———. (ed.) (2011). *The Catholic Church and the World Religions: A Theological and Phenomenological Account*. London: Continuum.

D'Costa, Gavin, Paul Knitter, and Daniel Strange. (2011). *Only One Way? Three Christian Responses on the Uniqueness of Christ in a Religiously Plural Word*. London: SCM Press.

Feil, Ernst (ed.). (2000). *Streitfall Religion: Diskussion zur Bestimmung und Abgrenzung des Religionsbegriffs*. Studien zur systematischen Theologie und Ethik, 21. Münster, etc.: Lit.

Fitzgerald, Timothy. (2000). *The Ideology of Religious Studies*. New York and Oxford: Oxford University Press.

Fredericks, James L. (1995). "A Universal Religious Experience? Comparative Theology as an Alternative to a Theology of Religions." *Horizons* 22: 67–87.

———. (1999). *Faith among Faiths: Christian Theology and Non-Christian Religions*. New York: Paulist Press.

———. (2003). "The Catholic Church and the Other Religious Paths. Rejecting Nothing that is Good and True." *Theological Studies* 64: 225–54.

———. (2010). "Introduction." In: Francis X. Clooney (ed.). *The New Comparative Theology: Interreligious Insights from the Next Generation*. New York: Continuum. pp. ix–xix.

Grünschloß, Andreas. (1999). *Der eigene und der fremde Glaube: Studien zur interreligiösen Fremdwahrnehmung in Islam, Hinduismus, Buddhismus und Christentum*. Hermeneutische Untersuchungen zur Theologie 37. Tübingen: Mohr Siebeck.

Hedges, Paul. (2010). *Controversies in Interreligious Dialogue and the Theology of Religions*. London: SCM.

———. (2013). "Discourse on Discourses: Why We Still Need the Terminology of 'Religion' and 'Religions'." *Journal of Religious History* 38/1: 132–48.

Hick, John. (1997). "The Possibility of Religious Pluralism: A Reply to Gavin D'Costa." *Religious Studies* 33/2: 161–66.

———. (2003). "Theology of Religions versus Philosophy of Religions." In: Timothy W. Bartel (ed.). *ComparativeTtheology: Essays for Keith Ward*. London: SPCK. pp. 24–32.

Hintersteiner, Norbert. (2001). *Traditionen überschreiten. Angloamerikanische Beiträge zur interkulturellen Traditionshermeneutik. Mit einem Vorwort von Robert J. Schreiter*. Vienna: WUV Universitätsverlag.

Kiblinger, Kristin. (2010). "Relating Theology of Religion and Comparative Theology." In: Francis X. Clooney (ed.). *The New Comparative Theology: Interreligious Insights from the Next Generation*. London and New York: Continuum. pp. 21–42.

Masuzawa, Tomoko. (2005). *The Invention of World Religions: Or, How European Universalism Was Preserved in the Language of Pluralism*. Chicago and London: University of Chicago Press.

Nehring, Andreas. (2006). "Religion und Gewalt—ein leerer Signifikant in der Religionsbeschreibung. Überlegungen zur religionswissenschaftlichen Theoriebildung." In: Friedrich Schweitzer (ed.). *Religion, Politik und Gewalt: Kongressband des XII. Europäischen Kongresses für Theologie 18.–22. September 2005 in Berlin*. Veröffentlichungen der Wissenschaftlichen Gesellschaft für Theologie 29. Gütersloh: Gütersloher Verlagshaus. pp. 809–21.

―――. (2008). "Religion und Kultur: Zur Beschreibung einer Differenz." In: Andreas Nehring and Joachim Valentin (eds.). *Religious Turns—Turning Religions: Veränderte kulturelle Diskurse—neue religiöse Wissensformen*. ReligionsKulturen 1. Stuttgart: Kohlhammer. pp. 11–31.

Nostra Aetate (1965). Available at: http://www.vatican.va/archive/hist_councils/ ii_vatican_council/documents/vat-ii_decl_19651028_nostra-aetate_en.html.

Race, Alan. (1983). *Christians and Religious Pluralism*. London: SCM.

Rettenbacher, Sigrid. (2005). "Theologie der Religionen und komparative Theologie— Alternative oder Ergänzung? Die Auseinandersetzung zwischen Perry Schmidt-Leukel und Klaus von Stosch um die Religionstheologie." *ZMR* 89: 181–94.

Schmidt-Leukel, Perry. (1993). "Zur Klassifikation religionstheologischer Modelle." *Catholica* 47: 163–83.

―――. (1996). "Die religionstheologischen Grundmodelle: Exklusivismus, Inklusivismus, Pluralismus." In: Anton Peter (ed.). *Christlicher Glaube in multireligiöser Gesellschaft: Erfahrungen Theologische Reflexionen Missionarische Perspektiven*. Immensee: Neue Zeitschrift für Missionswissenschaft. pp. 227–48.

―――. (1997). *Theologie der Religionen: Probleme, Optionen, Argumente*. Beiträge zur Fundamentaltheologie und Religionsphilosophie 1. Neuried: Ars Una.

―――. (2005). *Gott ohne Grenzen: Eine christliche und pluralistische Theologie der Religionen*. Gütersloh: Gütersloher Verlagshaus.

―――. (2007). "Limits and Prospects of Comparative Theology." In: Norbert Hintersteiner (ed.). *Naming and Thinking God in Europe Today*. Currents of Encounter 32. Amsterdam and New York, NY: Rodopi. pp. 493–50.

Sharma, Arvind. (2005). *Religious Studies and Comparative Methodology: A Case for Reciprocal Illumination*. Albany: State University of New York Press.

Simmel, Georg. (2013 [1908]). *Soziologie. Untersuchungen über die Formen der Vergesellschaftung*. 7th ed. Berlin: Duncker & Humblot.

Smith, Wilfred Cantwell. (1963). *The Meaning and End of Religion*. New York: MacMillan.

Stausberg, Michael (ed.). (2009). *Contemporary Theories of Religion: A Critical Companion*. London: Routledge.

Stietencron, Heinrich von. (1993). "Der Begriff der Religion in der Religionswis-senschaft." In: Walter Kerber (ed.). *Der Begriff der Religion*. Fragen einer neuen Weltkultur 9. Munich: Kindt Verlag. pp. 111–58.

Stosch, Klaus von. (2007). "Comparative Theology as an Alternative to the Theology of religions." In: Norbert Hintersteiner (ed.). *Naming and Thinking God in Europe Today*. Currents of Encounter 32. Amsterdam and New York, NY: Rodopi. pp. 507–12.

(2012). *Komparative Theologie als Wegweiser in die Welt der Religionen*. Beiträge zur Komparativen Theologie 6. Paderborn: Schöningh.

Winkler, Ulrich. (2012). "Reasons for and Contexts of Deep Theological Engagement with Other Religious Traditions in Europe: Toward a Comparative Theology." *Religions* 3: 1180–94.

PART 4

Some Responses to the Christian Theology of Religions

∵

CHAPTER 18

A Jewish Response to the Christian Theology of Religions

Reuven Firestone

While the varieties of Judaism lived by Jews for the past two millennia are profoundly different from Israelite monotheism,[1] all forms of Judaism are naturally and deeply influenced by worldviews expressed in the Hebrew Bible. One such aspect of biblical worldview that profoundly influences all Jewish expressions to this day is the acute particularism of Israelite monotheism. That an expression of monotheism would lack a universal perspective might seem an oxymoron. Nevertheless, the following represent a few of the many sources that seem to confirm the distinct particularism of early monotheism:

> And I say to you: You shall possess their land, for I will give it to you to possess, a land flowing with milk and honey. I, the Lord, am your God who has set you apart from other peoples... you shall be holy to Me, for I the Lord am holy, and I have set you apart from other peoples to be Mine.
>
> LEV. 20:24–6

> You are a people consecrated to the Lord your God; of all the peoples on the face of the earth, The Lord your God chose you to be His treasured people.
>
> DEUT. 7:6

> Happy is the nation whose God is the Lord, the people He has chosen to be His own.[2]
>
> PSALM 33:12

Of course there are counter-verses that call for Israel to help the stranger, that exclaim that God is the creator of the heavens and the earth and all that is

---

1 By 'Israelite monotheism,' I mean the varieties of religious practice and belief represented by the Hebrew Bible. These are sometimes referred to as 'Biblical Judaism' to distinguish it from 'Rabbinic Judaism' and other forms of post-biblical Judaism such as Kara'ite Judaism.

2 Many more supportive verses could be cited.

© KONINKLIJKE BRILL NV, LEIDEN, 2016 | DOI 10.1163/9789004324077_020

therein, the God of all peoples, etc.—but these cannot take away from the consistent sentiment that the God who created the entire universe is the God of Israel[3] with an exclusive relationship with his chosen people. How can a religious community that adores a universal God, creator of the entire universe from the heavens above to the earth below, live out a theology that seems to be unconcerned with the remainder of humanity?

In order to respond adequately to the question, I must first call attention to the contextual nature of theological thinking. Affected by history, culture, language, and many other factors, theology represents a spiritual and intellectual consideration of the human condition in relation to the transcendent—but always within particular settings.[4] In fact, there can be no doubt that a Christian theology of religions was impossible before the unique developments of the past century. The theologies articulated in the Hebrew Bible reflect their own contexts, just as theologies today reflect ours. The earliest theologies of the Hebrew Bible were worked out within the context of a tribal world. Israel emerged into history after the great empires of Egypt and Mesopotamia, but during a hiatus in their imperial power when dozens of indigenous peoples populating the area we know today as Turkey, Lebanon, Syria, Israel, Palestine, and Jordan lived as extended kinship communities (Killebrew 2005: 13–4, 21–92). Life in the ancient world in which Israel was situated was tribal. All communities or nations were what we would call today ethnic, organized according to kinship. Every individual was part of a family, every family part of an extended family, every extended family part of a clan, every clan part of tribe, and every tribe part of 'nation' or confederation of tribes. That society was conceived of tribally is clear from the language. The Hebrew of the Bible, for example, refers to clans or tribes not only as *shevet* or *mateh*, but also *beit av*—literally, 'the father's house,' certainly a patriarchal term (Ex.6:14; Num. 3:30; Josh.14:1, etc.). A tribe or even an entire people or nation, however, can also be called *ummah* a term deriving for the word for mother (Gen.25:16; Num.25:15;

---

3 I use the term 'Israel' in this essay as it is used in traditional Jewish literature and thought. It refers to the community and people who have been named Hebrews, Israelites (or 'Children of Israel'), Judeans and Jews in various genres of Jewish discourse through the ages. Unless noted specifically, the term does not refer to the modern state, which official name is 'The State of Israel' and which means something like 'The modern national polity of the Jews.'

4 See, for example, the "Christian Theology in Context" book series currently under production by Oxford University Press, which examines "... theological thought in its full social, historical, and political context. Each [volume] attempts to show the close relationship between knowledge and social practice, rationality and cultural location."

Psalms 117:1, etc.). Another term for a people or nation is 'am, which may be related to the Semitic root for paternal uncle.[5] These are all terms of kinship, expressions of tribalism and a tribal orientation to the world.

There were many powers that ruled the universe in those ancient days— powers that controlled the weather, brought forth fertility, and so forth. They were not omnipotent powers. They worked together or at odds with one another, and they were open to influence by humans. They accepted human offerings and reciprocated in response. In addition to the nature deities, there were gods that protected nations and peoples—for compensation—because they were not omnipotent. They needed to eat, and the offerings of humans were relished for their sweet aromas. When properly worshiped, these tribal gods would protect their peoples (Albright 1968; Cross 1973; Smith 2002).

The Moabites, for example, lived to the east of Jerusalem and southeast of ancient Israel. When they went to war with their Israelite neighbors, their god Kemosh helped the war effort.[6] The Israelites, meanwhile appealed to their own god (2 Kings 3:15–20), who might assist them. When a tribal nation lost a battle, it could have been because their god was not enthusiastic about helping his community of followers. Perhaps their offerings were not adequate, perhaps their words of love and loyalty to their deity were not sincere. The relationship between human and divine in those days was mutual—and some Jewish theologies retain aspects of that relationship to this day.

Let us consider the particularities of sacrificial offerings in the ancient Near East. How did one send an offering to a particular deity when smoke always rises in the same basic direction and arrives at the same basic place? One needs to designate something like a postal code for the offering in order to ensure that the correct god received the correct offering. This was certainly one of the motivations for the development of liturgy. The gods had proper names, known to their people, who used them in their litanies of invocations and supplications when they sent off their offerings to the proper address. The tribal confederation that called itself the Tribes of Jacob or the Children of Israel, like all other tribal nations in those days, had its own particular god. His name is derived from the three Semitic root letters h.w.h., which in that particular order convey the meaning of existence or being. The name of the Israelite god was once pronounceable, probably something like Yahweh. It meant roughly

---

5 This occurs in the Arabic, 'amm.
6 See the inscription of the Mesha stele (Moabite Stone), in Pritchard (1958: 209–10); and compare with 2 Kings Chapter 3.

'life-giver,' 'source of being,' 'maker of existence,' or the like. This was 'the God of Israel,' a common term used often in the Hebrew Bible. The God of Israel was not a universal God in the earliest period of Israel's existence as a people or nation. Israel's god seems not to have been much different in size and strength from Moav's god Kemosh or Ammon's god Milkom. But for reasons that continue to be debated, the people of Israel began to conceive of their god in increasingly universal terms. During the long period of transition from polytheism to monolotry or henotheism to monotheism, the community split into factions, some which were loyal to the ancient theology, while others were convinced that the God of Israel was really the creator God of the entire universe and the only real heavenly power that could respond to prayer. Those who conceived of God as the only divine power eventually won the day, but the transition to monotheism does not seem to have been smooth nor to have occurred fully until the end of the period of the classical prophets—that is, sometime in the sixth century BCE at the very earliest (Fox 2006: 326–45). Some would argue that the battle over 'true monotheism' continued through the end of the biblical period and beyond, and that the ongoing tension between Christians and Jews reflects to some extent the problematic of Trinitarian views of monotheism in relation to Jewish views of monotheism as formulated during the period of the Second Temple.

I return now to the historical context of early Israelite theology, which emerged in an ethnic world characterized by tribal enmity that probably originated in intense competition for meager resources in a difficult physical and political environment. This was an existential competition, and it was expressed in a variety of ways which included a kind of tribal theology. Every people or nation had its own tribal god that could advocate and even go to war on behalf of its community of worshippers. So did Israel. The Israelite god was a tribal god, with a personal name known to its people and a special and unique relationship to that population. When the transition to monotheism was complete, what originated as a tribal deity became recognized as the One Great God of the universe. Nevertheless, the now universal God still remained the tribal god of Israel with a very special personal relationship with its beloved devotees. The notion of God's special chosen relationship with Israel was too deeply embedded in the traditions of a people and in its sacred literature and scripture, both of which had emerged before the transition to monotheism was complete to be forgotten or ignored. In fact, that special relationship between God and Israel characterized by divine election remains a primary aspect of Judaism to this day. It also disturbs many Jews, an issue to which I will return shortly.

One interesting aspect of the relationship, however, changed with the monotheizing of God. That is in the name. When the tribal god of Israel was comprehended as the God of the universe, it made no more sense to relate to Him on a first name basis (I am using traditional theological assumptions here, so God is mostly male). And there was no need to designate a particular address for offerings so that it would go to the right god because it was realized that there were no other gods. Names have power, and knowing names projects power, as we have all experienced when in the uncomfortable situation of bumping into someone who knows our name while we do not know theirs. So it must have seemed preposterous by the Second Temple Period for a Jew (the survivors of the destruction of the First Temple are now called Jews) to call God by a proper name—and perhaps dangerous as well. So Jews began to avoid referring to God by the *tetragrammaton*. That became the *nomen ineffabile* (Jerome's term, but used earlier by Philo) (Jerome 1970; Philo 1906). Sometime perhaps in the third century BCE, the custom emerged through which Jews would refer to God through the idiom of the plural, 'royal' form of the appellation 'my lord.' That word is *Adonai*. When one reads biblical texts as at least some of them were originally intended—that is, as references to a tribal deity—one can sometimes observe a different kind of meaning than we may assume in our contemporary readings. Traditional Jews today will not even articulate that substitution of *Adonai*, for the same reason they refuse to use the *tetragrammaton*, except in prayer.

So here we encounter an interesting dilemma. With the monotheizing of God, Jews were confronted with the problem of reconciling the early personal, intimate and absolutely particular layer of biblical theology with the comprehensive, but often less immanent universal layer found in the later strata of the Hebrew Bible. It was not easy, it was not completely successful, and Jews struggle with the problem of intimacy and transcendence to this very day. One of the results of this early history of God is that Jewish monotheism retains a considerable measure of the ancient particularity along with its absolute faithfulness to monotheist universalism. This complex correlation is exhibited by a general Jewish disinterest in the theologies and the fates of other religious communities.

That Jews by and large have not been terribly concerned with the religions of other peoples is a residue from ancient Israelite tribalism. I should add that the Jews represent perhaps the only surviving tribal religious tradition of the ancient world. The Moabites and Ammonites and all the other 'ites' of that world have disappeared—they are extinct. They were assimilated first by the forced marches of the Assyrian and Babylonian empires, which mixed administrative and educational classes of nations and even moved whole populations to foreign lands. Survivors were then enticed by the allure of Hellenism; those that survived Hellenism were captivated by Roman cultural as well as military imperialism, and finally, many of those few who held on were converted by Christian universalism. But while those Jews who continued to identify as Jews were profoundly influenced by all these, they continued to retain a distinct sense of the old tribal worldview. They are not genetically tribal, to be sure, because of the great amount of genetic mixing and the welcoming of converts over the millennia. But Jews retain a sense of tribal kinship, despite the fact that anthropologists and historians have demonstrated that kinship is a powerful relationship constructed more out of myth than reality (Anderson 1983; Geary 2003; Patterson 2010). Nevertheless, the tribal nature of Jewish identity has stuck and remains firm, which is one reason why it has been so difficult to figure out exactly who or what the Jews are. A religion? Not exactly. A people? Perhaps to a certain degree though it is unclear what a 'people' means. A nation? Jews have vigorously argued the meaning of that term since the emergence of Zionism. A race? After WWII and the Holocaust the answer is a resounding 'no.' But all the usual designations for identifying human communities do not fully fit the bill in describing Jews.

Some Jews did not resonate with the general lack of concern for the religious and spiritual condition of others that is ubiquitous in the Hebrew Bible. One group of such Jews eventuated in Christianity. The tribal nature of monotheism found in the Hebrew Bible was understood by this community to have been superseded or fulfilled in the quite different nature of Christian monotheism, which became deeply concerned with the spiritual condition of all humanity. The result of that transformation brought an entirely different perspective to relations with non-believers, a perspective that has sometimes brought abundant solace and comfort, and at other times caused enormous violence and harm.

Jews as a whole have never expected or even hoped for the entire world to become Jewish. There are a few cases in the Hebrew Bible that may be read as universal appeals, but they are limited both in number and in scope. One famous passage is often cited to support the notion of a biblical view of a universal peace and a future of tranquility, harmony and unity. I read it as a rare example of Hebrew biblical absolutism. Consider Isaiah 2, paralleled in Micah 4:

> In the days to come, the Mount of the Lord's House shall stand firm above the mountains and tower above the hills; and all the nations shall gaze on it with joy. And the many peoples shall go and say, "Come let us go up

to the Mount of the Lord, to the House of the God of Jacob; that He may instruct us in His ways and that we may walk in His paths." For instruction shall come forth from Zion, the word of the Lord from Jerusalem. Thus He will judge among the nations and arbitrate for the many peoples. And they shall beat their swords into plowshares and their spears into pruning hooks; nation shall not take up sword against nation. They shall never again know war.

ISAIAH 2:2–4

When one reads the passage in the original Hebrew, one cannot help to sense that the peaceful scene described here seems like the *pax romana*, a totalitarian peace enforced by the rule of arms in the name of the God of Israel. It is the Israelite 'God of Armies'—the euphemistic 'Lord of Hosts'—who establishes the calm.[7] All the peoples in the world accept the God of Jacob—that is, the *Israelite* God—who will instruct the world.

The term, 'judgment' (*mishpat*) can be an attribute of harsh judgment in the Hebrew Bible, so when God will "judge among the many peoples," it is not a reflection of what we might consider compassionate justice. If you are uncertain whether or not to accept this translation, then look at the Hebrew parallel that is used to strengthen the idiom: *vehokhiach legoyim 'atzumim*, meaning "and rebuke the most powerful national-tribes." Then "*they* shall beat *their* swords into plowshares and *their* spears into pruning hooks." I do not see that the people of Israel are being referred to here. What is the result? "Nation shall not lift up sword against nation. They shall never again know war." The consequence will be that "everyone shall sit under their grapevine or fig tree and with no one to terrify them ...." True, all will benefit, but that is "... because it was the Israelite Lord of Armies who spoke."

This is an exceptional text because of its militant universal outlook. The militant texts of the Hebrew Bible are usually quite local in perspective, with the goal simply of establishing a limited geographical safe-haven for the undisturbed practice of monotheism in a world that was, outside of Israel, completely and absolutely polytheistic.

In the steppes of Moav, at the Jordan near Jericho, the Lord spoke to Moses, saying: "Speak to the Israelite people and say to them: When you

---

7   See 1 Sam. 17:45, where the 'Lord of Host' is parallel with 'God of the armies of Israel'–*elohey ma'arkhot yisra'el*. See also the common parallel of 'God of Armies' with 'God of Israel' (Jer. 35:17, 38:17, 44:7, 1Sam.7:27, etc.).

cross the Jordan into the land of Canaan, you shall dispossess all the
inhabitants of the land. You are to destroy all their figured objects, all
their molten images you are to destroy, all their high-places you are to
annihilate, that you shall take possession of the land and settle in it, for
to you I have given the land to possess it."

Numbers 33:50–3

The ancient Israelite theologies naturally changed and evolved in relation to
changes in history—in technology, interaction with other peoples, political
and social developments, etc. And like all human communities, the community of Israel factionalized as people responded in their own unique ways to
the changes. Some of those whose worldviews included increasing concern
for the religious views of non-Jews formed factions, some of which eventually broke away entirely and evolved into an independent religion: Christianity.
Most other Jews were satisfied to try as best they could to act out their understanding of the divine will and leave others to themselves.

The Hebrew Bible has nothing positive to say about the religious behaviors of the various peoples among whom the Israelites lived. I mean that
in both senses of the word "positive." It was neither affirmative of the rites,
rituals and beliefs, nor was it particularly specific about them. There are a
few exceptions of particularly odious practice such as the "passing through
fire" of children to the god known as Molekh, or of the wayward practices
of Israelites themselves who were backsliding to the ways of the "nations
roundabout" (*kol hagoyim saviv*) such as those listed in 2 Kings, when King
Josiah cleaned up the idolatrous practices that had become common in
Jerusalem and even within the Temple itself (2 Kings 23:4–11). Mostly, however, the Hebrew Bible seems hardly to care about the religious notions
and practices of neighboring peoples, as long as they did not impose them
on Israelites or influence Israelite practice. Non-Israelites can observe their
religion any way they wish, as long as they do not try to engage Israel in
their activities.

As might be expected, Rabbinic Judaism, which emerged to become dominant only centuries after the destruction of the Second Temple, has a somewhat different perspective. It was profoundly influenced by the end of Jewish
political autonomy, the end of religious authority over Jerusalem, Hellenism
in general and the Hellenistic monotheism of Christianity in particular. Something akin to what I referred to above as an oppressive tendency in the yearn-
ing of Isaiah and Micah can be found also in Rabbinic liturgy, and it may have
arisen there in part as a response to similar Christian sentiments. But in Jewish

liturgy it is expressed as a statement of desired unity rather than a requirement for salvation.[8]

Like the Hebrew Bible, Rabbinic literature is very concerned with the behaviors of Jews but hardly concerned with their thoughts—or if you will, faith beliefs. One can believe anything one wishes as long as one responds to the Divine imperative by observing God's commandments. The Hebrew Bible lays down the law in a number of places. The Talmud quantifies them. It comes up with the number of six hundred and thirteen commandments, three hundred and sixty-five negative commandments that correspond with the days of the year, and two hundred and forty-eight positive commandments that correspond with the number of bones in the body (Babylonian Talmud, Makkot 23b s.v. Rabbi Simlai).

The Rabbinic Jew is obligated to take on 'the Yoke of the Commandments.' This is a behavioral requirement, which is intimately associated with having taken on 'the Yoke of the Kingdom of Heaven,' an idiom that conveys spiritual surrender to the divine will. This is the essence of mission. The mission of the Jew is to serve God. How does one know how to do that? By responding to God's directive, given in the form of commandments—*mitzvot* in the language of Judaism. Taking on the Yoke of the Kingdom of Heaven is clearly a faith commitment, but the notion of faith in this term is not identical to the usual Christian notion of faith. The Jewish notion is grounded on *yir'ah*—awe of the profound and overwhelming power and presence of God. This includes the assumption of a World to Come, but there is little agreement regarding its description or the criteria necessary to arrive there. Spiritual surrender is articulated by fulfilling divine commandments, an act of love and duty. Such behavior is not carried out in order to gain something in return. In fact, the very beginning of a central tractate of the Mishnah includes an ethical caution voiced by Rabbi Antigonus of Socho: "Be not like servants who serve their master in order to receive a reward, but be like servants who serve their master without the condition of receiving a reward, and let the awe of heaven be upon you" (Mishnah *Pirkey Avot* 1:3). This awe of heaven does not refer to worry or concern for a heavenly afterlife but simply and entirely to awe of God, for the idiom, "awe of heaven" (*yir'at shamayim*) is the same awe that is articulated in the act of taking on the Yoke of the Kingdom of Heaven. Faith in divine salvation remains a vague assumption and is developed dogmatically only among

---

8 The three daily prayer services end with a prayer beginning with "We therefore hope..." which expresses longing for a future when the world will be united under the rule of the One Great God and ending with "on that day God will be one and His name will be one."

medieval Jewish theologians who were responding to the intellectual and religious challenges of their Christian and Muslim neighbors (Stroumsa 2009).

Most important, faith and belief are realized through acts. When one carries out a commandment one is acting on faith in God's wisdom and direction through the giving of *mitzvot*. One acknowledges this by reciting a liturgical formula of blessing: "Praised are You Lord our God, sovereign of the universe, who has sanctified us through divine commandments and commanded us to ... [fill in the blank]." Absolute commitment to the unity of God is expressed though obedience to the Divine Will by living out God's *mitzvot*.

This formulary did not develop in a vacuum. By the period of the Talmud when this idiom developed, Jews could not possibly ignore the religious practices and ideas of Gentiles because Jews were spread throughout the Diaspora. They were no longer living in their own land under their own rulers but were living everywhere as a minority among other communities. God could love the Jews by showering them with commandments. But God is the creator of all creatures. What about those Gentiles among whom the Jews were so thinly spread and with whom they were living so intimately? A number of traditions developed in Rabbinic literature to explain God's special relationship with Jews that is unshared with other peoples, and many of these are constructed around the notion that of all the peoples of the earth, only the Jews accepted God's offer of the divine commandments (Babylonian Talmud *Avodah Zarah* 2b; Lamentations Rabbah 3:1; Mekhilta *bahodesh, parsha A* (on Ex.19:2); Pirkey de'Rabbi Eli`ezer 41, etc.). A significant problem nevertheless remained. Since the divine commandment became not only the *conditio sine qua non* of Jewish identity but also the essence of relationship with the Creator, and since the loving and merciful God created all humanity, did God have no blessing also for Gentiles? To put it another way, could God so abhor Gentiles that he would not require of them even a few of his loving commandments?

A trajectory of Jewish thought emerged in Rabbinic Judaism that relates to non-Jews through the idiom of the Children of Noah (*B'ney Noach*) and the Seven Commandments of the Children of Noah, known as the Noahide Laws. According to this tradition, God did indeed give all humanity certain commandments. Non-Jews are obligated to observe only seven, which represent the very basic expectation of human morality (Tosefta, *Avodah Zarah* 9:4; Babylonian Talmud *Sanhedrin* 56a). They require:

1. The prohibition of idolatry (worship of idols but not necessarily owning images).
2. The prohibition of murder.
3. The prohibition of theft.

4. The prohibition of sexual immorality.
5. The prohibition of blasphemy.
6. The prohibition of eating flesh taken from a living animal.
7. The requirement of maintaining courts to provide legal recourse.

Gentiles who observe these commandments are presumed to have a portion of the World to Come in the same way that Jews who are engaged in the many more commandments established by Rabbinic Judaism have a portion of the World to Come. Tradition is not in agreement about what should be done about those who do not practice these commandments. Should Jews require mission to the Gentiles? There has been very little discussion about this in traditional or modern sources.[9] As noted previously, the mission of the Jews is to serve God by living according to the Torah. Jews were happy to accept converts, to be sure, but since Jewish missionizing was forbidden and then became a capital crime under both Christian and Muslim rule from the fifth century onward, it was not an option or even much discussed. Maimonides, the great twelfth century polymath, under the influence of Islamic ideas, requires war against all nations that do not practice these seven minimal commandments, but his policy was of course impossible to enforce, and his position was disputed by other scholars who could not agree with his viewpoint (Firestone 2012: 119–23). Modern Jewish thinkers attempted occasionally to emphasize mission, but these were also responses to the universalism of Christianity and the increase in Jewish assimilation.[10]

Given these views, one can readily understand that there was hardly a need to develop a Jewish theology of religions. The question was raised only in the modern period and in response, like so many other developments in modern Judaism, to a modern world in which Jews have been trying so hard to be accepted as normal. Jews have no need to develop a theology of religions because non-Jews are not by Jewish definition damned. They may be considered wrong, sinful, or inferior in one way or another, but they are not consigned to divine retribution by virtue of their not taking on Jewish systems of behavior and

---

9   For some traditional sources associating Abraham with mission to bring idolaters to the unity of God, see Bereshit Rabbah 39:14; 48:8; Babylonian Talmud *Sota* 10a-b; Avot d'Rabbi Natan 12; Pirkey d'Rabbi Eliezer 25.

10 The 19th century Orthodox Rabbi Samson Raphael Hirsch advocated a mild form of mission (see his commentary to Numbers 29:13, Hirsch 1867–78). Alexander Schindler, president of the liberal Union of American Hebrew Congregations urged in 1978 that Jewish communities reach out to the non-Jewish partners Jewish married couples for conversion but not for a larger mission (http://urj.org/about/union/history/schindler/?syspage=article&item_id=61140). For the view of one contemporary Orthodox thinker, see Krinsky 2013.

belief. Nonetheless, while non-Jews are not presumed to be damned, they are not necessarily loved either. The ambivalence about the status of non-Jews is articulated classically in the following Rabbinic passage:

> Rabbi Eliezer says: No Gentile (lit. *goy* 'nation') has a part in the world to come, as it says (Ps. 9:18): *The evil ones will return to Sheol, all the nations who forget God.* 'The evil ones will return to Sheol' refers to the evil among Israel.[11] Rabbi Yehoshua said to him: "If Scripture had said, *The evil ones will return to Sheol, all the nations* and then was silent, I would agree with you. But Scripture says, *who forget God.* Thus there are righteous among the Gentiles who have a part in the world to come."
>
> TOSEFTA *SANHEDRIN* 13:2. Cf. Babylonian Talmud, *Baba Batra 12b*

This and many other passages from Rabbinic literature echo the generally negative perception of Gentiles articulated in the Hebrew Bible, but they do not consign them to damnation by virtue of their not belonging to the Jewish people, believing in Jewish religious notions or practicing Judaism (Porton 1988). The predominant view of Judaism is that the righteous of all peoples have a share in the next world (*`olam haba*). It is right behavior—and not right belief—which determines one's fate. Negative references in Rabbinic literature to Gentiles are based on the experience and observation of a powerless minority living among Gentiles who could and did take advantage of the Jews' powerlessness. They are not derived from false belief. Theological 'truth' and proper faith are not major issues in Jewish religious ideology and practice. Jews, therefore, are typically not bothered by other people's faiths, as long as they leave Jews alone.

One might naturally ask, then, why would Jews become involved in interreligious dialogue? The most direct answer, though incomplete, is because Christians are. From the beginning of the long process of Western Jewish emancipation from their degraded pre-modern status, some or even many Jews felt the need to demonstrate that they are civilized and acceptable to non-Jews. Ernest dialogue is a statement and demonstration of concern and belonging. A related explanation, perhaps cynical but certainly realistic, was

---

11   Therefore, the remainder of the sentence referring to "all the nations" requires that they are also destined to damnation. Rabbi Eliezer's reading, it should be pointed out, goes against the contextual function of biblical parallelism, which equates the two phrases. The contextual reading equates "the evil ones" with "the nations who forget God." In contrast, Rabbi Eliezer's reading sees two separate entities: (1) "the evils ones" are the evil among Israel, and (2) all the Gentile nations.

articulated by a rabbinic colleague professionally involved in interreligious dialogue for decades who responded to the question of why Jews should engage in dialogue with Christians: "so they won't kill us." Jews need to interact with non-Jews in order to correct dangerous negative stereotypes and assumptions. This is necessary to fend off the kinds of distortions about Jews that have so often lead to violence directed against them. Jews were involved in an interreligious dialogue of sorts also in the Middle Ages when they developed Jewish expressions of systematic theology and a significant apologetic literature in response to the conversionary pressures of Christianity and Islam. The underlying impetus for engagement was the religious threat and intellectual influence that were wielded by religious authorities in power. A significant theological literature has been developing also in the modern period, but as in the Middle Ages, it did so at least in significant part as a response to outside conversionary and intellectual pressure.

There also exist more positive motivations for Jewish engagement in dialogue, and some of these derive directly out of Jewish religious tradition. Judaism has always placed a great emphasis on learning, and little or no learning is forbidden. The same collection of aphorisms cited above to demonstrate the importance of serving God without thought of reward teaches, "Who is (truly) wise? One who learns from everyone" (Mishnah *Pirkey Avot* 4:1). Commentaries on this tradition stress the wisdom of learning not only from those who are more learned but also those who are less so. There is no limit from whom one can learn, and this may apply to non-Jews as well as Jews.

Another important notion in Judaism is encapsulated in the term 'for the sake of peace' (*mipney darkhey shalom*). A list of acts that are prescribed for the sake of peace includes allowing poor Gentiles along with the poor of Israel to collect the gleanings and dropped produce of the harvest, for the sake of peace.[12] And in a different passage, "Our Rabbis taught: We sustain the non-Jewish poor with the Jewish poor, visit the non-Jewish sick with the Jewish sick, and bury the non-Jewish dead with the Jewish dead, for the sake of peace" (Babylonian Talmud, *Gittin* 61a). These can be seen as merely pragmatic acts designed to protect Jews living among Gentiles, thus fitting under the category of "so they won't kill us." Maimonides, on the other hand, seems to understand the requirement differently:

---

12   "One does not restrain poor pagans from collecting the gleanings, forgotten pieces and what is left on the corners of fields for the sake of peace." Mishnah *Gittin* 5:8. Some manuscripts have 'idolaters' rather than Gentiles (`ovdey kokhavim or `ovdey elilim in place of *goyim*).

The Sages commanded visiting the sick of the pagans and to bury their dead together with the dead of Israel and to support their poor along with the poor of Israel for the sake of peace (*mipnei darkhei shalom*). For it is said: "God is good to all and His compassion extends to all His creatures" (Ps. 145:9). And it is said: "Its ways are the ways of pleasantness and all its paths are peace" (Prov. 3:17).[13]

HILKHOT MELAKHIM 10:12

Walter Wurzburger suggests that Maimonides' citation of the Psalms and Proverbs passages absent in the Talmudic references conveys the view that proper relationships with Gentiles are not established merely to promote Jewish self-interest or even preservation. While this motive might be meritable enough on its own right, Wurzburger sees Maimonides' reason here as an act of *imitatio Dei*, for "His compassion extends to all His creatures" (Wurzburger 1994: 50–51).

Reaching out to non-Jews may not be required or encouraged according to biblical commandments or their Rabbinic extension. Nevertheless, engaging positively with non-Jews falls under the category of *tikkun* or *tikkun ʻolam*, literally, 'repair of the world.' The words *tikkun* or *takkanah* in Jewish jurisprudence refer to an act or practice that is engaged, not because it is required directly by God through the *mitzvot*, but in order to prevent social discord (Mishnah *Gittin* 4:2). Engagement between Jews and non-Jews in order to promote peaceful relations and to improve our communities, countries and the world as a whole has been sanctioned and encouraged by most sectors of the Jewish community, from the most liberal to many in the world of Jewish Orthodoxy (Sacks 1997).

Rabbi Joseph B. Soloveitchik, spiritual mentor of thousands of American-trained Orthodox rabbis and universally acknowledged as the intellectual leader of 'Modern Orthodoxy,' wrote an essay on dialogue in the early 1960s while the Vatican was engaged in the process leading up to the 1964 *Nostra Aetate* (Soloveitchik 1964).[14] Acutely conscious of the centuries of religious contact with Jews initiated by the Church for the purpose of conversion, and the history of antisemitic persecution culminating in the unspeakable horrors of the Holocaust, Rabbi Soloveitchik limited all dialogue to engagement on issues of economic, social, and scientific concern. Any discussion of faith or

---

13   See also *Hilkhot Avodat Kokhavim* 10:5; *Hilkhot Matnot ʻAniyim* 7:7.
14   The essay is entitled "Confrontation," and was delivered at the 1964 Mid-Winter Conference of the Rabbinic Council of America in response to requests by Christians to enter into dialogue with Jews.

theology was forbidden because of the history of religious debate and disputa-
tion that was intended not for spiritual learning and growth but for religious
coercion and conversion. Forty years later, Rabbi Soloveitchik's position was
addressed by a panel of Orthodox rabbis in order to explore the issues raised by
that watershed essay in the light of changing circumstances.[15] The intervening
years has seen a significant movement among a number of Christian churches,
organizations and leaders toward interest in a dialogue of mutual respect, and
a genuine desire to learn rather than preach. In such cases of authentic aspiration for learning and mutual understanding, increasing numbers of Jews,
including Orthodox Jews, are becoming engaged in dialogue.

To conclude, due to the particular nature of Jewish monotheism and the
particulars of Jewish history, Jews have not generally felt the need to interact
religiously with non-Jews, but have historically always engaged with non-Jews
in virtually all other ways. The two aspects of Christianity that have been the
driving forces of religious engagement with other faith communities—mission
and the development of systematic theology—have not been driving forces in
Jewish tradition. Nevertheless, there are authentic Jewish religious rationales
for interreligious engagement including dialogue, which range from learning
and refining spiritual knowledge to improving the world in which we live. The
driving mission or motivation for Jewish religious practice is the obligation to
serve God by living out God's precepts through conduct and behaviors which
develop our humanity as Jews and fellow travelers in a world of God's creation.
As both Jews and God's creatures, we are responsible to one another and for
participating in the advancement of all humanity—what in Jewish parlance
is called *yishuvo shel ʾolam*—an untranslatable idiom that means something
like 'restoring the world' or 're-adjusting the world.' The perfection of religious
thought is not a significant motivator for Jewish engagement. Jews can live
productively and peacefully with others who believe very differently, as long
as different beliefs are not imposed upon them. On the other hand, living out
God's precepts is more satisfying and meaningful when one feels that one has
a sense of the source of divine wisdom and practice. God has many faces, and
the very existence of many religions attests to the difficulty and complexity involved in making sense of the divine essence. Learning from others in an open
and non-coercive environment can be a noteworthy means of getting closer to
or deriving a better understanding of the Source of all being.

---

15   https://www.bc.edu/dam/files/research_sites/cjl/texts/center/conferences/soloveitchik/
      index.html#2.

Bibliography

Albright, William Foxwell. (1968). *Yahweh and the Gods of Canaan.* New York: Doubleday.

Anderson, Benedict. (1983). *Imagined Communities.* London: Verso.

Cross, Frank Moore. (1973). *Canaanite Myth and Hebrew Epic.*Cambridge, MA: Harvard University Press.

Firestone, Reuven. (2012). *Holy War in Judaism: The Fall and Rise of a Controversial Idea.* New York. NY: Oxford University Press.

Fox, Nili. (2006). "Concepts of God in Israel and the Question of Monotheism." In: G. Berkman and T. Lewis (eds.). *Text, Artifact, and Image: Revealing Ancient Israelite Religion.* Atlanta: Scholars Press, Brown Judaic Studies. Pp. 326–45.

Geary, Patrick. (2003). *The Myth of Nations: The Medieval Origins of Europe.* Princeton: Princeton University.

Jerome. (1970). "Letter to Marcella in Response to her Query about the Names of God." In Isidorus Hilberg (ed.). *Sancti Eusebii Hieronymi Epistulae.* 3 volumes. New York: Johnson. Ep. 25. Available at: http://epistolae.ccnmtl.columbia.edu/letter/427.html. Last accessed 20 September 2013.

Hirsch, Samuel Raphael. (c. 1867–1878). *Commentary on the Pentateuch to Numbers 29:13 on the Mission of Israel.* Available at: http://berkleycenter.georgetown.edu/quotes/ samson-raphael-hirsch-i-commentary-on-the-pentateuch-to-numbers-29-13-i-on -the-mission-of-israel-c-1867-1878.

Killebrew, Ann. (2005). *Biblical Peoples and Ethnicity.* Atlanta: Society of Biblical Literature.

Krinsky, Alan. (2013). "Orthodoxy and Mission." *Conversations: The Journal of the Institute for Jewish Ideas and Ideals* 17: 59–64.

Patterson, Lee. (2010). *Kinship Myth in Ancient Greece.* Austin, TX: University of Texas.

Philo. (1906). "De Vita Mosis," iii. 519, 529. As cited in article: "Names of God." In *Jewish Encyclopedia.* Available at: http://www.jewishencyclopedia.com/articles/11305 -names-of-god. Last accessed 20 September 2013.

Porton, Gary. (1988). *Goyim: Gentiles and Israelites in Mishnah-Tosefta.* Atlanta: Scholars Press.

Pritchard, James (ed.) (1958). *The Ancient Near East.* Volume 1. Princeton: Princeton University Press.

Sacks, Jonathan. (1997). "*Tikkun Olam*: Orthodoxy's Responsibility to Perfect G-d's World." Available at: http://advocacy.ou.org/1997/tikkun-olam-orthodoxys-respon sibility-to-perfect-g-ds-world. Last accessed 25 March 2014.

Smith, Mark S. (2002). *The Early History of God.* Grand Rapids, MI: Eerdmans.

Soloveitchik, Joseph B. (1964). "Confrontation." *Tradition: A Journal of Orthodox Thought* 6:2. Available at https://www.bc.edu/dam/files/research_sites/cjl/texts/cjrelations/resources/articles/soloveitchik/. Last accessed 24 September 2013.

Stroumsa, Sarah. (2009). *Maimonides in His World: Portrait of a Mediterranean Thinker.* Princeton: Princeton University Press.

Wurzburger, Walter. (1994). *Ethics of Responsibility.* Philadelphia: Jewish Publication Society.

CHAPTER 19

A Muslim Response to the Christian Theology of Religions[1]

Haifaa Jawad

Introduction

In an era of globalisation characterised by information technology, increasing interconnectedness, and intensifying conflict between popular, liberal, secular values and strident religious affiliation, the question of religious diversity can no longer be seen as merely academic. Religious diversity, in principle and in practice, has not only gained a new political urgency; it has been catapulted to the centre-stage of international relations and now figures as a key theme in the articulation of policies of states, international organisations, and NGOs throughout the world. For many minority faith-based communities around the world the question has practically become one of life and death; while for the growing minority of Muslims in the West, the issues concerning religious pluralism help to shape the debates about the essential nature of Muslim identity, the contribution that Muslims can make to civil society, and the extent to which Muslims can or should be integrated or assimilated within Western democratic polities.

In such a highly charged context, the issue posed here—the Muslim response to the Christian theology of religions—has acquired acute political as well as religious importance. I have to confess that it has not been easy to write this essay on Muslim responses to the various Christian formulations pertaining to the religious Other. For, to begin with, there is of course no single Christian 'theology of religions'; instead, there are a host of Christian theological perspectives in terms of which non-Christians are located and defined. So it is virtually impossible to present a single coherent Muslim response to these divergent, and often contradictory, Christian theologies of religion. The threefold typology given by Alan Race (1983)—exclusivism, inclusivism, and pluralism—much commented upon in this volume, shows us well the range of possible perspectives on this theme within Christian thought. Gavin D'Costa (1986) gives us an excellent evaluation of all three mutually exclusive positions,

---

1 I am grateful to Reza Shah-Kazemi for his extensive comments on the first draft of this essay.

while also putting forward in subsequent works—especially *The Meeting of Religions and the Trinity* (2000)—his own preferred way of responding to and respecting religious diversity through his own interpretation of the role of the Holy Spirit in non-Christian religions. This differs from the pluralism of John Hick which seeks to see all religions as responses to a common Real/divine reality.

It is clear that the majority of Muslim theologians down through the ages fall into the exclusivist category. In contemporary discourse there are several scholars who would refer to themselves as pluralists, such as Muhammad Arkoun (1987), Hasan Askari (1985), Mahmoud Ayoub (2004), Farid Esack (1997), and Abd al-Aziz Sachedina (2001). But, as Thomas (2013) has recently argued, the overall result of such efforts is not an open-ended appreciation of the non-Muslim Other as such, but a subtle 'inclusivism'. The Other is evaluated in terms of Islamic criteria: an Islamic conception of *tawhīd*, or the unitive affirmation of divinity; and an Islamic conception of revelation, whereby God despatches His prophets one after the other, and reveals His message through these prophets in the form of a discourse which is then registered as a text. While I would agree with Thomas that, particularly in the cases of the three examples studied by him (Arkoun, Ayoub, and Faruqi), these efforts fall short of a Muslim 'theology of religions', if this is understood as respecting the non-Muslim Other in all their 'otherness', it nevertheless appears that the view of the Muslim perennialists (Chittick, Eaton, Lings, Nasr, Schuon, Shah-Kazemi) has not been taken sufficiently into account in his evaluation. Among the perennialists, it is Seyyed Hossein Nasr who has expounded the universality of Islam in the most scholarly manner, and in so doing, I believe, has given us some foundations for a contemporary 'Islamic theology of religions'. These foundations are built upon by Reza Shah-Kazemi, who applies the perennial approach more systematically to the Qur'an through traditional Sufi exegesis. In so doing, he shows that the Sufi approach to *tawhīd* celebrates the uniqueness of each of the revelations, and so respects the Other in all their otherness, this being one of the metaphysical implications of *tawhīd*. This argument will be assessed later, along with the question of whether the Muslim perennialist perspective amounts to an 'Islamic theology of religions'.

At this point, we need to step back a little and to consider this paradox: despite the existence of a high level of religious tolerance in the Islamic tradition (as compared with other polities in the pre-modern period), there is not a discipline within Islamic theology that can be labelled a 'theology of religions'. Why, one might ask, has a theological articulation of *religious pluralism* not accompanied the socio-political and legal tolerance of the empirical phenomenon of *religious diversity* in Islamic history? In attempting to answer this question the most important point seems to be this: there would appear to be a kind of *implicit* theology of religious pluralism operating throughout Islamic history, a theology which was never fully articulated and rendered explicit by the theologians of Islam, even if the mystics of Islam often sung its praises in their poetry and in some of their prose writings, and even if the jurists of Islam applied this implicit worldview in their dealings with non-Muslims. This implicit theology, or what can be called a 'pluralism-in-practice', was present from the very beginning, its premises being found in the Qur'an and in the conduct of the Prophet. It should be noted that by religious pluralism this paper means a tolerance and acceptance of co-existence on a socio-political level, alongside a theological recognition of the continued validity of other religions as embodying their own value in relation to the Islamic tradition.

Religious Diversity vs Theological Pluralism

In the Prophetic period the worldview underlying a pluralist theological perspective certainly existed, even if it was not articulated as such. For, as Cantwell Smith strongly asserted, Islam is the only Abrahamic faith which, from its very inception, contained a sophisticated and nuanced understanding not just of religion (*dīn*) but of religions (*adyān*). In his famous work, *The Meaning and End of Religion* (Smith 1978: 80–118), he claims that Islam is unique among religions as regards its approach to the phenomenon of religious diversity. Islam alone acknowledges 'religion' as a category: it is one religion among others, one *dīn* among many *adyān*. By contrast, religions like Christianity see themselves as religion as such, in a category of its own, or *sui generis*. It would be useful to quote here from the Jewish scholar Bernard Lewis, making a similar point to Cantwell Smith:

> Islam, from the beginning, recognized that it had predecessors, and that some, having survived the advent of Islam, were also contemporaries. This meant that in Muslim scripture and in the oldest traditional theological and legal texts, certain principles were laid down, certain rules were established, on the treatment of those who follow other religions. This pluralism is part of the holy law of Islam, and these rules are on many points detailed and specific. Unlike Judaism and Christianity, Islam squarely confronts the problem of religious tolerance, and lays down both the extent and the limits of the tolerance to be accorded to the other

faiths. For Muslims, the treatment of the religious other is not a matter of opinion or choice, of changing interpretations and judgments according to circumstances. It rests on scriptural and legal texts, that is to say, for Muslims, on holy writ and sacred law.

LEWIS 1998: 120

Lewis is echoing here the view held among most objective western scholars of Islam, who recognised the degree to which religious tolerance was practised by Muslims throughout Islamic history. This religious tolerance was not only extremely high, by medieval standards, it was also the norm.[2] Episodes of religious persecution were seen as deviations from this norm, as Lewis notes: "Until the seventeenth century, there can be no doubt that, all in all, the treatment by Muslim governments and populations of those who believed otherwise was more tolerant and respectful than was normal in Europe" (1998: 129). Such a statement would have appeared a truism in the last century, but in today's post-9/11 period, it seems astonishing to say that for well over a thousand years, Muslims were 'more tolerant and respectful' of the religious Other than Christians were. It is worth quoting Lewis further: "there is nothing in Islamic history to compare with the massacres and expulsions, the inquisitions and persecutions that Christians habitually inflicted on non-Christians, and still more on each other. In the lands of Islam, persecution was the exception; in Christendom, sadly, it was often the norm" (Lewis 1998: 129).

Norman Daniel, author of the influential *Islam and the West: The Making of an Image*, states very daringly: "The notion of toleration in Christendom was borrowed from Muslim practice" (Daniel 1966: 12). Taking these points of view together, it is possible to ask the question: to what extent is the 'Christian theology of religions' itself a response to the Muslim *practice* of religious tolerance, a practice in which an implicit conception of the legitimacy of religious diversity is embedded, even if there is no fully-fledged theological doctrine of religious pluralism? Before turning to our main discussion—Muslim responses to Christian theology of religions—it might be useful to point out some manifestations arising out of this implicit 'theology of religions' in Islam.

As noted, the very first Muslims were fully aware that the religion being revealed to them through the Prophet was one among other religions. Such a

---

2 For convincing expositions of the role played by tolerance in the Islamic tradition, see the works of Khaled Abou El-Fadl (2002) and Reza Shah-Kazemi (2012); and the article by Hamza Yusuf (2005).

perception could hardly be avoided given the numerous, repeated references in the Qur'an, some positive, some negative, to religions other than the new religious dispensation being revealed through the Qur'an itself. In a moment, we shall evaluate some of these key verses, but for now it would be worth mentioning an incident in the life of the Prophet which graphically proves the existence of an implicit 'theology of religions': his invitation to the Christians of Najran to perform their liturgy in his mosque in Medina (Guillaume 1968: 270–277).

The visit of the Najrani delegation, led by a Bishop, is largely commented upon within Muslim sources in relation to the disagreement between the Christians and the Prophet in relation to the Sonship of Jesus, and the termination of that debate through the revelation to the Prophet to challenge the Christians to a mutual imprecation: the curse of God would be upon the liars:

> Indeed, with God the likeness of Jesus is as the likeness of Adam: He created him of dust, then He said to him, Be, and he was. This is the truth from thy Lord, so do not be one of those who waver. And whoever disputes with you concerning him [Jesus], after the knowledge which has come to you, say: Come, summon our sons and your sons, our women and your women, and ourselves and yourselves, then let us pray and invoke the curse of God upon the liars.[3]
>
> Q 3:59–61

The Christians refused to take up this duel (*mubāhala*). But what is not so frequently commented upon is the fact that, despite this theological disagreement on the fundamental dogma of Christianity, the Prophet invited the Christians to perform their liturgy in his mosque. Here we can see a kind of tacit 'theology of religious pluralism' being put into practice. Muslims may disagree with certain tenets of Christianity; but this disagreement need not imply a rejection of the religion of Christianity *per se*. Christians may well believe in the Trinity, in the Incarnation, etc.—doctrines rejected by the Qur'an; but the rejection of these doctrines by Muslims cannot imply a root-and-branch invalidation of the Christian faith as a whole. On the contrary, theological disagreement can (and I would say, must) go hand in hand with respect for the Christian faith as such, and tolerance as well as respect for Christians who practise their faith: any position other than this contradicts the premise of 'religious pluralism'

---

3 All translations from the Qur'an are my own, based upon those of Abdullah Yusuf Ali, Muhammad Asad and M.M. Pickthall.

that is implied in the Prophet's invitation to the Christians of Najran to perform their prayers in his mosque. For Christians to pay the religious poll-tax
(*jizya*) to the Muslim state and receive political protection is one thing; but
for Christians to perform their liturgy in the Prophet's mosque goes well beyond the boundaries of a merely political tolerance. It is the expression of a
religious tolerance and respect which logically implies the acceptance of the
validity and authenticity—to some significant degree, at least—of a religion
very different from one's own; in other words, there is here a recognition of the
legitimacy of a religion which contradicts one's own as regards certain fundamental dogmas, as well as ritual practices. The Prophet's action embodies one
of the key premises and aims of religious pluralism. The roots of this implicit
religious pluralism are found in the Qur'an.

The Qur'anic Roots of Religious Pluralism

In any discussion of Muslim responses to religious diversity in general and
to Christian theologies of religion in particular, two essential factors need to
be taken into consideration: first, the Islamic view of revelation; second, the
context in which Islam arose and grew. The Islamic view of revelation and religious diversity is based on the understanding of the oneness of God manifested through multiple revelations and a long line of prophets. In this context,
"the oneness of God has, as its consequence, not the uniqueness of prophecy,
but its multiplicity, since God as the Infinite created a world in which there
is multiplicity and this includes, of course, the human order" (Nasr 2002: 9).
Islam sees both revelation and prophecy as vital and omnipresent, and asserts
that humanity was created from a single soul and then was multiplied into
different races, tribes, and nations: "O humankind, be conscious of your Lord,
who has created you out of one soul, and out of it created its spouse, and out
of the two spread a multitude of men and women" (Q 4:1). The purpose of this
diversity within the human race is the enrichment of mutual knowledge and
the attainment of piety: "O humankind, truly We have created you male and
female, and have made you nations and tribes that you may know one another.
Truly the most noble of you, in the sight of God, is the most pious of you. Truly,
God is Knowing, Aware" (Q 49:13).

   Human nature is singular, unique, and immutable, but it manifests itself
in diverse forms. On the one hand: "So set your purpose for the religion with
unswerving devotion—the nature [framed] of God (*fitrat Allāh*), according to
which He has created humankind. There is no altering God's creation. That is
the right religion, but most people do not know it" (Q 30: 30). The common

origin of humankind indicates, according to Nasr, "the profound unity within diversity of human nature, and therefore religion based on the message of Divine Oneness could not have been only meant for or available to a segment of humanity" (2002:16). The diversity of peoples and nations requires multiple revelations, and the Qur'an confirms that for every people, God has sent a messenger or a prophet, and a law and a way. This is affirmed in what is arguably the single most important verse of the Qur'an in relation to the purpose and the source of religious diversity, and must therefore figure as a key element in any Muslim theology of religious pluralism:

> To each among you We have prescribed a Law and a Way. If God had so willed, He would have made you a single community (*umma*), but He wills to test you in what He has given you; so compete with each other in all virtues. You will all return to God, and He that will show you the truth of the matters about which you differ.
>
> Q 5:48

From this verse one can infer that, for Muslims, religious diversity is divinely decreed: it is neither a mere historical accident, nor the result of human contingency. Rather, the diversity of religious revelation is a manifestation of the infinity of God.

The underlying aim governing all the revelations sent to humankind by God was to communicate the same essential message, that of *tawhīd*, the unity of God. While this may sound monolithic and levelling, it actually leads directly to diversity, for this same message of monotheism is delivered in terms of the different 'languages' of the people to whom it is sent, in different times and places. As the Qur'an explains: "We sent no messenger except [to teach] in the language of his people, in order to make things clear to them" (Q 14:4). The basic content of the Qur'an is identical to all other previous revealed books; they are all contained in a celestial archetype called in the Qur'an the *Umm al-Kitāb* (Q 43:2–3) or 'Mother of the Book'. Just as the unity of the human race implies the diversity of races, tribes, and languages, so the unity of the divine message implies a diversity of modes of revelation; and both of these modes of diversity, human and religious, are expressions of the diversity of Names and Qualities of God. Unity is the heart of diversity, and diversity is the expression of unity.

According to the Qur'an, all revelations convey the same basic message: to believe in one ultimate Reality, to surrender to, and worship, that Reality alone, and to perform righteous deeds. If there are some differences between these revelations, they are superficial, being contingent on differences in human nature, language, history, and other such relativities subject to change. What does not change from revelation to revelation is the basic message: belief in divine unity and the imperative of human virtue, and both of these principles are ingrained in the substance of the *fitra*, quintessential human nature, which, as noted above, is identified with the 'right religion', even if 'most people do not know it'. These two principles—faith in one God and righteous conduct—were articulated by the different prophets, by means of divine revelation which was adapted in a manner which would be intelligible to the peoples addressed by their respective revelation.

The diversity of religious revelation is in accord with the divine purpose underlying the diversity of the human race. The variety of races, nations, languages, and cultures constitute so many 'signs' (*āyāt*) of God, for those who reflect: "And among His Signs is the creation of the heavens and the earth, and the variations in your languages and colours; verily herein are signs of those who know" (Q 30:22). Special respect is given to the Jews and Christians, referred to as 'People of the Book': "Those who believe [in this revelation, the Qur'an], and the Jews, and the Christians and the Sabians—anyone who believes in God and the Last Day, and works righteousness: they shall have their reward with their Lord, on them shall be no fear, nor shall they grieve" (Q 2:62; this is repeated, in almost identical terms, at 5:69).

But this respect for fellow believers among the 'People of the Book' should not be seen as exclusive. For the Qur'an asserts not only that God has sent a messenger to every single *Umma* (Q 10:47), but also that "We have sent messengers before you; among them are those We have told you about, and those about whom We have not" (40:78). Here, the open-ended aspect of qur'anic pluralism is to be noted: the implication is that the category of those who are saved—"anyone who believes in God and the Last Day and works righteousness"—must not be restricted by the boundaries of the Abrahamic tradition. There is an invitation to explore, without prejudice, all the religions of humankind, and to be prepared, in principle, to accept their validity, however different they may appear to be from Abrahamic faiths. These differences are the result of the different conditions of the communities, who need to receive the divine revelation in a manner that is intelligible to them. As Ayoub puts it: "Each messenger had to let the message entrusted to him by God speak the truth as it related to the condition of his people" (Ayoub 2004: 100).

A careful study of the Qur'an reveals that its worldview is dominated by an implicit religious pluralism, one that affirms the divine purpose underlying the diversity of religions and asserts the imperative to live in peace and harmony with people of other faiths. Within this global religious perspective it is the Christian and Jewish heritages that share the most with Islam, insofar as

Islam regards itself as part of the Abrahamic tradition that forms the essential branch or the main fountain of monotheism (Nasr 2003: 2). Jesus, Mary, and the Hebrew Prophets are deeply respected, even venerated, by Muslims around the world, and are regarded as prophets within the Islamic universe of revelation. There are many foundations shared in common by these three religions: the belief in the Oneness of Ultimate Reality; prophecy; sacred revelations; sacred history; and all the major ethical principles such as the sacredness of life, respect of the revealed laws, respect for human dignity, fairness and equity in human dealings, compassion towards neighbours and the implementation of justice and equity. Although there have been many Muslim critiques of Christian and Jewish doctrines, the vast majority of Muslims who abide by the teaching of the Qur'an, have revered the Jewish Prophets, as well as Jesus and Mary. Indeed, Islam "envisages itself as the complement of those religions and the final expression of Abrahamic monotheism, confirming the teachings of Judaism and Christianity, but rejecting any form of exclusivism" (Nasr 2002: 42).

The qur'anic discourse on the People of the Book goes as far as privileging them, referring to them as points of reference for those who do not understand and need to understand. It informs those Muslims who had some doubt about the true nature of the message of Muhammad to ask or consult those people who had previous revelations and read the scripture before them. It asserts: "And before you the Messengers We sent were but men to whom We granted inspiration: if you do not understand, ask of those who possess the message [i.e., the People of the Book]" (Q 16:34). By the same token, the Qur'an urges the People of the Book to join hands with the Muslims and emphasise the common ground between them, that is the belief in the oneness of God and not to associate any one with Him, so that they could live in peace and harmony with each other. Here is what the Qur'an has to say in this context: "O People of the Book! Come to common terms as between us and you: that we worship none but God; that we associate no partner with Him; that we erect not, from among ourselves, Lords and patrons other than Allah. If then they turn back, say: bear witness that we have submitted" (Q 3:64).[4] To strengthen their connection with the People of the Book, the Qur'an instructs Muslims to have dialogue with them in the "best or most beautiful manner" (Q 16:125), and to assure them that

---

4   The interfaith initiative known as 'A Common Word between Us and You', which started in 2007, was based on this verse. It has been acclaimed as the most successful Muslim-Christian dialogue in history, hundreds of conferences, seminars, lectures, etc. resulted from it. See for details www.acommonword.com.

they too respect and believe in the validity of their revealed books. The Qur'an also says, reinforcing the thrust of this approach to dialogue: "And dispute not with the People of the Book, except with what is more seemly; unless it be with those of them who inflict wrong; but say, we believe in the revelation which has come down to us and in that which came down to you; our God and your God is One; and it is to Him we submit" (Q 29:46).

There is no doubt that the Qur'an also criticises some of the scriptural inter-pretations and doctrinal teachings of the People of the Book. An example of this in the Qur'an is when it is said that some of the People of the Book failed to accept or acknowledge the authenticity of the message of Muhammad (Q 3:110); in doing so, the Qur'an reprimands them for concealing the truth (Q 5:15). Another more serious criticism, especially against Christians, is the misinterpretation of their scripture that led to the belief in the Trinity and the divinity of Jesus (Q 5:17, 73, and 116). The Qur'an moreover, tends to be exclusivist in some verses as "the religion in the sight of God is Islam" (Q 3:19), and "If anyone desires a religion other than Islam, it will not be accepted from him; and in the Hereafter he will be among the losers" (Q 3:85). On the basis of these criticisms and statements some have stated that the qur'anic approach to the People of the Book has been ambivalent, in the sense that while it has positive statements about them, on the other hand it rejects some aspects of their belief systems. In response to first two points, Ayoub stresses that despite some criticisms, the Qur'an does leave space for discus-sions among the pious of the three faith groups. For him, the Qur'an does not criticise "the faiths of Jews and Christians or Judaism and Christianity as such. It always qualifies critical statements with: 'Some among the people of the book or a group of the people of the book'" (Ayoub 2004: 102). We shall discuss in the final section the way in which the Muslim traditionalists deal with these verses.

To conclude this section: the implicit pluralism within the Qur'an and the prophetic conduct manifested itself within a context which was itself already pluralistic. The Hellenistic-Christian philosophical tradition inherited and re-worked by Muslims helped Islam to become "nourished by the rich heritage of ancient Greek philosophy, Eastern Christian spirituality, as well as the Bibli-cal religious morality of Judaism," according to Ayoub (2009: 4). Stating that Islam's historical position—coming after the great religious traditions of Juda-ism, Christianity, and Zoroastrianism—contributed to its religiously pluralistic theology, he makes this important claim: "Islam evolved into one of the most universalistic religious civilisations of the world." This claim is corroborated by numerous objective non-Muslim scholars of Islam, two of whom were cited above, Smith and Lewis.

In light of the Islamic conception of revelation and religious diversity, and given the direct contact, on the ground, between Islam and the major world religions—initially Judaism, Christianity and Zoroastrianism, and then Hinduism, Buddhism and Confucianism, etc.—the Muslims were, historically, able to interact and deal with these religions and their followers within the framework of an implicitly universalist worldview. This worldview was one in which religious diversity was accepted as normal, and in which not just tolerance but also peaceful coexistence flowed naturally. There may have been periods of intolerance and persecution, but, as noted by scholars such as Lewis, these were exceptions to the rule. Judged by the standards of the time, the tolerance of religious diversity manifested by Muslims throughout its history until relatively recent times was remarkable.

The Non-Existence of an 'Islamic Theology of Religions'?

Despite the relatively pluralistic worldview of the Qur'an and its clear willingness to engage in dialogue with the people of the book, and despite the rich historical encounter with other world religions, Muslim theologians did not take the issue of religious diversity seriously and therefore did not develop a distinct discipline of the theology of religions within the wider field of theology. In other words, we have to admit that the implicit conceptions of religious plurality expressed through tolerance of the religious Other have not resulted in a satisfactory theology of religious pluralism either historically or in the contemporary period.

As noted above, Muslims lived almost always within a setting characterised by religious diversity. Many educated Muslims throughout the course of Islamic history felt, either out of a sense of religious duty, a sense of charity, or simply intellectual curiosity, that they should become acquainted to some degree at least with the main perspectives of other religions. In this context one thinks of the regular theological debates between Muslims and non-Muslims that took place in Baghdad at the court of the Caliph al-Ma'mun. During these discussions scholars from various faiths and traditions freely presented their respective views and attempted to overtake or excel one another in argument. Also, we are told that the Caliph al-Ma'mun used to take a personal interest in visiting the monasteries around the capital Baghdad to enjoy the scenery and relative coolness of these ancient buildings. It is said that he was familiar with church ceremonials and, even, that he might have secretly converted to Christianity (Thomas 2013: 249). This tolerant and open world of interreligious understanding was mirrored in one way or another in different parts of the

Muslim world, and was not confined only to the elite communities but also was reflected, to some degree at least, and with inevitable fluctuations, in the general attitude of ordinary Muslims towards the People of the Book and other faith groups. For despite what has been said about some of the constraints imposed on the People of the Book through the pact of the "protected people status" (*dhimma*), in real terms, these rules were rarely enforced in a systematic way, demonstrating that the application of these regulations were the exception rather than the rule. I would argue that these restrictions were contrary to the spirit of the Islamic ethos, and find little justification in the primary sources—the Qur'an and Hadith, as we hope to demonstrate below.

Also, it was quite normal to observe that members of other faith communities moved upward in terms of social mobility and reached positions of seniority with no real constraints placed upon them. There is ample evidence of this in the historical records of personal physicians, medical experts, translators, philosophers and officials in the caliphal offices who were from Christian, Jewish, and Zoroastrian backgrounds. While these persons might be notable and distinct from the wider setting, and while the overall picture might not be ideal by modern standards, nonetheless, judged according to pre-modern criteria, Muslim tolerance of non-Muslims was of a very high order.

The qur'anic view of the universality of religion together with these global historical encounters with other religions, enabled Islamic civilisations to develop a broad and cosmopolitan religious view which was quite unique, in comparison with the other religions in the pre-modern era. This global religious view is still alive and continues to form part of the worldview of those traditional Muslims, who have not assimilated modernism nor reacted against it in the form of radicalism or fundamentalism. Within this global view both Jewish and Christian traditions have the closest affinity with Islam (Nasr, 2002: 40).

Taking the above into consideration, one would expect Muslims to be at the forefront in dealing with the problem of religious diversity. But this is not the case as we stated earlier and there are many reasons for this, among which we shall mention three:

(1)   Traditionally, Muslims looked at the issue of religious diversity in *legal* terms and dealt with it within the context of Islamic jurisprudence, the Sharia, rather than as an issue within *kalām* or scholastic theology. Looking at the classical Islamic sciences such as those of the Qur'an, Hadith, *fiqh, tafsīr* and *kalām,* one clearly notices the absence of an independent discipline that focuses solely on the question of religious diversity. This may be due to the fact that for Muslims the Sharia sciences were

traditionally considered more important than theology, as it is with the
Law and not theology that Muslims came into contact on a daily basis
in all their activities. In the modern context, it is difficult to conceive
of a mind-set wherein the Law—that is, the Sharia (and the study of it:
fiqh)—comprises not simply legal rules and regulations, but an ethical
framework that so dominates Muslim life, that it is akin to a moral codex
imprinted in the mind and hearts of ordinary Muslims and thus governs
all outward formal conduct while fashioning inner ethical intentions.
Within this context, Muslims "often thought that the issue of determining the status of those who live within the domain of Islam is a practical
problem, i.e., it arises when a certain group of people or individuals are
classified for administrative purposes. They did not consider it as an issue of faith. That is because ultimately only God can know who has a
genuine faith in God, and therefore deserves salvation" (Aslan 1994:186).
The Sharia continues to occupy the attention of Muslims more than any
other aspect of their faith right up to the present day. This can also be attributed to the fact that the Sharia, in contrast to theology, continues to
play a role in preserving, no matter how formal or artificial it may be, the
unity of the community intact.

(2) The Muslim view of the history of religion in general seems to have pre-
cluded a need to consider the concept of diversity, or to view this concept
within the universal notion of *tawḥīd* (not simply 'unity' but 'unifying
oneness'). For normative Muslim belief holds that Islam is the last form
assumed by religion in the current cycle of human history; while its
founder is the final prophet, and the revelation which he transmitted is
the final one, it is also part of the long chain of revelations that preceded
it, with all previous revelations and their prophets being expressions of
the one and only Truth, that of *tawḥīd*, which thus lies at the heart of all
revealed religions and which Islam was revealed to confirm. In its final
revelation of the truth of *tawḥīd*, Islam is seen as sealing the universal
religious message and so it:

> signifies the return to the primordial religion and names itself accord-
> ingly (*din al-fitrah*, the religion that is in the nature of things, or *din al-
> hanif*, the primordial religion of Unity)... This primordial character of
> the Islamic message is reflected not only in its essentiality, universality
> and simplicity, but also in its inclusive attitude toward the religions
> and forms of wisdom that preceded it.
>
> NASR 2003: 4–5

This understanding of Islam as a fulfilment of previous revelations,
together with being, until relatively recently, a successful global force,

may have added to a sense of fulfilment (overflowing into a kind of triumphalism) and therefore diminished the sense that there was any need to engage theologically with the question of religious diversity.

(3) The general belief that was and continues to be prevalent to this day amongst exclusivist Muslims—always in the majority—is that although other religions, especially Judaism and Christianity are revealed religions, they are no longer reliable religions, and certainly not compared with Islam. Muslim exclusivists regard Islam as being more faithful to the spirit of the primordial revelation and therefore more attuned to the Truth than other religions. This sense of Islam being the final embodiment of the ultimate, one and only Truth, is closely connected with the doctrine of 'distortion' (*tahrīf*), namely, the belief that the Jewish and Christian scriptures have been tampered with, and no longer faithfully reflect their inaugurating revelations. However, as Ayoub argues, what the Qur'an appears to mean by *tahrīf* is not the actual alteration or distortion of the texts by the different faith traditions but erroneous interpretations or meanings. Had this been the majority opinion of the term, one might have envisaged more meaningful and open dialogue between the different faith traditions (Ayoub 2004: 101–102).

Contemporary Muslim Perspectives on Religious Diversity

The advent of modernity, followed by globalisation that has led to the revolution of information technology and the breakup of the once homogeneous 're-ligious universe' has generated an entirely new situation to people of all faiths. In a world of discourse formed by the ever-intensifying and ever-accelerating transmission of knowledge and information, the boundaries that previously separated religions from each other have gradually become porous. People now know far more about the people of other faiths than they did in the past, and different belief systems are confronted with each other on a much wider scale than ever before. The question of how to relate to other faiths thus assumes major significance. Many different responses have been forthcoming from various intellectual and theological currents. To simplify: secularists assert that all religions are relative, and thus none are either absolute or true; dogmatists assert that their particular religion alone is true and thus absolute, and that all others are false; universalists advocate a view that all religions are relative when compared with the Absolute, of which they are just different expressions, and thus can lead one back to the Absolute. These religions, the universalists assert, are absolutely necessary, despite their unavoidable relativity.

On this basis, one is then compelled to acknowledge not only the validity of one's own religion or belief system, but also to be tolerant and open to the values revealed by other religions.

For Muslims, this perspective raises many challenges, since for most of their history, the faith and identity of Muslims was tied up with their dominance in terms of their relationship with non-Muslims. However in the contemporary scene, Muslims are suffering from the combination of a long term intellectual decline together with the absence of charismatic leadership, which has inhibited the creativity of responses to the theological issues raised by the complexity and acuteness of the phenomena flowing from contemporary religious multiculturalism.

Nonetheless, there has been a variety of approaches to the problem of religious diversity among Muslims; we are prevented by time and space from surveying all of them, and will restrict ourselves to giving an overview of the salient features of the following four groups: fundamentalists, conservatives, modernists, and traditionalists—the latter will receive particular attention, as they appear to offer the most promising way forward for an Islamic theology of religions.

(1)   The fundamentalist/exclusivist approach to other religions is the least representative among ordinary Muslims though currently it appears to have the most vocal representatives. One need not go any further in reference to the writings of this group than the work of Maryam Jameelah. In her *Islam versus Ahl Al Kitab*, for example, she argues that peace and reconciliation between different religions under the current circumstances are unattainable in the absence of the political dominance of Islam (Jameelah 1989: 409–412). The position of this group, asserting as they do that Islam alone is true and thus absolute, does not hold out much hope for religious dialogue, let alone a theology of religions.

(2)   As regards the conservatives, they accept the classical understanding of Islam as the fulfilment of previous faiths and believe that they should perform *da'wa*, that is, invite non-Muslims to embrace Islam, without, however disrespecting non-Muslims should they not convert. Hence, the relationship between them and Muslims should be based on mutual acknowledgement and respect for the major religious differences between them. Any compromise on these main differences would not be acceptable to the conservatives. They stress that cooperation and dialogue between Muslims and the people of other faiths must be maintained for the sake of social and political harmony. This harmony could be achieved through the following steps: the recognition and acceptance that the

phenomenon of religious diversity is the will of God, and that disagreements in the realm of religion are best left to the Hereafter. In other
words, reconciliations of these differences are left to God, rather than humans, to judge, in accordance with the words of Q 5:48, cited above: "He
that will show you the truth of the matters about which you differ." Here
and now, cooperation and co-existence on the practical plane between
the two sides must continue and be respected and cultivated.

Secondly, conservatives emphasise the need to base dialogue with
non-Muslims on the common ground of their respective scriptures,
rather than focus on the issues that divide them. The 'A Common Word'
initiative, noted above, is an example of the kind of initiative favoured
by conservative Muslims: it does not 'give anything away' in terms of
fundamental Muslim beliefs, but is nonetheless open to dialogue so that
differences of religious perspective are discussed in an open and peaceful rather than an aggressive way. One underlying aim of the initiative is
that Muslims should work together with non-Muslims against common
enemies such as atheism and other -isms that deny the existence of the
Ultimate Reality. Furthermore, Muslims should cooperate with people of
other faiths on common issues such as oppression, injustice and exploitation irrespective of race, religion, ethnic background or nationalities; common agreement should be reached between Muslims and non-Muslims
on spreading the spirit of forgiveness and mercy and fight all forms of intolerance and bigotry. For them, all humanity has a common origin, and
this entails a deep respect for the dignity of that common origin irrespective of the religious backgrounds. This position has been well expressed by
the Egyptian scholar Yusuf al-Qaradawi (Qaradawi 2007: 65–71).

Qaradawi, and his fellow-conservatives, reject the classical status of
the People of the Book as *dhimmi*, considering this notion as one that
belongs to a particular historical context; since this context has changed
there is no justification to continue this mode of hierarchical classification (Qaradawi 2008: 84–85). It is worth mentioning that this group
strongly opposes the position adopted by the fundamentalists that
Muslims should not interact with non-Muslims; they criticise them and
claim that they are ignorant of the overall Islamic understanding of
proper relations with people of other faiths. This group stresses that Islam acknowledges not only the Divine origin of non-Muslim scriptures
but also encourages Muslims to actively interact with those of other religions, to the extent that Islam permits Muslim men to marry women
from the People of the Book; the close blood relationships that result by
necessity entails legal and moral responsibilities. Despite the advocacy

of cooperation, this group insists upon the mutual recognition of the major differences between their beliefs and those of other faiths, so that all interaction would take place on the basis of a clear understanding of religious difference. While being laudable on the political and social level, this kind of religious conservatism has not produced anything that could be labelled as an 'Islamic theology of religions'; rather, it is more concerned with the political and social imperatives of Muslim coexistence with non-Muslims.

(3)   The modernists constitute the third and most powerful group (at least within western academia), that has dealt with religious diversity. This group includes figures such as Abdululaziz Sachedina, Mohammed Arkoun, and Farid Esack. Their approach aims mainly at reformulating Islamic principles in order to accommodate the norms of the modern world and the assumptions and expectations of modern thought. This group tends to highlight those ideas and notions within Islamic thought that are in tune with the premises of modernity while ignoring all ideas and principles that appear to be in direct conflict with them. Irrespective of their intellectual background, modernists tend to reject tradition, especially traditional exegesis, in order to make the case for religious pluralism—understood here as the meaningful coexistence of religious diversity, that is Diana Eck's understanding of pluralism. In other words, they "seek to debunk and dispute authoritarian theological discourses" (Rizwi 2004:31) that they think both obscure and disable proper religious understanding. For example, Sachedina in his attempt to find a public sphere for religious pluralism that protects the rights of religious minorities, tries to rethink political imagery in Islamic and democratic societies (Rizwi 2004:28). His approach is to make the Muslim past relevant to the present, by downgrading religious exclusivism and conservatism, and affirming the unity of humankind, which the Qur'an stresses, and through the emphasis that humanity essentially worships one God. Further evidence of pluralism is the notion of *fitra* (the primordial human nature) that unites all religious and religiously conscious people, the imperative for ethical propriety as a criterion of success for any religious community, and the fact that the Qur'an stresses that it was God's will to have diverse religions. The modernists add mutual self-improvement that would remove intolerance (based on Q 5:48) which forms the ethical basis for religious freedom together with the freedom of conscience based on the primordial nature of humanity. For the modernists, qur'anic ethics demand that humankind practise universal forgiveness and toleration,

abandoning violence in favour of a moral struggle. Moral struggle leads to the path of freedom, fulfilment and the removal of religious exclusivism.

Farid Esack's concern is to "negotiate a space in modern liberal democracy for religious communities such as Islam as peaceable, moral partners in a just, socially equitable and free society" (Rizwi 2004: 29). Esack's approach to religious pluralism is fashioned by a kind of liberation theology. The context in which he developed his approach was the apartheid setting which he experienced in South Africa. Esack advocates a hermeneutical method that aims at the contextualisation of the Qur'an within specific social-historical situations. As he puts it: "all readings of any texts are necessarily contextual. If the word of God is at all interested in being heard and actualised, as all Muslims would insist, then the Qur'an has to be contextual" (Esack 1997: 255). To justify his approach he argues that "belief in the relevance of the Qur'an is not the same as belief in a text which is timeless and spaceless" (Esack 1997: 49). For him, the text is bound to its time and space; and in order to achieve justice and religious solidarity, texts must be interpreted by human beings within their specific time and space, so that they can correspond to contemporary realities. His aim is to have a qur'anic hermeneutic that can respond effectively to the social, economic and political realities of oppression and exploitation. Traditional tafsir or interpretations of the Qur'an, he says, are oppressive and do not allow room outside Islam and in most cases they are used to support illegitimate or oppressive orders. New contextual interpretations of key qur'anic passages are essential to allow for tolerance and religious solidarity with the other. He insists this is inevitable for any Muslims serious about applying the message of the Qur'an to contemporary pluralistic settings.

Arkoun, another prominent Muslim modernist, urges us to adopt a new approach to religion and offers radical suggestions on how religion should be taught if it is to lead to greater interreligious understanding. He argues that the revealed texts need to be re-evaluated and read from different angles— sociological, philological, historical, contextual, etc. His aim is to view all religions as strictly equal, given that they have all received revelation from a single source—this brings him into line with Hick's brand of pluralism. Moreover, no community can claim to have received the totality of revelation; what each community has received can only be partial and fragmentary, given the fact that the ultimate Truth is beyond all forms of revelation and ineffable. Despite Arkoun's claim to objectivity and impartiality in relation to all religions, however, I agree with Thomas' evaluation: Arkoun presupposes a fundamentally Islamic conception of revelation, however much he appears to accommodate the non-Muslim Other (Thomas 2013: 167). According to Thomas, modernists such as Arkoun, Esack and Sachedina may try to present a form of Muslim pluralism, but they fail to fully appreciate the non-Muslim Other in all their true 'otherness.' Instead, they 'include' the Other within an essentially Islamic paradigm: even if they have an expanded conception of tawhīd, their views of the religious Other are dominated and permeated by a clearly recognisable qur'anic perspective on the nature of divine revelation.

I would add that these scholars try so hard to become pluralist that they oppose all traditional approaches to Islam, ignore all exclusivist verses of the Qur'an, and therefore alienate the overwhelming majority of conservative and traditional Muslim scholars. It is difficult to see how these modernists will have any success in convincing those who most need to be won over to the idea of an 'Islamic theology of religions': the overwhelming majority of Muslims— scholars, theologians, jurists and lay Muslims alike—who believe firmly in Islam as the only fully normative and fully efficacious religion.

Muslim Traditionalists

Gai Eaton, a leading Muslim traditionalist, described Reza Shah-Kazemi's work *The Other in the Light of the One* as "a pioneering masterpiece" (Eaton, in Shah-Kazemi 2006, backcover). It certainly has articulated the traditionalist or 'perennialist' perspective[5] in a more systematically 'qur'anic' manner than any other work in the perennial school. Shah-Kazemi dedicates his book to his spiritual guide, Martin Lings, probably because it was Lings who most explicitly expressed the principles of the perennial philosophy in Muslim terms (see for example Lings 1993: 22–23). The founders of the school, Frithjof Schuon and Rene Guenon, although practising Islam as members of a Sufi order, express the perennial philosophy in terms of all the major religious traditions, and Islam is not given a privileged position. In the writings of Eaton, Lings, and Nasr, however, Islam is clearly the primary religious source of reference. They adhere to the universality of the perennial philosophy, but they express this universality mainly through Islamic sources. But, because the basis of their expositions is metaphysical and therefore universal, I would find it difficult to refer to their writings as constituting an 'Islamic theology of religions'. All three writers stick to the distinction made by Schuon and Guenon between metaphysics—defined as 'supra-confessional', esoteric, and universal—and

---

5 For a good overview of the perennialist or traditionalist school, see Oldmeadow (1998).

theology—defined as 'confessional', exoteric, and exclusivist (see Schuon: 1993). For these writers, to say 'theology' is to say 'exclusivism'; so the only kind of 'theology of religions' envisaged by them would be one in which tolerance and respect for other religions would be infused into an exclusivist attitude; or into an 'inclusivist' one, whereby other religions are seen as 'Islamic' to the extent that they conform to the principles of *tawhīd* and the qur'anic conception of revelation. So here, the Muslim perennialists would be in agreement with the position of Thomas, as noted above: Muslim theologies of the religious Other are either exclusivist or inclusivist, even if they are described as pluralist. But the Muslim perennialists would add that the theological conception of *tawhīd* is not the only one to be found within the Islamic tradition, and would insist on the importance of a metaphysical or mystical conception of *tawhīd*, and how this can lead to a different conception of the religious Other.

Shah-Kazemi appears to be aware of the problem of defining his work in terms of theology, and for this reason states that the perspective he adopts in *The Other in the Light of the One* cannot be put into any of the categories of the tripartite schema formulated by Alan Race, i.e., exclusivism, inclusivism, and pluralism (1983). In the "Introduction" to his book, Shah-Kazemi (2006: xxiv-xxvi) explains the reason why his approach requires a different category:

> The position argued for in this book cannot be fitted into any of these categories. It can instead be characterised as 'universalist': a position which shares with pluralism the basic premise that the major religious traditions are valid paths to salvation, but parts company with the pluralist in asserting that this salvific efficacy stems from the fact that these religions are divinely revealed, not humanly constructed. While many of the aims and motives of the pluralists are laudable and deserve support, this does not mean that one has to agree with all its premises and concomitants; in particular, one disagrees with the kind of pluralism which is constrained to deny the uniqueness of each religion in order to subsume them all under some putatively 'global theology'. For it is by the same token constrained to contradict the self-definition of all the religions.[6]

---

6 In his recent important contribution, Khalil (2012) likewise goes beyond Race's categories, and refers to 'universalists', but not in the same sense intended by Shah-Kazemi. For Khalil, universalists are defined as those who believe that all souls eventually end up in Paradise, even after a long stay in Hell, if they are sinners. See the review by Firestone (2014) of both this book and the volume edited by Khalil (2013) which includes a chapter by Shah-Kazemi, "Beyond Polemics and Pluralism: The Universal Message of the Qur'an," 87–105.

He continues by stating that his universalism differs from 'inclusivism' in asserting that, though there is indeed a single religious essence underlying all outward forms, the differences between these outward forms are irreducible, because they are revelations of God. From this point of view, he argues, "the very otherness of the Other is rigorously maintained and respected, rather than being domesticated and appropriated as part of oneself or one's formal religion, and thereby in practice denying its otherness" (Shah-Kazemi 2006: xxv). The next point he makes explains the reason for the rather unusual title of his book, *The Other in the Light of the One*:

> Rather, the Other in its very otherness, in all its particularities, in all its irreducible difference, is respected not simply out of a sentiment of religious tolerance, but on the basis of a perception that the Other is an expression of the One. The One reveals itself in diversity and infinite differentiation; it does not deny or abolish differences on the plane of its infinite unfolding. The difference between oneself and the Other is therefore simultaneously upheld and transcended: upheld on the plane of irreducible form, and transcended only on the supra-phenomenal plane of the divine Principle itself in which all differences are embraced and unified.
>
> SHAH-KAZEMI 2006: XXV

Readers of the perennialist school authors will recognise here the influence of the perspective referred to by the title of one of Schuon's best known works, *The Transcendent Unity of Religions* (1993).[7] Shah-Kazemi also refers to Nasr's essay, "Islam and the Encounter of Religions" (Nasr 1972: 123–52) as "a wide-ranging application of the principle of 'transcendent unity of religions' from the point of view of the Islamic tradition as a whole" (Shah-Kazemi 2006: xvii). Shah-Kazemi's book clearly follows in the footsteps of Nasr's Sufi adaptation and expression of the perennial philosophy. Nasr's vision of Sufi esoterism is cited by Shah-Kazemi as follows:

> The Sufi is one who seeks to transcend the world of forms, to journey from multiplicity to Unity, and from the particular to the Universal. He leaves the many for the One, and through this very process is granted the vision of the One in the many. For him all forms become transparent, including religious forms, thus revealing to him their unique origin.
>
> NASR 1972, cited in SHAH-KAZEMI 2006: XVIII

---

7   T.S. Eliot wrote of this book that "I have met with no more impressive work on the comparative study of Oriental and Occidental religion."

Chapter 2 of Shah-Kazemi's book, entitled "The Reality of the One and Dialogue with the Other" can be seen as an elaboration of this Sufi vision of *tawhīd*.

Here, again, one notes the importance of the distinction between theology and metaphysics: for the theologians of Islam, *tawhīd* is fundamentally a statement about the oneness of God; whereas, for the Sufis, it is a statement about the nature of Being. This has significant implications for the conception of the religious Other. Basing himself chiefly on the qur'anic exegeses of Ibn 'Arabi, 'Abd al-Razzaq Kashani, and al-Ghazali, Shah-Kazemi draws out the implications of the notions of the 'multiple One' (*al-wāhid al-kathīr*) and 'unique multiplicity' (*al-kathīr al-wāhid*). The most important point he makes here, as regards the implications of ontological or metaphysical *tawhīd* for the religious Other, is the following:

> Thus we are invited to contemplate the vision of the One in the many, and the many in the One.... From this perspective, one sees through the aspect of multiplicity to the real unity that each phenomenon replicates in its own way—to the oneness which gives it all its reality, and without which it is reduced to nothingness. To see the One in the many is thus to see the Real in the very heart of appearances, the Absolute in the relative: all relativities are thus so many projections of the one and only reality. And to see the many in the One is to perceive, on the one hand, that the One embraces all as *al- Muhīt*, 'the All-Encompassing'; and on the other hand, it is to intuit the roots of all phenomena "on high", that is, within the Absolute; it is thus to re-integrate all phenomena within their unique source. The One is both absolute—hence exclusive of all relativity; and it is infinite—hence inclusive of all existence.
>
> SHAH-KAZEMI 2006: 88

This view of metaphysical *tawhīd* implies that the One reality is present within every single phenomenon, making it unique and irreducible to any other phenomenon. Each particular thing manifests the Universal, while at the same time being different from all other particulars. As applied on the plane of religions, the religious Other must be 'integrated' (the true, or literal, meaning of *tawhīd*, as Shah-Kazemi insists repeatedly) into one's vision, in all its 'otherness,' in all its particularity as a unique revelation of the One (Shah-Kazemi 2006: 137–139). The difference between this perspective and a conventional 'theological' conception of how other religions are to be 'integrated' within *tawhīd* is clear. Whereas for the theologian, the religions of the Other can be seen as true religions only to the extent that they approximate the religion of Islam; for the Sufi, all religious forms without exception are seen as expressions of the One. It is upon this vision that Ibn 'Arabi's famous poem "The Interpreter of Desires" or *Tarjuman al-Ashwāq*, is based:

> My heart has become capable of every form: it is a pasture for gazelles and a convent for Christian monks,
> And a temple for idols and the pilgrim's Ka'ba and the tables of the Tora and the book of the Koran.
> I follow the religion of Love: whatever way Love's camels take, that is my religion and my faith.
>
> Ibn 'Arabi 1978: 52, cited in SHAH-KAZEMI 2006: 192–3

If we were to stop here, we would have a vision of esoteric universalism that appears to metaphysically embrace, in the 'heart', all possible religious forms; but Shah-Kazemi draws our attention to Ibn 'Arabi's own commentary on these lines: "No religion is more sublime than a religion based on love... This is a peculiar prerogative of Muslims, for the station of perfect love is appropriated to Muhammad beyond any other prophet, since God took him as His beloved" (Shah-Kazemi 2006: 199). It would appear that behind the poetic mask of universality there lies the face of an exclusivist theologian. But Shah-Kazemi demonstrates that this combination of universalism and exclusivism is in fact typical of most of the Sufis, referring to Rumi and Shabistari as examples. Rumi is well known for his poetic expressions of universality, but less well-known for his invitation to Christians to enter Islam. Shah-Kazemi cites this passage from Rumi's *Discourses*, in which Jarrah, a Christian asserts his belief that Jesus is God because his 'books' tell him so:

> That is not the action or the words of an intelligent man possessed of sound senses... Certainly, it is right that ... the Lord of Jesus, upon whom be peace, honoured Jesus and brought him nigh to Him, so that whoever serves him has served his Lord, whoever obeys him has obeyed his Lord. But inasmuch as God has sent a Prophet superior to Jesus, manifesting by his hand all that He manifested by Jesus' hand and more, it behoves him to follow that Prophet.[8]
>
> SHAH-KAZEMI 2006: 200

---

8   Shah-Kazemi notes that Muhammad Legenhausen cites this passage (1999: 108–109) as evidence that Rumi "was by no means a reductive religious pluralist of the sort Hick makes him out to be." Shah-Kazemi adds that he agrees with Legenhausen's critique of Hick's religious pluralism "from a strictly orthodox Muslim point of view." Here, again, we note that Shah-Kazemi is not pretending to mount an 'Islamic theology of religions.'

To appreciate the logic by which the Sufi universalist is also, apparently, an exclusivist, we need to go back to Shah-Kazemi's "Introduction," and the reason why his approach cannot be placed into any of Race's three categories. Above, it was noted that his 'universalism' cannot be equated with 'pluralism' or 'inclusivism'; it cannot be seen as a form of 'exclusivism', either, but nonetheless it does include some aspects of 'exclusivism'. Finally, as regards the 'exclusivist' position, even though universalism clearly transcends one type or aspect of exclusivism—the denial of the validity of other faiths—it evinces a certain solidarity with another type or aspect of exclusivism: the notion that one's own religion is normative and binding. Reconciliation of these two apparently contradictory positions is one of the main aims of Shah-Kazemi's book; his success in this effort is debatable—we will return to this criticism below.

Shah-Kazemi does not cite the writings of Schuon in his effort to reconcile the apparent contradiction between universalism and exclusivism;[9] rather, it is Ibn 'Arabi that gives him the key for the reconciliation, through this ontological principle: "Part of the perfection of existence is the existence of imperfection within it, since, were there no imperfection, the perfection of existence would be imperfect because of the absence of imperfection within it" (Shah-Kazemi 2006: 296, citing Chittick 1989: 296). This conception of being is then applied to the distinction between universalism and exclusivism: a universalism which excludes exclusivism is itself exclusivist. There must be a place within an authentic universalism for exclusivist perspectives. Shah-Kazemi takes full advantage of this principle, and applies it to key qur'anic verses in accordance with this hermeneutical principle of Ibn 'Arabi:

> As far as the Word of God is concerned, when it is revealed in the language of a certain people, and when those who speak this language differ as to what God meant by a certain word or group of words due to the variety of possible meanings of the words, each of them—however differing their interpretations may be—effectively comprises what God meant, provided that the interpretation does not deviate from the accepted meanings of the language in question. God knows all these meanings,

---

9 In various works Schuon has shown that whereas universal metaphysics (esoterism) transcends exclusivist theology, as esoterism transcends exoterism, or essence transcends form, he also insists that there can be no effective realisation of the esoteric essence outside the framework of a particular exoteric form. One must practise a single religion 'exclusively.' This is a crucial part of his articulation of orthodoxy, understood as a protective framework, a 'seal' of authenticity, for any esoteric path of self-realisation. See Schuon (1961: 13–52, and 1981: 15–47).

and there is none that is not the expression of what He meant to say to
this specific person.

CHODKIEWICZ 1993: 30

In Chapter 3 of his book, entitled "Islam: Quintessential and Universal Submission," Shah-Kazemi applies these ontological and hermeneutical principles to the interpretation of the meaning of Islam. As is well known, in the
writings of Muslim pluralists the word is taken to mean 'submission' and this
principle of submission to God tends to eclipse the idea of Islam as a particular religion. The verse: "Truly, religion with God is Islam" (3:19) is therefore
interpreted to mean that universal submission is what is intended, not the
particular religion bearing that name. But Shah-Kazemi maintains that, in
terms of Ibn 'Arabi's hermeneutics, there is no need for mutual exclusion between the two interpretations. The universalist can adopt a position in which
the exclusivist interpretation is not seen as invalid, but as being intended by
God for that interpreter. The universalist does not have to adopt that point
of view himself, but he cannot say that it is wrong or invalid. But the universalist will adopt for himself the point of view that the particular religion,
Islam, is one manifestation of the universal principle of submission. But he
would add, in accordance with Ibn 'Arabi and Rumi, that the particular religion Islam is indeed the best manifestation of this universal principle. This
leads to what I regard as Shah-Kazemi's strongest argument: the universalist
does not undermine the principle of *da'wa*, the call to embrace Islam which
is so important a part of the duty of the exoteric/exclusivist Muslim. Rather,
this call is made precisely on the basis that Islam is the most universal of all
religions, seeing the truth and holiness within all religions that have been
revealed by God:

> In other words it should be possible to present an 'invitation' to study the
> universality that is undoubtedly present in the Qur'an, together with the
> profound Sufi perspectives on key Qur'anic verses, as a most—possibly
> the most—effective and appropriate manner in which to 'call' people to
> Islam. In an age dominated by the opposition between atheism and reli-
> gion, when 'religion' often appears as but another form of bigotry, chau-
> vinism, and exclusivism, and when secularism appears on the contrary
> as the only ideological antidote to such narrowness—in such a context,
> the explicit universality of the Quranic revelation stands out as a brilliant
> *spiritual* corrective to religious bigotry. It is a revealed 'invitation' to com-
> bine depth of conviction with breadth of spiritual vision; a depth of con-
> viction that calls out to be plumbed intellectually and spiritually, rather

than just defined dogmatically, and a truly panoramic scope of spiritual perception, one which encompasses all revealed faiths, without dissipating, in the name of tolerance, into an unthinking acceptance of all ideas as equally 'true.'

SHAH-KAZEMI 2006: 235

It seems to be the aim of Shah-Kazemi to 'open up' traditional, conservative, exclusivist Muslims to the religious Other, doing so in a way that does not undermine their fundamental beliefs, or their need to call people to embrace Islam. His nuanced approach to universalism incorporating particularism, and thereby allowing for traditional *da'wa,* is certainly an important bridge between metaphysical universalism and theological exclusivism. But his success in terms of spiritually embracing and relating to the religious Other in all its otherness—and therefore his success in a key element in any 'Islamic theology of religions'—seems to me to run counter to his aim of 'opening up' Muslim exclusivists both to the religious Other and to Sufi/perennialist hermeneutics. He states this aim as follows (2006: 262):

The task for the Muslim universalist who sees the need to include the particularist even while *spiritually* 'going beyond' particularism, is to affirm conservatism at the same time as opening it up, both inwardly and outwardly, to the Other. This is best done by compromise and not confrontation; that is, by reinforcing and building upon the strong tradition of tolerance in Islam, encouraging an openness to dialogue, while helping to cultivate an appreciation of the deeper aspects of the religion of the Other—that is, giving evidence of the devotion, virtue, piety, beauty and sanctity residing in other religions. All of this, we believe, is far more likely to cultivate those resources within conservative Islam which constitute such a crucial bulwark against fanatical, extremist interpretations of Islam.

But here, one has to ask the question: can traditional Muslim exclusivists really be expected to take on the radical universalism espoused by the Sufis, when it comes to particular qur'anic denunciations of, for example, Christian dogma? Here, I believe, there is a contradiction in Shah-Kazemi's approach: his very success in opening up to the non-Muslim Other, in all its uniqueness and all its true otherness and difference from Islam, undermines his effort to positively influence the exclusivists in their attitude to the non-Muslim Other. I would therefore argue that even if his book, and the Muslim traditionalist approach in general, does give us some important points of departure, it does not help much in articulating a doctrine that can be accepted as *theological*. That is, a doctrine that can be recognized and taken seriously within the tradition of Muslim *kalām*, scholastic theology. It is very unlikely that he will meet with much success in convincing Muslim theologians of the need to respect the religions of the Other in all their otherness, at the same time as accepting these religions as revelations of one and the same God, and therefore leading to one and the same summit.

Shah-Kazemi seems to be aware of this problem, and cites such examples as the late Shaykh of al-Azhar, 'Abd al-Halim Mahmud (d. 1978), who read and highly approved of both Guenon and Schuon (Shah-Kazemi 2006: 264). However, one has to take note of the fact that this openness to the 'supra-confessional' perspective of Guenon and Schuon seems to have more to do with their critique of modernism than their universalism. Also, it would seem that 'Abd al-Halim was the exception that proves the rule: since his death in 1978, nobody of his 'exoteric' authority has manifested such a degree of appreciation of the perennialist school. So, even if Shah-Kazemi, Nasr, Lings, Chittick, and Eaton have given us the most promising approaches to the religious Other within an Islamic framework, their efforts should be defined in terms of universalist metaphysics, or perhaps 'mystical theology', and as such will not have much credibility in the eyes of upholders of traditional Muslim scholastic theology, or *kalām*.

However, we should remember that, as noted above, scholastic theology does not play in Islam the central role that it plays in Christianity. Rather, it is the Sharia that takes centre-stage. In the traditional Islamic universe, theology was always firmly subordinated to the formal Law, in practical terms; but it was also at least partly subordinated to spirituality or mysticism, wherever the Sufi tradition was well established—which means most of the Muslim world for the past millennium, that is, until modern times. This has been the case largely thanks to the monumental influence of one man: arguably the most important 'mystical theologian' of Islam, al-Ghazālī (d.1111). In the first book of his massively influential 40-book work, 'Revival of the Religious Sciences' (*Ihā' 'ulūm al-dīn*), al-Ghazālī states that the scholastic theologian, *al-mutakallim*, is restricted in his vision and knowledge to the outward or formal aspects of belief. He has no spiritual knowledge (*ma'rifa*) of God, according to al-Ghazālī, unless he undergoes spiritual purification which alone leads one to authentic knowledge of God's nature and His acts (al-Ghazālī, 1992: 34). For al-Ghazālī, despite its necessity as a shield against heterodoxy, theology acts like 'a veil' over the heart, which is the organ of spiritual vision. Whereas theology veils, mysticism (or Sufism) unveils. Purification of the heart opens up insights not just into the essential nature of God, but also into His acts (*af'āl*). Given that the revelations of God are among His 'acts', it is possible that mystical unveiling through Sufi practices opens up the 'eye of the heart', enabling it to see the different revelations of God in a light which is supra-theological or metaphysical. This is what one observes in the poetic expressions of Rumi and Ibn 'Arabī, noted above. But Ibn 'Arabī also states the fruits of his vision in terms which lend themselves to theological discourse:

> Messengers were sent according to the diversity of the times and the variety of the situations. Each of them confirmed the truth of the others. None of them differed whatsoever in the roots by which they were supported and of which they spoke, even if rulings differed... The governing property belonged to the time and the situation, just as God has declared: "To every one of you We have appointed a right way and a revealed law" (5, 48). So the roots coincided, without disagreement on anything.'
>
> Cited by CHITTICK 1994: 134

It seems that there is a bridge linking mystical vision and theological discourse, this bridge being the notion of the divine 'act', in al-Ghazālī's terms, and that of divine self-disclosure (*tajallī*), in Ibn 'Arabī's terms. For Ibn 'Arabī, all the revealed religions are so many 'acts' of God by which He reveals something of the 'hidden treasure' of His Essence. In a complex diagram depicting the modalities of self-disclosure, in which each element is both cause and consequence, he presents the phenomenon of religious diversity as one element in the unfolding kaleidoscopic self-disclosure of God. This diagram is given in Chapter 48 of his *al-Futūḥāt al-Makkiyya*, and contains, in circular form, the following interlinked statements, each being the cause of what comes next, and the consequence of what came before, in the never-ending cycle of divine self-disclosure:

· The revealed religions are diverse only because of the diversity of the divine relationships
· The divine relationships are diverse only because of the diversity of the states
· The states are diverse only because of the diversity of the times
· The times are diverse only because of the diversity of the movements
· The movements are diverse only because of the diversity of the attentivenesses
· The attentivenesses are diverse only because of the diversity of the goals
· The goals are diverse only because of the diversity of the self-disclosures

- The self-disclosures are diverse only because of the diversity of the revealed religions
- The revealed religions are diverse only because of the diversity of the divine relationships

CHITTICK 1994: 157

Another major point which helps to show the theological implications of a mystical vision of religious diversity is that Ibn ʿArabī, in common with most Sufis, firmly ground their mystical vision in the principles, ideas, and terms of the Qurʾan (as has been so ably demonstrated by Massignon, in his 1954 classic work, *Essay on the Origins of the Technical Language of Islamic Mysticism*). From this point of view, it might be argued that the Muslim perennialists, Chittick and Shah-Kazemi in particular, have helped to articulate the universalist, inclusivist, and pluralist implications of the mystical perspectives on the religious Other contained within the Qurʾan; even if their efforts cannot be seen as an expression of a credible Muslim theology of the religious Other. It seems that we are still waiting for the formulation of an ʿIslamic theology of religions' which is fully open to the Other as the Other, while at the same time remaining firmly and recognizably within the tradition of Islamic *kalām*.

Bibliography

Abou El-Fadl, K. (2002). *The Place of Tolerance in Islam*. Boston: Beacon Press.

Askari, H. (1985). "Within and Beyond the Experience of Religious Diversity." In J. Hick and H. Askari (eds.). *The Experience of Religious Diversity*. Aldershot: Gower Press. Pp. 191–218.

Arkoun, M. (1987). *The Concept of Revelation: From the People of the Book to the Societies of the Book*. Claremont, CA: Claremont Graduate School.

Aslan, A. (1994). *Religious Pluralism in Christian and Islamic Philosophy: The Thought of John Hick and Seyyed Hossein Nasr*. Abingdon: RoutledgeCurzon.

Ayoub, M. (2004). *Islam: Faith and History*. London: Oneworld.

―――. (2009). "Christians and Muslims in the Qurʾan and Muslim Tradition." In: Stephen R. Goodwin (ed.). *World Christianity in Muslim Encounter*. London and New York: Continuum. Pp. 3–15.

Chittick, William C. (1989). *The Sufi Path of Knowledge: Ibn al-ʿArabi's Metaphysics of Imagination*. Albany, NY: State University of New York Press.

―――. (1994). *Imaginal Worlds: Ibn al-ʿArabī and the Problem of Religious Diversity*. Albany, NY: State University of New York Press.

Chodkiewicz, M. (1993). *An Ocean Without Shore: Ibn Arabi, the Book and the Law.* Transl. by D. Streight. Albany, NY: State University of New York Press.

Daniel, N. (1958). *Islam and the West: The Making of an Image.* Edinburgh: Edinburgh University Press.

———. (1966). *Islam, Europe and Empire.* Edinburgh: Edinburgh University Press.

D'Costa, G. (1986). *Theology and Religious Pluralism.* Oxford: Blackwell.

———. (2000). *The Meeting of Religions and the Trinity.* Edinburgh: T & T Clark.

Esack, F. (1997). *Qur'an, Liberation and Pluralism.* Oxford: Oneworld.

Firestone, Reuven. (2014). Review article. *Journal of Qur'anic Studies* 16/2: 142–49.

Al-Ghazāli (1992). *Iḥyā' 'ulūm al-dīn.* Beirut: Dār al-Jīl.

Guillaume, A. (1968). *The Life of Muhammad: A Translation of Ibn Ishāq's* Sīrat Rasūl Allāh. Oxford: Oxford University Press.

Jameelah, M. (1989). *Islam versus Ahl al Kitab: Past and Present.* Delhi: Taj Company.

Khalil, M.H. (2012). *Islam and the Fate of Others: The Salvation Question.* Oxford: Oxford University Press.

———. (ed.). (2013) *Between Heaven and Hell: Islam, Salvation, and the Fate of Others.* Oxford: Oxford University Press.

Legenhausen, Muhammad. (1999). *Islam and Religious Pluralism.* London: Al-Hoda.

Lewis, B. (1998). *The Multiple Identities of the Middle East.* New York, NY: Schocken.

Lings, M. (1993). *What is Sufism?* Cambridge: The Islamic Texts Society.

Massignon, L. (1954). *Essay on the Origins of the Technical Language of Islamic Mysticism.* Transl. B. Clark. Notre Dame: University of Notre Dame Press.

Nasr, S.H. (1972). *Sufi Essays.* London: George Allen & Unwin.

———. (1996). *History of Islamic Philosophy, Part 1.* London and New York: Routledge.

———. (2002). *The Heart of Islam.* San Francisco: Harper Collins.

———. (2003). *Islam: Religion, History and Civilisation.* New York: Harper Collins.

Oldmeadow, Harry. (1998). "Metaphysics, Theology and Philosophy." *Sacred Web* 1.

Qaradawi, Y. (2007). *Fiqh al-Aqalliyāt,* Cairo: Dar al-Shorouk.

———. (2008). *Reasons for the Change of Fatwas in our Contemporary Situation.* Cairo: Dar al-Shorouk.

Race, A. (1983). *Christians and Religious Pluralism.* London: SCM Press.

Rizvi, S.H. (2004). "A Primordial *e pluribus unum*? Exegesis on Q.2:213 and Contemporary Muslim Discourses on Religious Pluralism." *Journal of Qur'anic Studies* 6: 21–42.

Sachedina, A. (2001). *The Islamic Roots of Democratic Pluralism.* Oxford: Oxford University Press.

Schuon, F. (1961). *Stations of Wisdom.* London: John Murray.

———. (1981). *Esoterism as Principle and as Way.* Bedfont: Perennial Books.

———. (1993). *The Transcendent Unity of Religions.* Wheaton, IL: Theosophical Publishing House.

Shah-Kazemi, R. (2006). *The Other in the Light of the One: The Universality of the Qur'an and Interfaith Dialogue*. Cambridge: The Islamic Texts Society.

Shah-Kazemi, R. (2013). "Beyond Polemics and Pluralism: The Universal Message of the Qur'an." In: M.H. Khalil (ed.). *Between Heaven and Hell: Islam, Salvation, and the Fate of Others*. Pp. 87–105.

Smith, Wilfred Cantwell. (1978). *The Meaning and End of Religion: A Revolutionary Approach to the Great Religious Traditions*. London: SPCK.

Thomas, D. (2013). "Islam and the Religious Other". In: D. Cheetham, D. Pratt, and D. Thomas (eds.). *Understanding Interreligious Relations*. Oxford: Oxford University Press. Pp 148–71.

Yusuf, H. (2005). "Generous Tolerance in Islam and its Effects on the Life of a Muslim." *Seasons: Semiannual Journal of Zaytuna Institute* 2.2: 26–42.

CHAPTER 20

A Buddhist Response to the Christian Theology of Religions

Mark Owen

Introduction

Considering the fairly general nature of the title of this contribution, it would be prudent to begin with a number of caveats, and the recognition of inevitable presuppositions. My own interest in Buddhism began over twenty years ago as a visitor to Thailand, where I began to learn more about Buddhism through books aimed at aspiring Buddhist practitioners, academic texts, and by spending time in several monasteries learning meditation techniques. I returned to Thailand on several occasions but also began to spend an increasing amount of time in India. Subsequently I have spent the last fifteen years frequently visiting and working predominantly in Tibetan communities in India, where I have regularly attended teachings, had audiences with learned monks, and generally learned more about Tibetan religion and culture. Today my interest in both Thai and Tibetan Buddhism remains strong, and, as an academic with a particular interest in Buddhism, I try and take the wisdom from both to help shape and improve my research, thoughts, and actions.

From an academic perspective my background was initially in the broad discipline of religious studies, progressively specializing in Eastern religions and Tibetan Buddhism. However, more recently, my work has focused on the role of religion in conflict and peace,[1] with a particular interest in Buddhism, conflict transformation and peacebuilding (see for example Sivaraksa 1992, 1993; McConnell 1995; Galtung 1995; Chappell 1999; Kawada 1999; Neumaier 2004; Mun 2007). My current work looks at the complex relationship between simplified constructs of religion as either inherently good or inherently bad, and the complex religious dynamics that often exist in situations of conflict 'on the ground' (and it will become apparent how this interest has influenced this chapter). This work is underpinned by the strong conviction that religion can play (and often has played) a positive role not only in situations where religion is an apparent driver of conflict, but also in conflicts where religion is

---

1   For more information on this area see seminal texts by Appleby (2000), Gopin (2000), Hertog (2010).

not negatively involved. In view of my interests in religion and peacebuilding, which explores how religions can play a more positive and sustainable role in understanding and transforming deadly and structural conflict, dialogue within and between religions is an issue that is fundamental to my own research.

Given the strong practical dimension of this work, and the belief that Buddhists have an important role and responsibility to participate actively in peacebuilding, my approach to this task could be seen to have a resonance with more engaged forms of Buddhism. Engaged Buddhism is a socially aware, non-violent movement and practice, rooted in concepts such as interconnectedness and universal compassion, and sees Buddhists as having the ability to contribute positively to a broad range of issues such as the environment, economics, ethics, politics, as well as peacebuilding.[2] My approach and understanding then is perhaps analogous to that of James Fredericks, who suggests interreligious engagement must be useful to contemporary Christians (2004), and my brief appraisal of the theology of religions from a Buddhist perspective will seek to understand and evaluate what practical and applicable value it may have, and therefore to what extent it might be considered a worthwhile endeavor in the engagement within and between different religious traditions.

One of the principle points of this slightly self-indulgent introduction is to emphasize the potentially complex nature of the formation of many Buddhists' beliefs and understandings. John D'Arcy May and Perry Schmidt-Leukel, in their introduction to Schmidt Leukel's *Buddhist Attitudes to other Religions* (2008), rightly interrogate the terms 'theology' and 'religion' but surprisingly uncritically adopt the terms 'Buddhism' and 'Buddhists.' However, as Lai and von Brück note in their study of the 'multicultural history' of Buddhist Christian dialogue, "there is neither *the* Buddhism nor *the* Christianity, and certainly not an *essence* of each, but always just a web of communication processes and shifting images" (2001: 237). However, the existing tendency in discussions on Buddhism and the theology of religions to talk of Buddhists and Buddhism in the abstract, as if we know what this means, fails to acknowledge existing scholarship from Buddhist studies which addresses this issue in a critical and thoughtful way (see for example Gethin 1998: 1–27).

A popular Tibetan saying approximates to, "As every valley has its own language so every teacher has their own doctrine." Whilst this arguably overstates the case when looking at many Buddhist traditions, evidently Buddhism in common with most other religions incorporates a myriad of different ideas, views, beliefs, and traditions, in many different cultures, countries, and

---

2 For more information on the theory and practice of Engaged Buddhism see Keown et al. (2003); King (2009); Moon (2004); Queen (2012); Sivaraksa (1992a, 2005).

contexts. Therefore it is important to acknowledge that the account presented here in no way claims to be representative of all or any Buddhist traditions or communities, but is a product of my own experiences and understandings; and therefore when I talk about a 'Buddhist perspective' it is my own partial and conditioned definition to which I am referring. That said, this is in no way intended to underplay this contribution through a sense of modesty. On the contrary it is my intention here to recognize the unique and individual nature of religious belief and experience; an important issue, which I will return to in due course when examining a Buddhist critique of the theology of religions 'project'.

A 'Buddhist' Approach to the Theology of Religions

It is possible to approach this task in a number of ways. Buddhist responses to the theology of religion debate (or challenge) have often taken the form of attempts to construct a 'Buddhist theology of religions,' with a focus on, or engagement with, Alan Race's now well established 'typological frame-work' of exclusivist, inclusivist, and pluralist categories, or variations on that theme.[3] Often a judgement is then made as to which category/s is/are most justifiable from a 'Buddhist' perspective.[4] As the debate has become nuanced, scholars such as Abraham Veléz de Cea (2012) have also sought to redefine the underlying presumptions on which the debate (and typology) is founded, shifting them in a more 'Buddhist' direction. There have also been attempts to 'creatively reinterpret' Buddhist traditions in order to bring them into dialogue with contemporary issues and comparative engagement (Hirota 2000). Most if not all of these endeavors have drawn on Buddhist teachings, philosophy and scripture, to underpin their presumptions and conclusions; with Kristen Kiblinger's inclusion of historical examples of Buddhist interreligious engage-ment a welcome addition (2005).

All these forms of inquiry are important and valid modes of study; and it is not my intention here to repeat what has already been done by other scholars with more knowledge and expertise in this area than myself. However, what I would (and am about to) argue is that there are a number of underlying prob-lems and 'discursive formations,' which existing studies have failed to ade-quately recognize and address when constructing representations of Buddhist

---

3   For an in-depth discussion on the development of Race's typology see Hedges (2010).

4   See for example Abe (1995); Kiblinger (2005); Schmidt-Leukel (2008); Makransky (2011); amongst others.

attitudes towards other religions. Consequently, in this chapter, I endeavor to offer a Buddhist critique of some of the assumptions underpinning the broader theology of religions project. I will ask whether from a Buddhist perspective systematically considering and developing responses to other religions is seen as a necessary or legitimate endeavor, and whether Buddhists really consider (any more than many Christians) many of the issues and questions that theology of religions scholars engage with.

That said, in attempting this task, I will inevitably also engage at least indirectly with the theology of religions typology. "As Mark Heim, John Thatamanil, and Kristen Kiblinger have argued, behind any interest (or disinterest) in learning from other religions lies a theology of religions that is either conscious or unconscious" (Makranksy 2011, 120). Clearly the extent to which constructing a theology of religions is seen as valid or worthwhile presupposes a certain position and attitude towards other religions; for example exclusivist responses invariably critique the theology of religions project, whereas an acceptance of the necessity and relevance of a theology of religions arguably infers an inclusivist or pluralist position. That said, addressing and engaging directly with these categories is not my main aim. I would also add finally that some of the issues raised here are by no means exclusive to a Buddhist perspective. Many of the points explored could be equally applicable if approaching this subject from another religious perspective or indeed none at all; although I would argue that it is valid to address these issues as a Buddhist constructing this critique.

Buddhist Sympathy for a Theology of Religions

The theology of religions project was driven initially by the need to consider the reality of increasing interaction with other religions, and the perceived threat to Christianity from other competing truth claims (Knitter 2004:1). Alan Race has argued that, "[G]lobal awareness entails that the religiously committed can no longer imagine their particular religion alone holds the key to the meaning of life and the truth about Ultimate Reality" (2001:164). The endeavor to seek different ways of engaging other religions is also underpinned by the implicit assumption that an exclusive attitude towards other religions is negative and this rejection can only lead to increased tension and conflict, whilst conversely a more open inclusivist and pluralist approach will help mitigate disputes between religions, engender greater respect and co-existence, and in turn make for a more harmonious global community and existence. In addition to building greater mutual respect and tolerance, scholars also regularly

claim that, if done in the right way, engagement with other religions can enhance one's own spiritual understanding and practice.

So how might we/I view these ideas and presumptions from a Buddhist perspective? Perhaps inevitably both similarities and differences can be seen to
exist between Christians and Buddhists over the underpinning motivations
for developing a theology of religions. Parallels can (and have) been drawn
between Christian and Buddhist teachings on love and compassion (*karuṇā*),
whilst, in addition, Buddhist concepts of nonviolence (*ahiṃsā*), interdepen-
dency (*paṭiccasamuppāda*), and the Bodhisattva ideal can be seen to support
an attitude of openness towards people from all backgrounds. There is also
ample work in the area of comparative theology, both from Buddhists and
Christians, which would seem to support the presumption that engagement
with other faiths leads to a greater mutual understanding and respect, and
deepens understanding of each other's and our own religion (see for example
Abe 1995; Lai and von Brück 2001; Fredericks 2004; Schmidt-Leukel 2005;
Ingram and Streng 2007; Thompson 2009; amongst others).

Furthermore, a theology of religions is evidently as much about self-understanding, self-inquiry, and self-evaluation as it is about learning about other
religious traditions. Constructing a theology of religions demands that we reflect profoundly on our own identity, how we perceive the 'other' and the relationship and interaction between those different identities; and indeed how
those identities are conceived of and constructed in the first place. This kind
of deep self-reflection and search for profound insight is something that many
Buddhists would, or certainly should, relate to and appreciate. It is exactly this
kind of deep self-analysis, and analytical deconstruction of the self and others
that the Buddha advocated in his teachings, and, for Buddhists, understanding
how we perceive and interact with the 'other' (Buddhists or non-Buddhists) is
an important and worthwhile exercise. That said, as I will argue shortly, this
does not necessarily advocate a more inclusive or pluralistic approach to other
religious traditions.

Buddhism has also not been immune to increasing encounters with alternative religions and beliefs systems, and the challenges this potentially brings. As
Masao Abe (1995) noted nearly twenty years ago, Buddhists in many traditions
have also begun to feel more of a threat to their identity and a challenge to
their beliefs. Today around the world we can see Buddhist engagement with
other religions bringing a wide range of both positive and negative outcomes;
from constructive participation in interreligious dialogue and multifaith
activities around the world, to complicity in intra and interreligious disputes
and deadly violence in countries such as Myanmar, Sri Lanka, and Thailand
(see for example Deegalle 2006; Juergensmeyer and Jerryson 2010; Tikhonov

and Brekke 2012). Furthermore, there is also a long history of (sometimes violent) intra Buddhist conflict, and Buddhists have periodically wrestled with how to reconcile what are ostensibly very different beliefs and practices between Buddhist traditions. Therefore, any endeavor which can serve to prevent tension, end conflict, and bring about lasting and meaningful reconciliation must for Buddhists be seen as an important and worthwhile venture.

'Buddhist' Critique of the Theology of Religions

Given the openness to interpretation of Buddhist scriptures and the flexible nature of key doctrines,[5] as Kiblinger has demonstrated (2008), it is a relatively easy task to select areas of Buddhist scripture, philosophy and/or Buddhist teachings that support a preferred position in relation to other religions; whether this be exclusivist, inclusivist, pluralist, or any variation on these themes. However, the questions remain; what is the point of this exercise and what good will it actually do? And how do these abstract constructions relate to the experience and practice of Buddhists on the ground? Whilst undoubtedly there are a number of good reasons why Buddhists should engage with other religions, and indeed many historical and contemporary examples of Buddhist inclusivism and pluralism towards other religions can be found (see Kiblinger 2005), in my experience this is not an issue that occupies the thoughts of many Buddhists, or is seen as a high priority. Therefore, in this section I will explore briefly the possible reasons for this incongruity, as well as begin to explore from a Buddhist perspective what the implications are for a theology of religions.

Throughout its history Buddhism has come into contact, and to some extent competition, with numerous other religions such as Jainism, Hinduism, Daoism, Zoroastrianism, the Shinto tradition, Judaism, as well as more recently, Islam and Christianity. Arguably, due to its traditional emphasis on inner spiritual development, as opposed to outward social engagement, it has developed an innate ability to adapt and synthesize with other cultures, contexts, and religions. For example, in Nepal, Buddhist and Hindu beliefs and practices are intricate and multi-faceted; and throughout Asia and beyond we can very easily find similar examples of where Buddhism exists in complex relationships with other religions. As a result, in contrast to the neat boundaries between

---

5   I am thinking for example of Mahayana Buddhist doctrines like the 'two truths', which postulates a difference between ultimate and relative truths, and skilful means (*upāya kauśalya*), where a teacher might adapt their teachings to best suit the needs or understandings of their pupils.

religions a theology of religions often implies (even in more nuanced typologies), in fact in many countries where Buddhism is prominent the relationship
between religions and cultures is often much more syncretic, dynamic and
complex. The kind of simplistic dichotomies often presupposed in a theology
of religions bear little relation to the lived experience of many Buddhists, and
therefore the type of systematic and considered reaction a theology of religion
might describe often does not occur.

Masao Abe has also noted that Buddhism displays a significant degree of
diversity in terms of its practice and scripture (1995: 18). Whilst he suggests this
predisposes Buddhism to a more pluralistic outlook, I would argue that the dif-
fuse nature and structure of Buddhism also means in fact that the challenges
presented by other religions do not impact on, and pre-occupy Buddhists, in
quite the same way as presumed by the theology of religions debate. So, for example, whilst contradictions and challenges might be viewed and formulated
by some scholars as a challenge to the whole Christian tradition, a challenge
to one Buddhist tradition or school is not necessarily seen as a threat to all
Buddhists or the whole of Buddhism. As a result, except in scholarly circles, interreligious engagement and experience is unlikely to stimulate the same sort
of systematic response we see in theology of religions seminars, debates, and
publications.

I would also suggest that for some Buddhists the perceived need to engage
with other religions, and certainly accept their truth claims as equally valid,
would to some extent be interpreted as a form of self-doubting, and indeed
as disrespectful to your teacher. For example, in the *vajrayāna* tradition, the
teacher is considered indispensable for attaining realization and as a living
manifestation of the Buddha: "the teacher is representative of the Buddhas,
and therefore devotion to the Buddhas largely comes down to devotion to
one's personal guru" (Ray 2001: 168). Therefore, unless a teacher has specifically instructed pupils to engage with other faiths and religious beliefs, and
acknowledge and accept them, it would be unthinkable to presume that other
religious instruction holds equal authority. In fact, despite the often popular
rhetoric that Buddhists are encouraged by the Buddha's teachings to constantly question and learn for themselves, this is not the reality in many Buddhist
cultures. Buddhists monks and laity are often taught by rote, and deference to
the teacher is the expected norm.

Furthermore, if the pursuit for a Buddhist theology of religions is an exercise to encourage religious actors to shift towards a more inclusive/pluralistic
point of view, I am not convinced that all Buddhists would see that as always a
useful or positive development. Hakamaya Noriaki has argued that "Buddhists
should not give in to a compromising and mushy 'tolerance' that uncritically

accepts all things ...." Similarly, Hans Küng has proposed the "problem of an easy, cheap tolerance in Buddhism." "There is a danger," he says in agreement with Hakamaya, "of uncritical assimilation, of an opportunistic attitude of compromise, of a dangerous lack of discrimination and insufficient resistance to some highly dubious Western 'achievements'" (cited in Kiblinger 2005: 3). I would be inclined to argue that attitudes towards other religions requires careful consideration of the context or circumstances, and an open and accepting attitude towards other religions cannot necessarily be assumed to be relevant or appropriate in all circumstances.

I am thinking particularly here of the problems Buddhists have experienced and still experience in contexts where Christian conversion is aggressive, and a retreat to an exclusivist position can assist in protecting existing religious and cultural identities. As John Makransky notes, "[T]he traditional Buddhist allergy to the notion of learning important religious things from religious Others, including Christians, has been exacerbated in the modern period by the Asian experience of Western colonialism, which many experienced, in part, as an aggressive assault by Christian missionaries on indigenous Asian beliefs in support of the Western domination of their societies" (2011: 123). The Tibetan case is also a pertinent example. Whilst the Dalai Lama is often held up as a model of religious pluralism, in fact, in practice, the Central Tibetan Administration and many members of the Tibetan exile community (as well as Western supporters) put considerable effort into protecting Tibetan religion and culture from being 'degraded' through dilution and syncretism. In fact it can and has been argued that this insular attitude and the perpetuation of their unique identity underpin the Tibetan struggle for meaningful autonomy (Lopez 1999; Anand 2000).

Often put forward as supporting the need for a theology of religions is the somewhat simplistic assumption that misunderstandings between religions have the potential to cause interreligious tension and conflict (Fredericks 2004: 14). In fact existing evidence does not support this assumption, and whilst a religious dimension to conflict can certainly make conflicts more difficult to solve and more deadly (Svensson 2012), rarely is difference over religious belief or doctrine a primary driver of conflict (Appleby 2000). In fact it is possible to argue that the converse is true, and that there is a very real danger that the religious dichotomies implicit, and often explicit, in a theology of religions, have the potential to reinforce stereotypes, and, from a Buddhist perspective, dualistic thought; notwithstanding that in the most extreme forms of pluralism a deconstruction of dualism is seen to lead to deep spiritual understanding and empathy. A pertinent example of the potentially negative impact can be seen in Nepal where religious and ethnic tensions have arguably been exacerbated by international efforts to establish interreligious committees and dialogues. This has perpetuated a process of conscious identification with one particular religion in a context where previously notions of religious identity were often more fluid, and has contributed to the proliferation of identity politics in Nepal, where individuals and groups are now more firmly divided along ethnic, religious, and caste lines than ever before (Owen and King 2013).

Paul Hedges recognizes a similar phenomenon in China, where Buddhist and Daoist teachers increasingly emphasize to their congregations the need to 'belong' to only one religion (2010: 95). However, whilst Hedges acknowledges the "lingering effects" of Western imperialism, he also in my view correctly recognizes that accusations of imperialism are not straightforward. Indeed it is equally disempowering to suggest that religious actors from other cultures are not in some way actively complicit in the process of creating their own religious and cultural identities. However, rightly or wrongly, for some Buddhists there would be (and is) a nagging presumption that the theology of religions project is a subtle form of neo-colonialism, and pressure to conform and adopt a Buddhist theology of religions fails to value traditional and indigenous ways of engaging with other religions, or indeed the choice not to. Furthermore, we cannot ignore the post-modern critique that engagement with other religions and cultures, and the subsequent process of re-presenting those experiences are replete with issues of power and authority (Alvesson and Skoldberg 2000; Davies 2002).

All of the problems identified above have their roots in the complex realities of lived religion, whereas arguably what a theology of religions generally proposes is how religious adherents should/could engage with other faiths from a doctrinal, scriptural, theological, philosophical perspective. So how do these two different dimensions of religious belief and practice relate to one another? Drawing on work in Buddhist Studies, Philip Almond, amongst others, has convincingly argued that the predominant cultural discourse of the Victorian era significantly determined western understandings of Buddhism (1998). As a consequence of "Protestant presuppositions" (Schopen 1997: 1–22) and attempts to portray Buddhism as a philosophical system analogous to European humanism (Strong 2004; Trainor 1997), textual sources were prioritized over all other forms of evidence (Lopez 1995) and aspects of Buddhism were assimilated in so far as they correlated with normative Victorian ideas and values (Almond 1998). Facets for which there was no obvious scriptural support were rejected and vilified.

As Gregory Schopen notes, a conception of Buddhism predominantly derived from textual and scriptural sources inevitably resulted in an idealized notion of what constituted Buddhist practice (1997: 1–22). This construct was subsequently used as a yardstick against which to determine the historic demise of 'classical' or 'authentic' Buddhism, and as a premise from which to critique existing Buddhist traditions. In recent decades in the field of Buddhist studies, there has been an almost universal refutation of the view that textual evidence ever offered unparalleled insight into an 'authentic' form of Buddhism, or indeed that such a phenomenon ever really existed (see Schopen 1997; Almond 1998; Germano and Trainor 2004; Strong 2004; Swearer 2004, amongst others). The luxury of hindsight has enabled scholars to clearly identify and elucidate the problems associated with Victorian scholarship. Early scholars' work on Buddhism has been consistently critiqued for being more representative of their own socio-cultural and religious context than offering an accurate depiction of Buddhist beliefs and practices. Scholars now increasingly recognize that in fact "[T]his material records what a small, atypical part of the Buddhist community wanted that community to believe or practice" (Schopen 1997:1). I would argue that attempts to construct a Buddhist theology of religions based on scriptural evidence face similar problems. It is difficult to escape the fact that a Buddhist theology of religions cannot account for the wide diversity of Buddhist beliefs and practices, and ultimately presents an artificial construct, the result of a predominantly abstract academic exercise.

A further fundamental flaw in a theology of religions approach is the tendency to draw on personal experiences and beliefs to construct a systematic and universal framework for engaging with other religions. We can see a good example of this in Kenneth Tanaka's contribution in Schmidt-Leukel (2008: 69–84), where he begins by acknowledging the subjective and partial nature of his work, but then proceeds to move from the specific to the general without any recognition of the problems inherent in doing so. It can of course be argued that religious scholars and leaders have always sought, and indeed should continue to, inspire (in this instance) Buddhists to find more constructive and pro-active ways of engaging with the 'other.' However, to my mind there is something problematic about using Buddhist scripture, ideals, or philosophy to construct a model or ideal against which to measure the appropriateness of Buddhists' modes of interaction with people of other religions. Unavoidably this process contains implicit value judgements, and itself becomes a process of exclusion.

Conclusion

As scholars (or practitioners), acknowledging the partial and subjective nature of our work should in no way be seen as a weakness. In fact I would strongly agree with Daniel Capper who argues that "[A] reflexive self-consciousness on the part of the researcher is essential for textual, social scientific authority, rather than an obstacle to such authority" (2003: 236). However, it is not simply enough to acknowledge the subjective nature of our work and then "press on regardless;" it is imperative to recognize the significant impact this has on our representations and conclusions. In a chapter this size addressing such a broad subject it would be naïve to think it is possible to draw any definite conclusions. Therefore, the primary purpose of this chapter has been to draw on existing work in the theology of religions, and the experiences and practices of Buddhists, to interrogate and problematize some of the implicit assumptions that underpin the theology of religions. All the issues raised require much greater reflection than can be afforded here.

That said, it is possible to argue from a Buddhist perspective that the aspirations of increasing understanding of ourselves and others; preventing or de-escalating tensions and conflict; and enhancing our own spiritual experience and practice, are important and worthwhile endeavors. However, as Kiblinger notes, "in our excitement to search Buddhism for treasures to import, and amidst Christian theologians' efforts to formulate justifications for inclusive stances, have we forgotten something obvious? Clearly, many want to include Buddhists, but do Buddhists want to be included?" (2005: 1). I would suggest that perhaps inevitably some but not all are willing participants, and careful consideration of the context is important and appropriate when considering whether or not Buddhists should engage in more inclusive practices. It is also important not to exclude or demean Buddhists (or non-Buddhists) who do not agree with or appreciate the presumed advantages of engaging meaningfully with other religious traditions; and unfortunately, intended or not, this is often implied in Buddhist (and non-Buddhist) constructions of a theology of religions.

I would also conclude by adding that a sense of perspective is extremely important. Much of the rhetoric in the theology of religions focuses on the rich benefits engaging with other religions can bring. Speaking as someone now theoretically and practically engaged in peacebuilding processes, there are undoubtedly times when we desperately need to conceive of ways for people of different faiths to communicate constructively. However, it is all too easy to over-play the importance of our work. Religious identity is not always an important or appropriate means of bringing people back together after conflict, and in some cases concentrating on and emphasizing religious difference can exacerbate tensions. Indeed the kind of deep intellectual inquiry articulated in theologies of religions is a luxury that people directly involved in conflict situations are not open or amenable to.

Finally a pertinent question that I often wrestle with in my own research on religion and peacebuilding is: do we need to have a deep understanding of another person's religion in order to have a profound understanding of their humanity, and to have empathy and compassion for them and their situation? Time and again the evidence shows that the answer is sometimes … but not necessarily. Courageous and inspiring acts have been carried out by religious people of all religions and none, and by people of faith who have no inclination to meaningfully explore outside of their own religious boundaries. People can and regularly do fundamentally reject another person's religious beliefs and traditions, and yet still live together in peace and harmony; an important insight to remember when considering the value of a 'Buddhist' theology of religions.

Bibliography

Abe, M. (1995). *Buddhism and Interfaith Dialogue*. London: Macmillan Press.

Almond, P.C. (1988). *The British Discovery of Buddhism*. Cambridge: Cambridge University Press.

Alvesson, M., and K. Skoldberg. (2000). *Reflexive Methodology: New Vistas for Qualitative Research*. Thousand Oaks and London: Sage.

Anand, D. (2000). "(Re)imagining Nationalism: Identity and Representation in the Tibetan Diaspora of South Asia." *Contemporary South Asia* 9/3: 271–87.

Appleby, S. (2000). *The Ambivalence of the Sacred: Religion, Violence and Reconciliation*. Carnegie Commission on Preventing Deadly Conflict. Lanham, MD: Rowman and Littlefield.

Capper, D. (2003). "Scientific Empathy, American Buddhism, and the Ethnography of Religion." *Culture and Religion* 4/2: 233–53.

Cea, A.V. de (2012). *The Buddha and Religious Diversity*. London and New York: Routledge.

Chappell, D. (ed.). (1999). *Buddhist Peacework: Creating Cultures for Peace*. Somerville, MA: Wisdom Publications.

Davies, C.A. (2002). *Reflexive Ethnography: A Guide to Researching Selves and Others*. London and New York, NY: Routledge.

Deegalle, M. (ed.). (2006). *Buddhism, Conflict and Violence in Modern Sri Lanka*. London and New York: Routledge.

Der-lan Yeh, T. (2006). "The Way to Peace: A Buddhist Perspective." *International Journal of Peace Studies* 11.1: 91–112.

Fredericks, J.L. (2004). *Buddhists and Christians: Through Comparative Theology to Solidarity*. Maryknoll, NY: Orbis Books.

Galtung, J. (1993). *Buddhism: A Quest for Unity and Peace.* Honolulu: Dae Won Sa Buddhist Temple of Hawaii.

Germano, D., and K. Trainor (eds.). (2004). *Embodying the Dharma: Buddhist Relic Veneration in Asia.* New York, NY: State University of New York Press.

Gethin, R. (1998). *The Foundations of Buddhism.* Oxford: Oxford University Press.

Gopin, M. (2002). *Between Eden and Armageddon: The Future of World Religions, Violence, and Peacemaking.* New York and Oxford: Oxford University Press.

Hedges, P. (2010). *Controversies in Interreligious Dialogue and the Theology of Religions.* London: SCM Press.

Hertog, K. (2010). *The Complex Reality of Religious Peacebuilding.* Plymouth, MA: Lexington Books.

Hirota, D. (ed.). (2000). *Towards a Contemporary Understanding of Pure Land Buddhism.* New York, NY: State University of New York Press.

Ingram, P., and F. Streng (2007). *Buddhist-Christian Dialogue: Mutual Renewal and Transformation.* Eugene, OR: Wipf & Stock Publishers.

Juergensmeyer, M., and M. Jerryson. (2010). *Buddhist Warfare.* Oxford: Oxford University Press.

Kawada, Yoichi. (1999). *From Inner Peace to World Peace: A Buddhist Perspective.* New York, NY: St. Martin's Press.

Keown, D., C.S. Prebish, and C. Queen. (2003). *Action Dharma: New Studies in Engaged Buddhism.* London and New York: Routledge.

Kiblinger, K.B. (2005). *Buddhist Inclusivism: Attitudes towards Religious Others.* Aldershot and Burlington, VT: Ashgate Publishing Limited.

———. (2008). "Buddhist Stances Towards Others: Types, Examples, and Considerations." In: P. Schmidt-Leukel (ed.). *Buddhist Attitudes to Other Religions.* St Ottilien: EOS. pp. 24–47.

King, S.B. (2009). *Socially Engaged Buddhism.* Honolulu, HI: University of Hawai'i Press.

Knitter, P. (2004). *Theology of Religions.* Maryknoll, NY: Orbis Books.

Lai, W., and M. von Brück. (2001). *Christianity and Buddhism: A Multi-Cultural History of Their Dialogue.* Maryknoll, NY: Orbis Books.

Lopez, D.S. Jr. (1999). *Prisoners of Shangri-La.* Chicago, IL: The University of Chicago Press.

Luz, U., and A. Michaels. (2006). *Encountering Jesus and Buddha: Their Lives and Teachings.* Minneapolis, MN: Augsburg Fortress.

Makransky, J. (2011). "Thoughts on Why, How, and What Buddhists Can Learn from Christian Theologians." *Buddhist-Christian Studies* 31: 119–33.

McConnell, J. (1995). *Mindful Mediation: A Handbook for Buddhist Peacemakers.* Bangkok: Buddhist Research Institute and Manachula Buddhist University.

Moon, S. Ichi Su. (2004). *Not Turning Away: An Engaged Buddhism Anthology.* Boston, MA: Shambhala Publications.

Mun, C. (ed.). (2007). *Meditators and Mediators: Buddhism and Peacemaking*. Honolulu: Blue Pine Books.

Neumaier, E. (2004). "Missed Opportunties: Buddhism and Ethnic Strife in Sri Lanka and Tibet." In: H. Coward and G. Smith (eds.). *Religion and Peacebuilding*. New York: SUNY Press. pp. 69–92.

Niwano, N. (1982). *A Buddhist Approach to Peace*. Tokyo: Kosei Publishing.

Owen, M., and A. King. (2013). *Religious Peacebuilding and Development in Nepal: Report and Recommendations for the Nepal Ministry of Peace and Reconstruction*. Winchester: University of Winchester.

Queen, C.S. (ed.). (2012). *Engaged Buddhism in the West*. Somerville, MA: Wisdom Publications.

Race, A. (2001). *Interfaith Encounter*. London: SCM Press.

Schmidt-Leukel, P. (ed.). (2005). *Buddhism and Christianity in Dialogue*. London: SCM Press.

—— (ed.) (2008). *Buddhist Attitudes to Other Religions*. St Ottilien: EOS.

Schopen, G. (1997). *Bones, Stones, and Buddhist Monks*. Honolulu, HI: University of Hawai'i Press.

Sivaraksa, S. (1992a). "Engaged Buddhism: Liberation from a Buddhist Perspective." In: D. Cohn-Sherbok (ed.). *World Religions and Human Liberation*. Maryknoll, NY: Orbis Books.

——. (1992b). *Seeds of Peace: A Buddhist Vision for Renewing Society*. Berkeley: Parallax Press.

——. (2005). *Conflict, Culture, Change: Engaged Buddhism in a Globalizing World*. Somerville, MA: Wisdom Publications.

Strong, J.S. (2004). *Relics of the Buddha*. Princeton, NJ: Princeton University Press.

Svensson, I. (2012). *Ending Holy Wars: Religion and Conflict Resolution in Civil Wars*. St. Lucia, Queensland: University of Queensland Press.

Swearer, D. (2004). *Becoming the Buddha: The Ritual of Image Consecration in Thailand*. Princeton, NJ: Princeton University Press.

Thich Nhat Hanh. (2008). *The World We Have: A Buddhist Approach to Peace and Ecology*. Berkeley: Parallax Press.

Thompson, R. (2009). *Buddhist Christianity: A Passionate Openness*. Winchester and Washington: O-Books.

Tikhonov V., and T. Brekke. (2012). *Buddhism and Violence: Militarism and Buddhism in Modern Asia*. London and New York, NY: Routledge.

Trainor, K. (1997). *Relics, Ritual, and Representation in Buddhism: Rematerializing the Sri Lankan Theravāda Tradition*. Cambridge: Cambridge University Press.

Afterword: Persisting with the Typology and Pluralism

Alan Race

New Context of Interdependence

At Easby Moor, on top of the Cleveland Hills in North Yorkshire, and visible on a good day from my boyhood home some fifteen miles away, there is an obelisk with a plaque honoring the British explorer Captain James Cook (1728–1779). Cook was born at Marton-in-Cleveland and his boyhood home was at the village of Great Ayton which nestles below the hills. He was responsible for mapping the Pacific, New Zealand and Australia, thus radically altering western perceptions of world geography. The obelisk was erected in 1827 and the inscription reads:

> In memory of the celebrated circumnavigator Capt James Cook F.R.S. A man of nautical knowledge inferior to none, in zeal, prudence and energy, superior to most …. While the art of navigation shall be cultivated among men, whilst the spirit of enterprise, commerce and philanthropy shall animate the sons of Britain, while it shall be deemed the honour of a Christian Nation to spread civilisation and the blessings of the Christian faith among pagan and savage tribes, so long will the name of Captain Cook stand out amongst the most celebrated and most admired benefactors of the human race.[1]

That era has now passed. The colonialism it represented has been dismantled. No longer can we talk of "pagan and savage tribes" which are nothing more than labels of domination. No longer is the coupling of "civilization" and "the blessings of Christian faith" an easy marriage, for we are aware of the moral ambiguities which have accompanied such a coupling. We might admire the exploratory spirit of men like Cook, and there is every reason not to doubt his sincerity or integrity. But colonialism has passed.

There is a parallel argument to be made in respect of religious attitudes and religious colonizing. The obelisk demonstrates that other traditions have been imagined as "pagan and savage tribes," ready to be supplanted by superior Christian faith. Moreover, in the case of Cook's obelisk, Christian colonialism

---

1 See http://www.captcook-ne.co.uk/ccne/cookne/gtayton.htm.

has gone hand in hand with economic and political colonialism, and indeed provided the latter with transcendent purpose.

As with post-colonial politics we now have post-colonial religion. We have entered an era of interdependence, religiously as well as politically. We have learned to let go the making of others in our own image and we now feel the pull to celebrate and not lament our differences.

The birth of interdependence—economically, politically and religiously— has been painful and continues to be so. There has been talk of a 'clash of civilizations' and the rise of religiously-motivated violence expressed through nationalist causes. Given that civilizations have been largely religiously shaped through history, is it possible to envisage a positive experience of interdependence without some equally positive articulation of what cultural and religious difference might entail? Hans Küng famously said that we need a global ethic to accompany our newly emerging sense of global interdependence (Küng 1991). We also need global spiritual vision to go with it.

Other commentators have labeled our postcolonial world as a new era of axial consciousness. For example Ewert Cousins, following the historian and philosopher Karl Jaspers, describes the evolutionary emergence of human individual awareness as being integral to the rise of the world religions as movements for transformation in the world. A split developed between 'heaven' and 'earth,' between 'spirit' and 'matter,' and it encouraged the idea of the subjective spiritual journey as we have come to know it. But now we are facing the dawn of a second axial period, whereby the fragmentation of consciousness is being transcended by global consciousness. The first axial period produced remarkable results with differentiated cultures and religions. With the shift towards convergence, Cousins writes of what this means for the religions:

> Now that the forces of divergence have shifted to convergence, the religions must meet each other in center to center unions, discovering what is most authentic in each other, releasing creative energy toward a more complexified form of religious consciousness.
>
> COUSINS 2012: 75

The tasks and challenges of the theology of religions (ToR) fall within this larger dawning of a second axial period in history. Note this global consciousness will not be an undifferentiated, abstract form of life, but a more dynamic, because dialogical, form of consciousness. It will be concerned to recover some earlier dimensions of consciousness (such as ecological connectedness) but evolve to embrace a sense of interrelatedness between religions and cultures which hitherto has not been possible.

The possibilities within an emerging second axial period arise because of the universal thrust at the heart of first axial religions. The 'world religions' are precisely that—*world*—that is to say, applicable beyond the conditions of their origins. As such, a universalist thrust expects there to be religious awareness beyond any boundaries of particularity, and it is this expectation which creates the conditions for the second axial period. To date, the universalism of separate religions no longer requires monologic mission as its essential outward expression but invites a mutuality, initially of respect and then of giving and receiving of insight and truth.

Responding to Debates

Since the publication of the first edition (Race 1983) of *Christians and Religious Pluralism* (*C&RP*) the debate over how to interpret theologically and philosophically the fact of many religions—I should say 'world religions'—has spun off in many differing directions. One intention behind that book was to bring some order to what was then becoming a confusing field in the Christian ToR. Since then, however, the field has yielded even more products, such that the confusion has not abated but become a lively and heavily contested field of theological enquiry.

Any serious work in theological construction of course requires testing among peers. Therefore I am grateful for the many essays in this volume, for their critical appraisals in an endeavor which is no longer the final afterthought in the theological textbook. The significance of the many religions for Christian theology had already been articulated twenty years previous to *C&RP* by the masterly theologian Paul Tillich with great prophetic intensity, when he said at the end of his career that had he been starting afresh to write systematic theology he would have had to have the world religions as his interlocutor/dialogue partner. The Christian (or any other) theological and philosophical discipline has not yet fully arrived at this point even fifty years later, and apart from one or two notable exceptions (e.g. Raimon Pannikar, Wilfred Cantwell Smith, John Hick) it remains elusive as a direction of travel.

Since 1983 there have been a number of developments which have had a bearing on the ToR challenge. In this regard, I venture the following themes:

(1)   The rise of interreligious dialogue and the production of monographs and edited collections which began in earnest from the mid-1980s

onwards.[2] Harboring at least one assumption relevant for ToR—that dialogue depends on participants willing to learn not only 'about' but also
'from' their co-religionists—dialogue began generating a life of its own,
with a discourse and shape that complemented a debate which could all
too easily treat 'religion' in too reified a sense.

(2)   The growing contributions from feminist circles which first articulated
       a parallel treatment of 'other religions' with the patriarchal treatment of
       women by androcentric theologians from all traditions, and then moved
       to become more demanding that theologians of religions pay better at-
       tention to the more liberative aspects of their craft even as they accept
       others in dialogue.

(3)   The development of 'comparative theology,' which involves encounter,
       listening and learning from others with an openness to religious truth
       from different quarters and a willingness to absorb that truth into one's
       own system. Often comparative theology seeks to place ToR on one side
       in the pursuit of a dialogical-type outcome.

(4)   The setting forth of a critique of ToR on the grounds that it contains hid-
       den assumptions that are of a 'grand narrative' type; that is, it ignores
       the putative incommensurability between traditions and, once this is ac-
       knowledged, any grounds for focusing a ToR on a supposedly identifiable
       common transcendent source is misplaced.

(5)   Related to (4) is the emergence of what is sometimes named as a fourth
       category in the typology under discussion in this book, namely so-called
       'particularity.' This is the view which accepts the inviolable differences
       between traditions with the result that each tradition is 'particular' to
       itself and its cultural history, and therefore the exercise of interpreting
       religious plurality or making judgements about others theologically can
       have no real meaning or purpose.

In general I am inclined to the view that these developments represent concerns appropriate to the ToR, by broadening discussion and raising issues
which are pertinent in their own terms. However, apart from the critique
(4), none seems to alter the terms of reference of ToR as such and the typology by which I sought to canvas the Christian options. It is worth repeating
the oft-cited challenge posed by Cantwell Smith by way of maintaining focus

---

2   To cite one major publishing venture: during this period Orbis Books produced numerous
     collections of books of dialogue between Christian and other faiths, some single-authored
     and some edited collections, and books reflecting on the assumptions and purposes of dia-
     logue as an emerging theological endeavour.

"We explain the fact that the Milky Way is there by the doctrine of creation, but how do we explain the fact that the *Bhagavad Gita* is there?" (Smith 1998: 138).

Those who would abandon ToR as a valid enterprise have no answer to this question and presumably feel no need even to approach it. That seems to me an abdication of theology altogether, or at least a terrible narrowing of theology's rightful remit, let alone an avoidance of ToR. But those who face Cantwell Smith's question head-on are left with the options which fall into the typology under discussion; namely, that the *Bhagavad Gita* G has no validity as an inspiration for 'transcendent vision and human transformation' (my definition of what Christians know as 'salvation' or others as 'liberation,' etc.), or it has partial validity, needing to be completed (fulfilled) by a religious form which has advantages according to certain criteria of its own, or it has validity roughly on a par with the Christian outlook in so far as it has demonstrated its potential to be a well of lasting insight into the human condition and the divine life that comes in to light within it. These options of course correspond to the options within the typology which I am defending.

The essays in this volume, to varying degrees, raise questions about the continuing applicability of the typology, at least in its original form. Some suggest abandoning it and some redefining it. This makes for a lively debate. I wish now to respond in broad terms to some of the emergent themes which have appeared in the essays in this collection. They cohere with the developments which I outlined above but I hope to show that they do not alter the continuing applicability of the typology.

No Typology

One motive for abandoning the typology coheres around a puzzle about the term 'religion.' It is common to note that 'religion' is notoriously hard to define wholly adequately and in such a manner as to apply consistently to those movements of the human spirit which we have been used to calling 'the religions.' And without a good working definition of 'religion' how can there be a 'theology of religions'? I take these concerns, legitimate in their own way, to be an unnecessary muddying of what ToR involves. It is true that 'religion' does cover a varied range of activities, has shifted and evolved through time, and is internally plural for any one tradition. It is true that the phenomena which scholars study underline a high degree of particularity with regard to culture, custom and context, and it might be no accident that the Buddhist reflection in these papers brings this aspect of religious studies into the open. Yet, against the endless gnawing at the bone of 'religion,' there is nevertheless a sense in which a family resemblance model captures what we feel intuitively to be the case. Religions might not be the same but neither need we think of them as so-lipsistic activities, walled up behind their own cultural enclaves. The religions participate in a sense of transcendent purpose and recommend proposals for a transformed life in the light of it (even if that transcendent purpose is considered to spring from within a person rather than from outside impacts). These two movements alone justify the family resemblance idea. We may not be able to define 'religion' precisely but we know what we mean when we talk of it. Difficulties of definition are no deterrent to the ToR as such.

A second critique complains that the ToR asks too much of us in terms of choosing between the options. We do not know sufficient of one another or sufficient of how tradition shapes a person or exactly what transpires within a person when they pray or believe or practice, in order to make informed judgements about the religions. This kind of objection lies behind the championing of so-called 'comparative theology' as an alternative endeavor to ToR. But I do not know what level of sufficiency is needed or what sufficiency even amounts to in this context. Of course if we are ignorant of other traditions then this would indicate an insufficiency, but the levels of available information about the religions and potential for personal contact are such that we have no excuse for ignorance today. Paul Knitter makes the point that comparativists have indulged in much comparative work but as yet have been weak on absorbing any of the theological implications they might have gleaned from the exercise.[3] This leaves us wondering if 'comparative theology' is a kind of stalling mechanism on ToR itself. If comparative theology is concerned as much with the truth of a tradition, and not simply the study of tradition as phenomena, then ToR surely becomes unavoidable. Comparative theology is a potentially highly fruitful discipline, but if it is not able to explain how its fruits make a difference to the interpretation of plurality how can it function as an alternative to ToR. As it is, there is every reason for supposing that ToR would benefit greatly from comparative theology (as opposed simply to what was formerly known as comparative religion), and if comparative theology discerns value in other traditions this becomes a question knocking on the door of ToR in spite of comparative theology's best efforts to maintain a safe distance from it.

A third objection arguing for the end to ToR complains that the form of the typology is biased towards a pluralist outcome. Once the inadequacies of exclusivist and inclusivist views are exposed, it is supposed that the pluralist

---

3 As Knitter (2014: 20) says: "Where are the clear, creative, courageous conclusions as to what Christians can learn from these comparisons? What might need to be clarified or changed or discarded in traditional Christian doctrine?"

arrives on the scene in order to rescue a lamentable state of affairs. Although the objectors often add that the typology is value-laden and not neutral, it must be said that a neutral approach has never been envisaged. The typology is not simply a descriptive tool but arises out of the search for theological integrity vis-à-vis other religions. Neither is there bias, as each category must stand or fall by its own merits. I confess to finding this whole line of objection very strange. Gavin D'Costa's chapter in this collection perhaps comes closest to articulating this objection. For Gavin, the typology is biased because it relies on Enlightenment assumptions about universal values and pluralism is an example par excellence of the Enlightenment project in this area.

Gavin's well-rehearsed answer to the Enlightenment challenge is simply to reaffirm Christian tradition as a confessional matter: Christianity stands or falls by the doctrines of Incarnation and Trinity. This seems like an essentialist definition of tradition, but more than that, it strikes me as deeply uncritical. Incarnation and Trinity were developed in a certain context, and under many intellectual and political pressures. There have been many theological works deconstructing these doctrines as well as others supporting them. Certainly, ecclesiastical authorities pin their colors to these doctrinal masts, as Gavin has pointed out, but critical thinking has equally pointed out that many assumptions behind them are not easily shared by twenty-first century people. In these circumstances it seems arbitrary to complain that pluralists are post-Christians and that the typology which incorporates their position is therefore null and void. But to wall oneself up in essentialist Catholicism is itself an arbitrary act—and might not even be Catholic enough!

Modify Typology

It has repeatedly been said that the typology's three categories (*not* three paradigms, as some commentators in the past have written) do not properly delineate the options which exist in reality. In this collection the calls for modification come from two directions and involve the addition of a further category: the first call is observational and the second theoretical. Let me offer a response to both.

Calls for modification which are observational propose a category which has been labeled 'particularity' (Hedges 2008) or the 'mutuality model' (Knitter 2002). It is observational because the extra category gathers a number of writers for whom the three-fold distinctions do not fully correspond to the specific proposals from these writers. At the same time, the call is to 'loosen' the categories so that they function more heuristically, more a series of pragmatic headings under which some useful discussion might take place. 'Particularists' and 'mutualists' seek simply to set forth a Christian understanding of the human condition and its salvation, do not close down the possibilities of salvation being enacted outside of the Christian fold but at the same time refuse to endorse 'other religions' as potential vehicles of salvation as such. They are influenced by postliberal thought, refuse to countenance the philosophical universalist challenges of Enlightenment legacy, yet promote interreligious dialogue and 'openness' to other traditions.

My difficulty with incorporating 'particularity' into the ToR typology is simply that all the theologians for whom particularity is compelling generally desire to dismantle the typology itself, branding it variously as misleading or too abstract or a Christian imposition of categories. So James Fredericks, a strong proponent of particularity, has famously averred that there should be a moratorium on TofR.[4] I do not doubt that there is a category of theologians and others who deserve sincere and serious engagement but they are not interested in questions of whether or not 'other religions' are 'vehicles of salvation' and it is this question which classically lies at the root of the ToR discipline itself. Discussions about interreligious relations, dialogue and comparative theology all canvas pertinent questions and issues, but let them be what they are: discussions in these areas though not a category in ToR. As it is, it is often noted how particularism often eventuates in a form of exclusivism: they are unwilling to surrender their absolutism and refuse to entertain other traditions even as potential vehicles of 'transcendent vision and human transformation.' The 'openness' espoused by particularists and mutualists remains an admirable personal disposition, even if also rather vague, but again it is not ToR.

A second call for redefining the typology is centred on a category 'pluralist inclusivism,' spelt out forcefully by Abraham Veléz de Cea in this collection.[5] The reason for the category lies in dissatisfaction with (a) an alleged incompatibility between the shape of the typology's categories and what they describe and the phenomenological facts of those traditions which are reluctant to envisage a sense of 'transcendent substance'—particularly from manifold Buddhist perspectives around the world—behind the world's religions, and (b) the need for a category between any of the usual forms of inclusivism (stimulated originally by Karl Rahner's 'anonymous Christianity') and usual

---

4   As Fredericks writes: "Although abandoning attempts to erect a systematic theology of religions may be difficult for Christian theologians to accept, honesty to our current situation requires this of us" (1995: 83–4).

5   It is a view which was first brought to the literature, though in different form, from an Indian context by K.P. Aleaz (2005), and in his earlier book, *Religions in Christian Theology* (2001).

pluralist accounts which are deemed to be a step too far from a Christian perspective.

Regarding (a), the fact that Buddhist forms, or other 'non-theistic' forms, might not necessarily share a common view about what it is that confers nirvana or satori, and therefore cannot fit the categories of the typology, does not mitigate against the typology applying to Buddhism. Pluralism operates with a basic distinction between that which is beyond words and categories (what John Hick called 'transcategoriality') and the representation of what is beyond description in forms of human and cultural instantiation. Some Buddhists might be content, Abraham contends, for there to be many equally valid mediators of ultimate reality, so long as we do not specify any relatedness to a transcendent reality which might be assumed to be 'of substance,' no matter how varied that 'substance' might be globally speaking. What is needed, he avers, is a category we could name as 'pluralist inclusivism.' This concern seems to me not to take sufficient cognizance of the basic distinction between ultimate reality which is transcategorial and the varied experienced interpretations/reflections of this in the many religions. It is not the case that even a rehoned version of the tripolar typology, such as that submitted by Perry Schmidt-Leukel (2005), and to which Abraham takes exception, represents the imposition of Christian concepts which have relied on a substantive essence of ultimate reality as envisaged by most Christian theologians. If such a reliance was the case then this most certainly would rule out Buddhism's place in the typology. But this is to ignore the distinction which pluralists proffer between ultimate and embodied reality.

Regarding (b), it seems to me that a decision simply has to be made between inclusivism and pluralism. If a strong case for inclusivism can be made—and there are those who claim this (see, e.g. Cheetham 2008)—then this should be embraced. But if the case is not convincing then some form of pluralism must step in to take its place. Sometimes an argument is put forward which seeks to retain a qualified absolutism inherent in inclusivist views and yet allows for 'openness' to other traditions, an openness which might lead to clarification or correction of the inclusivist choice. Apart from puzzling over what exactly 'openness' entails, with its potential vagueness (e.g. does it include being prepared to surrender absoluteness?), the inclusivist choice cannot escape the accusation of wanting Christian faith (or any other) to be *a priori* superior. Again, most inclusivists shy away from the description 'superior,' but it seems to me to be built into the structure of the category. Therefore is it not best to own up to superiority and build a case which is happy to embrace it, with the implication that how that might be received by other traditions and dialogue partners would be a matter for them? From my perspective, I do not see how inclusivism can escape the basic accusation of superiority.

Dialogue

Critique of the typology has occasionally revolved around the issue of interreligious dialogue: in what sense does the typology hinder or facilitate dialogue? Strictly speaking, the three options inform dialogue from their standpoints. So exclusivists would seek to convert people of other faiths or at least point out their deficiencies from the point of view of being effective contexts of salvation; inclusivists would seek lines whereby trajectories of thought and experience in other tradition could be brought to climactic realization in Christianity; pluralists would search for complementarities or analogous pattern of thought and action between traditions. Some might think this exposition rather formalized and that dialogue as it happens between partners does not follow this style or pattern in reality. This may be so, but it is the structure of ToR which informs the dialogue either in the open or 'behind the scenes.' In this sense ToR is significant for interreligious dialogue irrespective of whether or not dialogue partners own up to the theology which informs their stance in the more theoretical sense.

When it is suggested that the typology should be reinterpreted in order to render interreligious dialogue more palatable for those whose theoretical, if personally hidden, position entails either the replacement or the fulfilling of other traditions then it is likely that ToR discipline will be downgraded or be rendered a sub-set of something called 'interfaith relations.' When this happens ToR has been effectively sidelined.

For me, the goal of dialogue is best captured by the following remarks of Stanley Samartha, the great Indian theologian and first Director of the Subunit on Dialogue at the World Council of Churches:

> If the great religious traditions of humanity are indeed different responses to the Mystery of God or Sat or the Transcendent or Ultimate Reality, then the distinctiveness of each response, in this instance the Christian, should be stated in such a way that a mutually critical and enriching relationship between different responses becomes naturally possible.
>
> SAMARTHA 1991: 86

Even so, it remains a vital issue as to how such a relationship might be possible given the different phenomenal differences between traditions. In this respect,

the doyen of interreligious dialogue, Leonard Swidler, has written how differences could be of three kinds:

> Such differences may be (1) *complementary*, as for example a stress on
> the prophetic rather than the mystical, (2) *analogous*, as for example,
> the notion of God in the Semitic religions and of sunyata in Mahayana
> Buddhism, or (3) *contradictory* where the acceptance of one entails the
> rejection of the other, as for example, the Judeo-Christian notion of the
> inviolable dignity of each individual person and the now largely disap-
> peared Hindu custom of suttee, widow burning.
>
>   SWIDLER 2014: 23

It is important to have these distinctions in mind, for we easily assume that difference means either contradiction or straight incommensurability.

Absolutism

There is often a methodological divide in the literature on ToR. Top-down
approaches assume the givenness of classical formularies and seek to bring
those formularies into relationship with new information coming from our
evolving global religious consciousness. The results usually issue in a version
of exclusivism or inclusivism. This is because at root there is a reluctance to
surrender the absolutism at the heart of classical formularies. Even those who
'universalise' the symbol of 'Christ,' as signalling 'divine reason/wisdom/spirit'
inspiring different religious responses throughout the world, are bound by
the structure of the argument to place Christian faith as the supreme religion.
The doctrine of the incarnation has always functioned in this way at least
from the fourth century onwards. On the other hand, bottom-up approaches
are prepared to admit that new information combined with critical thinking
more generally make for a substantial reconfiguring of approaches in ToR. In
this sense the shift to a pluralist option is more a function of the bottom-up
methodology than it is of being slave to Enlightenment rationality as some
critics have warned.

   Further, it is not the case that pluralists are bound to revise their Christian
commitments in order to accommodate themselves to a new 'grand narrative'
encompassing all world religions. The opposite in fact is the case: revisions
in Christian understanding, including in the central doctrines of Incarnation
and Trinity, are part of a cluster of bottom-up perspectives which now includes new information from the many religions. Pluralists are not abandoning

Christian faith for some agnostic transcendent vagueness but accept that theological revisions already underway for two hundred years—including contextual insights, biblical and doctrinal criticism, and the recognition that all our language and formularies are necessarily limited—now need to take account of vibrant religious awareness from other traditions which have stood the test of time.

The problem for ToR is the sense of absolutism which has accompanied religious commitment, whether Christian or other. Can we give it up in the light of new realities and new contexts? But what would Christian faith be without the absolutism of its language? It is often in Jewish-Christian dialogue that these questions come into strong focus. Theologians and churches have been moving in the direction of non-absoluteness, as is evidenced by the surrender of the doctrine of supersessionism in the light of the holocaust, a more historical appreciation of the New Testament literature and an appreciation of living Judaism as opposed to a fossilized view from perceptions in the past. If we have done that in relation to Jews and Judaism—and the Jewish-Christian matrix has been the dominant framework for theologizing about other traditions too—then why not give it up in relation to others as well? It seems logical. But what will happen to identity and what will happen to Christian truth? Theologians worry about its survival.

There is another reason for giving up absolutism, and it has little to do with other religions. The doctrine of revelation which is meant to secure a sense of God-givenness about Christian identity and truthfulness has undergone significant reshaping over the last two centuries. There is less directness about revelation than we once thought. In response to critical thinking with regard to scriptures, belief systems and practices, and in the face of new learning in every sphere from the sciences to the humanities, whatever it is that God gives through the language of revelation, it is always a matter of experienced response. "God is greater than the mind," said Augustine, but the full implications of this insight perhaps had to wait until modernity for them to become apparent. The mind has been not passive but proactive in interpreting human experience. Epistemology might be a complex enquiry but most would agree that we come to know as a matter of interpreting experience rather than implantation. The role of the mind in organizing sense data, in cognitive psychology and the sociology of knowledge is well-known and is a point largely accepted. It is part and parcel of the bottom-up approach to theology and other disciplines. There is a freedom in the interpretation of experience which operates such that the ambiguity of experience (is 'this' from God or not?) can point in more than one direction in terms of the truth of the matter. Nothing is forced: revelation is a relationship of gratuitousness on both sides of the human-divine divide. If we now add to this general principle the fact of many world religions then we can see why the absolutist doctrine cannot really be sustained. It is changes in the way we think theologically which have created the opening towards a reassessment of the meaning of religious plurality, and once the goodness, truth and beauty of others has been recognized, then it is best to let absolutism slip away.

We might supplement this shift in Christian understanding with the insight, borrowed from Cantwell Smith, that what really matters when a Buddhist bows down to a Buddha image and a Christian says a rosary and a Muslim recites the Qur'an is what is going on inside the Buddhist, Christian or Muslim as these actions are performed, for this is where significance and revelation occur. It is the relationship or experienced response which counts. Revelation has cognitive value but there are reasons for imagining that revelation might be taking place under different cultural conditions more than we are used to imagining, and it is that 'more than' which propels us to dialogue and to a ToR which reflects the experience of our changed perceptions and experiences.

Pluralism

Suggesting that other traditions are significant, however, is not quite the same as what is reflected in the Stanley Samartha citation I gave above. Samartha has a conditional 'If' at the beginning of his sentence. 'If' the traditions are different responses to the mystery of what theists call God .... We do not know if the different traditions really are different responses to that mystery, in the sense of being beyond reasonable doubt. But there are good reasons for thinking they may be so. The religions have sustained their followers through time, they have underpinned civilizations, they have moved the hearts of people to great acts of compassion and altruism, and they have provided what I call 'transcendent vision and human transformation.' Moreover, just as Christians have the tenacity to trust their religious experience, to trust that what has been glimpsed is of ultimate worth and has a bearing on the truth of how human beings should live, so by the same token can we accord that same capacity for trust to other followers in other traditions. But of course what we trust and what tumbles out in terms of intellectual explanation and exploration will be different—necessarily so, because what we experience is shaped by variations of time and place. Religious people do experience the world differently; we are not variations on the same theme. But that doesn't mean that we do not in some sense share a common source of inspiration, or revelation if you will. In this respect I think that Rosemary Ruether's perception sums up the pluralist prospect:

> Each religion, like each culture, is a unique configuration of symbolic
> expressions that has been shaped by the total experiences of people,
> their particular histories, and ecological settings. Although there is much
> overlap among religions, they also represent a broad spectrum of pos-
> sible ways of experiencing the divine. Some may focus on the historical
> struggle for justice, some on the renewal of natural processes, some on
> mystical ecstasy.
>
> RUETHER 1987: 141F.

Each experiences the whole. We are not talking about pieces of a jig-saw
puzzle where the religions represent different pieces and all you have to do is
put them together for a whole picture. We each experience the whole—but we
do so in distinct and partial ways, and they are ways which the human capability for empathy and the willingness to stand in the shoes of the other creates
the prospect for mutual accountability for truth through dialogue. Why should
the facts of phenomenological difference lead us to expect that only incommensurable difference between us can be the real measure of truth? To me,
that just seems odd.

Returning now to Samartha's conditional 'If.' The 'If' is there because pluralism as an approach in ToR is an hypothesis not a certainty. It has the power of
explanation unless and until a better one is proposed. Let me repeat here an
eight point outline of what pluralism entails, an outline I have published previously since *Christians and Religious Pluralism* (see Race 2001: 31ff.):

1.   The authenticity and truth of the Christian Way is based on the validity of
      the religious experience it embodies; i.e. the basic Christian affirmation
      of 'transcendent vision and human transformation' is trustworthy as real
      experience and it has cognitive implications.
2.   This Christian act of trustworthiness can be extended to others on the
      basis that other religious contexts too provide a framework for 'transcend-
      ent vision and human transformation'; i.e. there is no reason to doubt the
      validity of the religious apprehension of other religious traditions and
      every reason to accept their integrity.
3.   The spiritual fruits of the many faith-traditions seem comparable: all
      have inspired saints and holy figures who have been active on either indi-
      vidual or sociopolitical levels (or both), and all have demonstrated their
      share of complicity in support of different kinds of social ills, such as rac-
      ism, war, sexual prejudice, and so on; i.e. the comparability of spiritual
      fruits suggests a common source of inspiration, however this is portrayed
      in different traditions.

4. The distinction occurring in all faith-traditions between the 'unknowabil-
    ity' and the 'knowability' of Ultimate Reality in terms of symbolic/iconic
    forms is the key distinction which allows for the hypothesis of Ultimate
    Reality to be experienced and conceptualized in different symbolic/icon-
    ic forms according to cultural history; i.e. Ultimate Reality as ineffable is
    yet the deeper ground of the varied manifestations of ultimacy glimpsed
    through the varied lenses of the historical and cultural forms of the reli-
    gions themselves.

5. Theologies and religious philosophies have evolved within particular
    cultural environments, reflecting the limitations of these environments,
    but the faith-traditions now need to develop new directions for their the-
    ologies and philosophies in order to account for the wider picture en-
    compassed by religious plurality. In Christianity, this entails formulating
    Christian belief in a manner which respects the integrity of other tradi-
    tions; i.e. the effectiveness of Christian belief need not depend on theo-
    logical interpretations which are treated as necessarily absolute and/or
    exclusive.

6. Criteria for distinguishing between good and bad religion, and between
    true and false religion need to be developed; i.e. in order to dispel the
    relativist caricature that 'anything goes' pluralists have an ongoing task to
    specify critically the grounds on which certain manifestations of religion
    are more and less acceptable.

7. Each tradition has both an adequate and inadequate grasp of the rela-
    tionship between particularity and universality; i.e. each particular vi-
    sion of the universal availability of Ultimate Reality is an adequate (if
    also conditioned and partial) view of the whole yet complementary to
    other equally adequate (if also conditioned and partial) perspectives of
    the whole.

8. Belief systems are practical means for achieving the religious ends of
    'transcendent vision and human transformation.' While this entails that
    many metaphysical and other disagreements between traditions will
    remain it does not invalidate the basic picture of complementarity; i.e.
    patterns of what constitutes complementarity can be pursued through
    critical dialogue, in mutual respect and without prejudice.

Clearly, Pluralism in ToR is not a form of 'we're all talking about the same thing
underneath and so let's just mix up the phenomena.' It is not that, because
what we are imagining are different responses to different *manifestations* of
the same transcendent reality. This is a point frequently missed by critics but it
is crucial for the pluralist case. It is the transcendence of ultimate reality which

relativizes traditions and not simply the recognition that our religious forms are necessarily culturally contextual.

In the modern, democratic, critical-minded and plural-conscious world, clinging to religious absolutism seems unsustainable. This is not to say that there are not those who perpetuate it still. But the shift which has been underway, perhaps since the Second World War, now places the *onus probandi* on those who wish to defend absolutism rather than its detractors. From a Christian viewpoint, changes in the notions of revelation, together with the fruits of dialogue and a greater receptivity to the integrity of others, witness to the prevailing impact and power of the shift itself. None of this means that we are abandoning the continuing need to distinguish between good and bad, adequate and inadequate, true and false religion, but we do that work now together. "God transcends the mind," said Augustine. That is just as well; otherwise we are in danger of idolatry. I am suggesting that it is idolatrous now to think that religious absolutism from one perspective can trump the salvific validity of the world religions.

Bibliography

Aleaz, K.P. (2001). *Religions in Christian Theology*. Kolkata: Punthi Pustak.

Aleaz, K.P. (2005). "Pluralism Calls for Pluralistic Inclusivism." In: Paul F. Knitter (ed.). *The Myth of Religious Superiority: a Multifaith Exploration*. Maryknoll, NY: Orbis Books. Pp. 162–75.

Cheetham, David. (2008). "Inclusivism: Honouring Faithfulness and Openness." In: Alan Race and Paul Hedges (eds.). *Christian Approaches to Other Faiths*. SCM Core Text series. London: SCM Press. Pp. 63–84.

Cousins, Ewert. (2012). "Religions of the World: Teilhard and the Second Axial Turning." *Interreligious Insight* 10.1: 75–86.

Fredericks, James. (1995). "A Universal Religious Experience? Comparative Theology as an Alternative to a Theology of Religions." *Horizons* 22: 83–84.

Hedges, Paul. (2008). "Particularities: Tradition-Specific Postmodern Perspectives." In: Alan Race and Paul Hedges (eds.). *Christian Approaches to Other Faiths*. SCM Core Text series. London: SCM Press. Pp. 112–35.

Knitter, Paul. (2014). "Good Neighbours or Fellow Seekers? Dealing with the Plurality of Religions in the Twenty-First Century." *Interreligious Insight* 12.1: 10–26.

———. (2002). *Introducing Theologies of Religions*. Maryknoll, NY: Orbis Press.

Küng, Hans. (1991). *Global Responsibility*. London: SCM Press.

Race, Alan. (1983). *Christians and Religious Pluralism: Patterns in the Christian Theology of Religions*. London: SCM.

———. (2001). *Interfaith Encounter: the Twin Tracks of Theology and Dialogue*. London, SCM.

Ruether, Rosemary Radford. (1987). "Feminism and Jewish-Christian Dialogue: Particularism and Universalism in the Search for Religious Truth." In: John Hick and Paul F. Knitter (eds.). *The Myth of Christian Uniqueness: Toward a Pluralistic Theology of Religions*. Maryknoll, NY: Orbis Books. Pp. 137–48.

Samartha, Stanley. (1991). *One Christ—Many Religions: Toward a Revised Christology*. Maryknoll, NY: Orbis Press.

Schmidt-Leukel, Perry. (2005). "Exclusivism, Inclusivism, Pluralism: the Tripolar Typology—Clarified and Reaffirmed." In: Paul F. Knitter (ed.). *The Myth of Religious Superiority: A Multifaith Exploration*. Maryknoll, NY: Orbis Books. Pp. 13–27.

Smith, Wilfred Cantwell. (1998 [1962]). "The Church in a Religiously Plural World." In: Wilfred Cantwell Smith. *Patterns of Faith Around the World*. Oxford: Oneworld.

Swidler, Leonard. (2014). "Interreligious Dialogue: its Origin and Meaning." *Interreligious Insight* 12.2: 8–33.

Index of Subjects

Index of Names